CONSUMERS IN THE BUSH

McGill-Queen's Rural, Wildland, and Resource Studies Series
Series editors: Colin A.M. Duncan, James Murton, and R.W. Sandwell

The Rural, Wildland, and Resource Studies Series includes monographs, thematically unified edited collections, and rare out-of-print classics. It is inspired by Canadian Papers in Rural History, Donald H. Akenson's influential occasional papers series, and seeks to catalyze reconsideration of communities and places lying beyond city limits, outside centres of urban political and cultural power, and located at past and present sites of resource procurement and environmental change. Scholarly and popular interest in the environment, climate change, food, and a seemingly deepening divide between city and country, is drawing non-urban places back into the mainstream. The series seeks to present the best environmentally contextualized research on topics such as agriculture, cottage living, fishing, the gathering of wild foods, mining, power generation, and rural commerce, within and beyond Canada's borders.

CONSUMERS IN THE BUSH

SHOPPING IN RURAL UPPER CANADA

Douglas McCalla

MCGILL-QUEEN'S UNIVERSITY PRESS

Montreal & Kingston • London • Ithaca

© McGill-Queen's University Press 2015

ISBN 978-0-7735-4499-4 (cloth)
ISBN 978-0-7735-4500-7 (paper)
ISBN 978-0-7735-9709-9 (ePDF)
ISBN 978-0-7735-9710-5 (ePUB)

Legal deposit first quarter 2015
Bibliothèque nationale du Québec

Printed in Canada on acid-free paper that is 100% ancient forest free (100% post-consumer recycled), processed chlorine free

This book has been published with the help of a grant from the Canadian Federation for the Humanities and Social Sciences, through the Awards to Scholarly Publications Program, using funds provided by the Social Sciences and Humanities Research Council of Canada.

McGill-Queen's University Press acknowledges the support of the Canada Council for the Arts for our publishing program. We also acknowledge the financial support of the Government of Canada through the Canada Book Fund for our publishing activities.

Library and Archives Canada Cataloguing in Publication

McCalla, Douglas, 1942-, author
Consumers in the bush : shopping in rural Upper Canada / Douglas McCalla.

Includes bibliographical references and index.
Issued in print and electronic formats.
ISBN 978-0-7735-4499-4 (bound).–ISBN 978-0-7735-4500-7 (pbk.).–
ISBN 978-0-7735-9709-9 (ePDF).–ISBN 978-0-7735-9710-5 (ePUB)

1. Consumers–Ontario–History–19th century. 2. Shopping–Ontario–History–
19th century. 3. General stores–Ontario–History–19th century. 4. Consumption
(Economics)–Ontario–History–19th century. 5. Ontario–Economic conditions–
19th century. 6. Ontario–Social life and customs–19th century. 7. Ontario–
Rural conditions–History–19th century. I. Title.

HF5429.6.C32O58 2015   381'.10971309034   C2014-907273-2
                                                C2014-907274-0

To the memory of Kazuo Kimura (1947–2007)

CONTENTS

ILLUSTRATIONS

TABLES

APPENDICES

ACKNOWLEDGMENTS

I am delighted to acknowledge obligations accumulated in writing this book. Initial funding for the research was provided by grants from the Social Sciences and Humanities Research Council of Canada. The program was carried forward under the auspices of a Killam Research Fellowship awarded by the Canada Council and during my tenure as Canada Research Chair in Rural History at the University of Guelph.

Laura Zink and Annette Fox were responsible for record linkage and gathered and coded the original account book data, a herculean task given the limitations of spreadsheet software then available. Subsequent checking and work with their data and the original sources have only reinforced my appreciation of their accomplishment in turning daybooks into data. I benefited also from their engagement with the larger research objectives of the project as our encounters with the evidence prompted reflection on and adjustment of initial hypotheses. Erin Stewart-Eves, Beth Yarzab, Jeralyne Manweiler, Jon Studiman, and Josh MacFadyen all provided excellent research assistance as the data posed ever-widening questions; Erin also did superb work in systematically rechecking data sets.

The work was greatly assisted in early stages by Rosemary Ommer, Robert Sweeny, and Robert Hong; their work on Newfoundland was an inspiration and their generous advice to Laura, Annette, and me was immensely helpful. Normand Séguin, Serge Courville, Jean-Claude Robert, and their colleagues at the Centre interuniversitaire d'études québécoises were likewise encouraging from the start. Participating in

CIEQ has offered a privileged window on some of the liveliest historical scholarship I know and provided a sympathetic audience for several of my tentative explorations in consumption history. Ruth Sandwell and Colin Duncan read drafts of most of the core chapters and gave just the right kind of advice on what needed to be done with them.

Colleagues in history at Trent University and the University of Guelph likewise provided willing audiences and constructive criticism as the project developed. Catharine Wilson and Kris Inwood have been consistently supportive; I can only begin to express my gratitude for the ways in which they have sustained my commitment to the work. While visiting at Guelph, Royden Loewen was equally encouraging; his scholarly engagement has continued to provide an example to aspire to. The book could not have been written without all of this support; its flaws and limitations, however, are entirely my responsibility.

Papers from this project have been presented at CIEQ, meetings of the Canadian Network for Economic History, the Business History Conference, the Canadian Historical Association, the Department of Economics at Queen's University, and the Niagara Historical Society. My thanks to all for these opportunities. Elements of the argument have appeared in the *Material History Review* (now the *Material Culture Review*), *Agricultural History*, and *Ontario History*; I am grateful to the editors of these journals and their publishers, Cape Breton University Press, the Agricultural History Society, and the Ontario Historical Society, for permission to incorporate revised versions of these essays here.

None of this would have been possible without the business accounts that sustain this study. Full credit to the Trent University Archives, Queen's University Archives, and the Archives of Ontario for recognizing the promise of these materials – and to staff at all three for their professionalism and for making their archives such ideal places for a historian to work.

It has been a pleasure throughout to work with McGill-Queen's University Press. I owe a particular debt to Kyla Madden for her sustained engagement and support, sharp and constructive advice, and remarkable efficiency at every stage. Helen Hajnoczky has been consistently helpful and equally efficient. Claude Lalumière has been an ideal editor, very professional, and at all times a pleasure to deal with. His perceptive and patient work in addressing the intricacies of all the numbers and tables deserves special acknowledgement. Here I also thank readers for the Press for their responses to the manuscript and suggestions for improvement; if I have not always succeeded in following the latter, I nevertheless took them seriously and the book benefited greatly from the review process.

Work on the project was interrupted by a year in Japan as visiting professor at the University of Tsukuba. This was a transformative time for Anna and me (and for this research), thanks to the warmth of welcome by colleagues, neighbours, and students (notably Toshihiro and Reiko Tanaka and Aya Fujiwara, exemplary guides and mentors then, friends and colleagues since) and the extraordinary generosity of our hosts, Kazuo and Ruri Kimura. I deeply regret that I did not finish this book in time to share it with Professor Kimura.

Finally, and above all, my thanks to Anna McCalla for living with and supporting this program too.

CONSUMERS IN THE BUSH

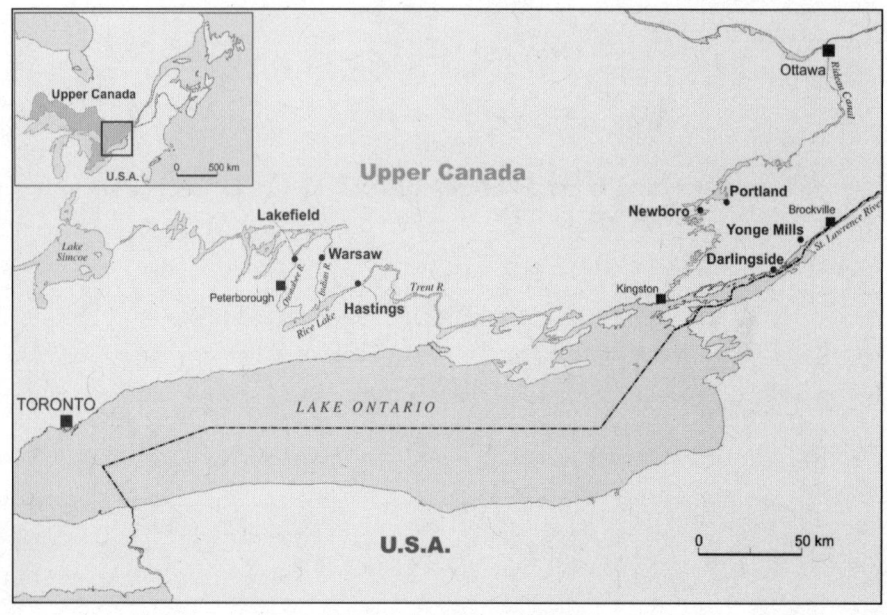

Figure 0.1   Location of stores, in bold. (Map by Marie Puddister)

PREAMBLE:
CONSUMERS IN THE BUSH

The details are not the details. They make the design.
Caption, Stedelijk Museum, 2013[1]

On Thursday, 1 September 1808, the storekeeper at Yonge Mills began a new daybook, marked number 3. Settlement of the township of Yonge, on the St Lawrence River in Leeds County, had been underway for about a decade by then, and the store itself had been open since spring 1807 (for the location of this and other stores, see figure 0.1). The milling complex with which it was associated had probably been open longer.[2] The owner of the mills, the store, and a store founded in 1802 in the region's main village in the adjoining township of Elizabethtown was Charles Jones (1781–1840), a member of a leading Loyalist family in the area, and later a prominent figure in business and politics on the provincial stage.[3]

It is not Jones who interests us, but his customers. Through the goods they charged to their accounts we can open a window on their consumption, their material lives, and the economy that they were making. To identify buyers, we draw upon other local data (for details on record linkage and on the selection of customers for study, see appendix D). From local tax rolls and lists of households, we know that these people were representative of the rural population that constituted the overwhelming majority of Upper Canadians – farmers, artisans, labourers, rural entrepreneurs, and their families. To illustrate, we begin with four men who all owned land in Yonge Township (although only one met the threshold we have used to define a farmer in this period, having 5 or more acres in cultivation).[4] John Cronk and Daniel Patterson each had

50 acres, but no house on their properties. Patterson had no land in cultivation and no livestock; Cronk had one horse and two cows, and 1 acre in cultivation. Archibald Kincade owned 10 acres, 4 of which were in cultivation, and a round log house. Silah Robins, who owned 120 acres, had 16 acres under cultivation and, a key asset for an early farmer, a pair of oxen. But he too lived in a round log house. Robins's household included eight others, four men and four women. Cronk's household included just two others, both women, and Kincade's just one woman; Patterson was not listed in the household census.

Cronk was the first of these men to appear on 1 September, charged for a quart of rum at 35 cents and 7.5 yards of bed ticking at $1.10 per yard.[5] The next entries were for Robins, seven yards of bed ticking, also at $1.10 per yard; two pieces of calico, seven yards at 50 cents and six yards at 53 cents; plus vest and trimming worth $1.43. The book then returns to Cronk, charged 50 cents for cash paid to his daughter and $2.27 for Margaret O'Neill's purchase of a piece of calico. Patterson was charged 13.7 cents for "balance on rum," as if the rest had been paid in cash; later in the day he would twice be charged 35 cents for a quart of rum. Kincade followed, credited with $1.00 paid in cash.[6]

The book then comes back to Robins, who purchased a handkerchief (40 cents), three-quarters of a yard of "imitation" at 70 cents per yard, a paper of pins (30 cents), 1.5 yards of broadcloth ($1.80 per yard), some thread and buttons (20 cents), 4.5 yards of "russell" at 60 cents per yard, one skein of silk thread (8.3 cents), a fine comb (40 cents), another handkerchief (this one 45 cents), a dozen needles (10 cents), and three skeins of silk at 10 cents each. Except for the comb, all of Robins's purchases were textiles, sewing supplies, and finished cloth products, with the six kinds of fabrics adding to a total of about 27 yards.[7] Later in the day there would be two more charges to Robins's account, 35 cents for a quart of rum and 43.3 cents for a quart of spirits (a more costly rum). In total these purchases amounted to about $25, the second largest expenditure of anyone that day at the store.

So the accounts continue. That day's entries record purchases by sixty-four customers, including twenty-five families whose transactions we have recorded for the ensuing year. In total, eighteen of the latter purchased fabrics, more than 145 yards of at least nine distinct fabrics, seven purchased a total of at least twelve quarts of rum, and so on. The 121 itemized transactions for these people were the first of more than 2,900 recorded on the accounts of the seventy people we selected for study here.

Among them, they purchased at least 180 different products, many of which came in varied forms.

The daybook from which this information comes listed transactions as they took place, with the customer's name, items purchased, unit prices, and total values. In a business of any sophistication, this information was the first step in accounting; the more permanent record was the firm's ledger, in which accounts were maintained for at least long-term customers.[8] At some stores details of purchases were copied to the ledger, but usually, as was the case at Yonge Mills, the ledger noted only the total obligation for the day with a cross-reference to the daybook. To know what people actually bought, therefore, daybooks are the better source. But, as these few transactions suggest, the data in even a single daybook represent an almost overwhelming body of information. This, no doubt, is one reason why not many historians have used them systematically.

Yet it is the very specificity of these details that is their attraction. The inspiration for the research was a desire to know "ce que *faisaient* les gens" ("what people *did*"), as Tom Wien emphasizes in paying tribute to the accomplishment of Louise Dechêne.[9] Through retail accounts, we can begin to answer, for Upper Canada, a key question in the history of consumption posed by Carole Shammas: "*who* consumed *what* and *when?*"[10] Based on that information, we argue the importance of adding consumption in the countryside to the main narrative of Canadian settlement history, which has been almost exclusively oriented to production. That settlers shopped at all is our first story. To interpret what they shopped for is the challenge. What do the pieces of various sizes of various fabrics, sewing supplies, and alcohol that we have already encountered – and the hundreds of products we will encounter in ensuing chapters – tell us about consumption and material life in Upper Canada? What can we learn about economic practices from details of transactions? Already, for example, we have seen that goods had prices, that cash could be involved in store transactions, that goods for third parties might appear on someone's account, and that women were visible in the accounts.

As a way of considering the implications of such detailed information, we will set the evidence against stories others – contemporaries and later historians – have told about goods and consumption in Upper Canada. Doing that confirms some stories. Others, however, are clearly not literal statements of fact; they require to be understood as myths and metaphors. Consider, for example, a story about a product we have already encountered; set in Fitzroy Township, on the Ottawa River upriver from Bytown (Ottawa), it is compelling both for its account of a specific object – a needle – and for its image of overall pioneer living standards.

> The incident of the lost darning needle illustrates ... the circum-scribed life of these pioneers ... At the time of which this is written there was but one of these needles in [Fitzroy] township. Many homes there were whose darning and mending depended upon the safety of this little household convenience, and darning and mending were the pioneers' devices for saving the expense of new clothes. It passed from one shanty and log house to another, following the convenient rule that each housewife could have its use for a day once in each three or four weeks. Another could not be procured, except on a special visit to the District Town of Perth, and that was nearly sixty miles away. But there came a day when the needle was lost. The neighbours were sum-moned and informed. The usual sniffs and glances ... came from among the half-dismayed women as they gathered to discuss the calamity. Mrs Dickson had lost the needle while on a visit to Squire Landon's grist mill, and it must be somewhere along the way. And so the neighbourhood turned out – the women, the boys, the girls, for the men were mostly absent from the settle-ment engaged elsewhere ... gaining by other means of livelihood what yet the partially cleared farms could hardly yield. And just as the quest seemed almost useless ... the sharp eyes of a little girl rescued the precious darning needle from a trodden tuft of grass, and there was general rejoicing in the settlement.[11]

For all its specific detail, this story is entirely unlikely. If needles were so useful, could any family afford not to have its own? If there was a mill nearby, why was the nearest store so far away?[12] As we have seen, needles were sold by country stores, at a cost in 1808 of just 10 cents per dozen. Even if there was no store, peddlers, whose stock in trade undoubtedly included needles, might have visited. That is, it is not believable that any-one had to travel sixty miles to acquire needles. Few if any settlers can actually have gone that far into the bush; but, however far they went, it is impossible to believe that they would have been so improvident as not to bring something this vital and inexpensive. Why then repeat the story here? Because it illustrates the power of stories: that sophisticated historians could cite it as literally true suggests that it fit their under-standing of the trajectory of settlement in Upper Canada.[13] As we will see, they are not alone; stories like this are deeply embedded in accounts of the making of rural Canada. By considering the details of what people actually bought, we tell a different story, one that situates them fully in the global consumption economy of their time.

1

CRUSOE IN UPPER CANADA? STORIES OF RURAL CONSUMPTION

> We begin to get reconciled to our Robinson Crusoe sort of life, and the consideration that the present evils are but temporary, goes a great way towards reconciling us to them.
>
> Catharine Parr Traill, 20 November 1832[1]

Catharine Parr Traill was among the most perceptive of contemporary writers on settlement in Upper Canada. So her description of her new life in the "backwoods" is of great interest. Writing for readers she imagined as "the wives and daughters of emigrants of the higher class who contemplate seeking a home amid our Canadian wilds," she chose an image they would immediately recognize, which depicted the family as if, like Crusoe, it was alone on an island – isolated, surrounded by the unknown, deprived of the usual supports of civilization, and fending for itself.[2] Just two sentences later, however, she sharply qualified the story; far from being self-sufficient, the Traills were "dependent upon the stores for food of every kind."[3] Their reliance on stores cannot have been unusual. In the mid-1820s, tax assessors counted 470 merchant shops in Upper Canada, the equivalent of one for every 349 people (a rate that was consistent throughout the settlement era).[4] As most Upper Canadians lived outside the main urban centres, there could only be so many stores if people in rural areas, like the Traills and the people we encountered in the preamble, were buying from them.

Given the number of stores in the province, the story of Crusoe-like self-sufficiency would be of mainly literary interest except for its power; it is the basic starting point of many Canadian narratives of settlement.[5] In one version, living "at or near subsistence levels" was a condition that rural families like the Traills hoped was temporary and that they or their children could sooner or later "rise above."[6] Another version makes self-sufficiency a goal and a strategy, as people seeking independence struc-tured their lives to minimize their engagement in markets.[7] Whichever was the case, if self-sufficiency is the main element in the story of settle-ment, it pushes stores to the edge of the narrative. Even when exchange is recognized in that narrative, it is often understood as involving "trad-ing," "bartering," and "haggling," processes essentially different from the buying and selling of commerce in later periods.[8]

A similar story has been told in American history; to many histori-ans, as we discuss below, the idea that colonial America was a world of "self-sustaining economic communities" has had tremendous appeal.[9] That appeal is even stronger in popular narratives. For example, the much-loved and widely recommended *Little House* series of children's books, sold in the tens of millions and translated into dozens of lan-guages, tells of "an America made prosperous and energetic by individuals from self-sufficient families, people dependent on no one ... a society in which the only legitimate ties were neighborliness."[10]

At the other extreme, stores and markets are central to a very differ-ent narrative of Canadian settlement. In this account, ordinary fishing, lumbering, farming, and aboriginal men and women throughout British North America required credit from merchants to buy "goods, seeds, and animal feed," "equipment and provisions," without which they could not survive. Needing supplies, families were deeply vulnerable to a commer-cial system based on unequal exchange, which entrapped them in a "network of dependency" and on "a treadmill of debt."[11]

Buyers and the goods they bought are the focus of this book. As we will see, the purchases of rural Upper Canadians provide no indication of the retail pricing practices imagined in the story of unequal exchange. Nor do they leave much room for Robinson Crusoe. If they were to suc-ceed, the families who settled Upper Canada, like rural people everywhere, had to have his versatility, resilience, and self-reliance; but imagining them as isolated from the currents of the global economy would entirely misrepresent their experience. Pioneering was complex, difficult, and risky; it would have been impossible if settlers actually had to live outside the markets through which those currents flowed. As Laurel Thatcher Ulrich writes in her brilliant study of "the age of home-spun" in New England, "There was no period when [people there] were disconnected from the larger Atlantic economy."[12]

To say this returns us to the original cornerstone of Canadian eco-nomic history, the conclusion to Harold Innis's *Fur Trade in Canada*, which explicitly rejects the Crusoe story, except as a goal to strive toward. "The migrant is not in a position immediately to supply all his needs and to maintain the same standard of living as that to which he has been accustomed, even with the assistance of Indians, an extremely fertile imagination, and a benevolent Providence such as would serve Robinson Crusoe or the Swiss Family Robinson on a tropical island. If those needs are to be supplied he will be forced to rely on goods which are obtainable from the mother country."[13] Innis focused on the exports that would pay for these goods and on the character of colonial economies built around them; his argument shaped an understanding that Canada was "an export-led staple-dominated economy producing raw materials ... for external markets" that "imported more than it exported."[14] In this book, we explore the other side of the story, the imported goods that Innis calls "needs"; Peter Russell calls "essential needs";[15] and Allan Greer, in his study of Samuel Jacobs's store in the Richelieu Valley in the later eighteenth century, calls "real needs." "Year in, year out," Greer writes, "the range of goods demanded by rural customers remained remarkably stable. Consumer demand was rather inelastic as it was dominated by the real needs of the population, mostly habitants."[16]

In thinking about consumption, markets, and exchange in settlement economies, many historians base their story on dichotomies. They contrast needs with luxuries, traditional with modern, informal with formal, independence with dependence, "neighborhood exchange" with "the market principle," "local" with "long distance" exchange, "non-capitalist" or "pre-capitalist" with capitalist, merchant with industrial capital, products with "commodities."[17] Each of these words and all of these pairings pose "genuinely complex issues of language and culture."[18] One complexity is that they seldom denote precise and mutually exclusive categories; rather, they shade into one another, overlapping and connecting in ways that blur apparently clear distinctions.[19] Where evidence is placed depends also on perspective. To one writer on pre-Revolutionary America, that colonists' per capita consumption of goods imported from outside their colony equalled or exceeded one-quarter of per capita annual incomes suggests very substantial engagement in the international marketplace; to another, the data represent a "stunning reliance on imported goods"; to a third, they define a pre-eminently local world, in which "most ... basic needs" were produced locally.[20] Evidence of the kind we consider cannot resolve such variation in interpretation. But in identifying actual goods and how they were purchased, it reveals ambiguities and complexities in processes that are frequently understood in dualities.[21] Consider, for example, a standard distinction, between local and non-local: imported goods such as textiles and hardware, when used in production of goods for sale, were actually essential to local exchange.[22] Moreover, even what might appear to be purely local and domestic – what families produced for their own use with their own time, labour, and materials – was influenced by knowledge of what goods could be bought, from whom, and at what price.[23]

Besides dichotomies, we need to recognize two underlying considerations in the historical literature on consumption. First is the challenge of reconciling stories that single out a specific dramatic change, described as a transformation or revolution, with "the ubiquity of markets and the virtual universality of exchange activity" in the very long term.[24] Second, there is deep disagreement on the main direction of long-term change. As two leading authorities note, "Much of the scholarly literature on consumption has taken a moralistic attitude towards consumption, sometimes positive, but more usually negative."[25] In the former story, the underlying trend was to higher living standards and a culture of choice, abundance and well-being through a consumer capitalism in which an ever-widening proportion of the population, including women, both as workers and shoppers, willingly participated.[26] In the latter, the outcome was "the rampant materialism of [modern] society," a world in which demand is shaped by impersonal and powerful global corporations, whose strategies, advertising, and branding entirely frame our possibilities.[27] For the period studied in this book, one of the central interpretations of rural America is a narrative of profound loss; it tells of previously autonomous, independent families and communities being subordinated to the market and to capitalism.[28]

Stories of dramatic change in consumption begin long before Upper Canadian settlement. Thus, Beverley Lemire, writing of the early cotton trade, speaks of "[n]ew consumer forces ... at work in England in the late seventeenth century";[29] and Neil McKendrick opens a pioneering book in consumption history with the blunt declaration, "There was a consumer revolution in eighteenth-century England."[30] He finds this in changes in wealth, behaviour, attitudes, and ideas: luxuries became normal and everyday, shopping became routine, and fashion became prominent far beyond the elite and the metropolis. Widely adopted by "middle-ranking households,"[31] such changes were also selectively taken up by families farther down the social scale. Jan de Vries agrees that in this period, "The evidence for growth in consumer demand is ... compelling, and it cannot be explained away as a phenomenon restricted to a small social group, a few goods or a brief period of propitious price and wage movements."[32] These changes happened in a period when real wages did not rise and without revolutionary technological breakthroughs on the production side. To explain the paradox, he invokes not a consumer but an "industrious revolution." Focused on changes in household behaviour that allowed greater consumption, this concept is particularly pertinent to us because it integrates households' production for themselves and for markets with consumption of purchased goods, and it recognizes that families could vary what household members did and the intensity of their work.[33]

A similar story of revolution has been told for the British colonies in America.[34] Thus, T.H. Breen describes a "mid-eighteenth-century transformation" marked by "the flood of imports that found its way into even the most humble provincial households" creating a "spectacularly new material culture [that] provided a social and economic framework ... in which people could work out for themselves the implications of core liberal values which we now associate with modernity."[35] There were inequalities in wealth, income, and living standards and variations within and among regions, but colonists all participated in this new world of goods.[36] In rural New England, Gloria L. Main argues, "a remarkably resilient" farm economy grew despite the limitations of the land, partly by "greater efficiencies in farm production" but "perhaps just as important was the availability of new consumer goods that encouraged families to expand their indoor tasks and work 'smarter.'"[37] The latter can be seen, for example, in the eighteenth-century transformation of weaving in New England; initially a male artisan's trade, it became a female, household-based skill. Rising consumption of store-bought goods did not rule out, indeed could be reinforced, expanded or changed by home production, including in bourgeois families. It did not imply a linear, or indeed any, trend away from home production. And there was always a relationship between the time and effort put in and the value and desirability of the output.[38]

Given this account of the eighteenth century, it comes as a surprise that another American story situates the key dramatic change after the Revolution, in a "market revolution" that brought local worlds increasingly within, and under the power of, external forces.[39] This interpretation imagines earlier rural Americans as collectively, if not individually, self-sufficient and sees their world as a subsistence-oriented moral and com-munitarian economy whose values placed it outside, and resistant to, capitalism.[40] To make this argument, it is necessary to define the exten-sive and diverse market-oriented activities of rural families, including buying, selling, and renting land and working for wages, as falling out-side capitalism and within a world of "subsistence production, neighborly exchange, sale of surpluses, and movement to new lands."[41] Christopher Clark sums up works in this tradition by contrasting capi-talism's "search for profit in the marketplace" with families' orientation to succession and land accumulation for "succeeding generations."[42] A Canadian work in this tradition extends this definition, making capital-ism "a relentless search for profit."[43] Another Canadian study defines "the capitalist mode" as involving "specialized production for ... sale on an impersonal market."[44] Clark's own definition of rural capitalism looks elsewhere, focusing specifically on "the set of social relations in which labor is ... divorced from the ownership of the land, tools, or materials that form the means of production."[45] That seems to deny the presence of such labour earlier, and it excludes many farm families, even far into the twentieth century.

To the north of New England, in Lower Canada, Gilles Paquet and Jean-Pierre Wallot also locate the core transition in the late eighteenth and early nineteenth centuries, but they see it positively. This, they argue, marked "the transition from an essentially subsistence society ... to a society transformed by the market," "an important discontinuity [that] transformed Quebec's socioeconomy at the turn of the nineteenth cen-tury[:] modernisation and the establishment of a commercial capitalist system."[46] Using, among other evidence, a sample of probate inventories, they document sharp increases in the wealth both of rural merchants and of habitants, whose ownership of goods grew substantially during even the brief period between the early 1790s and 1807–12. By then, as the existence of numerous villages likewise demonstrates, commerce reached far into the countryside.[47]

A third account of the history of consumption delays the really important transition in the structure of capitalism and market activities until very much later, the last third of the nineteenth century, when what one author calls "the transition from a simple to a complex market soci-ety" occurred.[48] For Britain, it is argued, this was when "the coming of the mass market" brought an "ever-widening range of choices" to most people.[49] Something like this image informs an overview of Canadian consumption history that pictures the later nineteenth century as "a formative moment in Canadian consumer history [when] some of Canada's inhabitants became interested in shopping for, purchasing, using, and enjoying commodities."[50] In Keith Walden's vivid account of the process in Toronto, this was when ordinary people became modern, learning through and responding to profound changes in technology, economy, and culture, as new goods and new experiences increasingly drew them into the "vortex of consumer capitalism."[51] At the heart of the new was the massive urban department store, "the palace of consumption."[52] Shopping in one of these stores, Walden suggests, was an essentially different experience from shopping at the country general store.

Even these changes were not the central drama according to a fourth approach to the history of consumption. In this version, that had to wait until the twentieth century, when, as another Canadian overview puts it, "many citizens ... could, for the first time, allow themselves to purchase goods beyond strict necessities."[53] This view echoes a powerful argument in American history that sees "a new kind of consumer society" created in the twentieth century.[54] A representative work stresses that it was in "the post-World War II period ... [that] mass consumption was extensively reshaping the nation."[55] For Canada, a leading textbook takes a similar view; for rural Canada in particular, it depicts a "transformation from subsistence to consumer society" only after 1945. Indeed, it has been argued that the era of "mass consumption" in Canada did not begin until after 1955.[56]

Summing up this sequence of revolutions, Jan de Vries writes, "Over and again, historians have ushered Western man, or a large subset thereof, out of an Edenic world of customary and traditional consumption patterns."[57] One reason that so many dramatic transformations have been found is that this is how historians prefer to frame their stories. But as they have added revolutions and extended the period in which substantial changes in consumption patterns can be demonstrated, historians have collectively made the concept of a revolution in consumption increasingly elusive.[58] With this in mind, seventeenth-century historian Sara Pennell has argued for a shift in emphasis, toward continuities (and the everyday): "to be forever seeking out a possibly mythical point of consumer take-off is arguably a quest with diminishing returns. Instead we should be seeking out continuities to understand better when significant change actually occurred within the practices, as well as the ideologies, of consumption. This surely means more attention to the quotidian, which of course is less freighted with desire, and usually less materially present to us now, than to 'luxury' and 'splendour.'"[59]

Finding the quotidian has, however, been a challenge. "There is very little historical research on the rate of diffusion of consumer goods," Carole Shammas has noted.[60] In a rich study of the Hudson River Valley in the first half of the nineteenth century, Martin Bruegel agrees: "We know little about patterns of consumption in rural areas."[61] Although historians have been aware of the issue, the difficulty, as Jan de Vries points out, is to find evidence that will allow us "to examine consumer behavior directly, by measuring the volume and value of actual purchases."[62] That is the objective of this book, which seeks to understand "how things were used, where, and by whom."[63] It grows from our earlier research on imports at the wholesale level and from a larger study of the entire provincial economy.[64] For evidence of farm marketing, the latter drew on country store accounts to see how farm families paid their bills. But it did not ask the question that prompted this book: what had they bought in the first place?

To put this differently, this book asks what goods were important enough to people that they would go into debt in order to have them. What could their purchases say about their priorities and their lives? From this perspective, even purchases that might seem "mundane and prosaic" – and perhaps self-evident – were nevertheless important.[65] This follows the view of John Brewer and Roy Porter, who write in introducing their foundational collection of essays that "Every object in the world of goods was emblazoned with meaning."[66] To attempt a comprehensive account of the meanings of every purchase would, obviously, be an impossibly large task.[67] To begin with, few if any goods have simple and unambiguous meanings.[68] Moreover, specialists in material history are better placed than we are to visualize goods and their uses – for example, historians of textiles and domestic life will know what could be made from a specific length of a particular fabric and what that might say about dress, table settings, and bedding.

Still, making sense of goods requires a context. For that, we draw on (and attempt to tell) stories about consumption. These encompass narratives both of overall living standards, such as the Crusoe image or the idea that demand was stable and inelastic, and of specific goods, such as the lost needle. Such stories can be found in every kind of source, both from the period and in modern writings. Among the latter, we include textbooks and popular histories, in part because they are where most people encounter history; if specialists are to get beyond essentially private scholarly arguments, they need to address popular understandings. Moreover, such accounts often point to larger historical issues; for example, the persistence of references to self-sufficiency demonstrates how a familiar story can overwhelm evidence and analysis.

Our data confirm some stories and question others. Thus, purchases of alcohol at one of the stores simultaneously support and challenge a common understanding of alcohol consumption in pioneer society. Other stories are unlikely, such as those emphasizing extremes – both of deprivation (such as the lost needle) and abundance. The latter could involve luxury goods that were seldom or never purchased or depict an overall pattern of settler wealth that the evidence makes unlikely.[69] Many of these stories come from nineteenth-century works: reminiscences, tributes to pioneers, emigrant narratives, guides to intending emigrants, and travellers' accounts – standard literary genres whose conventions need to be recognized if their descriptions are to be used.[70]

Historical writing likewise has its genres and conventions. Notably, stories of revolutionary transformation derive their drama from contrasting before and after. Often, however, this entails stylizing the earlier period, a tendency encouraged also by standard historical periodization, which provides conventional breaks in the narrative, and by the practical requirements of research, which lead to a concentration on evidence from a specific period.[71] The many revolutions in consumption are a case in point. When historians investigate a period others have understood as an almost timeless "before," [72] they find a complex world that needs to be understood in its own terms. In the process, they may also suggest more anticipation of the changes to come and more ways that the later resembles the earlier than the stylized version imagined. Whether an emphasis on continuity adds nuances to transitions that others have represented in sharp contrasts or changes our understanding in fundamental ways cannot be conclusively resolved by the evidence we explore here. But we will see that even if people bought less, bought different things, and lived in a different technological and cultural universe in 1800 than in 1900 (or in 1900 than in 2000, for that matter), they always knew why, where, and how to shop, to buy, to use credit, and to consume.

That is, we begin with the fact that Upper Canada was settled after all the changes in consumption during the eighteenth century. Emigrants from rural Britain and Ireland came from a rapidly changing society. Depending on their circumstances, they could have widely differing experiences of, and perspectives on, consumption and material life in the world they left, but they did not opt out of that world when they moved. A minority, likely a small one, of intending farmers were like the Traills, bourgeois families aiming to maintain a living standard that no longer seemed possible at home. Others came with some means, with the idea of bettering themselves. Not even the poorest had ever lived entirely outside the reaches of a market economy. And the underlying structures of that market were capitalist.

In contrast to the United States, which had been developing for more than 150 years, Upper Canada was a new society, begun in the 1780s. Many of its first settlers were Loyalists who came from the frontier rather than the now well-developed coast. But they too can readily be imagined as wanting to live within the late-eighteenth-century world of goods. By then, for example, the leading groceries had fallen dramatically in price. Using Carole Shammas's reasonable definition (which set the threshold at a level of imports that would permit one-quarter of the adult population to consume them at least once daily), they were now "mass consumed" both in England and the colonies.[73] Unlike newly opening areas on the American frontier, however, Upper Canada was primarily oriented to Britain. This reflected imperial power, which had kept the territory under British control; imperial trade policy, which until the 1840s was mercantilist; and, above all, Britain's industrial leadership and centrality in global trade and finance.[74] As demonstrated by American industries' demand for tariff protection in our period, for many goods the United States was not the lowest cost producer.[75]

In his ambitious book on consumption and revolutionary politics in eighteenth- century America, T.H. Breen lists "six major categories" of "evidence of consumer behavior": the writings of travellers and officials, museum artifacts, archaeological findings, probate inventories, customs records, and newspapers.[76] As he notes, each has strengths and limits. Descriptive sources such as official documents, the press, and private letters provide possibilities, yet collectively they are full of contradictions, and they frequently say more about the observer than the observed. For the material and visual record, the realities of production and preservation mean that the finest artifacts and society's upper echelons tend to be best documented; and ordinary people and their possessions are underrepresented. Hence researchers seeking a more comprehensive view of consumption and material life in the eighteenth century have turned to probate inventories. Prepared as part of settling estates, they covered a rather wider spectrum of the whole population and have been made to yield a sophisticated picture of colonial wealth and living standards.

Business account books are conspicuously missing from Breen's list of sources (and from many other lists, too). Even when used, they are often cited anecdotally rather than exploited systematically. The value of accounts is that they document actual buyers and catch the immediate flow of transactions – their frequency, sequence, and combinations – revealing "mundane, day-to-day, small-scale exchanges of things in ordinary life."[77] They are particularly helpful in understanding the diffusion of goods that disappeared through consumption, such as groceries and chemicals, and by wear and tear, such as textiles and crockery.

Here a contrast can be drawn with probate inventories, which recorded a stock, what the deceased possessed, but cannot say when or how goods were made or acquired, may not speak to how they were used (and how frequently), may not disaggregate some categories of goods, and will not record goods once possessed that had already been disposed of.[78] They are subject also to both unknowable and systematic biases, which raise issues concerning how they represent the world of the living. These include variations in inventory quality and coverage (by region, over time, among inventory takers, and among categories of goods, for example); biases by wealth, age, and gender; and complexities of valuation. Historians and economists have developed approaches to manage all of these; even so, it has been argued that the many assumptions necessary to arrive at usable conclusions mean that researchers prefer to "avoid the use of probate data unless alternative sources are unavailable."[79] Account books are one such alternative for Upper Canada. As it happens, some probate inventories survive for the colony, but the extent of coverage and their character have been little investigated; and although they have been used in studying wealth distribution, they would be very challenging to use to understand consumption in any detail.[80]

It is not that no one has used retail accounts as sources for rural history; indeed, this book was inspired by pioneering studies that have used them imaginatively to investigate several rural settings in British North America across a span of 150 years. We have already cited Elizabeth Mancke, who tracked the dealings of 175 women in the daybook of Edward Dewolf's store at Horton Landing, Nova Scotia, over ten months beginning in December 1793. Noting that there are "hundreds of extant account books available," she commends them as a source for "a more nuanced understanding of women's work."[81] Béatrice Craig has taken an impressively comparative approach, using accounts from mid-nineteenth-century New Brunswick, Maine, and Lower Canada, alongside census evidence, to reveal complex patterns of rural production and exchange, such as widespread production of homespun on a commercial scale, with "profit, not self-sufficiency, [as] the goal."[82] Accounts are vital to her argument for "the emergence of a consumer society at Madawaska" in the years around 1860.[83] A number of studies have used account books to analyze credit, the character and significance of customer indebtedness, wage and labour arrangements, and hierarchies of consumption and power.[84] Robert Sweeny's comparative treatment of the general ledgers of the Ryan and Templeman stores at Bonavista, Newfoundland, in 1889–91 catches the many nuances of families' engagement with one another and the commercial system, as they manœuvred to make their lives and earn their livelihoods; the result is to highlight the complexity of processes long seen as simple. As he writes, "what was typical was variety."[85] Because it focuses on what people purchased, one of the most directly relevant studies in terms of this book is Claude Desrosiers's analysis of Joseph Cartier's ledger at St Hyacinthe in the mid-1790s.[86]

These authors share an understanding of the potential of account books, and all provide sophisticated accounts of the challenges they pose for the researcher. These begin with the sheer quantity (and sometimes obscurity) of information in even a single account book; for example, the two firms Sweeny studies for Bonavista each generated one thousand to fifteen hundred intensely detailed pages of accounts per year.[87] In the circumstances, it is reasonable to focus intensively on one place or firm and a short period.[88] If the objective is to cover several locations and a longer period, another strategy is required. Ours is to use selected stores in a few places, to consider a sample of customers at each, and to focus on a single year of transactions.[89]

Another issue is what the records cannot show. Obviously they do not show all that a family possessed; nor, as we will see, did a store's accounts show all that someone bought. Indeed, Craig argues, "the fact that customers did not limit their purchases to a single store makes it impossible to use the store books to uncover individual consumption patterns."[90] But, she goes on to demonstrate with rich specificity, they suggest possibilities. If, for example, some people bought a particular product, others might also have done so, if not at that store or in that year. For some goods, we can confirm this speculation by drawing on published Canadian data on imports (available beginning in 1850; see appendix C). This need not mean that everyone bought an identical set of goods; like Sweeny, we argue for the importance of variation. Just one of the elements of variation – that people bought at more than one store – refutes a powerful and persistent version of the unequal exchange argument, that the wealth and prominence of individual merchants was based on their having "effective local monopolies."[91]

This book represents an experiment in bringing retail accounts fully into the study of consumption. Proposed as an illustration of possibilities and an encouragement to imagine ways of systematically approaching this type of source, it contributes to the debates about trends and transitions in consumption and market orientations by showing how some rural families used a specific store. Whatever else they were doing at the store, their purchases placed them within extended, often global, commodity chains.[92]

In the Canadian literature on these issues, the system that delivered these goods is usually defined as merchant (as opposed to industrial) capitalism, and it is true that within Upper Canada, except for the colony's new railroads, factory-based local industry had just begun to appear in 1861. On the other hand, our stores were associated with mills and lumber operations, the colony's principal rural industries, which could be substantial in scale (figure 1.1); and labourers were part of their work force and clientele.[93] And of course many purchases were the products of British industry. Moreover, to the extent that the dislocations of the nineteenth-century British and Irish economic universe that propelled much migration to Upper Canada after 1815 were the result of industrial capitalism, the colony itself was created in that context.[94] During the period covered in this book, the industrial revolution was transforming much of the British economy; the steamboat, the railroad, and the telegraph were developed, dramatically advancing the speed and regularity of transport and communications within North America; and Upper Canada's population grew more than twenty-fold.

This study began with a focus after these developments, at the end of the settlement era, during a period widely understood as "an era of fundamental change."[95] We focused on Peterborough and Leeds counties as places where forest and farm economies were closely combined, census manuscripts survived, and store accounts were available. By linking accounts to the census, we could obtain information on the families, occupations, and farms of the clientele. In the townships around our stores, land clearance was still very much in progress. The proportion of

Figure 1.1 The mill at Delta. Built in 1810 and described by the Rev. William Smart in 1817 as "unquestionably the best building of the kind in Upper Canada," this mill, in the south of Bastard Township, Leeds County, would have been familiar to many customers of Benjamin Tett and Samuel Scovil. See Gourlay, *Statistical Account of Upper Canada*, 270; and www.deltamill.org (accessed 13 October 2013). (Author's photograph, 1994)

occupied land under culture in 1861 ranged from one-third to one-half, below the levels found in the core of the province, around and to the west of the head of Lake Ontario, but very much in line with the proportion for the province as a whole. We then extended the research backward in five individual cases (discussed in the next chapter and appendix D). We reverse this order in discussions below, beginning each chapter with evidence from 1808–09, as early in the settlement era as our data allow. It would have been possible to multiply cases and regions, but, as the data swiftly mounted, it seemed more practical to stop at ten cases and see what they would yield.

The most immediate result is two lists to which we will refer throughout. Appendix A records almost 400 products and services bought by five or more people, of which almost 50 – including tea, sugar, tobacco, salt, gunpowder, nails, window glass, axes, scythes, handkerchiefs, blankets, shoes, cups and saucers, cotton and wool fabrics, thread and needles, ribbons and buttons – were bought by seventy-five or more families (about 10 percent of our buyers). Readily imagined as "needs," they are singled out for particular attention. Appendix B includes another 270 goods that had fewer buyers. To catch the range of goods, we organized both lists into nine main categories (of which four are further subdivided). Classifying some goods provided challenges:[96] for example, a single product description could cover many distinct products with widely varied uses, the actual use of some products is uncertain, and some categories overlap. Notably, distinguishing locally produced goods and services from imports proved vital in considering the local market, yet understanding a few local goods (whiskey, maple sugar, homespun woolens, and locally made clothing) required that they be discussed in chapters focused on imports. The three main constituents of a general merchant's stock of imports – dry goods, groceries, and hardware – are the subjects of chapters 3 to 5. At most of our stores, they represented about two-thirds of the value of customers' purchases. We address most local goods and services in chapter 6. Finally, we consider three remaining categories in chapter 7, goods for the home, footwear, and a residual group of other goods. Footwear too was locally made, but differentiated from other clothing by the materials involved, the skills of shoemakers, and, as we will see, its transformation in the 1850s from a local to a regional product.

Each category of the lists is organized by the year in which products first appeared and the total number of buyers. Many of the principal goods bought at the stores in 1861 prove already to have been widely purchased in 1808, and most were by 1842, a finding that invites reflection on stories of a mid-century revolution. Equally, this chronology questions stories whose arc runs from isolation and self-sufficiency to market involvement: the array of goods that people purchased widened over time, differentiating details of everyday material life in 1861 from 1808, but the timing of the appearance of new goods on the lists makes clear that rural buyers were well aware of developments in the market and open to buying new goods.[97] Despite many changes in consumption during the period, one of the main findings is how much, rather than how little, consumption in 1808 resembled consumption in 1861 for rural Upper Canadians.

2

PLACES, STORES, AND PEOPLE: VILLAGE STORES AND THEIR CUSTOMERS

General stores were an integral part of the life of the villages of Upper Canada, handling most of the needs of a local population. In fact, they functioned as small department stores. The shelves inside this store are designed to show the wide variety of goods that were available at the time of Confederation ... It was important that the storekeeper understood the needs of the townspeople and farmers, for they relied on him to import all the goods they might need throughout the year. It was also essential for the storekeeper to be able to extend credit for up to a year at a time as it was common for farmers to pay all their bills in the fall, after harvest.

Description of Crysler store, Upper Canada Village[1]

Anyone who has visited a heritage village representing nineteenth-century life has seen a country general store of the kind we consider here. To the modern eye, they seem small; and our photograph of Thomas Darling's store (figure 2.1) confirms that image.[2] Yet as the guide to Upper Canada Village points out, they contained substantial and varied stocks. An inventory of Darling's store, for example, taken on 1 April 1858, runs to over five hundred lines filling more than twenty-two pages.[3] The sequence of the list suggests the organization within the store. Dry goods came first, eight pages of textiles (almost 2,300 yards of about 30 distinct fabrics), clothing, and sewing supplies; they accounted for about half the inventory's total value of two thousand dollars. Housewares dominated the next few pages, followed by footwear (which needed only a few lines); hardware and more housewares (which must have been shelved in close proximity) took up five of the next seven pages, with other kinds of goods, including more sewing supplies, also listed in this section; two pages followed that mainly recorded imported groceries; entries on the final page included panes of glass of different dimensions, more hardware, and

Figure 2.1   Thomas Darling's store. In 1861, our sample of fifty-seven customers purchased goods worth more than $1,800 from this modest building at a landing on the St Lawrence River. It sold more than 260 different products then. The store, still standing in 2008, has since been demolished. See www.ltihistoricalsociety.org/darlingside.html (accessed 13 October 2013). (Author's photograph, 1994)

forty-six pounds of cheese. An inventory at Tett's store (dated 30 October 1851) also runs to about five hundred lines and has much the same sequence. It ended with footwear and shoemaking supplies, except the last two lines were for a total of 174 pounds of butter.[4] Here, too, dry goods represented half the almost eighteen-hundred-dollar total of the inventory. From Catharine Parr Traill's account of depending on stores for food, we might have expected entries for the main Upper Canadian foods, but the only local foods recorded, indeed the only perishable items, were the closing entries for cheese at Darling's and butter at Tett's. Although a few other local products were listed, the inventories confirm that the main role of the country general store was to sell imports.

Not surprisingly, many goods were found on both inventories. Each stocked opodeldoc, for example, a product we return to below. Even so, the lists are anything but identical.[5] For example, Darling recorded fabrics such as cambric, cashmere, linen, orleans, plaid, and silk that Tett did not; and Tett's list included fabrics not on Darling's list, such as homemade flannel and cloth, bagging, jean, and satinette. A partial explanation for these variations is that the store might have been out of stock at the time the inventory was taken. Darling sold jean and satinette in 1861, as it happens; and in 1842, Tett sold linen and silk. Neither stocked alcohol; as we will see, that was normal. But neither inventory recorded tobacco either, and it was among the most commonly purchased products at both stores in the year we selected for study. This is a useful reminder that inventories catch stock at a particular moment and do not necessarily reflect the role of products or entire categories of goods in the lives of customers.

When Benjamin Tett began business, he quickly learned that a rural clientele expected credit.[6] There are traces of cash transactions in his and other daybooks, but it is unlikely that they were a large part of the business of any of our stores. Our main focus is on purchases rather than payments; but we should note that, in picturing the "harvest" as the source of rural income and autumn as the usual time for payment, Upper Canada Village oversimplifies the rural economy, because customers could earn income in many ways. To begin with, not all were farmers. Even for farmers the season for cutting hay, a product they might sell, came before the wheat harvest. And the harvest was only one step toward the sale of a wheat crop; threshing, having it ground, and selling the resulting flour were often winter activities. Butter, eggs, wood and wood products, meat, and wool also had different seasonal patterns from wheat. Moreover, winter brought the possibility of earning income from off-farm work. These patterns could vary with the specifics of the local economy, to which many factors – such as soil quality, climate, and the proximity of larger urban centres – contributed. The demand for imported goods might likewise have varied, particularly between the richest and poorest rural areas. Even so, there is no reason to think that the transactions we consider could not have occurred at any village store in Upper Canada.

Still, it is important to this study that they took place at specific businesses in particular places (table 1). The stores were established early and their long lives suggest they were well integrated in their settings. Their owners, if not already locally prominent, soon became so. That, plus family continuity, helps explain the survival of their records. Just as important was the survival of buildings; none of these places experienced the systematic destruction that accompanied urbanization and the redevelopment that transformed larger towns and cities in the ensuing 150 years.

Like many rural businesses, ours encompassed more than just the store on which we focus, and the store was not necessarily the leading element of the business. Tett's 1851 inventory, for example, went on to record almost $2,400 in the stock of his lumbering operations; just its draught animals – five horses and eight yoke of oxen worth almost $750 – equalled the value of the store's stock of textiles. How the related enterprises were owned, managed, and represented in the store accounts varied both among stores and over time. The day-to-day roles of the owner in the store must likewise have varied, from active management to distant supervision. Even in the former case, other staff – such as a clerk or book-keeper and someone to help with heavy work – were required.[7] Where the relationship was obvious, we sought to exclude employees, as well as the owner and his immediate family, from the customers we selected for study. As it happens, several people we included proved to have close associations, a theme to which we return in later chapters.

THE SETTLEMENT ECONOMY

Rural development in Upper Canada combined rapid expansion of land occupied and of the proportion of that land actually used for farming. Throughout our period, new farms were being made and existing farms expanded. The first case comes from very early in that process. In 1808, Upper Canada's population numbered less than 60,000, and land taxed as under culture totalled about 200,000 acres. By 1828, the year of our second case, 3.6 million acres of land had been taken up in Upper Canada, although just 18 percent of that was in actual use. Fourteen years later, in 1842, 6.2 million acres were occupied, of which 28 percent was in use. In the province's heartland, which extended from Prince Edward and Northumberland counties west to Oxford and around Lake Ontario to the Niagara River, the proportion of occupied land in use passed 50 percent by 1851; and in 1861, two-thirds of occupied land was in culture in six of these core counties. Across the province as a whole, however, only 45 percent of all occupied land was being used for crops and pasture (plus gardens) in 1861 (table 2). By then, there were about 1.4 million people in the province, over 6 million acres were in crop or pasture, and most of the potentially useful agricultural land in the province had been occupied. Upper Canada had a well-developed urban network, which was reinforced and intensified during the 1850s by the construction of railways. Yet this remained a strongly rural economy. As late as 1871, at least half the population was directly engaged in farming; and many others, such as blacksmiths, carpenters, and millers, were integral elements of the farm economy.[8]

Most of the customers at our stores who could be found in the manuscript census lived in the eleven townships reported in table 2. In Leeds, settlement of the front, along the St Lawrence, began in the Loyalist era. At the rear, settlement came later, after the War of 1812, encouraged in part by imperial policy, including the construction of the Rideau Canal through the area. That was also when the Peterborough region was opened, again initially prompted by the imperial government, which sponsored a substantial group of Irish emigrants to settle there.[9] Neither county would develop to the level of the provincial heartland, but they were attractive enough to settlers that they continued to grow by voluntary immigration. On the other hand, at the end of our period, less than half of all the land in four of our townships had even been taken up, an indicator that much of it was extremely unpromising for agriculture. Some of this land could, however, provide forest products, as could land occupied but not cultivated, recorded as woodlands in the 1861 census.

In table 2, we include the number of holdings of fifty or more acres in each township in 1861. These ranged from 158 in Escott, the smallest township, to more than 300 in three other townships in Leeds. This provides a rough indicator of the number of farms, although a working farm could be smaller than this, not all holdings of this size were actively farmed, and some of those with such holdings reported other occupations to census enumerators and may well have worked mainly off-farm. Indeed, some of those reported as farmers may also have had other occupations. Nor do aggregate data speak to the variety of farms and family strategies. It can be said, however, that most farm families practiced some form of mixed farming, growing a variety of field and garden crops for on-farm consumption by the family and its livestock and for sale in nearby and more distant markets. Livestock included working animals – horses and oxen – and cattle, pigs, and sheep that supplied products for on-farm consumption and for sale. Most farms were also engaged in the forest economy, using their own and possibly also crown land, producing for family consumption (for heat and for building) and often also for the market. Some members of farm families also were employed by others in this sector. Members of our samples provide multiple examples of the forms such market participation could take. Thus, twenty families supplied ashes to Samuel Scovil (for the production of potash); several purchased supplies from the Fowlds for timber shanties; twelve supplied Thomas Darling with wood that he sold as fuel for steamboats on the St Lawrence; four sold maple sugar to Benjamin Tett; and eight earned credits at Thomas Choate's in 1851 by hauling lumber during January and February from his saw mill to Peterborough and to Lake Ontario. On the other hand, that only a minority in each of these samples can be directly shown to have engaged in these activities confirms the variety of rural families' strategies and practices.[10]

PLACES AND STORES

Because we wanted to explore consumption by the province's rural majority, we sought the records of businesses with a primarily rural clientele, hence located outside the principal towns. In Leeds County, as we noted in the preamble, the main centre began as a village on the St Lawrence in the township of Elizabethtown. Designated as the centre of the Johnstown District (which then encompassed Leeds, Grenville, and Carleton Counties), it was renamed Brockville in 1812; by the 1840s, its population exceeded 2,000 and in 1861 it was 4,100.[11] Our Leeds cases come from stores west of Brockville, two at the front and two at the rear of the county.

Yonge Mills, source of our first two samples, was in Yonge Township, about fifteen kilometres to the west. It was built by Charles Jones (1781–1840), whose father, Ephraim, came from a prominent Massachusetts landholding family. A Loyalist, Ephraim had quickly emerged as a local leader – he was elected for Grenville to the first Upper Canadian Legislative Assembly, for example. Like many such figures, he rapidly accumulated land holdings – by 1812, he owned more than 11,000 acres of land in twelve townships. After schooling in the United States, Charles began to acquire local offices.[12] But there were many with claims on such positions and few of these posts paid substantial incomes. Nor did unimproved land generate much income. Commerce was one of the most obvious alternatives. Charles opened a store in Elizabethtown in 1802, and a few years later turned his attention to a mill site in Yonge (on Jones Creek), where a substantial head of water could be created at a point which sailing vessels could reach from the St Lawrence, a few kilometres downstream. Either then or subsequently, the mill was built to a larger capacity than local harvests justified, reflecting Jones's intention to conduct a province-wide grain business. Buying wheat farther west, he would have it shipped for milling, then export flour downriver.[13] For our purposes, it is the mill's local role that matters; it ground wheat from area farmers, and the site also provided the other principal mills for a rural community, a saw mill and one for carding and fulling wool.[14] The mills were the attraction around which a small village grew, including a store that Jones opened in 1807. In 1828, the year of our second sample, Jones was named to the province's Legislative Council, a mark of his standing within the colony's Tory elite. His grain business would unravel in the later 1830s, but the village, the mill, and the store remained. In 1851, the *Canada Directory* reported it as having a population of 175.[15]

The other sample from the front of Leeds comes from the next townships west of Yonge, the Front of Leeds and Lansdowne (which were jointly administered) and Escott. Although they began to be settled in the late 1780s, the Canadian Shield, which here reaches right to the St Lawrence, tended to discourage settlement until relatively late.[16] Thomas Darling (1814–1883) arrived from Scotland in 1837 and acquired a farm along the St Lawrence between Gananoque and Brockville; from a narrow landing, he soon began to sell wood to passing steamboats. In 1845, he added a store to the enterprise.[17] When the Grand Trunk Railway came through a decade later, a few kilometres inland, Darling opened a second store at its nearest station, Lansdowne Village. The railway did not supplant the river, however, and river steamers still used wood for fuel. Hence the Darlingside store continued well into the 1880s. In a typical year, Darling sold around three thousand cords of wood.[18] At the prices he paid his suppliers, this represented more than four thousand dollars in earnings, some of which were spent at the riverside store whose 1861 accounts we use.

Following the War of 1812, the British government sought to increase the security of military communication between the two Canadas by sponsoring settlement in the rear of Leeds County and building the Rideau Canal. Our two cases here are from stores founded when the Canal opened. The first was owned by Benjamin Tett (1798–1878), who arrived from Somerset about 1820. With an English grammar school education, he began life in Upper Canada by establishing a school at Perth. In 1827, he was named as a paymaster on the canal works and began to extend his business links, for example with Thomas McKay, a leading contractor. Later, Tett would act as agent buying wheat for McKay's New

Figure 2.2   Benjamin Tett's mill in Bedford Township. Today an attractive lakeside home, this was once a gristmill, part of Benjamin Tett's milling complex at the outlet of Devil Lake. In 1842, Tett had a saw mill at this location that figures in a variety of ways in the daybook of the store at Newboro, eight kilometres away. (Author's photograph, 1994)

Edinburgh flour mill in Bytown.[19] In 1831 Tett acquired, or built, a saw mill in Bedford Township in adjacent Frontenac County, at the outlet of Devil Lake (see figure 2.2), and added a store to the complex in 1832.[20] By 1833, he had been joined in Canada by two brothers, one of whom took charge in Bedford, which allowed Tett to open a second store at Newboro (also known as the Isthmus), a lock on the canal at the boundary of North and South Crosby Townships. He purchased most of his stock in Montreal, to which the Rideau Canal gave access by steamboat. He sometimes bought from merchants in Brockville, about sixty kilometres to the east by road, and he used the canal to send lumber to Kingston. Besides lumber and the wheat sent to Bytown, he handled other local produce, notably potash, which he shipped to Montreal. Tett's ambitions are suggested by his unsuccessful candidacy for Leeds in the provincial election of 1836. Much later, he was elected to the provincial assembly (serving from 1858 to 1863) and then to the first Ontario legislature (in 1867).

Portland was founded at the same time as Newboro, in Bastard Township, just to the east along the Rideau – and not quite so distant from Brockville. Our records come from Samuel Scovil's store, a business that, like Tett's, had been established in the 1830s. Scovil, who had been born in adjoining Kitley Township, began as an employee of the store, then acquired it from its current proprietor, Philip Wing, in 1846. He would operate the business for another thirty years.[21]

The main urban centre of its region, Peterborough was granted a post office in 1829 and designated as the centre of the newly created Colborne District in 1841. Despite its inland location, it grew to match Brockville in size, with over 2,200 people in 1851 and almost 4,000 in 1861. Two of our samples in this region are from Thomas Choate's store in Warsaw, almost on the boundary between the townships to the east of Peterborough, Douro and Dummer.[22] Choate (1809–1900) was born near Cobourg, his family having moved there from New Hampshire in 1798 with their cousins, the Burnhams (who became the principal family of the region). Trained as a millwright in New York State, he came to Dummer in 1834–35 to complete work on a saw mill, a grist mill, and a woolen mill on the Indian River, which were being developed for his uncle, Zacheus Burnham of Cobourg. Choate opened a store there in 1836 and became the first postmaster of the village, which he named Warsaw, in 1842. He assumed other kinds of local leadership as well, for example as school commissioner and as a prominent temperance advocate. The mills burned in 1858 but were quickly rebuilt. They were on a scale appropriate to a local operation: in 1861 the saw mill's output was 150,000 feet and the grist mill produced 1,600 barrels of flour.[23] Choate himself oversaw the business until his retirement in 1889; it continued in the family into the 1920s.

We also have two samples from the Fowlds store at Hastings (until 1852 Crooks' Rapids). It was on the boundary of the counties of Peterborough (Asphodel Township) and Northumberland (Percy Township), at the outlet of Rice Lake, where the potential to generate waterpower had been recognized even before settlement of the region began. Henry Fowlds Sr (born 1790) had come with his family to New York State from Scotland in 1821, moved to Upper Canada in 1834, then settled in Asphodel in 1836. There he soon became associated with two leading local men, both also closely linked to Zacheus Burnham: Richard Birdsall, surveyor of the region, and Dr John Gilchrist, physician, politician, and local mill owner and developer. With Gilchrist, the senior

Fowlds owned a mill at Westwood, on a creek flowing into Rice Lake. Then, in September 1851, the family purchased the milling rights at Crooks' Rapids from the Hon. James Crooks, together with over one thousand acres of land.[24] Henry's three sons, James, Henry Jr, and William, under the business name of James S. Fowlds and Brothers, quickly developed a retail store and extensive mills, including a grist mill that could grind 25,000 bushels of wheat annually, a sawmill capable of sawing 2.5 million feet of lumber, and a carding and fulling mill. They also owned a steamboat, the *Forest City*, which ran between Hastings and Peterborough, and Henry Jr was the local postmaster.[25] By the 1860s, and probably earlier, the brothers ran timber shanties, through foremen or contractors, in Dummer and nearby Methuen Townships. In their ventures, they dealt with several banks, notably the Bank of Montreal branch in Peterborough. Their other orientation was to Lake Ontario, particularly through Cobourg, and from there to Montreal, source of most imports, and to New York State, destination of many exports. By 1861 they had invested $7,000 to transform one of their grist mills into a cotton mill and were extensively engaged in local property development. The scope of this business – and its extensive reliance on credit – exposed it to multiple risks, and this led to its bankruptcy in February 1865. The immediate cause was fire: several mills had been destroyed in 1863, and the store burned in 1864.[26] Following a compromise with their creditors, notably the principal dry goods supplier in Montreal, the brothers were able to continue in business, with milling and other timber operations; and the family retained its local prominence.[27]

Our other sample in this region comes from Lakefield, at an excellent waterpower site at the head of the Otonabee River above Peterborough, on the boundary between Smith and Douro. It is closely associated in Canadian literary history with the Strickland family, beginning with Samuel, who began to farm in the area in 1831 and became the most prominent figure in the community; his sisters, Catharine Parr Traill and Susanna Moodie, both lived in Douro for a time in the 1830s, and Catharine returned in 1857 (and is included in the 1861 sample). Although the first saw and grist mills were built here in the mid-1830s, the real takeoff for the village came after 1851, when Zacheus Burnham laid out the best mill site.[28] A post office, called North Douro, was established in 1856; a grist mill opened in 1857 on the Smith side; and a saw mill capable of cutting seven million feet per year opened in 1858.[29] John

Christopher Sherin (1827–1901), whose records we use, commenced business here in 1855 as a "general dealer in dry goods, groceries, provisions, &c. &c."[30] Sherin had been born near Cobourg, his parents having emigrated from Ireland in 1822. With his brother Samuel as bookkeeper, he would operate the store until 1881, then again from 1885; by then, his family's business affairs extended widely, for example into extensive lumbering and later into land dealings in Minnesota and the Canadian west.

One of our first findings was that the retail trade was highly competitive; this has implications for how people shopped. In the first place, people could buy at other nearby stores. Except at Yonge Mills and Darlingside, there were other local retailers besides those whose records we use: in the 1840s, for example, there were three other stores at Newboro, two at Portland, and one at Warsaw, each a village with a population of at most one hundred.[31] Lakefield and Hastings developed slightly later but grew quickly to populations of as much as five hundred in the 1860s; even in 1858, there were at least two other stores in the former and four in the latter. There were also other nearby villages to which many farmers had more or less equivalent access. Farmers in Douro, for example, were close to both Lakefield and Warsaw; those in south Dummer or north Asphodel were close to Norwood, which even in the 1840s had three stores plus other rural services.

In the second place, people could also shop in larger places. In the early 1840s, Smith's *Gazetteer* reported that Brockville, readily accessible from the front of Leeds, had as many as twenty-four stores and Peterborough had at least thirty, if we include retailers such as grocers and druggists who might have represented competition for part of the trade of a general country retailer. In Leeds, the 1851 *Canada Directory* noted that the trip by stage coach from Yonge Mills to Brockville cost 50 cents. From Warsaw (twenty-five kilometres) or Lakefield (fifteen kilometres), the return trip to Peterborough could evidently be done in a day when travel conditions were favourable. From Hastings, Peterborough was accessible during the navigation season by steamboat; Cobourg, a highly developed commercial centre on Lake Ontario with about thirty stores, was forty-two kilometres away. From the rear townships of Leeds, towns on the St Lawrence like Brockville and Gananoque were too far for a day return but nevertheless accessible.[32] And there were closer and larger villages along the Rideau system such as Perth and Smith's Falls, each with about a dozen stores.

CUSTOMERS AND SAMPLES

In order to study a number of stores without accumulating unmanageable quantities of data, we decided to focus on selected customers at each store and to record all transactions on their accounts over a year.[33] To identify customers, we targeted census years (initially 1861, to which we then added examples from 1851 and 1842) and locations where the personal and agricultural schedules of the manuscript census survived. We recorded every name found in the accounts, then sought these people in the census for adjacent townships (see appendix D for further information on the samples).[34] The 1854 case was the closest to 1851 that we could obtain from the Fowlds store; intended to complement our 1861 sample from this business, it was linked to the census of 1851–52. It also represents an experiment in using a ledger as the basic source and is the only case not drawn from a daybook. For 1808–09 and 1828–29, there was no province-wide census, but we could link to local censuses (lists of heads of households and counts of other members in age categories) and township assessment rolls (which recorded property subject to taxation: land owned and used, housing, and livestock).

In most cases we found at least two-thirds of customers (see table 3 for a summary of samples and linkages).[35] The exceptions were Fowlds's store, where we linked only 54 percent of customers in 1854 and 59 percent in 1861, and Tett's, where we found only 40 percent of customers. The latter was a special case, because we lacked census manuscripts for the three adjacent townships in Frontenac County, which bordered the Rideau Canal at Newboro. Some of our failures to link someone were because we found more than one person of the same name in adjacent townships. These duplications could sometimes be resolved, such as when more than one member of a family made charges to the same account, but more often we did not have enough cues to permit a decision. In these cases at least we know that the customer lived in the vicinity of the store. There were many more cases where we did not find customers' names in the census at all. It is striking that people sufficiently known to qualify for credit at a store were not caught by the census. Almost certainly that primarily reflects the extent of movement in rural society. More than half of those not linked in 1861, the most systematic provincial census to that point, did not appear in store accounts until after census enumeration for the area had been completed. At Darling's, in fact, only four of the thirty-one not linked appear in the daybook before mid-March.

For the eight samples linked to the census, we sorted the names of linked customers by occupation and household size. In our first three trials of this process, all in 1861, we drew samples consisting entirely of linked customers; thereafter, we also included some unlinked customers, who were listed alphabetically prior to selecting the sample. As explained in appendix D, we took names at regular intervals from the lists of linked and (in seven cases) unlinked customers, making sure to include at least one of each occupation. The aim of structuring the sample in this way was to catch the variety of actors in local economies. For 1808 and 1828, lacking information on occupation, we sorted by household size and assessed value of property (but for subsequent analytic purposes we estimated numbers who were farming by setting an arbitrary threshold of having five or more acres actually cultivated).[36]

Making occupation the priority meant that non-farm customers were somewhat overrepresented by comparison with the most common occupations, farmers and labourers. Even so, half or more of the linked members of all but two samples were farmers. Many (sometimes all) of those in the "no occupation" category were women, and some women thus were caught in our initial selection. We decided, however, to make women's accounts a particular focus; this led to including additional (in five cases all) women's names to the samples. Typically, a daybook recorded entries under the name of the account holder, with the identity of the person actually in the store added if the account holder was not present. But in three 1861 cases (Fowlds, Scovil, and Darling), the daybook recorded the person present, even if the transaction would subsequently be debited or credited to the household head or other account holder. For these stores, we added other members of the families of anyone caught in our initial sample process. This reflected that, for many purposes, the household or family was the basic unit of consumption, as was evident when charges were ultimately to a single account.[37] This should not be read as implying that individuals did not have their own reasons for making purchases.

The outcome of the selection process was ten lists of customers whose accounts we would record in detail. Samples do not necessarily mirror the exact distribution of the larger population on every observable variable (birthplace, religion, livestock holdings, etc.), but they do span the range for every variable with similar enough distributions to suggest that in these terms the samples of linked customers are representative of the linked group as a whole. As an indication of this, in table 3 we provide a summation of data on household size and extent of land being cropped. Going further, to present these distributions in more detail and to incorporate all the others we could add, would encumber the text and, as will be evident in ensuing chapters, would not contribute to the analysis.

In drawing the samples, we took no account of indications of a customer's intensity of engagement with the store, such as references to multiple ledger pages for a single customer. The samples thus include accounts that varied widely in value and in frequency of transactions. In fact, a majority of the accounts proved to be very modest. Except in 1808–09, the median account was fifteen dollars or less, and the bottom quarter of the distribution had debits of four dollars or less (table 3). As we argue below, these modest accounts must have represented no more than a small share of these families' actual consumption of store-bought goods. On the other hand, every store had some very substantial accounts. At seven stores, the largest account alone totalled more than 10 percent of debits; and at all the stores the ten largest accounts represented 40 percent or more of total debits. At two, the ten leading buyers accounted for two-thirds of the value of purchases. In subsequent chapters, we will pay particular attention to these customers.[38] As can be seen in the difference in value between the largest and the tenth largest, even their accounts varied widely. Some, for example, had large accounts because of quite particular transactions, whereas others bought goods in all the main categories.[39] Yet even the largest of the latter accounts, as far as we can judge, do not represent all that these families would have purchased during a year. To make sense of what they were buying, and why, we turn in the ensuing chapters to a detailed examination of the goods purchased and the patterns of buying them, dividing our discussion into five main categories of goods and the stories that have been told about them.

3

FASHION IN THE COUNTRYSIDE?
TEXTILE AND CLOTHING PURCHASES

It is unlikely that the majority of women in Canada, leading active lives in towns, villages, and small communities, succumbed to the dictates of fashion, except for church on Sundays and special occasions. One could wish that more everyday clothing survived to prove this point.

K.B. Brett, 1980[1]

Upper Canadian settlement coincided closely with the industrial revolution in Britain, in which the mechanization and exponential expansion of cotton output were a fundamental element; dry goods (textiles, textile products, and sewing supplies) were vital to the business of a general store – as we saw in chapter 2, they represented half the value of inventories at Darling's and Tett's; and cottons such as calico and bed-ticking were among the 1808 purchases we noted in the preamble. Yet cotton is hardly visible in most accounts of textiles in Upper Canada.[2] One explanation for this omission is suggested by our quotation from Katharine B. Brett: the clothing that has survived does not represent what people actually wore. Our evidence, of a kind that has not generally been available to textile historians, can help to address that problem. And by documenting clothing that people bought and the fabrics from which clothing was made, it also provides a perspective on fashion in rural women's lives.

Like other research for museum and living history settings, Brett's aim is to represent the past visually.[3] As she points out, however, artifacts can produce an unlikely vision of the everyday: indeed, in her contribution to the Canada's Visual History series, more than half the images of dresses and children's outfits are of silk (yellow silk, figured silk, ribbon silk, tartan taffeta, etc.), and many others are of luxury fabrics such as velvet, satin, and fine white muslin.[4] Textiles of other kinds have an equivalent orientation. Thus, Dorothy and Harold Burnham's classic work on hand-weaving in Canada warns that its rich illustrations are unrepresentative: "Most of the weaving done," they point out, "was plain material for sheets, blankets, and clothing, produced in great quantity both professionally and domestically. Being plain and utilitarian, little remains; it is the patterned coverlets that were always special that have been treasured, although their frequent survival gives an unbalanced picture of what was actually made."[5]

A second explanation for the invisibility of cotton is that the literature on textiles in the settlement era has a "strong bias towards a 'homespun' or romanticized interpretation."[6] In this powerful narrative, country people did not buy fabrics at all. This was the story told by a leading Nova Scotia lawyer and politician, who spoke in 1865 of "the great body of the settlers in the country, whose backs are covered with woollens of their own production – whose feet are shod from the hides of their own cattle – whose heads are covered with straw from their own fields – who sleep between blankets of their own wool and their own weaving – on feathers from their own farmyards."[7] This story has had equal appeal to many modern writers; it can be found, for example, in the standard history of women in Quebec: "The majority of women wore country fabric, which they spun, wove, dyed, and cut."[8]

In her account of country clothing, Brett avoids romanticization. Homespun was a function of a lack of alternatives: "shipments were infrequent and popular items quickly ran short."[9] "Of necessity," she writes, "clothing was frequently produced from homespun as part of the largely self-sufficient domestic farm economy."[10] She relates this understanding to the fashionable products that survive by making silk represent fashion in an otherwise largely homespun world. "Women in the rural areas, cut off from the outside world, had little time to bother with changes in style … These busy and practical women spent most of their time in simple and serviceable dresses, of gingham or printed cotton when available, but more often of home spun and hand woven wools and linens … which they made themselves. What thought they had for fashion was displayed in the best silk dress, the pride of every woman who owned one."[11] As time went by, improved communications transformed women's situation. Now supplies were "more readily available … there were more ready-made goods in the shops" and the "practice of making everything possible in the home, as well as making over and making do, were no longer a necessity."[12]

Other studies of textiles in the settlement era also focus on homespun. Thus, the account of "cloth and clothing" in Marjorie Griffin

Cohen's influential analysis of women's work and markets in nineteenth-century Ontario is devoted essentially to cloth. Doubting that the earliest pioneers had appropriate land and the time and resources to protect flocks of sheep, Cohen pictures them striving towards self-sufficiency in the production of woolens and linens. Although she recognizes that many women continued to produce woolen cloth and flannel at home after the mid-nineteenth century, her story otherwise parallels Brett's: "Expending time on home production of cloth became less rational as alternative and cheaper methods of supplying it were available [w]ith a more integrated local economy."[13] At the same time, her account of homespun sets it within, not outside, the market. Raw wool was bought and sold, and "home" production had many commercial dimensions: carding of wool and fulling of cloth done at local mills, spinning and weaving done for hire, and cloth-making and knitting done for sale. Women and families placed a value on their work and time; they were aware of alternatives, including the price of goods at stores; and not all had the appropriate resources for home production.

In the same period in Lower Canada, probate inventories demonstrate that rural families tended to possess much more limited quantities of clothing than did urban dwellers; nevertheless, most owned at least some made from imported British textiles.[14] The latter was entirely compatible with home cloth production; indeed, a substantial majority of rural households owned spinning wheels. On the other hand, especially in the Montreal area, a much smaller proportion owned looms, and almost no one owned more than one loom. Still, a rising proportion of rural inventories included looms, implying that an increasing number of rural families were taking up weaving. Hence David-Thiery Ruddel speaks of "the trend towards self-sufficiency in domestic textile production ... in the early nineteenth century."[15]

Another perspective on homespun shows that some production was not oriented to family consumption at all, but to sales in the marketplace. It was actually a relatively expensive specialized fabric suitable for rural work settings, including lumber camps; in New Brunswick, as Béatrice Craig shows, that market continued long after 1850.[16] Indeed, the manufacturing schedules of the 1871 census reveal that handloom weaving was very much an income-generating trade for some rural families. In Leeds County, a decade after our last samples there, many women and some men conducted market-oriented woolen handloom weaving using local wool and, for mixed fabrics, imported cotton warp.[17]

Craig's research, like ours, draws on accounts that record textile and clothing purchases. From these, she argues that "Madawaska people were not impervious to fashion. They just did not let it run their lives." She places particular emphasis on "[n]ew patterns of consumption [that] emerged at Madawaska ... between the late 1850s and 1863."[18] For Upper Canada, fashion was undoubtedly important earlier than that, as Elizabeth Jane Errington shows in her study of "the growth of an indigenous fashion industry in Upper Canada."[19] By the 1830s, newspaper notices demonstrate that the principal towns had a number of dressmaking and millinery shops, many smaller communities had at least one, and many women worked in others' homes or from their own to supply ready-made and made-to-measure items of clothing, including the "newest fashions" as one advertisement stressed. Errington's main focus is on the women who ran these enterprises, and she does not explicitly estimate how much of the province's clothing and accessories they might have supplied. But it is clear that their markets must have extended beyond the province's tiny elite and into the countryside.

If we take silk as a first indicator of fashion, we can confirm its availability by drawing on published trade statistics. Canadian imports of "silks, satins, and velvets" were valued at more than $700,000 per year at the beginning of the 1850s and almost $900,000 a decade later (for these and the following data, see appendix C). It gives a context for these figures to know that the comparable annual value of imports of cottons ($3.5 million in 1850–52 and $5.3 million in 1860–62) was five to six times higher and that the value of woolens ($2.7 million and $4.1 million) was four times higher. Linen was less important than any of these categories; imports were $355,000 per year in 1850–52 and only $309,000 in 1860–62. Taken together, the value at the port of entry of all fabrics imported into Canada was equal to about four dollars per capita in 1851 and slightly more in 1861. This figure will serve later as a rough benchmark in assessing leading customers' purchases. Both wool and flax, of course, might also be produced in Canada. Indeed, wool was. But, on the whole, linen was not; in 1851, the census reported home linen production in Upper Canada of less than 15,000 yards (of which the two counties studied here accounted for less than 500 yards).[20]

This chapter begins before these data and focuses particularly on dimensions of textile use that they cannot specify, individual fabrics and their buyers (see figures 3.1, 3.2, and 3.3). The accounts confirm Brett's skepticism about extrapolating from elite fashion to the larger society;

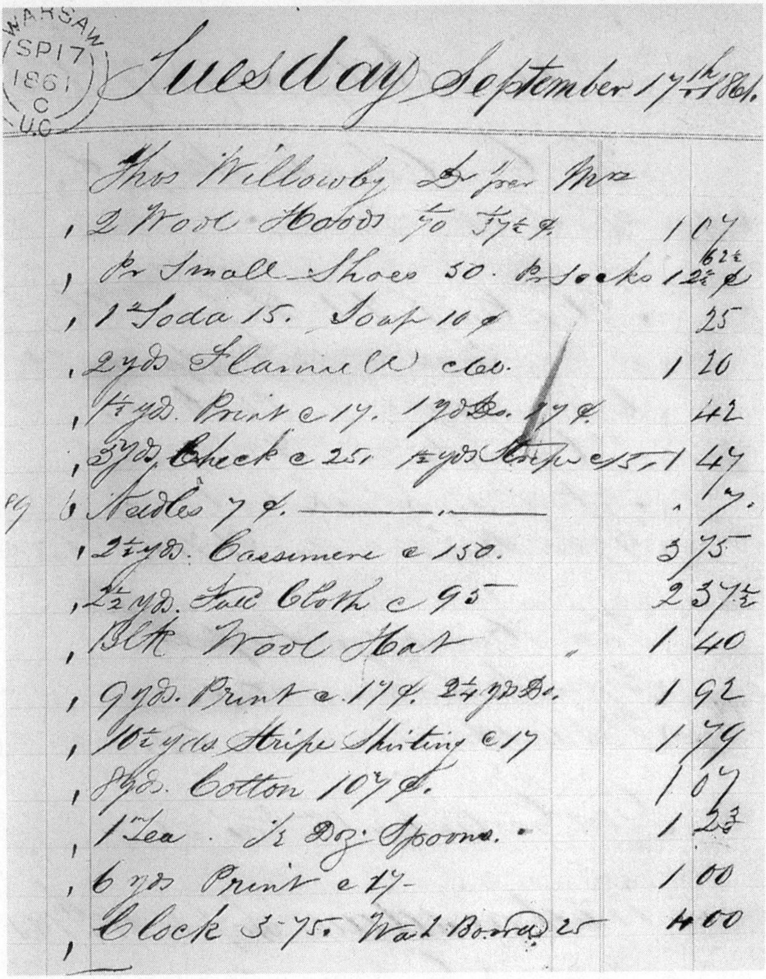

WARSAW SP 17 1861 C U.C

Tuesday September 17th 1861

Thos Willowby Dr per Mrs

2 Wool Hoods	1 07
Pr Small Shoes 50. Pr Socks 12½	62½
1 Soda 15. Soap 10	25
2 yds Flannel @ 60.	1 20
1½ yd. Print @ 17. 1 yd Do. 17	42
3 yd. Check @ 25. 1½ yds Stripe @ 15	1 47
Needles 7	7
2½ yd. Cassimere @ 150.	3 75
2½ yd. Fall Cloth @ 95	2 37½
Blk Wool Hat	1 40
9 yd. Print @ 17. 2¼ yd Do.	1 92
10½ yds Stripe Shirting @ 17	1 79
8 yd. Cotton 10½	1 07
1 Tea. ½ Doz Spoons.	1 23
6 yds Print @ 17	1 00
Clock 3.75. Wash Board 25	4 00

Figure 3.1 Purchases by Mrs Thomas Willoughby at Choate's store, 17 September 1861. An exceptionally large textile order, this list includes twelve pieces of eight different fabrics, totaling almost fifty-two yards and costing $15.00; although most were cotton, the seven yards of woolens (cassimere [cashmere], flannel, and home-made cloth) represented almost half of this value. Sarah and Thomas Willoughby were in their twenties and had no children. The cleared land on their farm was devoted largely to pasture for cattle; they reported no sheep to the census taker. They also purchased ready-made clothing – socks, two wool hoods, and a wool hat – and a washboard (see chapter 7). (Photograph by Michael Cullen, Trent Photographics)

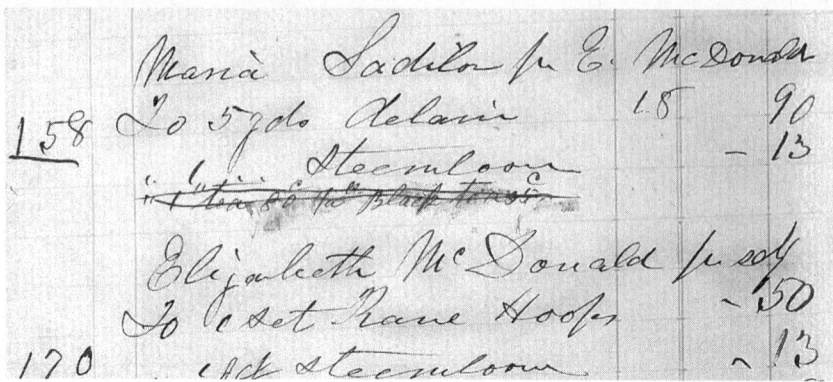

Figure 3.2   Purchases by Elizabeth McDonald, Sherin's store, Lakefield, 9 February 1861. Purchases on someone's account were frequently made by a third party; here Elizabeth McDonald bought fabrics for herself and Maria Sadler. Elizabeth (sixteen years old) and Maria (fifteen) were "servant maids" in the household of Robert Strickland, a farmer and entrepreneur. On other occasions, Maria made purchases for Elizabeth. The set of "kane hoops" suggests awareness of current fashions. The numbers next to their entries indicate that they had independent accounts; often, in such cases, the employer's account was charged. (Photograph by Michael Cullen, Trent Photographics)

luxury fabrics were seldom purchased in the countryside. On the other hand, they support Errington's analysis, by suggesting that rural women were never as isolated as many images of pioneering imply and that most rural families shopped at more than one store. Beyond these specific points, purchases of imported fabrics from the earliest period and continuing rural woolen production beyond 1861 deny the basic tenet of the homespun story, that it was a simple function of isolation and physical scarcity that necessarily gave way to purchases in the marketplace as the economy grew and communications improved.

In her study of "backwoods consumers," Béatrice Craig estimates minimum annual textile consumption at 7.5 yards per person (i.e., 45 yards per family of six). Textile historian Adrienne D. Hood uses 42 yards per year for a household of six in her study of late eighteenth-century Pennsylvania; this was the minimum "just to replace essential apparel that had worn out."[21] Hood's estimate is based on 16.5 yards for the father, 13 for the mother, and 3 for each child. That would have provided one or two work shirts, a pair of work trousers, and a pair of drawers for the man, plus a coat and waistcoat every second year; a short gown, an apron, and a shift for the woman, plus a petticoat every second year; and some new clothing for children, whose other clothing was hand-me-

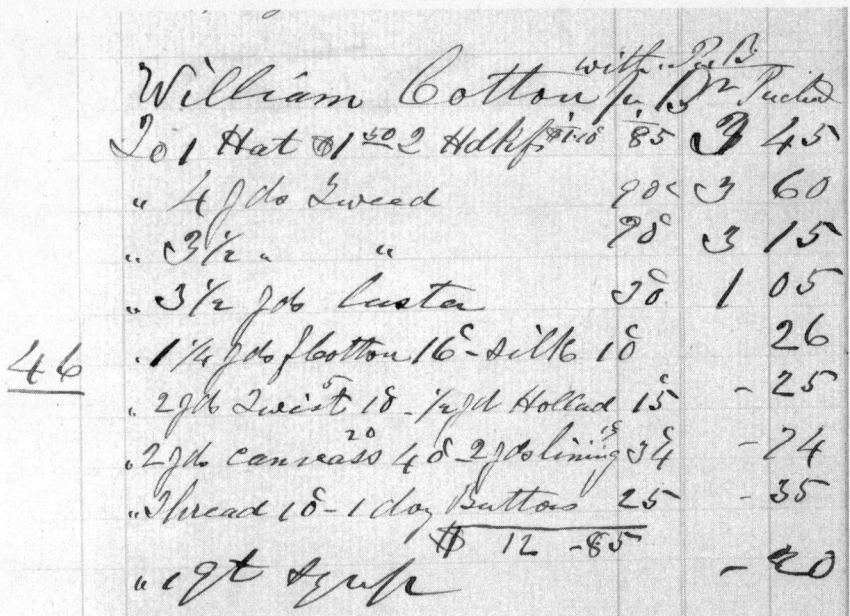

Figure 3.3   Purchases on William Cotton's account, Sherin's store, Lakefield, 8 June 1861. William Cotton was a twenty-four-year-old carpenter with a wife and a two-year-old son. Here he is charged for almost seventeen yards of six different fabrics, including two pieces of tweed (a new textile term that first appears in our samples at mid-century) worth $6.75, along with assorted sewing supplies. These purchases were by a third party, possibly another customer named Pri[t]chard; we have no indication of his relationship to Cotton. Another mystery, addressed in chapter 4, is the purchase of syrup. (Photograph by Michael Cullen, Trent Photographics)

down or made from reused fabrics. Textiles, of course, had many other uses: bedding, draperies, towels, table linens, and floor coverings in the home; and bags, covers, and other products in farm and other work settings. All were subject to wear. In addition, those who followed fashion had other reasons to buy fabrics.

Our analysis takes forty yards per household as a threshold to indicate relatively extensive purchasing or production of textiles. This is low for large households or those with several adults and slightly high for a couple without children, but it is convenient in summarizing data for a sample containing households of all sizes. The list of fabrics in appendix A is grouped by type of fibre, presented in sequence by the year each first appears in the samples then ranked in descending order by the total number of buyers in all samples. Related goods – sewing supplies and ready-made clothing – are listed in their own categories. With the exception of some homemade and fulled cloth, shown separately in the table and bought in 1842 and at two stores in 1861, fabrics and most of the other goods were imported from Britain by Montreal merchants who supplied country retailers. The list includes forty-nine fabrics purchased by at least five buyers, although no store sold all of them. More than thirty others appear in store accounts but purchased by fewer buyers (these are listed in appendix B).

Categorizing fabrics is complicated. The same name might be used for fabrics made from different fibres; some names may be alternatives for, inclusive of, or subsets of others; standard reference books sometimes disagree on the implications of a term; usages changed and overlapped; and the account entries themselves sometimes are incomplete, confusing, illegible, ambiguous, and even mistaken. For example, "cotton" might be a fabric, thread, or yarn (also called warp); usually these can be distinguished by price and by the unit, yard, skein, and ball (or pound or bunch). The main definition of cambric in the *Oxford English Dictionary* is "a kind of fine white linen," but it could also be "an imitation made of hard-spun cotton yarn"; "drilling" (called drill in store accounts) might be either "a coarse twilled linen or cotton fabric"; and sheeting was a "stout cloth of linen or cotton." Indeed, 1808 imports to the Yonge Mills store included some "cotton cambric," Fowlds's store in 1854 sold "cotton drill," and Tett's sold "cotton sheeting." Satinette could be "an imitation of satin woven in silk, or silk and cotton ... [or] a fabric woven with a cotton warp and woollen weft, with a satin-like surface"; and bombasine was "a twilled dress-material, composed of silk and worsted, cotton and worsted, or worsted alone."[22] Flannel was a woolen fabric, but imitations in cotton could also be found, like the "cotton flannel" purchased from Sherin's store in 1861. Such variations reflect the textile industries' constant search for "new fabrics in a never-ending stream of design, colour, and texture."[23] In these and other cases, our bias is not to underestimate the importance of the linens and luxuries that are so prominent in many stories. Hence, we record all cambric, drill, and sheeting as linen, all satinette and bombasine as luxury fabrics, and all flannel not explicitly cotton as a woolen. The most important uncertainty is the relationship between calico (found in 1808 and 1828 and at two stores in 1861) and print (found in 1842, both 1850s samples, and four stores in 1861). That one store, Fowlds's in 1861, recorded sales of both indicates that there was a distinction between the two textiles, yet the fact that only one store made it seems to suggest a variation in language more than in the product itself.[24] To avoid confusion, the two are presented separately.

As much as possible, the categorization in appendix A follows the language of the accounts. In particular, "cotton" (the individual fabric, not the category) includes all transactions in which this term was used, even if an occasional adjective such as stripe or check might have led to including it with fabrics called just "stripe" or "check."[25] The few transactions recording specific broadcloths, such as fearnought, kerseymere, coating, and trousering, have been included in the main woolen category, which was simply "cloth" (but these products have also been listed separately in appendix B). A residual uncertainty is that the prices for some "cloth" were less than most flannels and broadcloths; to avoid underestimating the importance of woolens, these have been counted with woolens. If this is incorrect, the low end of the price ranges for cloth would be higher and woolen yardages slightly lower; values would not be much affected.

Textiles represented just over one-quarter of the value of all purchases at Yonge Mills in 1808–09. Customers bought nineteen different fabrics, of which sixteen are included in appendix A.[26] These included cotton, calico, muslin, cambric, linen, sheeting, cloth, and flannel. In total, sample members purchased about 950 yards of material, in 275 pieces.[27] Cottons alone were 620 yards, worth over $310; wool cloth and flannel were about 180 yards, worth over $230; and linens were about 130 yards, worth almost $100. Purchases of readymade items such as handkerchiefs, shawls, hats, socks, gloves, and mittens totalled $101; and supplies for sewing and trim, such as thread, buttons, ribbons, and lace, totalled $84. Some fifty different customers bought at least a yard of fabric; the median yardage among them was fifteen, and the median value, when that is the ranking criterion, was almost $11. Of the remaining nineteen customers, eleven bought some other sewing or clothing item.

Much of this information is summarized in table 4, which presents selected information on the buying of textiles and related products in each sample: number of purchasers and their combined purchases in terms of yards, values, and number of different fabrics; the relative roles of cotton and wool; number of buyers and values of sewing supplies and ready-made clothing; and the proportion of total purchases accounted for by these products. To represent buyers who might be imagined as having made more (or most) of their purchases at the store, it provides the number of buyers who purchased 40 or more yards, the combined yardage for the ten leading buyers, and the yardage and value for the leading buyer(s). For example, at Yonge Mills in 1808, the ten families who bought the most fabric purchased 472 yards, and seven bought 40 or more yards.

Farmers were prominent in stores' clientele and in our samples. At Yonge Mills, more than half of the twenty-six buyers in 1808–09 who were at or above the median purchase of fifteen yards were farmers (that is, had at least five acres in cultivation). Three of the four principal buyers were farm families, including Thomas Freel, who had twenty cultivated acres; his family of seven led all textile buyers in both value and volume. His account (summarized in table 5) was charged for purchases of more than twenty pieces totalling 73 yards of ten different fabrics. These began on 1 September with 5 yards of cotton, and 4.5 of "imitation," a product found only in the 1808–09 accounts. There were transactions on Freel's account on fifty-four days between then and late June 1809, on eleven of which additional fabrics were purchased: flannel, woolen cloth, velvet, Russian sheeting (a British product despite the name), Lancashire sheeting, cotton, calico, linen, cambric, and "divinity."[28] Totalling almost $63, these fabrics included 33 yards of cottons worth about $16, 18 yards of wool and flannel worth almost $27, and 13 yards of linens worth about $13. The Freels bought $14 worth of ready-made products (a blanket, three shawls, two hats, two handkerchiefs, and one pair of gloves); as it happens, several of these transactions were the most expensive purchases of these goods.[29] They bought thread (including silk thread) on thirteen occasions, twenty-eight buttons, a thimble, and assorted needles, pins, and ribbons. Clearly much sewing went on in this household. What each of these purchases might have been turned into is largely beyond the scope of this research, although lengths give at least some hints, an issue to which we return below.[30] The Freels also bought a pound of indigo, and they were charged 46 cents for wool carding in 1808. Altogether these transactions represented more than two-thirds of their $129 in purchases for the year, a total that made theirs the fourth-largest account.

Such detail is meant to give a sense of the flow of textile buying. It also gives a different sense of the idea of "needs" to see them spelled out intensively and in sequence, and a different sense of the idea of rural isolation to see that transactions could be so frequent. This pattern was typical of large accounts. It is impossible and unnecessary to analyze every account, every purchase of thread or needles or a handkerchief, in this fashion. But some further examples serve to provide a sense of variation.

Samuel Tollman, whose purchases of about $135 slightly exceeded Freel's, was head of a household of five; he was not assessed as having any land. There were transactions on his account on forty-one days during the year, on four of which textiles were purchased, a total of 17.5 yards of cotton, calico, and check worth about $10. The Tollmans also purchased thread, binding, and pins, together worth 57 cents, on three other days. Despite the scale of their account, the fabrics they bought ranked only just above the median at this store by yardage and below the median by value. This is a reminder that the correlation between account size and the purchase of fabrics was never tight: it was possible to have a large account and limited textile purchases.

Joseph Proctor, head of a three-person household, was one of the most substantial farmers, with twenty-nine of his sixty-four acres in cultivation. Charges to his account during the year included 7.25 yards of four different fabrics plus thread, twist, tape, four dozen buttons, a handkerchief, and a half pound of indigo. Among the fabrics were 3.75 yards of woolen cloth; at almost ten dollars, this represented more than one-quarter of the charges on his account. Yet as we will see, he was also engaged in home woolen production. [31] And in August, he was credited $1.50 for thirty pounds of lamb, the only such credit.

Of the four women with accounts in their own names, two bought textiles. Catherine Leach, whom we could not find in the tax rolls, bought about twenty-one yards of cotton and four of cambric; and Widow Abigail Comstock, head of a family of five with twenty acres under culture, bought sixteen yards of four kinds of fabrics worth twenty dollars during the year. In yardage, Comstock's purchases were just above the median among those buying fabrics; in value, Leach was the median, with purchases worth almost eleven dollars.

Altogether, only seven customers bought forty or more yards, our threshold of minimum family requirements. Were the others all self-sufficient, making their own cloth? The accounts provide some additional information on this question, in the form of charges for wool carding in 1808 and 1807 that were transferred from the mill accounts to the daybook in May 1809. Among them were thirteen sample members. Besides Freel, these included Proctor, charged about $3.40 for carding in 1807 and 1808, which represented as much as fifty pounds of wool; Leach, whose charge for carding represented at most four pounds of wool; and

Comstock, whose combined carding accounts for the two years represented up to twenty-one pounds of wool. Of all customers, only Caleb Seaman Jr, charged $3.80 in 1808, had enough wool carded to make sufficient cloth to approach Hood's estimate for textile requirements for his family of six.[32] Proctor and Comstock's charges for carding implied wool production well below this level, although combining their purchases and an estimate of what they made would bring them almost to it. Eight of the thirteen carding customers were farmers; four others, like Leach, were not found in the tax rolls or census. It is still possible they had access to land or they might have bought wool. Other producers may have paid for carding before these charges were entered, carded their own wool, or had it carded at another mill. Still customers without land or with little land in cultivation were not well placed to keep a flock of sheep. They were evidently buying fabrics somewhere.

In 1808, Charles Jones imported 336 pieces (about 8,100 yards) of some forty different fabrics.[33] A number were likely sold only at the store in the village of Elizabethtown, because half of all the products recorded in the invoices were not purchased at Yonge Mills. But they involved only 42 pieces.[34] Of all these pieces, no more than 6 were luxury fabrics, taffeta, velvet, velveteen, and what was called bombasette (which is included with bombasine in appendix A). The invoices confirm the seasonality of imports emphasized by Brett: all the 1808 textiles were shipped upriver between late July and early November. At this store, there was something of a seasonal pattern also to purchases: September 1808 and August 1809 were peak months for yardage purchased.[35]

The main fabric, accounting for more than 70 percent of the 8,100 yards, was cotton. This should not surprise us; industrialization of cotton production in Britain was well under way by 1808. These invoices, like the purchases in 1808–09, prove to be representative of patterns in subsequent samples. In value, cotton was the leading fabric at all stores except Fowlds's, and in yardage it accounted for almost three-quarters of the more than 14,000 yards of fabrics purchased from all ten stores. Next most important both in 1808–09 and in the whole study were woolens, at over 1,500 yards. They cost very much more per yard than cottons (a yard of woolen broadcloth, however, was half again as wide as other fabrics). Thus they ranked closer behind cotton in terms of value than the yardage data would suggest. The other textiles ranked lower: in total, the ten samples record purchases of up to 1,600 yards of linen, about 800 yards of "mixed" and what we have called "other" fabrics –

and about 220 yards of eleven luxury fabrics, six of which appear in appendix A.

After 1808–09, each succeeding case adds new fabrics to the list. Although yardage and values were sharply lower at Yonge Mills in 1828–29 than twenty years earlier (indeed the lowest at any store), this sample adds seven fabrics. Cottons accounted for more than two-thirds of yardage and over 40 percent of the total value of textiles. Next by value were woolens: just twenty-seven yards of flannel and broadcloth were purchased, but they represented one-third of the value of textiles. Other purchases included several fabrics listed in the luxury category: silk, satinette, crepe, and bombasine. To be sure luxury fabrics are not underestimated, three indecipherable entries that seem to begin with "bomb" are also counted here, although their prices were relatively low. These and bombasine were purchased in pieces large enough for dresses, but pieces of the other fabrics (table 6) were all small; the thirteen purchases of silk, crepe, satinette, and muslin amounted to just ten yards, bought by nine different buyers.

At this store, only Ann Graham reached our threshold for substantial textile purchases. We were unable to locate her in the census and tax rolls, so do not know how many she was buying and sewing for; but she bought exactly forty yards of fabrics, on thirteen days between November 1828 and June 1809: two of the indecipherable pieces; three pieces of check; four of calico; five of cotton; and small pieces of muslin, cambric, and sheeting. In total these cost nine dollars, about half the total value of her purchases in the year. Her other purchases included a very few sewing supplies: a frock pattern, a pair of knitting needles, a thimble, one yard of tape, and one skein of thread.

The next largest textile account here purchased thirty-one yards, and another seventeen bought between ten and twenty-nine yards. The median in this sample was only seven yards. For those whose household size is known, only six bought as much as three yards per capita. Obviously, people were obtaining most of their textiles in other ways. Even so, fortynine different customers bought fabrics, and another nine bought some other clothing or notions. One bought indigo, the only dye purchased. This daybook also provides a few glimpses of fabric making: one person charged for carding, three buyers of cotton yarn which might have been used with wool in weaving, and one charged for a pair of wool cards.

The most striking development since 1808 was the sharp drop in prices for the ten cotton and linen fabrics that were purchased in both years. Prices for each in 1828 ranged from as little as one-quarter of the 1808 prices to just over one-half.[36] In every case, the highest price for any transaction in 1828 was equal to or substantially below the lowest price in the range for that fabric in 1808. Lower prices reflected the deflationary trend after 1815; but these prices were also substantially lower in real terms. Prices of local agricultural products were not as high in 1828 as in 1808, yet none had fallen as much as the prices for these textiles.[37] By contrast, woolen prices had declined little if at all: flannel ranged from 35 cents to 80 cents in 1808 and from 45 cents to 70 cents in 1828; cloth cost from 70 cents to $3.20 in 1808 and from $1.50 to $5.50 in 1828. These comparisons are perhaps sufficient to explain why woolens were a higher priority for families making cloth for themselves than linen; indeed, linen prices in 1828 make it difficult to believe home production could have been justified in financial terms.

Customers in 1842 purchased thirty-eight different fabrics, fifteen of them new to the list in appendix A. The leading customers here purchased many more textiles than had members of the two previous samples, and textiles accounted for more than a third of all purchases, the highest proportion at any store. The leading ten buyers at Tett's bought 894 yards of fabrics, and the median yardage was twenty-one yards. Yet although customers here bought more than double the yardage of the 1808 sample, lower cotton and linen prices meant that the values in table 4 (for total sales and for the largest and median textile accounts) were far below the equivalent 1808 figures.

The leading buyer (in terms of quantity and value) was Christopher Chant, a tailor with a family of nine. Most debits to his account were by his wife, daughters, or a son. They bought 139 yards of fourteen different fabrics worth thirty-three dollars, a total of more than forty pieces, many very small (table 7). About 110 yards of this material was cotton (grey, print, muslin, moleskin, shirting, and stripe). Of the remainder, only homemade cloth (which, at one dollar per yard, was the most expensive of all the fabrics purchased), merino, and flannel were woolens; evidently the family had other sources for them. Chant was also debited for a total of eleven dollars in sewing supplies and readymade items, the latter including a pair of silk gloves and a fur hat that alone was worth $4.50. In addition, he or a member of his family bought sixteen yards of fabric (in as many pieces) plus assorted sewing supplies that were charged to the accounts of six other customers. Among his credits at Tett's were twenty-five dollars for making various garments, including four coats, a vest, a suit, some "clothes," and a pair of trousers. Obviously these transactions give only a glimpse of his pursuit of his craft; from what we know of work processes, his clients would have provided the cloth for him to work with.

In 1842, we can draw on the census for information on flocks and cloth production (see table 8). Of the forty-two landowners in this sample, thirty-four reported owning sheep, a total of 460 of them, and producing almost 1,200 pounds of wool. Of the sheep owners, twenty-nine reported making cloth, as did two families that did not own sheep. In total, they produced almost 500 yards of fulled cloth and over 600 yards of flannel, with eleven having an output of forty or more yards. Yet, as shown in the table, more than 80 percent of cloth makers also bought fabrics, a total of 664 yards; in fact, six purchased forty or more yards.

Seven of the ten leading textile buyers (by yardage) could be linked to the census; four owned sheep, and two of them produced woolens. Richard Leach, who combined cabinetmaking with a substantial farming operation, reported forty acres in crop; twenty-three sheep; and production of sixty pounds of wool, forty-nine yards of fulled cloth, and twenty yards of linen (which was more than half of all the linen reported by members of the sample). He had a joint account with Robert Leach, a shoemaker; they purchased ninety-six yards of eight different textiles (table 7), which ranked them third by yardage (and seventh by value).[38] Next in rank in terms of yardage was Timothy Cavanagh, also a shoemaker and farmer, who had six sheep and produced ten yards of fulled cloth and twenty-two of flannel. The six members of his household (who almost all appear as buyers) purchased a total of sixty-nine yards of grey (unbleached) cotton and twelve yards of nine other fabrics, most in very small pieces (table 7). In total, these fabrics were worth $18.36, or almost 40 percent of his account. Among the $4.60 in sewing supplies were three pounds of cotton yarn, likely used for making homemade cloth. Such cases indicate that, for those who kept sheep and made wool cloth, making and buying were part of an integrated strategy.[39]

Evidently that strategy might involve selling some cloth. Such local exchanges need not have involved a merchant middleman, but Tett's accounts give a glimpse of them. Seven customers, including Chant, purchased a total of twenty-one yards of "homemade" cloth, at a cost of between 90 cents and $1.10 per yard.[40] Two people purchased a total of four yards of locally made flannel, which cost 60 cents per yard (more than the 40 cents to 50 cents charged for imported red flannel). There were also two buyers of small amounts of "Canadian cloth" at 40 cents per yard. Besides Cavanagh, five others bought cotton yarn, mainly in the form of a "bunch" at between $1.33 and $1.67; the four who were linked all owned sheep (although two did not report production of flannel or fulled cloth).[41]

At the Choate store in 1851, fabrics accounted for just 14 percent of purchases. Still, some twenty-six different fabrics were purchased, including four additions to the list in appendix A. One element in the modesty of textile values is that no pieces of broadcloth, indeed almost no woolens at all, were purchased from this store (just nine yards of flannel and small pieces of merino and delaine). Cottons, particularly print and plain grey cotton, represented three-quarters of the value, and over 80 percent of the volume. The only luxury fabrics were two tiny pieces of alpaca (which, at 40 cents per yard, actually were not that expensive) and one yard of crepe (60 cents per yard).

This store was in an area where many weavers had settled, although few gave this as their occupation in the census.[42] But many of its customers were engaged in wool production, as can be seen in table 8. Fully 90 percent of those found in the agricultural census owned sheep, a total of 468 of them, producing more than 1,400 pounds of wool. All but five sheep owners reported making cloth, a total of more than 1,200 yards, three-quarters of it flannel. Three-quarters of makers also bought fabrics, but only 383 yards in total; and only one bought as much as 40 yards.[43]

The local wool economy is also visible in store accounts. For example, six customers bought a total of 40 pounds of the cotton yarn or warp used in making mixed fabrics, no one's purchases large enough to suggest output at commercial scale.[44] Thirty fabric buyers (including six of the ten leading buyers) were charged for carding and/or fulling.[45] Carding charges were for 360 pounds of wool, and fulling accounts totalled 220 yards. Obviously the former was a small fraction of the wool reported on the census by sample members, but the latter was closer to the 300 yards of fulled cloth the census reported. Even so, there was no simple correlation between accounts and the census: seven customers who reported fulled cloth output on the census were charged for fulling; nine were not. And another nine of those charged for fulling did not report fulled cloth on the census. Moreover, although carding and fulling were both necessary in the production of woolen cloth, only five customers had charges for both.[46]

One such account was for George McMullen. Head of a six-person household, he was the only weaver in the 1851 sample, with a small farm and flock (six acres of land in cultivation and four in pasture, and five sheep) and output of just 20 yards of flannel. He was charged on 6 October for five pounds of cotton yarn and on 28 October for carding eleven pounds of wool. As these details suggest, the work he did in plying his trade does not appear in the census or the accounts; like other artisans, he would have worked on materials supplied by his customers.[47] He was himself a substantial buyer of fabrics, ranking sixth by yardage and seventh by value, buying over 5.4 yards of linen and 27 of cotton (mainly print and plain cotton, plus small pieces of stripe, gingham, and muslin).

Six more fabrics are added to the list from 1854 purchases at the Fowlds store in Hastings. In this fast-growing village, customer purchases of woolens equalled cottons in terms of value; the 150 yards of woolens cost about as much as almost 1,000 yards of cottons.[48] Yet as data in table 8 indicate, there was also extensive wool production in this area. In the 1852 census, about three-fifths of landholders had sheep, and over 80 percent of them reported producing cloth, including nine who produced forty or more yards of fabric. Four of these did not buy any textiles here, but they were tiny accounts with only minor purchases of any kind of goods.

At the other extreme, two of those who made cloth in 1851 ranked as the leading textile buyers in this sample (table 9). Edward Oakes, in fact, was the leading buyer in any pre-1861 sample.[49] A yeoman whose farm in Percy, not far west of Hastings, had a total of thirty-five acres in crop in 1851, he owned ten sheep and produced 40 yards of flannel then. This was a large and very active account, with charges to it on 104 days during the year. On 25 of these, someone purchased textiles, a total of 259 yards of fourteen different fabrics, worth $72, almost one-quarter of all debits. A partial explanation for these purchases is that the Oakes household was very large, with twelve members. The second leading buyer, Michael Hoolihan, also headed a large household. He had twenty-five acres under cultivation on his farm (not far from Oakes) in 1851, when he reported nine sheep and production of eighteen pounds of wool and 16 yards of fulled cloth. For the ten persons in this household, purchases totalled 152 yards of eleven different fabrics, at a cost of $36. In each of these cases, cotton was the dominant fabric, accounting for 80 percent of Oakes's yardage and 90 percent of Hoolihan's.

We have gone into such detail on the first five samples to introduce themes as they first appear in the data. We address our 1861 evidence primarily through an overview of the longer history of textile consumption and production in the province that incorporates all our data. Although they represent half of the entire sample, the five stores in 1861 add only four new fabrics to the list in appendix A: derry (linen), denim, factory cotton, and fulled cloth (a local woolen, purchased by six buyers at two stores). They have a larger impact on appendix B, adding fifteen fabrics to it. Without extending the study to later years, we cannot know whether these were the beginning of a trend and would subsequently be more widely purchased, which would parallel Craig's argument for "the emergence of a consumer society at Madawaska" at just this time.[50] Or they might be read mainly as an indication of the wide variety of fabrics available in the province. In 1861 as before, cottons were the most common fabrics (with the qualification that at Fowlds's store then, woolens exceeded the value of cottons). Among all our customers, just over 500 bought at least one piece of fabric, a total of more than 14,000 yards, in about 3,800 pieces. Over half of this yardage was accounted for just by the 10 leading buyers in each sample. In total, 117 customers bought 40 or more yards; one-third of these were at two 1861 stores, to which we return below.

Several fabrics listed earlier were not purchased in 1861. These include fustian and osnaburg (last seen in 1842), saxony (seen only in 1842), and merino (seen in 1842 and 1851). As none had been extensively purchased, however, it is difficult to interpret their disappearance. On the other hand, the lengthening list of fabrics includes several that were newly developed in the period, with the implication that at least some Upper Canadians were keeping up with textile trends. These appear on the list in 1851 or 1854 and were purchased at several stores by a considerable number of buyers. Among them were two woolens, tweed (a term that the OED says came into general use by 1850) and delaine (the 1830s); two mixed fabrics, orleans (1837) and cobourg (the 1840s); and one that we have classed as a luxury fabric, alpaca (1841).

Appendix A records many fabrics that Brett discusses and helps to address the unknowns of which she writes. For example, cotton print was one of the most widely purchased of all fabrics. Some 190 customers bought a total of more than 2,300 yards; and 1,050 yards of calico were purchased by 101 customers.[51] By contrast, gingham was purchased by only 28 customers, who bought a total of 114 yards, including just five pieces large enough that they might have made a dress. Muslin, a total of 198 yards, most of it in pieces of a yard or less, was purchased by 83 customers from all ten stores. Luxury fabrics, so prominent in the fashion literature, were purchased, but volumes were limited and, as with muslin, pieces were small. There were 19 silk buyers (a total of 29 yards); 3 satin buyers (3 yards); and 31 velvet buyers (29 yards). There were no purchases of taffeta. Another luxury fabric was satinette, with 22 buyers (63 yards). That these fabrics were purchased at several, or even most, stores suggests that the small quantities actually purchased reflected not physical scarcity but the demands of a rural clientele.

There were variations in appearance, quality and character, often very wide ones, within many specific fabrics (figure 3.4). Thus, there were fourteen different prices for print and nine different prices for cloth in Tett's 1851 inventory. In some cases, a remnant or a very small piece may have produced an unusually low or high price per yard. In others, the price range may actually cover distinct products. For example, the lowest priced transactions in crepe, velvet, and silk were more likely imitations or trim, not pieces, but we included them in the count (above) to ensure we did not underestimate the place of luxury fabrics. It should be re-emphasized, however, that the most expensive fabrics were the best woolens, which even in 1861 cost over three dollars per yard.

All of this evidence supports a fundamental textile story: that some men and most women sewed; for the latter, like the former, sewing was "an important skill," which should not be taken for granted.[52] Another indication of the extent of sewing is the frequency of purchases of sewing supplies, which make up most of the forty products listed under notions in appendix A. Thread (265 buyers), buttons (217 buyers), ribbons (182 buyers), and needles (106 buyers) were among the most commonly purchased of all goods. "Spool," which first appears in 1842 and was bought by 183 buyers in all subsequent samples, was thread on a spool.[53] These products were diverse, their variations reflecting what buyers wanted for their specific purposes. Thus, the 1808 import invoices discussed above list fifteen different threads (from number seven to number fifty, plus shoe thread) and three kinds of much more expensive sewing silk (black, blue, and cloth); buttons at fourteen distinct prices, the most expensive of which were specified as gilt (three prices), plated, and coat; and Holland tape at five different prices.[54]

Some products – gilt buttons, for example – were more than just functional. Ribbons, as Ann Smart Martin demonstrates, "were quickly changing indices of fashion," often selected by women "for themselves, a relatively inexpensive treat to update a wardrobe or entwine the body

Figure 3.4 Pieced quilt, made at Penetanguishene, Upper Canada, ca 1850-60 (detail). Few everyday textiles survive from Upper Canada, but a quilt such as this can suggest the substantial variety of fabrics available to rural women. In this detail, at least four-teen different fabrics are visible. According to the Royal Ontario Museum catalogue, "the majority are small prints. Most of these are cotton, but there are some wools and some union fabrics (cotton warp, worsted lustre weft)." (Royal Ontario Museum, 967.169, negative 74TEX303)

or hair."[55] Because store accounts seldom describe notions in detail, price is the main indicator of variation and of the possibility of fashion. Thus, the 75 yards of ribbon charged to twenty accounts in 1808–09 had twelve different prices. At least seven buyers were women (three were wives and four, identified by first name – Cynthia, Ginny, Rachel, and Betsy – were likely daughters in the two families whose accounts were charged for their purchases). Just one entry recorded what kind of ribbon was purchased, 4 yards of velvet ribbon charged to George Trickey at $1.00 per yard. There were two other purchases at that price, and one at an even higher price (Thomas Freel was charged $1.17 per yard for 3.5 yards); considering that the next most costly ribbons were 35 cents per yard, the velvet surely was a luxury. More than half of all ribbon transactions were at much lower prices, between 10 and 20 cents per yard; these still could have been adornments and treats.

Every store sold ready-made textile products; in the ten samples, about half of all accounts made at least one such purchase (table 4). The most common was handkerchiefs, with 160 buyers in all ten samples. Hats, gloves, socks, shawls, mittens, stockings, and vests all were purchased in 1808–09 and at most or all stores thereafter. Here too products varied widely, reflecting use, style, and quality. There were many different prices for them in the 1808 import invoices, and sometimes specific descriptions: hats were for youths or men; handkerchiefs were children's, pocket, fancy, bandana, and "rain'd"; and gloves were lamb, beaver, and men's. Most of the thirty-two handkerchiefs purchased by customers in 1808–09 were priced at 75 cents or less, but nine cost from $1.00 to $1.50 – and one, bought by Thomas Freel, cost $2.50. Almost all the twelve hats cost between $1.40 and $3.50, except for one that cost $7.00, bought by Peter Cronk (who had this store's largest account). Women are explicitly noted as buyers of seven of the thirty shawls in 1808–09; most of these cost from 75 to 90 cents; the most expensive (which cost $1.00) were cambric or muslin.

Each later sample adds nuances to our understanding of these products. For example, in 1842, four of the five hats purchased were fur (the other was beaver); eight of the ten pairs of mitts were buckskin (the other two were specified as homemade); among the more than fifty handkerchiefs were many described as buff, checked, filled, neck, red, and silk; three shawls were buff, nine were cotton, and six were plaid or tartan (the latter cost from $1.60 to $2.50, at least four times the price of cotton shawls); stockings were black, cotton, worsted, woolen, silk, and homemade (the two latter, at 50 and 70 cents respectively, were the most costly); and gloves were wool and silk. Each sample also adds new products to the list, beginning in 1828 with braces and caps (both widely bought thereafter, with more than sixty buyers).[56] Neckties appear on the list in 1851, hose in 1854, and belts in 1861.[57] Some of the products were locally made, including socks, mittens, pants (twenty-two buyers at eight stores, beginning in 1828), shirts (twenty-one buyers at six stores, beginning in 1842), and coats (forty buyers, beginning in 1854 and at all stores after that).

These products were general necessities, subject to wear at varying rates, yet even the most frequently purchased were bought by only a minority of the clientele, in quantities too small for most families' complete requirements; and the largest accounts might not buy any. The limited range of women's wearing apparel is particularly striking. (It is possible that even the five entries for dresses were actually fabric for a dress.) Store credits show that some socks, mittens, and other local products were sewn (or knit) by local women and resold by the merchant.[58] Such transactions could also have involved custom-made goods, for example for the merchant's employees, or exchanges between maker and buyer that for convenience were effected through the store's books. As we discuss further in chapter 6, the transactions in locally made clothing give only a glimpse of what must have been much more extensive exchanges. Finally, although we have seen that one textile story stresses a mid-century transition toward ready-made clothing, that is not evident here. In 1861 just as in 1808, a few imported goods were part of what rural people wore, but most clothing was not purchased from stores; it was made, mainly locally.

Several other products relevant to textiles are listed elsewhere in appendix A, including blankets (in housewares), first bought in 1808 (thirteen buyers, five stores), and horse blankets (listed among other goods), which appear in 1842 (seventeen buyers, five stores). Pasteboard (also listed under other goods) appears in 1808; one of its main uses was making women's hats, and many of the thirty-six buyers (at six stores) were women.[59]

Dyes and related products are listed in appendices A and B as chemicals. Taking the different dyes together, there were 124 buyers (see table 4). The most widely purchased – and often the only – dyestuff was indigo, a total of 16 pounds purchased by 75 buyers at nine stores. Almost half of this was at Yonge Mills in 1808–09, where 7 pounds valued at a total of twenty-three dollars were purchased by 15 customers (including Freel and Proctor). What they might have done with this is suggested by standard accounts, which say that to dye a pound of wool, from one to eight ounces of indigo were needed.[60] At the lowest rate, and if all the indigo purchased in 1808–9 was used for dyeing, the maximum that might have been dyed was 112 pounds of wool.[61] And if we estimate that 2 yards of fabric could be produced per pound of wool, this could have produced no more than 225 yards of cloth.

In later samples, the most active indications of dyeing were at Scovil's store in 1861, where twenty-four customers purchased one or more of the three principal dyes sold here: indigo, madder (a red dye), and logwood (black). Buyers included eleven cloth makers, who together produced over five hundred yards of cloth (table 10). Based on one ounce of indigo or eight ounces of madder or logwood per pound of wool or cotton, these purchases would have dyed less than 120 pounds of fibre. That can be compared to the almost 1,700 pounds of wool that this store's sample members reported producing in 1861.[62] The homespun interpretation suggests that people might have found natural dyes locally. Doing that, then preparing them, was time-consuming; and dyeing with most barks and flowers required a mordant.[63] Of these, the most commonly purchased were alum (a total of fifty-two buyers) and copperas (with forty buyers), both purchased at almost all stores (on thirty occasions at the same time as a dyestuff).[64] Quantities were modest, however, and each had other uses besides dyeing. But even if, for example, all 42 pounds of alum were used for dyeing, that would have treated no more than 170 pounds of wool. Such evidence suggests that home dyeing was common but hardly universal, that it involved modest quantities, and that most of the plain cloth made or purchased was not dyed. Rather, someone wanting colour could buy it – in calico, print, stripe, check, plaid, red flannel, and other fabrics; in accessories such as handkerchiefs, shawls, and neckties; and in ribbons, braid, and other trim.

Clearly families were sewing, or having others sew. What they were sewing has to be inferred from our understanding of bedding and clothing, from the fabrics and supplies that people bought, and from other indicators such as piece sizes (summarized in table 11). For example, according to one nineteenth-century source, "a perfectly plain dress for a figure of medium size requires twelve yards of material."[65] And indeed one purchase from Sherin's store, by Mrs George Shields, was precisely 12 yards of "material for dress." Yet fewer than 150 of the 3,800 pieces of material purchased were of 12 or more yards, most women never bought a piece of this length, and at least half of those long pieces were the plainest of cottons. It seems likely, in fact, that many of the more than 800 pieces of from 5 to 11.9 yards were used for dresses. Among all pieces of 5 or more yards, not even 10 were fabrics in the "luxury" group (three bombasine, two satinette, one alpaca, and several illegible entries whose prices suggest they might belong in this group). That no women bought dress-size pieces of silk cannot prove that they did not have silk dresses. But if, for example, they shopped for silk and other luxuries such as velvet in larger towns or if they were able to have someone in Britain send such fabrics to them, that belies images of scarcity and deep isolation that are so common in standard accounts of early rural life.

Whether and how garments followed fashion are more difficult matters. We have already seen that new fabrics were purchased. Some other products also suggest that fashion mattered to some families. An excellent example, because they were "a necessary accessory if one were to follow the latest fashion" in the 1860s, are hoops and hoop sets, purchased by thirty buyers (including Elizabeth McDonald [figure 3.2]) at four of the 1861 stores.[66] It is more difficult to interpret very modest purchases of other products such as feathers and plumes (six buyers at all five stores in 1861) and others listed in appendix B, whose buyers were perhaps following fashion. These include dress patterns; crinoline sets; and victorins, a fur-edged neck tippet introduced in England around 1850 and fashionable in Montreal in the 1860s.[67] Several purchases suggest a concern for shape, such as whalebone (five buyers at three stores, from 1854) and corsets, stays, and stay laces, all in appendix B.[68] Almost all of the sixteen yards of jean bought by fourteen customers from Darling's store in 1861 was described as "jean, corset" (whether any of the thirty-nine yards of jean purchased by seventeen customers from six other stores had the same use is not known).

We have already noted the extent of wool production by members of the first five samples. In this, census data confirm, they were representative of their communities: the 1842 census reported that the Johnstown District produced over 100,000 yards of fulled cloth and flannel, equal to 3.2 yards per capita, and the Colborne District produced more than 30,000 yards (2.3 yards per capita). In Johnstown there was also 19,000 yards of linen production. That was a small figure (just over a half-yard per capita), and this was the only census to record any considerable linen output in the province.[69] But twenty years later Leeds and Peterborough counties were still substantial woolen producers; the 1861 census reported production in the former of almost 94,000 yards (2.6 yards per capita) and in the latter of over 40,000 yards (1.7 yards per capita).[70]

In table 8, we summarize the census data on sheep ownership and production of cloth by customers. From this information, it is evident that 1861 patterns in the countryside resemble those earlier; there had been no transition away from home cloth production. Many, usually most, landowners reported sheep, and most sheep owners also reported cloth production. The average output for all 202 producers was thirty-seven yards, and about 40 percent of makers produced forty or more yards in a year. At least some of the latter were likely producing cloth for sale as well as household use. That there was a market in local woolens is also implied by the relatively limited purchases of woolens from our stores by even those who did not produce any cloth or flannel. That there was also a market for wool itself is evident from Sherin's customers. Here only about half the sheep owners reported making cloth, and the non-makers reported more sheep, and more raw wool produced, than those who made cloth. Indeed, by 1861, Upper Canada had a growing export trade in wool.[71]

Many makers also purchased fabrics. It should be noted that the census tells us all of these customers' production but we know only some of their purchases; those who bought few or no textiles at our stores might have bought fabrics elsewhere. Still, 89 of the 202 makers bought 10 or more yards, and 34 of them purchased 40 or more yards. Except at Darling's, quantities produced greatly exceeded quantities purchased. At Darling's, however, makers purchased over 1,400 yards, almost twice what they collectively made. As this example suggests, making and buying coexisted, likely in a wide range of combinations.[72] It is doubtful that many cloth producers were, or intended to be, self-sufficient in textiles.

One further indication of cloth making is the purchase of cotton yarn or warp, required for weaving mixed cotton and wool fabrics. In total there were forty buyers of warp or yarn, at eight stores. The largest purchases, as at Choate's in 1851, averaged about five pounds. Such weaving was, evidently, not uncommon, but not large-scale and by no means universal. It was, rather, another choice in the spectrum of possibilities.

In each sample, as can be seen in the data summarized in table 4, there was wide disparity between the leading and the median buyer in volumes and values purchased. Because those who bought modest quantities at one store might have been large buyers elsewhere, however, the median is of limited value in representing overall textile consumption patterns. As a way of addressing this concern, we present data for each store on yardage purchased by the ten leading buyers. This group accounted for from 43 percent (at Tett's store) to 73 percent (at Sherin's) of total yardage. About half were among the stores' ten largest accounts, but it was possible to have a large account without buying many fabrics, and vice versa. About 40 percent (at stores for which the information is available) also owned sheep and/or made cloth. As on most indicators, the Yonge Mills and Choate samples were at the low end of the range for purchases. At the other extreme, the leading buyers at Fowlds's in 1861 purchased almost 1,900 yards, and at Darling's the total was almost 1,400; at these stores even the median for all buyers approached 40 yards. All ten leading buyers at Darling's, in the countryside, were farmers; and eight also produced cloth, a total of 252 yards. By contrast, in 1861 seven of the ten at Fowlds's store, in the largest of the villages, were artisans.

Table 4 also includes the highest value of fabrics purchased by one customer. Reflecting the price levels early in the century, the leading customer's account at Yonge Mills in 1808 ($62.56) was among the highest values, exceeded only in the two samples from Fowlds's store. To interpret these and other values, we can relate them to the standard of four dollars per capita in imported textile consumption suggested by mid-century trade data. This, it should be noted, was the value at the point of import rather than at retail. Excluding 1808–09 from consideration because price levels were higher then, we can consider per capita purchases in the other nine samples. For them, household size is known for the seventy-six (of ninety) leading buyers who were linked to the census. Of these, twenty-six bought fabrics worth more than four dollars per household member (as did fifteen buyers who ranked outside the ten leaders). More than half of these buyers, like Edward Oakes, discussed above, were customers at Fowlds's store. In 1861, in fact, all the leading buyers there exceeded this threshold. It is no coincidence that this is the store where woolens were most prominent in purchases.[73] At other stores, those exceeding the threshold of four dollars per capita were individuals or small households.[74]

Thus, although volumes purchased by the leading buyers in 1861 tended to be larger than earlier, only at Fowlds's and Sherin's did a majority reach the threshold of four dollars per capita. The most common context for extensive purchases was a large family that might have several income earners and more than one person sewing. That was the case for

Oakes and Hoolihan in 1854. At Darling's, the leading buyers were Nicklus Gilbert, who had ten persons in his household and bought 198 yards (of ten different fabrics) for $27; and James Deer, who had twelve in his household and bought 192 yards (of twenty different fabrics) for $42. As their examples suggest, it was possible to buy very large quantities of textiles without attaining the provincial per capita average by value.

In the eight samples for which occupations are known, there were about thirty men with what could be called bourgeois occupations (merchants, teachers, clergymen, doctors, engineers, and lumbermen). None were among the leading buyers; indeed, thirteen bought no fabrics and another nine bought minuscule amounts. A partial exception is Dr James Bingham, whose 24 yards purchased from Choate's in 1861 ranked him sixteenth in that sample. Among his purchases were seven yards of woolen cloth valued at $1.10 per yard, a piece of cloth worth $6.80, and the most expensive linen sold at any store in 1861 (2.4 yards at 79 cents per yard). On the basis of value, at almost $21 his was actually the leading Choate fabric account; as he was single, this was also the largest on a per capita basis for the entire study. These purchases, unusual for a bourgeois client at a country store, almost certainly reflect his links to the Choate family; in 1862 he would marry Thomas Choate's daughter.[75] Other than Bingham every one of the leading buyers at these stores represented ordinary levels of Upper Canadian society, the farm, artisan, and labouring families who constituted most of the economy. Their purchases suggest what other such families might have been buying at other stores, or at very least what they might aspire to.

If the account-holder was not present, the daybook normally recorded the identity of the buyer (figures 3.1, 3.2, and 3.3). Hence we often know that women were the actual buyers of fabrics, even if the charge was on the account of a husband, father, or employer. There were also women who had their own accounts, among them Catharine Parr Traill, whose writings are a key source on this topic. Respectfully accorded the occupation of "lady" in the census, she had an account at Sherin's that resembled those of the bourgeois men; the only fabric charged to her was a small piece (2.75 yards) of gray flannel, purchased by her son Walter. Like hers, many of the women's accounts proved to be very small.[76] Only 9 of the 105 women's accounts were charged for 40 or more yards of fabrics, among them Ann Graham, discussed earlier. Another twenty women purchased between 10 and 39 yards. About half the women were identified in the census or in accounts either as widows or as "Mrs," a title that must often have indicated widowhood as well. The others included several designated in the census as servants, but others must have been working in this capacity.

Some women, including in households whose accounts were in men's names, must have earned money by sewing, spinning, or weaving. Occasionally, such work appears on the credit side of the accounts. An example is the account of James Bush, a fifty-year-old customer at Fowlds's, listed in the 1861 census as a labourer. His textile debits of $88.95 were the second largest among all 502 sample buyers. His family of nine included five others who appeared in Fowlds's accounts: his wife (forty-seven years old), two sons, and two daughters. Among them, they purchased about 179 yards of fabrics, of twenty-six kinds, on forty-one days between March and December 1861. By value, their purchases of about 40 yards of woolens represented more than half their purchases; in yardage, cotton dominated (with 97 yards). They spent $4.40 on luxuries (one-eighth of a yard of "silk velvet," a small square of lustre, and 2.5 yards each of satinette and mohair). They also had a small account for carding and fulling ($1.50). Bush was credited with 16.5 days work for Fowlds (at $1.00 per day) and his son James Jr (aged twenty-four) with almost seven months work at $18.00 per month. Mrs Bush was credited with $23.75 by making four pairs of drawers, six pairs of overalls, twenty-six pairs of pants, nineteen shirts, and three vests; daughters Roselia (twenty-two) and "Miss" Bush were also credited for smaller amounts of sewing. The phrasing of these credits distinguishes them from the textiles they purchased, and the value of credits suggests payment for work only. But there is no way of knowing if the Bushes were transforming some of the purchased fabrics into clothing for sale to others, or sewing in part to be able to afford to have such fabrics for themselves. Nor can Fowlds's accounts tell us about other commercial sewing that they may have done.

In fact, retail accounts offer only the briefest of glimpses of market-related sewing, because those hiring a seamstress, dressmaker, or tailor purchased fabrics and other material themselves and paid only for the work done with the materials. Besides Chant, discussed earlier, there were eight other tailors in the samples. Among them, they purchased just 135 yards of fabrics: for example, Betsy Dorway, a widow and a customer at Scovil's, described as a "tayloress," bought 29 yards of five kinds of fabrics; and Kenneth Urquhart, a twenty-seven-year old bachelor, bought 30 yards of nine kinds of fabric at Sherin's. Urquhart was also the buyer of

21 yards of materials charged to another customer's account. No doubt some of the material purchased by sample members was transformed by someone working for pay, but it is impossible to estimate even orders of magnitude.

Few of the specific details of textile purchases in rural Upper Canada are likely to surprise specialists in the history of textiles in colonial North America. Even so, they offer a sense of proportion in reading – and sorting among the conflicting images in – the extensive anecdotal literature on consumption. When taken together, the data confirm some key stories while making others seem highly improbable. Among the latter is the idea that there was a transition in the countryside from self-sufficiency to market orientation. On the one hand, the principal kinds of fabrics and some standard ready-made items were available and purchased by many families even in 1808, including by many who also made cloth. On the other hand, even fifty years later, ready-made clothing (with the exception of footwear, which we discuss in chapter 7) was not a major part of the business of any of these stores, and if there was any trend away from cloth making it was limited and far from consistent. Even the Fowlds store, which had such large textile sales in 1861, was part of a business that included a carding and fulling mill. Nor is there any reason to think that families in the province's early years made more cloth than those we have met in 1842, 1851, and 1861. Imported products had prices; so did locally provided goods and services, such as those of the artisans who appear prominently among the leading buyers. Indeed, respondents to Robert Gourlay's 1817 statistical survey of Upper Canada could report the wages of women for housework and spinning, the price of sheep, the yield of wool per sheep, and the price of wool per pound.[77]

Two-thirds of sample households bought at least some fabrics. For those who bought little, the principal finding is that they did at least purchase textiles. On the basis of those who bought more, we are able to suggest orders of magnitude, although these families too might have made purchases elsewhere. All these buyers were representative members of rural and village society. On a per capita basis the value of most families' purchases did not exceed the provincial average, with the partial exception of principal customers at Fowlds's store, where woolens were more prominent among purchases. That it was in the largest village studied can serve also as a reminder that consumption was structured by class and that it was likely to be both greater and different in urban centres.[78] Specialists in textile history would undoubtedly read much more from what is (and is not) contained in the account books, such as interpreting the colours that are sometimes mentioned. To what extent, for example, would it be reasonable to associate black with mourning?[79] One thing is clear, however: it is unlikely that the standards and preoccupations of the provincial elite, about whom fashion historians are best informed, are a reliable indication of textile consumption by most people in Upper Canada, the vast majority of whom lived outside the main cities and towns.

Almost all the fabrics that people were choosing at the country store fall into the middle ground between the often-emphasized extremes, homespun and high luxury. At every store, individual cotton products were, in terms of yardage, the principal fabrics sold. In terms of values as well, cotton led by a wide margin, except at Fowlds's. One element of its prominence among purchases may be that it wore out more quickly than wool. That it wore reduced the likelihood of its surviving to be collected by museums. Its neglect may also reflect a tendency to think more about the harshness of Canadian winters and the need for warmth than of the heat of the Ontario summer (or to assume that linens took care of that, without demonstrating that there was sufficient domestic production in Upper Canada).

When women went to a store, they chose among products whose differences were visible. We can readily imagine them to have been as practical as Brett imagined, with an eye to value, in terms of price, quality, and purpose. That is entirely consistent with having an eye for fashion, in the context of their lives – in colour, in fabric, in what they intended to make (or perhaps to have made), in trim and accessories, and even in line and shape. During the period, new kinds of fabrics became available, stores found it paid to stock a greater number of fabrics, and quantities purchased rose. Particularly striking, because the evidence is from well before the mid-century boom, is the level of consumption of leading Tett customers in 1842. But the rise in purchases was selective; the many rural Upper Canadians who continued to make woolen cloth (and perhaps others who bought it from neighbours) were in a position to make fewer purchases of expensive imported woolens.

4

A WORLD WITHOUT CHOCOLATE: PURCHASES OF GROCERIES AND MEDICATIONS

OPODELDOC – LIQUID – Best brandy 1 qt.; warm it and add gum camphor 1 oz.; salammoniac and oil of wormwood, of each ¼ oz.; oils of origanum and rosemary, of each ½ oz.; when the oils are dissolved by the aid of heat, add soft soap 6 ozs.
Its uses are two [*sic*] well known to need further description.

Dr Chase's Recipes, 1867[1]

We begin with a quotation from the Canadian edition of a popular nineteenth-century compendium of medical and other recipes because of its explicit reference to everyday knowledge – knowledge that we no longer possess. This is an issue for many of the goods considered in this chapter, even if, for lack of space and knowledge, we can explore it only selectively. The OED defines opodeldoc as encompassing "various kinds of soap liniment" and as a remedy familiar as long ago as Paracelsus. One of its uses, according to a leading doctor's book of advice for mothers published in 1880, was for infants' bowel problems – not given internally, fortunately, but rubbed on the abdomen.[2] Another was as a rub for leg cramps during pregnancy.[3] Men also used it; it was, for example, carried in Northwest Company medicine chests.[4] Thirteen different customers bought opodeldoc, a total of fifteen transactions at five different stores, at a cost of 35 cents per bottle in 1828, 20 cents in 1842, and 15 cents in 1861.[5] The size of a bottle is not specified, but it was evidently filled in a pharmaceutical house in Montreal or in Britain. Clearly some Upper Canadians used opodeldoc. The puzzle is, in effect, how common it was for Canadian babies to have it rubbed on their abdomen. Did almost everyone have it at hand, although only a few happened to buy it from these particular stores, or did most not use it?

If we have to go to considerable effort to begin to identify the uses of a now-unfamiliar medication, we have the opposite problem with chocolate, today one of the most familiar groceries, a highly pleasurable part of daily routines, and one of the principal commodities in a global grocery economy involving tropical and sub-tropical foods, medicines, spices, and dyes that began to take shape early in the age of European expansion – an age of which Canada itself was a product.[6] Nineteenth-century Canadian cookbooks include recipes for chocolate as a beverage and in cakes, caramels, and custards.[7] Other references include the first Canadian novel (published in 1769), *The History of Emily Montague*: Emily writes from Quebec that "We, the ladies I mean, drink chocolate with the general tomorrow."[8] Travel writer Patrick Campbell mentioned "tea or chocolate" as an indispensable element in what he depicted as the high wages of even day labourers.[9] John Lambert, another traveller, spoke rather of chocolate as of "inferior quality," drunk mainly by "the French inhabitants."[10] Yet, at about the same time, Thomas Ridout's daily breakfast (from stores purchased at Quebec) on a voyage to England included "two or three cups of chocolate, coffee or tea."[11] A few years later, writing from the bush near Peterborough, Frances Stewart, a member of a well-known Canadian family of gentry pioneers, spoke of "some delightful chocolate," a treat before an early start on a winter journey, which had come in the "annual box" from England.[12] Taken together, these sources raise questions. Was chocolate mainly a beverage, as the quotations suggest, or was it consumed also in the other forms described in recipes? Was it so readily available that it was a routine part of breakfast, or so unusual that it required family connections in England to enjoy it? Who drank it – elite ladies, labourers, French Canadians, someone in a relatively prominent official family?

To these questions, our data provide an indirect answer: they suggest that rural Upper Canada was a world without chocolate. In ten thousand grocery transactions, not even one purchase of chocolate was recorded.[13] Trade statistics confirm this. In 1861, Canadian imports of cocoa and chocolate totalled less than 25,000 pounds, the equivalent of no more than one-sixth of an ounce (4.5 grams) per person.[14] Obviously chocolate was not a widely enjoyed everyday pleasure. That there are literary sources to suggest otherwise re-emphasizes the uncertainty of using such descriptive sources as evidence of how people lived.

Groceries are defined as "imported plant foodstuffs."[15] Like chocolate, they were not produced in western Europe and northern North America. They were distinguished from provisions, which were locally and regionally produced foods (and which we discuss in chapter 6). By the time settlement began in Upper Canada, some leading grocery products had become, as we noted in chapter 1, goods of mass consumption in England and Wales (and in America). Based on estimated net imports divided by the entire population, English tobacco consumption had by the end of the seventeenth century reached a relatively stable long-term level of two pounds per person per year. A century later, English sugar consumption had reached twenty-four pounds per person, and tea consumption was two pounds per person.[16] By then in France, as a sophisticated argument on the implications of Paris protests at rising food costs during the Revolutionary era notes, "what is most striking is that coffee and sugar had, by 1793, become 'needs' worth rioting about."[17]

Like most groceries, tea could not be grown in Upper Canada, although some pioneer advice books offered ingenious substitutes.[18] Because some tobacco was grown in the colony and maple sugar was widely produced, we might imagine the possibility of family or local self-sufficiency in both of them; but in fact sugar and tobacco were imported in large quantities. Mid-nineteenth-century Canadian trade data show that enough tea and tobacco were imported to allow English levels of consumption, 2 pounds of each per person per year (see appendix C); given the high proportion of the population living in rural areas, many rural dwellers must have reached this level.[19] The volume of imported sugar was below English levels but rising – 10 pounds per person in 1851, 16 pounds in 1861. These were the three principal groceries in the countryside; among all those listed in appendix A, they had the most buyers and accounted for about half of all grocery transactions and an even higher share of values. Was their prominence a consequence of mid-century commercialization? Evidently not. In 1808–09, forty-eight customers bought a total of 99 pounds of tea worth $153, thirty-four bought a total of 142 pounds of tobacco worth $70, and thirty-three bought 212 pounds of sugar worth $42 (table 12).

Salt, the fourth-ranked product in terms of numbers of buyers, is also included in table 12. It was not a "plant foodstuff," but like some other imported products that disappeared in everyday consumption – soap and candles, for example – it is most conveniently discussed with the main groceries. If most households required salt, as seems likely, it is an indicator that customers bought goods elsewhere that there were only eighteen buyers of salt in 1808–09 (with purchases worth $35). Salt was commonly purchased in bushels (priced at $2.00 to $2.10), but there were also purchases by the quart (at 7 cents each) and one "bag" (at $4.40). According to 1808 invoices, the two Jones stores purchased ninety-two barrels of "Liverpool salt" that year; it came in used potash barrels containing four minots each.²⁰ Later stores provide other units of retail sales, the barrel, the peck, and the pound – and describe the salt as coarse, fine, and table. All were distinct from "salts" (Epsom salts or containers for table salt; these appear elsewhere in appendix A). Other groceries purchased in 1808–09 included pepper (twenty-three buyers, twelve of whom also bought salt), snuff (fifteen buyers, eleven of whom also bought tobacco),²¹ allspice (seven buyers), ginger (five buyers), cinnamon (two buyers), and coffee (one buyer). These goods would appear in most, or all, subsequent samples.

That the principal groceries were so widely purchased in 1808–09 confirms that, as in contemporary Britain and France, they were part of many families' culture. On the other hand, of buyers whose household size is known from the census list of households, only a very few bought these goods from this store at the rate suggested by Canadian import data in 1851: just five tobacco buyers and one tea buyer. The latter was the store's largest account, Jabez and Stephen Andrews. The census reported Jabez's household as consisting of himself and three women. Tax rolls indicate they were not primarily farmers, as they had just two acres in cultivation. But if we add Stephen, who was not listed in the census, theirs was a five-person household. Their $220 in debits were incurred in transactions on 107 days in all twelve months. They were the leading buyers of both tea and tobacco and the second ranked for sugar. In total they were charged for 15.25 pounds of tea (in twenty-two transactions), 20 of tobacco (in ten transactions), and 24 of sugar (in fourteen transactions). These and other groceries accounted for more than a quarter of their account.

To explore the rhythm and extent of grocery consumption in 1808–09, we again focus on the ten largest accounts, which might be expected to have bought a higher percentage of their goods at this store. In 1808–09, these accounts equalled almost half of all debits.²² Nine of them bought tea, eight bought tobacco, and nine bought sugar. But only six bought all three, and they did so with varying frequency and in widely varying amounts (from as little as one-quarter pound of tea, a half-pound of tobacco, and four pounds of sugar). As we have seen, trade dropped sharply at this store in summer 1809.²³ In thinking about frequency and scale of purchasing, therefore, it is better to narrow the focus to the eight prime months for sales of these goods, from September to April. Other than Caleb Seaman Jr, whose account involved transactions on just thirteen days, the leading customers were in the store regularly and often in this period (seven in all eight months and two in seven), but only six bought tea, four bought tobacco, and two bought sugar in four or more of these months.[24] Among the other sixty sample members, just eleven bought one of these groceries in at least four months.[25]

Yet these are goods that we expect to be habitually consumed. It would be one thing if people bought in bulk, the image we have when we think of isolated farm families making rare trips to town to stock up. There are examples of what seem like this type of purchase, such as Seaman's 11.25 pounds of tobacco on 25 November and William Avery's 14 pounds of sugar on 25 March. But that was not the norm. Not one of sixty-two transactions in tea by the ten leading buyers exceeded 1 pound (and their average purchase was less than 0.5 pound); just six of their forty-three tobacco purchases were over 1 pound; and only eight of their forty-six sugar purchases were of 5 or more pounds.[26] Such modest and not very frequent purchases may suggest that people did not consistently consume these products; that they rationed their consumption, enjoying them only in certain contexts, such as on special occasions or seasonally or in a particular work setting; or that only one person in a household might have consumed a specific product, and he or she might have been present only for part of the year. Still, it seems likely that many, even of the leading buyers, also bought these goods at other stores.

Although daybooks seldom specify what kind of each product was purchased, price differences suggest variations in the actual products. For the two Jones stores in 1808, import invoices record a total of 2,900 pounds of three kinds of sugar at three distinct prices; over 900 pounds of four kinds of tea (most at 90 or 95 cents per pound), and 970 pounds of two kinds of tobacco at two distinct prices (see table 13). The sugar, most of the tea, and 60 pounds of the more expensive plug tobacco were purchased from Montreal merchants. Two chests of tea and the rest of the tobacco came from a supplier in nearby Ogdensburg, New York (where he obtained them is not known – an American source seems possible). At the retail level, there were three distinct sugar prices at Yonge Mills: most cost 20 cents per pound, but there were fourteen transactions at 16.7 cents and three at 33.3 cents. That nine of the ten customers who made purchases at a lower or higher price also bought some sugar at 20 cents per pound suggests that the variation was not by customer but by kind of sugar. For tea and tobacco, the main variation in retail prices was instead chronological. From 1 September 1808 until mid-January 1809, all tea was $1.40 per pound; after that, until May it was $1.80. Until early October 1808 and again for a month in midwinter 1809, tobacco was 45 cents per pound; from mid-October to mid-February it was 50 cents, and from mid-March to mid-June it was 46.7 cents.

ALCOHOL PURCHASES

We begin with tea, tobacco, and sugar because they are the most prominent groceries of the period and had the most buyers in the long-term. Indeed, about half of all buyers purchased tea and tobacco (see table 12). But the value of alcohol purchases exceeded the total for all three of these groceries in 1808–09 and equalled their combined total in 1828–29. In each year, alcohol accounted for 14 percent of the value of all purchases. The products were rum, spirits (a higher priced rum),[27] brandy, wine, and whiskey (see table 14). Whiskey is listed in appendix A with other local products (and its value is therefore excluded from grocery totals in table 12), but it is convenient to consider it here alongside imported alcohol. In 1808–09, there were fifty-four alcohol buyers and in 1828–29, fifty-six. In 1808–09, forty-nine customers bought $236 worth of rum; like other groceries, its price also rose during the winter, from 35 cents per quart in September 1808 to 40 cents in November and 55 cents from February to May, then fell back to 40 cents in August.[28] The price of spirits followed the same path, with a peak of 70 cents. As if stock was limited, all the brandy was purchased in September and October, at 50 cents per quart. Wine was priced at between 50 cents and 80 cents; from import invoices, we can identify it as "best port" and "teneriff." Whiskey, which cost 45 cents per quart (or $1.60 per gallon), was purchased only in May and June 1809, perhaps as a substitute for products that were out of stock; in any case, just ten quarts of rum were purchased then. In total, the 828 quarts of alcohol purchased equalled more than 15 quarts per buyer, but there was wide variation, from the 78 quarts bought by Jabez and Stephen Andrews, including all five kinds of alcohol, down to the 1 or 2 quarts bought by nine people.

Twenty years later, whiskey had become by far the leading form of alcohol, with 685 of the 815 quarts purchased. Its price was no more than one-third of what it had been two decades earlier, just 12.5 cents per quart for most of the year (and 15 cents from February to May 1829).[29] Rum now cost 25 cents per quart, and spirits 34 cents. Brandy prices, by contrast, had hardly fallen; it cost 43 cents or 48 cents per quart. And wine, most described as port, was just as costly as twenty years earlier, at 75 cents per quart. The only person to buy all five kinds of alcohol was James Adams, whose 53 quarts made him the leading buyer.

To interpret these purchases, we begin with four stories about alcohol in this period, the latter two from studies of Leeds County:

> By almost any standard, Americans drank not only near-universally but in enormous quantities. Their yearly consumption at the time of the Revolution has been estimated at the equivalent of three-and-a-half gallons of pure, two-hundred proof alcohol for each person ... After 1790, probably in response to anxieties generated by rapid and unsettling social and economic change, American men began to drink even more. By the late 1820s their imbibing had risen to an all-time high of almost four gallons per capita. [30]

> Whisky was often served to the family including the children, at breakfast. For the pioneer confronted with long hours of hard physical labour, alcohol was served as a stimulant; most community efforts such as the building "bees" were fueled by the ever-present pail of whisky; liquor flowed at wakes and weddings; court cases held in the local inns were often settled with the assistance of "ardent spirits"; banquets and dinners were noted for their many toasts. Men of position and even some clergymen were often "under the influence" towards the end of the day. Drunkeness was not considered a sin unless it significantly interfered with one's duty or occupation.[31]

> In British North America nearly every family kept a bottle in the house to "treat" guests and workmen, and community gatherings witnessed heavy drinking among all levels of society. Liquor was simply considered an absolutely normal accompaniment to whatever men did in groups. Before the late 1820s the only people who worried about heavy drinking were a few New England clergymen ... In Upper Canada bush drudgery and high grain

yields together produced a society as inebriated as that in Ireland and Britain.[32]

[Alcohol] … was the surest, quickest way for the isolated farmer, the bush worker, and the village claustrophobic to escape his environs. The long hours of manual labour, often alone or in the company of the same small family group, day in and day out, the omnipresent silence when out of doors, the cramped quarters indoors, especially in December, January and February, all dictated that a person sometimes had to hear a fair and inspiriting musik [*sic*], conveyed to him by alcohol.[33]

If the last of these stories presents a dark view of winter, others view it as the season of greatest leisure and of convivial celebrations.[34]

One explanation for such extensive alcohol consumption is that alternatives were lacking; and it has been argued that the reduction – or complete elimination in some settings – of the consumption of alcohol at and after the mid-nineteenth-century was "because alternatives had appeared … Coffee, tea, fruit juices, and carbonated beverages began to grace dining tables, picnics and banquets, steamship bars, and military canteens."[35] Another explanation takes the opposite view, contending that people had to be persuaded to drink alcohol. Thus, an influential analysis of rural society in the Richelieu Valley depicts merchants luring hitherto self-reliant people into new habits and into dependency: "For each merchant, rum was an important arm in the struggle with his competitors but, for the merchants as a class, liquor was just as important as a vehicle for making contact with the peasant economy and for expanding their foothold in the precapitalist world of rural French Canada. While Jacobs and the others were flooding the Richelieu in a tide of cheap rum, other Canadian merchants were finding alcohol just as useful in securing a share of the fur trade with the interior Indians, and for similar reasons."[36]

Every one of these stories has a critical tone, informed by a sense of the damage done by excessive alcohol consumption and by dependency related to it. They represent alcohol as absolutely abundant, at once an accompaniment to daily work routines and an escape from them. It was essential to leisure activities for men and, some say, for women and even children. It was consumed at public events such as bees, elections, and militia musters; at home, with or without company; and at the innumerable pioneer inns and taverns. It was consumed in all seasons, often to the point of intoxication. Not so clear, if people drank as continuously and excessively as some of these stories assert, are how they could justify such profligacy with their money and time; why they took so little account of the risk of accidents; how it was in employers' and merchants' interests to ply workers and customers with so much drink that they were often drunk; how this would encourage repayment of the debts incurred to buy alcohol; how work was actually accomplished; and what was the quality of that work.

Such questions justify the effort to explore what our data can be made to say about them. Larkin's figure of up to four gallons per year per person of full strength alcohol offers a benchmark in assessing ordinary consumption. In terms of the amount actually drunk, a much larger volume was implied – if the alcohol was one-hundred proof, that was equivalent to as much as eight gallons per year. As at least half the population in a fast expanding pioneer society consisted of children and youth, adult men, the prime consumers, must have drunk very much more. Hence estimates such as James Moreira's seem reasonable; in "seaport, garrison, and lumbering towns," he writes, "a 'moderate' drinker consumed a half pint of rum every day."[37] If we allow a day off on Sunday, that was 3 pints per week, or 78 quarts (19.5 gallons) per year.

Alcohol stories suggest at least two kinds of consumption: sociable, in public settings and when treating at home, and private.[38] Many also have a seasonal dimension. To explore both of these strands, we present data in table 15 on purchases by month and by size of purchase. In interpreting seasonality in the table, it is important to recall that there was little activity of any kind at the store in July 1809, whereas July 1828 was the year's peak month for alcohol sales. August and September were peaks in both years, and January and June were relatively low; in the other seven months, sales were substantial in one or both years. Larger purchases must often have been for collective consumption, rather than by just the buyer and his immediate household. In the table, therefore, purchases are divided into three categories: eight or more quarts at a time (i.e., two or more gallons), four to six quarts (there were none of seven), and three quarts or less (most were a single quart).

Purchases in the largest category were infrequent – there were thirteen in 1808–09, made by nine different buyers, and twenty-four, by eighteen different buyers, in 1828–29. These included the Andrews' purchase of twenty-four quarts of whiskey on 19 May 1809; Seaman's seventeen quarts of rum on 12 September 1808 and twelve quarts on 2 December; James Adams's total of thirty-two quarts of whiskey in an eight-day span beginning 4 May 1829; and Peter Trickey's sixteen quarts of whiskey and eleven of rum on 18 September 1828. At a rate of one-half pint per person per day, the alcohol bought by the Andrews and Trickey could have supplied about one hundred people for a day, enough for a large "festive" bee (or, of course, fewer people for a longer period).[39] Purchases of two or three gallons (eight to twelve quarts) would have supplied smaller groups. This sort of pattern is compatible with peaks in work, where a large group was required, or with the social settings often imagined. That many of these purchases were in the summer also seems to associate drink with outdoor work.

To examine the intensity, scale, and frequency of everyday alcohol consumption more closely, we provide additional detail on purchases by the principal alcohol buyers (table 16). In 1808–09, the two tenth-ranked buyers bought twenty-nine quarts of alcohol, and in 1828–29, the tenth ranked bought twenty-seven quarts. In the former year there was a rough correlation between large overall accounts and extensive alcohol purchases, and only one of the eleven buyers listed was not among the twenty largest accounts. In 1828–29, however, the accounts of four of the leading alcohol buyers ranked lower than that. Almost all large accounts included some alcohol, but the modesty of purchases by some makes it at least possible that they did not consume it routinely in large quantities.[40] Among all twenty-one buyers in the table, only the Andrews purchased enough to meet the requirements for the "moderate" drinker noted above, and their seventy-eight quarts were bought by two adult males. Their purchases cost them thirty-four dollars. Twenty years later, the leading buyer spent less than ten dollars and most of the leading buyers spent only about five dollars. The lower totals reflected a shift to whiskey from rum – an example of a local product replacing something imported – and falling prices for both.

For each customer listed in table 16, we provide information on total alcohol purchases, large volume purchases (of two gallons or more at a time), number of weeks in which he bought two or more quarts (i.e., exceeded a threshold of 1.5 quarts per week – this includes the large volume transactions), the total number of weeks in which he bought alcohol, and the total number of weeks in which there were debits to his account. The largest tended to involve both large purchases and regular purchasing of smaller quantities. In fact, seven (the Andrews, Cronk,

Jones, Busea, Tollman, Warren, and Russe) would still be on the list of leading buyers even if their purchases of two or more gallons at a time were excluded. Three (Trickey, Seaman, and Guild) made almost all their purchases in large quantities, whereas seven (such as Daniel and Calvin Patterson) never made a purchase of two gallons or more. A few (such as Benjamin Warren and Joseph Christmas) purchased alcohol in most weeks in which there were debits to their accounts; but others (like Elisha Mallory, James Brown, the Andrews, Francis Russe, and Calvin Patterson) had many weeks in which there were transactions on their accounts but no alcohol purchases. Among the twenty-one buyers in table 16, only two purchased alcohol in as many as twenty-six weeks, and half did so in fewer than thirteen weeks. All bought two quarts or more in a number of weeks, but only one had such transactions in even half of the weeks in which there were debits to his account. This was A. Thomson, who purchased thirty-four quarts in just seven weeks from 1 July to 16 August 1828, including one purchase of two gallons. There is no way to know whether he drank this all himself, but, if he did, his consumption would have been four times Moreira's rate, a level approached by no other customer.[41]

For others who bought systematically over extended periods, a rate of 1.5 to 2 quarts per week is more typical, for the weeks in which they bought alcohol. Even here there was considerable variation. Jeremiah Chichigran, for example, bought almost exactly 1.5 quarts per week (32 of rum, 6 of brandy, and 2 of spirits in twenty-five weeks, plus debits in another three weeks for "balance on" rum, transactions of unknown volume). But in eighteen of those weeks, he bought only a single quart (i.e., he bought 22 quarts in the other seven weeks, most of them in September and October). And in ten weeks, the debits to his account did not include any alcohol.[42]

Variations among customers can be related to stories that differentiate alcohol consumption by occupation, family status, and gender. Several leading buyers, including Chichigran (whose account shows him to be a cooper), Christmas (whose account was credited for at least twenty-eight days of work), Busea (credited for more than four months of work), and Russe, could not be found in the census and/or assessments, and it seems unlikely they were farmers; from the sound of their names, three may have been *Canadiens*, possibly seasonal workers. In fact, only a third of the men listed in table 16 had the five acres in cultivation that we have used to define farmers; and only Trickey was a really substantial one. Of the women sample members, only two purchased alcohol: Abigail Comstock, who bought six quarts of rum in 1808–09, and Hannah Whitney, who bought one quart of whiskey in 1828–29.[43]

We cannot assume that leading purchasers were not buying else-where, even in periods when they were buying extensively from this store, and we cannot draw conclusive inferences about the habits of those who bought less, or no, alcohol at these stores. But we can ask how close these stories come to the kind of systematic, constant, excessive drinking that standard stories suggest. For example, if we exclude purchases of over two gallons from the calculations, leading buyers in their most active periods of buying bought roughly at the rate estimated for a "moderate" drinker; and this allows us to ask if that might have been nearer the high end than the middle of the range for many men's everyday consumption. Similarly, the data allow the possibility that consumption varied in intensity and might even have stopped altogether at times.[44] Whether the leading buyers (and participants in events at which alcohol was served) spent much of the time in a state of intoxication depends on the strength of the rum and whiskey they drank and also on how we imagine consumption to have occurred: did it involve hard drinking at the end of a long work day or moderate drinking throughout the entire day? These stories confirm the possibility of seasonal variation in individuals' purchasing, but taken together they do not suggest strongly seasonal patterns.

Because one alcohol story was that alternatives were lacking, it is significant that almost without exception the leading alcohol buyers also purchased tea.[45] If they drank alcohol, that is, it was not for lack of choice. That all but one of the twenty-one men in table 16 bought more than one kind of alcohol and that some was considerably more expensive than the lowest priced whiskey or rum indicate a role for taste in our understanding of alcohol consumption.[46] Such evidence suggests that there is room for choice, moderation, and even abstinence among stories of alcohol in settlement society. This is not to deny the tragedies, waste, and violence linked to excessive alcohol use, but to argue the need to reflect closely on the stories, using evidence from actual lives. Our evidence thus reinforces the findings of the principal authority on alcohol in Upper Canada, Julia Roberts, who has demonstrated the interpretive possibilities when we imagine alcohol in colonial pioneer society in frames and contexts other than that supplied by what has been the standard source, literature from the temperance movement.[47]

In 1842, Tett's accounts record a number of purchases of alcohol, including a 40-gallon barrel of whiskey by William Bilton (a local innkeeper), 1.5 quarts of port by Thomas Canning, and some brandy and 1.5 gallons of gin by Peter Hassen (the only gin purchase in the entire study). After that, no sample member purchased alcohol from any of the stores. Had the countryside gone completely dry? It is unlikely. Mid-century directories list inns, taverns, or hotels in all our communities except Darlingside. Nor did indicators of alcohol consumption, production, and imports for the province decline in this period: the ratio established early in the colony's history of one licensed tavern for just over three hundred people remained until well after Confederation, and per capita output of provincial distilleries was sustained across the mid-century era despite its intense temperance movement.[48] Thus, it seems likely that the pattern of purchasing at our stores is attributable to alcohol becoming a distinct, licensed trade with its own channels. Indeed, several of Tett's alcohol debits (including Hassen's gin) indicate that the alcohol was actually from the store of William McDonald, a local grocer. Why none of our later stores was licensed is a separate question. Two of the merchants, Thomas Choate and Samuel Scovil, were very active in the temperance movement; perhaps the other three also made such a personal choice.

GROCERY PURCHASES, 1828–61

As with alcohol and with some of the textiles we considered in chapter 3, prices for the principal groceries had fallen substantially by 1828. The 1828–29 retail price for tea, 95 cents to $1.00, was no more than two-thirds of the 1808–09 price. Sugar had fallen by about the same amount; the lowest price was 10 cents per pound, as compared to 15 cents earlier, and the highest (loaf sugar) was 25 cents, as compared to 33.3 cents. Tobacco prices were now about half of their earlier levels (20 to 25 cents rather than 45 to 50 cents). These levels were generally representative of the ranges in subsequent years.

After 1808–09, each subsequent sample adds to the list of groceries in appendix A.[49] In 1828–29, these include soap, with nine buyers then, and candles, with one; both were widely purchased henceforth, at all stores. Two additions this year, molasses and vinegar, each had a single buyer; this modesty proves typical – in total there were only twenty-one buyers of the former and fifteen of the latter in all the samples, although each was purchased at a majority of stores. Groceries represented just 12 percent of total purchases in 1842,[50] yet there were a number of new groceries purchased then, and widely thereafter. These included currants, raisins, starch, saleratus (an ingredient in baking powder), mustard, and peppermint.[51] Two extensively purchased goods were added in 1851: soda (with 123 buyers; as accounts report washing soda as well, this was likely sodium bicarbonate, a new product at the time, used in baking, cooking, and perhaps beverages),[52] and rice (76 buyers, who bought a total of 410 pounds). The 1850s samples also add some goods that we have grouped to simplify presentation: candies (which include "sweets" and "bulls-eyes," 44 buyers) and fish (herring, codfish, whitefish, "split," and "fresh," with 35 buyers). Some of the fish could have been local.[53] Despite the weight of 1861 customers in the study, only one product was added then, syrup, bought by 46 customers at four stores; many made multiple purchases, even during a single month. Because it was sold in large volumes, sometimes by the gallon, it is listed here as a grocery product.[54] But if it was the "simple syrup" that medical advice books assumed people had on hand, a molasses-based product according to Dr Chase,[55] it would be better listed with medications.

This is probably the case for some other products listed as groceries, all of which appear on nineteenth century lists of home remedies or products used by physicians: ginger and cinnamon, on the list from 1808-09; mustard, cloves, cayenne, nutmeg, and caraway seeds, added in 1842; and essence of lemon, added in 1851. Although a number of these were purchased at many, or most, stores, quantities were so modest that they seem unlikely to have been standard flavours and seasonings for Upper Canadian country cooks.[56] Other potentially medicinal products include alcohol, especially brandy and wine, and chemicals such as madder and sulphur.[57] Indeed, sulphur and molasses supply the title of a book on "home remedies ... of the Canadian past."[58]

Few of the products added to the grocery list after 1808–09 were foods (just currants, raisins, rice, and fish), and the additions did not challenge the primacy of tea, tobacco, and sugar, which almost everywhere accounted for more than 60 percent of all groceries, and sometimes much more.[59] With some variation in numbers of buyers and volumes (for example, Darling's had much larger sales of sugar than other stores, and Fowlds's in 1861 had sugar sales in just a few months), the patterns of purchasing already described for 1808–09 prove to have been representative. Thus, it was normal for these goods to be purchased in relatively small quantities: 95 percent of all transactions in tea and tobacco involved from a quarter-pound to a pound, and 80 percent of sugar transactions were of less than five pounds (table 12). These modest transactions accounted for 80 percent of the volume of tea purchased, three-quarters of tobacco, and half of all sugar.

Tea and tobacco (and sugar, to which we return below) were consumed from taste, habit, and even (we might now say) addiction.[60] They were perhaps occasional luxuries for some, but many probably consumed them regularly. Yet only about a third of customers who bought tea and tobacco did so in as many as four months in a year (the threshold used earlier in discussing leading customers in 1808–09; see table 12). Almost 90 percent of the ten largest accounts at each store bought at least some tea and tobacco; but only about two-thirds even of these principal buyers did so in four or more months, and they did not necessarily buy both with equal frequency. Of all buyers whose household size is known, only about one buyer in ten bought tea or tobacco in amounts approaching two pounds per person per year, enough to meet English (and mid-century Canadian) standards of consumption. Does this mean that few people in the Upper Canadian countryside reached this standard? Judging by the 1851 and 1861 import figures cited earlier, that seems unlikely, because rural dwellers made up so large a proportion of the whole population.

Even among those who did reach this threshold, there was still considerable variation, in the mix of products purchased, scale of purchases, and pattern of buying. For example, at Sherin's store, the largest account was for George Shields, a blacksmith with eight people in his household. There were charges to his account on almost one hundred days, in every month, yet he bought nearly all of his 28 pounds of tea on two days, 14 pounds on 1 March 1861 and 12 pounds on 19 October (table 17). Shields bought 51 pounds of sugar in two transactions in early September (and 47 more in six transactions between 1 March and 19 December). He bought almost no tobacco, however, just 1.5 pounds in January. Similarly, Charles Watley, a farmer with a household of nine, bought nearly all his 20 pounds of tea in three transactions in January and August, yet there were transactions on his account on thirty-two days during the year, in all twelve months. The Watleys bought 15 pounds of sugar (and made 100); they never bought tobacco. George Bolton, a teamster with a three-person household, had an entirely different pattern: he bought tea and tobacco in every month, 23.5 pounds of the former in thirty transactions and 25 pounds of the latter in thirty-seven transactions. Such purchases were large enough on a per capita basis that it seems possible that there were other consumers besides the Bolton family. Their sugar purchases were not so exceptional, 56 pounds bought in twenty-seven transactions in eight months.

Some large volume purchases were definitely for social or work-related consumption, and others might have been. Thus, the leading tea buyer in all samples was David Rose, described in the census as a "lumberer," who bought sixty pounds of tea from the Fowlds on 9 February 1861; twenty pounds of tobacco on 28 January and another fourteen pounds on 18 February; and twenty pounds of sugar on 9 February (table 17). As the timing and quantities indicate, he was buying for a winter shanty operation, although only his tea purchases seem sufficient to constitute a supply for much of a season's operations.[61] Charges to another Fowlds customer, Andy Orr (recorded in the 1861 census as a labourer with a household of six), included several explicitly for a shanty located in Methuen Township, north of Hastings: eight pounds of sugar on 28 January, four pounds of tobacco on 7 October and again on 8 November, and one pound of tea on 31 July.[62] Other charges likely had a similar purpose, notably the fifty-nine pounds of tobacco he bought in three transactions in February (table 17). He and his wife bought nineteen pounds of tea, in nineteen transactions between February and December. That was enough for more than three pounds per person, but we do not know what proportion of the tea was consumed within their household.

One Sherin customer, the Reverend Percy S. Warren, Church of England minister in Lakefield, bought no tea or sugar but was the leading coffee buyer in the entire sample, accounting for more than one-quarter of all the coffee ever purchased, nearly all of it in two transactions late in the year (table 17). The other fifty-seven buyers combined bought just over one hundred pounds. Coffee was generally available, purchased at eight stores, but it was not a rival to tea.[63]

Strikingly, these bulk purchases seldom involved a discounted price. For example, Warren paid 25 cents per pound for his coffee, as did the eleven other buyers at Sherin's. Rose paid 80 cents per pound for tea. So did Shields and Watley in their earlier purchases. This was the normal price at both stores.[64] By autumn, when Shields paid $1.10 per pound, others were paying between $1.00 and $1.25. Rose paid 30 cents per pound for his tobacco purchases, as did Orr in one case; but Orr paid 40 cents for his next purchase. Through the first several months of the year, customers paid 30, 40, and sometimes 50 cents per pound at Fowlds's; a quality difference is thus implied. Only one of the prices in table 17 might have represented a discount. Shields (and one other customer) paid 8.3 cents per pound for a large volume purchase of sugar; Sherin otherwise charged 10 to 13 cents (including for Shields's other purchases).

MEDICATIONS

Even without counting the many potentially medicinal products already noted, the list of medicines in appendix A is as long as the main grocery list.[65] Nine were first purchased in 1828–29. The total value of all such purchases then was only about eight dollars, but twenty-three different customers bought at least one such product (table 12). Pills were the most common of the medications, bought by people at every store from 1828 on, a total of seventy-five buyers. They cost 45 cents per box in 1828; later, almost every box sold for 25 cents. Next came castor oil, purchased in all subsequent samples by a total of sixty-three buyers, and salts (often specified as Epsom), with thirty-eight buyers at six stores. Others included camphor, opodeldoc, calomel (mainly as calomel and jalap), paregoric, and bark. They had considerably fewer buyers, as did many of the fifteen medications added in 1842. Aloes, quinine, balsam, spike oil, squills syrup, pink root, and assorted ointments, plasters, and cordials were common, yet not widely purchased. The same can be said for the oils grouped here as "other"; individually, oils such as British, black, olive, and sweet would not have ranked very high in frequency.

What were all these products, and why did people take them? We can only selectively address so long a list, but it can be said that virtually all can be found in Dr Chase's recipes and in other general medical guides of the period. Many had multiple uses, often for animals as well as people. Knowing that a remedy like opodeldoc had been used for centuries, we might imagine these as representative of traditional (possibly even folk) practices. It is therefore important that many were part of progressive professional medical practice, prescribed by well-trained doctors applying their understanding of what worked as prevention or to cure or alleviate specific medical situations. For example, as Jacalyn Duffin writes in her account of the mid-nineteenth-century medical practice of Dr James Langstaff, in the countryside north of Toronto, "The most commonly recorded drugs in the 1850s include jalap, calomel, and tartar emetic (antimony potassium tartrate), all strong remedies with violent side-effects ... Calomel (mercurous chloride), a cathartic, was used for severe fevers, such as acute rheumatism and hepatitis, especially when accompanied by constipation ... Jalap ... had been a favourite of the pioneer physician-politician William 'Tiger' Dunlop ... who counselled that it, together with calomel, should be given unstintingly to the new immigrants to ward off colonial ills."[66]

No ordinary customer purchased the combinations of medicinal products that recipe books prescribed; someone wanting, say, opodeldoc bought it already made. This helps to explain the number of medicines that were branded (though some names represented a generally known formula rather than being proprietary). It is likely that many of the eight named kinds of pills recorded (see table 18) were variants on the generic ingredients also visible in the lists; for example, Cooper's Pills (purchased in both Choate samples) were a purgative that included calomel, tartar emetic, Castile soap, etc.[67] Vermifuges (sometimes specified as worm tea or worm candy) and products described as "pain killer," "pain destroyer," or "pain extractor" tell us of common problems. Several products were for ague, such as quinine and bark. Much of the latter was "Peruvian," although it also had other applications.[68] For emetics and purgatives, we know the treatment but not the illness. Some, perhaps, were taken as preventatives. Judging by Dr Langstaff's purchase of an "electric machine" in 1861, there was a fashion for things electrical then; indeed, one of the "other oils" was "electric oil," which appears in 1861, as does "galvanic fluid" (in appendix B). An advertisement for gargling oil (new in 1861 and purchased at all five stores, by a total of fourteen buyers) includes testimonials attesting to its efficacy for treating horses, saving the arm of a man who feared paralysis, relieving stiff knee joints and sore nipples, and treating chronic rheumatism.[69]

Opium was one of James Langstaff's most frequently used therapies. On our list, laudanum (an opium-based product) was purchased by five buyers from three stores, the first in 1842.[70] Tett and two other merchants also sold opium itself (listed in appendix B). There was laudanum in Godfrey's Cordial, which was the most commonly purchased of the cordials (accounting for at least eight of the twelve buyers, the other cordials being unspecified); and opium was the key component in paregoric.[71] Just among these four products, there were twenty-eight buyers (from eight stores) of something opium-based. On the other hand, and despite stories of addiction to medications for the narcotics (or alcohol) in them, there was only one repeat purchase of these products.

Indeed, among all these medications, frequent purchasers were uncommon; for example, just twenty-two families bought two or more boxes of pills in a year. Even among the most frequent buyers, purchases were not sustained on a full-year basis. Thus two Choate customers each bought eight boxes of pills, but mainly in quite concentrated periods (early winter in one case, high summer in the other; see table 19). At Scovil's the two customers who were the leading buyers of balsam had similarly varied patterns (one buying often in July and August, then a large bottle in November; the other buying none between 7 March and 3 October).[72] Overall, the main pattern is one of widespread purchasing. Taking all these drug and related products combined, a total of 283 households bought at least one of them (table 12). That is, although few medical products, seen individually, appear very significant, collectively they represent an important dimension of the country store's role.

Among the purchasers were three doctors. It is noteworthy that Benjamin Tett's store could supply Dr J.W. Miller with quinine, bark, gum myrrh, squills syrup, oil of vitriol (which we have, perhaps wrongly, included with vitriol on the chemical list), hartshorn (a form of ammonia), ether, and spirits of nitre (the latter three are in appendix B – in fact Dr Miller was the only buyer of ether and spirits of nitre in all the samples). Dr J.B. Wilson, on the 1854 list, was one of the buyers of opium and once bought an emetic. Dr James Bingham was one of the three buyers of olive oil (one of the "other oils" in the table) in 1861. From the modesty of their purchases, it is clear that these men did not use these stores as their main supplier of pharmaceutical products.[73]

MAKING AND BUYING

Groceries such as sugar, candles, and soap might also be made at home. Indeed, wick for candle-making was purchased by someone at every store, a total of seventy-five buyers (see table 20). Even as they confirm that home candle-making was common, such purchases also call into question stories that portray production as driven by necessity, as in the following: "Women had little choice but to be enterprising in the days when household necessities were not easily affordable at the general store … Such commonplace items as candle-wicking often had to be made in the farm kitchen ... The wicking was made from twisted linen or cord, soaked in a solution of borax, coarse salt, and water."[74] In this example, salt and borax (and probably linen) would themselves have had to be purchased. And borax, according to advice books, had many uses.[75] Yet there were just six buyers of it, all men, four of them blacksmiths; and five of the six buyers also bought candles and/or wick. In any case, it is unclear why anyone would make wick when it cost 15 cents per ball in 1842 and 9 cents in 1851.[76] Nineteen of those who bought wick can also be found among the sixty-six candle buyers (table 20). That is, as with textiles, making and buying were not mutually exclusive.[77] Rather than being about lack of choice, as our story of wick-making asserts, they actually reflected choices in the use of time and money – and in taste (such as in occasional purchases of more expensive spermaceti candles and Castile soap, although the latter might have been for medical purposes; as we have seen, it was a standard ingredient in medications).

About half of the farm households in the eight cases for which data are available made sugar (see table 20), as did some landowners for whom the census gave another occupation. There is variation among samples, but essentially this was as true in 1861 as it had been in 1842.[78] In total, sample members made over 17,000 pounds of maple sugar. The mean output was slightly over 100 pounds per maker, but with wide variation. The largest producer, William Lewis, a customer with a tiny account at Fowlds's store in 1861, made 1,000 pounds, and several made 400 to 450 pounds. Production at this level was likely market-oriented rather than just for the household. Indeed, modest amounts of maple sugar were among the sugar purchased at five stores, notably Yonge Mills in 1828–29, where about half of the 152 pounds of sugar purchased was explicitly recorded as maple sugar, sold at 10 cents per pound.[79] At the other extreme, some producers reported making very small volumes, as little as 5 or 10 pounds. Either they consumed very little sugar or they, like non-makers, acquired sugar in the marketplace. In general, as the data in table 20 indicate, few of those who made sugar purchased it in large amounts. For example, ten Sherin customers reported making a total of 832 pounds of sugar; seven of them also bought sugar, but only 37 pounds in total. The other twenty-two sugar buyers purchased 401 pounds. Even so, just three bought even 14 pounds per capita (and two of them were single men), a threshold still below the level of 16 pounds per person indicated by 1861 import data. There is a similar pattern for imported sugar at almost all the stores. Did these families do without or buy from local producers and at other stores?

The best confirmation that rural families consumed sugar at the level indicated by the general trade statistics is the Darling store, which alone accounted for one-third of the sugar bought at all stores. Thirteen of its customers made sugar, a total of 1,113 pounds. Unlike makers at the other stores, some of these families also bought substantial quantities. Nine of them bought almost half of the more than 1,000 pounds of sugar purchased (table 20); combining what they made and bought, four of these families reached a threshold of 16 pounds per capita. (So did one on the basis of what was made, and one couple on the basis of what they bought.) The highest indicated consumption was for the family of Marsey Chismore, which purchased 135 pounds of sugar and reported output of 100 pounds. In this ten-person household, that totalled 23.5 pounds of sugar per person, or almost exactly the *average* rate of consumption in England in 1800. This is one of the very few families for whom our data provide direct evidence that some rural Upper Canadians consumed sugar at that rate.[80] Even so, given Upper Canada's mainly rural population, many more of our customers must have reached this level.[81]

Beyond this basic, and perhaps obvious, conclusion, our evidence suggests others not visible in the aggregate data. First, it shows that at the beginning of our period the basic groceries – tea, tobacco, sugar, salt, and pepper – were already widely purchased and were likely routinely consumed. Second, it shows how such purchases actually were made, typically in small volumes, relatively frequently purchased, rather than in bulk.[82] Third, it strongly suggests a pattern like the one we have seen for textiles, that most buyers purchased at more than one store. Fourth, it extends and specifies our list of groceries beyond those individually recorded in the trade data; this is especially important for a long list of not-so-widely consumed goods, for which it can be relevant to know whether rural dwellers bought them – borax being an example. Fifth, it reveals change, in various ways, across the period. Besides the appearance of new products, the disappearance of alcohol is particularly noteworthy – although there is reason to believe that this was not because no one in these communities was drinking it by mid-century. Sixth, among all these goods, only salt seems in some absolute sense to have been a necessity; choice was involved in purchases that have usually been depicted as reflecting simple needs. Choice is evident in the variations in purchasing by the large accounts; most bought the three principal groceries, but some did not; and buyers did not necessarily buy them with equivalent frequency and in similar quantities. Choice is visible also in the variety of kinds of alcohol, sugar, tea, tobacco, and medications that people bought, and in where they bought them.

Details of patterns and variations for each commodity and for individual buyers could be multiplied almost indefinitely. The larger point is their normalcy: they show us some Upper Canadians doing some of their shopping to acquire products that formed part of the routines of their lives. Although we know only an uncertain portion of their purchases of groceries and medicines, the lists suggest possibilities and orders of magnitude. Some of the goods added to the list after the first sample were quite widely purchased: new foodstuffs – currants, raisins, and rice; new ingredients – such as saleratus and soda, which were among "the superb leavening agents that began to appear by the middle of the nineteenth century," with a real impact on bread-making;[83] and household products – soap, candles, and starch. Of the many other products, most were bought in smaller quantities and by fewer buyers, as if they were not so generally used. Opodeldoc seems to fit here. Medicinal products were nevertheless important, judging by how many people bought something in this category. Worries about health are, no doubt, universal, but responses were given specific shape by the products people chose to buy, including many new products. Medications are a reminder also that pain, illness, the fear associated with them, and the desire to treat them were very much part of everyday life.[84] Even when families made goods for themselves, as they continued to do in 1861, at levels that were equivalent to twenty years earlier, their decisions reflected judgments about how to allocate their resources, including time, and knowledge of what was available, from whom, and at what price. What they bought, made, sold, and did without were a function also of culture, which structured their priorities and the routines of daily life. Stressing that even in 1808-09 Upper Canadians bought groceries familiar to us does not mean that nothing changed either within the period or between then and today. As the absence of chocolate and the presence of opodeldoc vividly demonstrate, Upper Canada was a different world.

5

IRON IN A "WOODEN AGE": HARDWARE
AND RELATED PURCHASES

Much could be written of the pervasiveness of wood in ... domestic life;
the extent of dependence upon wood in farming was truly phenomenal.
Not only were houses, barns, outbuildings, wagons, and furniture made
of wood, but much of this was often done by the farmer himself.
Moreover, wood was pressed into service for many uses which in a less
wooded land could have been taken care of by different materials.

Brooke Hindle, 1975[1]

In telling the story of a nineteenth-century "wooden age," Brooke Hindle
places the techniques and technologies of wood at the heart of the
American rural economy. We begin with this idea because Upper Canada
relied at least equally on wood in the same period. This was not, however,
because iron and its products were unavailable. Iron was reported in two
categories in the mid-century Canadian trade statistics, iron and "manufactures of iron and hardware" (very modest quantities of steel were
also imported). Between 1850 and 1852, such imports averaged about
$2.7 million per year, equivalent to $1.49 per person in the two Canadas
(appendix C); two-thirds of the imports were manufactures. A decade
later, after an entire railroad system had been built using imported iron,
the total value of these products was much the same, albeit with a smaller
proportion of manufactures; in a larger provincial population, this was
equal to $1.21 per capita. Some iron was also supplied by the domestic
charcoal iron industry, but falling prices of British pig iron made primary
production of iron from Canadian deposits steadily less competitive. On
the other hand, low prices for iron contributed to the flourishing of new
foundries: by 1871, secondary iron manufacturing was one of the main
elements of Ontario's industrial economy.[2]

That iron imports were modest confirms the predominance of
wood in Upper Canada, for construction, transportation, tools for field
work, and heating. Because iron and coal are so closely associated with

nineteenth-century industrialization, reliance on wood might be read as evidence of underdevelopment, or even backwardness. For example, this might be how a British readership understood Catharine Parr Traill's 1833 account of the tools needed for farming (although she stresses the appropriateness of local farm technology): "A small farmer at home would think very poorly of our Canadian possessions, especially when I add that our whole stock of farming implements consists of two reaping-hooks, several axes, a spade, and a couple of hoes. Add to these a queer sort of harrow that is made in the shape of a triangle for the better passing between the stumps: this is a rude machine compared with the nicely painted instruments of the sort I have been accustomed to see used in Britain. It is roughly hewn, and put together without regard to neatness; strength for use is all that is looked to here. The plough is seldom put into the land before the third or fourth year; nor is it required."[3]

Contrast with practice elsewhere also informs William Wylie's rich study of blacksmiths, the principal metal workers in Upper Canada, which draws on many smiths' accounts. He recognizes that farmers were an essential market for blacksmiths, but places considerable emphasis on what farmers did not buy. "Particularly in the first years after settling, farmers restricted purchases of hardware to essentials. Whenever possible, they substituted wooden equipment such as hoes, drag teeth, and ploughs for more expensive iron and steel ware. Many settlers had grindstones and files which enabled them to do some of their hardware maintenance work without recourse to blacksmiths."[4] In his presentation, smiths (and, by implication, their clientele) represent a traditional, not a modern, economy. "The working world of the blacksmith at mid-nineteenth-century was in many ways not much different than it had been for centuries in Europe ... The survival of these activities in the nineteenth century was a temporary phenomenon facilitated by the limited economic development of Upper Canada."[5] Suppliers of costly "essentials," blacksmiths thus were a "survival" from a timeless past.

The idea that ironware was "more expensive" is often, as in Wylie's account, set in a story of what "hindered" development in Upper Canada, especially "the difficulties of transportation" that made for "high costs of importation" until the St Lawrence canals were built.[6] Indeed, barriers are central to most representations of this economy. "The main obstacle to settlement in Upper Canada" before 1812, the standard Canadian economic history text argues, "was the high cost of transporting products to market and bringing in equipment and supplies."[7] Yet the colonial economy grew for a half-century before the Rideau Canal was built and more than sixty years before the St Lawrence canals were completed. And blacksmithing continued long after. Among craftsmen, their numbers in Upper Canada were exceeded only by carpenters and shoemakers. Anything but a "survival," this was a craft in full expansion at mid-century – the census counted 4,200 blacksmiths in 1851 and almost twice as many in 1871.[8] Smiths tended to be generalists who produced and maintained a wide range of goods, but that role cannot have been a function of high transport costs for imports.[9] If the iron they used reached the backwoods, products manufactured from iron could also have borne those costs. Moreover, tools and other products made of iron were durable or semi-durable; if they could save time or effort, or allow doing important tasks that otherwise would not have been possible, they were investments justifiable in terms of the return they would generate.

In addition to carpenters and shoemakers, other rural crafts included coopers, masons, wagon makers, tanners, and saddlers and harness makers.[10] They used some imported goods but, unlike smiths, primarily relied on local materials, wood, leather, and (for the masons) stone. By examining actual purchases by such craftsmen and by farmers, this chapter seeks to translate the hardware categories in the trade data into specific goods and transactions, and to provide a longer term perspective on mid-century imports. It also understands wood as a basic resource for living, an orientation missing in a Canadian historiography that focuses almost exclusively on staple wood exports.[11] As the rapidity of American growth during the "wooden age" indicates, farmers' practice and the work of blacksmiths and other craftsmen should be read not as expressions of tradition and limited development but as appropriate choices in a rural economy where wood was abundant.

HARDWARE AND IRON

The goods considered in this chapter are listed in two sections of appendix A. There are fifty-nine hardware products, of which the twenty-seven purchased in 1808–09 include almost all of the most common goods – such as the nails, glass, and gun-related goods summarized in table 21. Another thirty-three products are listed as chemicals, the seven purchased in 1808–09 including five of the six most common ones. A further thirty-eight hardware products and six chemicals are listed in appendix B. In

1808–09, hardware and chemicals amounted to only 8 percent of all purchases, yet over 80 percent of buyers bought something in these
categories. In later samples, the value of hardware purchases was generally less than dry goods or groceries, and the value of chemicals was more
modest still. At four stores the two categories combined did not equal 10
percent of purchases (table 21). Still, almost five hundred sample members bought some kind of hardware, and almost three hundred bought
some kind of chemical. Although some of their purchases (tools and
building components for example) were durable and thus might survive
as artifacts or be recorded in inventories, these products often disappeared (or were transformed) in use.

Many of the products encompass goods that were diverse in character, quality, and purpose. Representing such variations in appendix A
would have been difficult, however, because account entries were seldom
specific. An example is knives, which rank second on the hardware list.
In 1808–09, thirty-nine were purchased by twenty-two buyers: three jack
knives, one pocket knife, three pen knives, and thirty-two recorded simply as knives. Import invoices indicate that the latter must mainly have
been of these three types, but prices overlapped and there is no way to
know which was which. Some might have been butcher or shoe knives;
modest quantities of both were imported this year, and they were explicitly mentioned in later samples. There were also variations within each
product, indicated in 1808 import invoices by differences in the wholesale price: four prices for pocket knives, four for shoe knives, and two
for pen knives.[12]

"Farmers made nails by the thousands during winter months around
the forge or fireplace" writes one American account of pioneering deeply
suffused by images of self-sufficiency.[13] Yet nails were among the most
common purchases; there were 23 buyers in 1808–09 and 278 in the ten
samples combined. In a wooden age, nails were indeed essentials. Saying
that does not, however, address what they were essential for – the kinds,
quantities, and actual uses. Most transactions were recorded simply as
"nails," but at least nine kinds are mentioned in accounts (table 22), with
varied prices and purposes; most also were available in different sizes.[14]
A few transactions in 1808–09 identify fourteen- and sixteen-penny nails
(both referred to as "plank nails" in import invoices), eight-penny, and
shingle nails.[15] All were sold by count, at a price per hundred for larger
nails and per thousand for smaller. Four men bought 600 or more, led
by Elias Tryan, who bought 300 fourteen-penny nails (at 33 cents per

hundred), 200 sixteen-penny nails (35 cents per 100), and 2,000 unspecified, evidently smaller, nails (at $1.80 per thousand), all on 19 September. Most buyers made smaller purchases, such as Zachariah Hagerman, who on 13 October bought 200 nails for 67 cents, 25 more expensive nails (at 50 cents per hundred), and a hammer (for 35 cents). This was one of three hammers purchased in 1808–09, all by men who also bought nails.

The 1828 sample adds cut and brass nails to the list of types. At $1.35 per pound, the latter were costly; there were only two buyers then, and such nails are recorded at only one later store.[16] Cut nails, on the other hand, were now standard for most building purposes. Available in many sizes, they were sold at every store simply by weight. Thanks to rapidly developing new manufacturing technology after 1800, they were cheaper than any other nails, and their price fell steadily across the period, from 12.5 or 13 cents per pound in 1828, to 8.3 to 10 cents in 1842, and 5 to 7 cents in 1861.[17]

Wrought nails continued to be purchased; they could cost twice as much as cut nails (the typical price was 12.5 cents per pound in 1851 and 1861), but evidently were preferred for some construction purposes. Rose nails, frequently purchased in 1842 (but not mentioned at other stores), were a type of wrought nail.[18] Later samples add pressed nails[19] and two specialized, relatively expensive products: boat and clout nails. Among the uses for the latter was "fastening a clout ['a piece of iron … fixed on an axletree to prevent wear'] on an axle."[20] The three buyers were a cooper, a blacksmith, and a carriage maker.

In the first two samples, volumes seem modest; the twenty-nine buyers in 1828–29, for example, purchased just over 100 pounds. Reflecting falling prices and the changing character of building, volumes tended to be much higher later. Notably, a few buyers made very large purchases (see table 23). In 1842 almost half the nails were accounted for by Stephen McCathron, a tanner, who bought 84 pounds of nails in spring and John Hubbard, a blacksmith, who bought a 72-pound keg in autumn. In 1854, four buyers accounted for about 60 percent of the nails. In 1861, John Sharpe bought one-quarter of the nails at Fowlds's; Thomas Hunt and Isaac Errott bought about half the nails from Darling's; and William Kyle bought more than one-quarter of all nails from Scovil's. The same pattern held at Sherin's, except here the value of hardware purchases far exceeded other stores, representing one-quarter of all debits. The 2,650 pounds of nails alone represented more than

6 percent of total debits. Three-quarters of these were purchased by three buyers (table 23), William Cotton, a carpenter, A. Morrow, a merchant, and Kenneth Urquhart, a tailor. The accounts of Morrow and Urquhart show that they were engaged in building projects (e.g., they were also charged for paint and window glass, and many charges on Morrow's account were by tradesmen, including Cotton).

Not all the largest accounts bought nails.[21] Still, it was evidently normal to have nails on hand for building and repairs. Like the routine purchases considered in previous chapters, they could be acquired in appropriate types and quantities when needed and from whichever store was most convenient. Bulk purchases suggest the requirements for larger-scale building; but, if that required nails in the quantities bought at Sherin's, our samples provide only glimpses of the transition from log to frame building during the period. It is striking that even Cotton, the leading buyer, did not buy nails on his own account after mid-May, although he continued to buy other kinds of goods.[22]

All of these nails were for wood. So were brads (listed separately in appendix A), a small, almost headless nail that could be sunk below the surface of wood and covered over; they were purchased by a few buyers beginning in 1842.[23] Shoemaking also required nails, such as shoe tacks (purchased in 1808 and all but one later sample) and sprigs (purchased in both Choate samples and at one other store in 1861).[24] For example, Thomas Riggs bought sprigs on three occasions in 1851. But he was the only shoemaker in the samples to do so; most buyers were actually farmers. Indeed, if shoemakers routinely used tacks and sprigs, they evidently bought them mainly from other sources.

Finally, nails were essential for shoeing horses and perhaps oxen. Horseshoe nails, a type of wrought nail, appear among purchases in 1842 and in all subsequent samples (table 22).[25] Sold mainly at 25 or 27 cents per pound, they were among the most expensive nails. The main buyers, perhaps not surprisingly, were the five blacksmiths listed in table 23. Yet even among them there was wide variation. Daniel Dwyer bought often, in small volumes, 43 pounds in almost as many transactions; the regularity and consistency of his purchases might suggest that these met his needs. George Shields bought much more, 150 pounds in two bulk transactions.[26] John Grant, John Hubbard, and Thomas Pomeroy (in 1854) bought only modest quantities. Yet Grant and Hubbard had the second largest accounts in their samples; unless they seldom worked with horses, they either made nails themselves or bought them elsewhere. For our purposes, the main finding is that they bought at least some horse-shoe nails and also nails of other kinds.

Others also purchased small quantities of horseshoe nails, such as five at Darling's who bought a total of four pounds and seven at Choate's in 1861 who bought a total of twelve pounds. Do such purchases indicate that some men's self-sufficiency extended to shoeing their own animals? Perhaps, but evidently that was not the norm: blacksmiths were widely present in rural society and farm purchases of horseshoe nails were infrequent. Possibly farmers kept nails for maintenance or to supply the smith when he worked on their animals, or else such nails had other uses.

Horseshoe nails are a reminder that horses and oxen were vital to the rural economy.[27] Appendix A also includes whips and related products (at every store from 1828 onward – and import invoices show they were stocked in 1808); trace and halter chains (among the most commonly specified types of chains, they were purchased in 1808 and at almost all later stores); curry combs (appearing in 1842 and then at most other stores); rasps (also 1842); and horse cards and brushes (1861).[28] This seems a limited spectrum of products, and none were all that frequently purchased. Even if many were durable, the implication is that harness and saddlery must generally have been acquired through other channels.

Iron itself was purchased at all ten stores.[29] In 1808–09, nine men bought a total of 144 pounds, in quantities ranging from 1 to 53 pounds, at a price of either 11.7 or 12.5 cents per pound. In 1828–29, nine buyers purchased a total of 205 pounds, the largest purchase being 65 pounds. Almost all iron was now just 5 cents per pound. It is significant that the decline in retail prices, which already were virtually as low as at mid-century, preceded completion of any provincial canals.[30] General deflation, declining ocean freight rates, and technological developments on the production side all contributed to lower prices.

Transactions were commonly recorded simply as "iron," but it came in many forms, for different uses. Some of the principal varieties can be seen in invoices for the almost three tons of iron imported by the Jones stores in 1808. They included bars of English iron, "Swedes" iron, and flat and square iron; and smaller quantities of sheet iron, hooping, coopers iron, and round iron.[31] In 1828–29, many purchases were explicitly of English iron. Later samples note additional types (table 22); many (such as Swedish iron, the highest quality) were evidently available earlier.

The leading buyers were blacksmiths (table 24), but again there was substantial variation among them. For Pomeroy (and also for David Latimer, listed on the census as a farmer, whose uses for almost a ton of iron are unknown), transactions recorded external suppliers' invoices; that is, the merchant was facilitating custom imports, not supplying iron from his own stock.[32] John Grant's account, with charges for nine different kinds of iron, is especially revealing on varieties; and George Shields's purchases of about three tons suggest the possible scale of a smith's iron requirements.[33] They must have had close relationships to the merchant for him to be able to anticipate the varieties and very large volumes to stock. But for most smiths in table 24, our stores cannot have been the main supplier. Indeed, John Hubbard, despite having Tett's second largest account, bought almost no iron there.

Most of the fifty-eight buyers were not blacksmiths or other metal tradesmen. Were such buyers able to work with iron, transforming it themselves, or did they buy to supply it to a craftsman? The story of pioneer winter nail-making, above, offered one explanation, but patterns in 1808 and 1828 resemble those at some later stores, when nails were very inexpensive.[34] Thus, in 1851, eleven others besides Edward Kennedy bought iron at Choate's, a total of almost three hundred pounds including three purchases of between fifty and sixty pounds. And in 1861, eight others besides Dwyer bought hoop, stirrup, round, and tire iron from Choate's, in smaller quantities. It is not impossible that some farmers cut nails in the winter, but clearly most did not – nor is it clear why someone would do so when most chose to purchase nails.

Purchases of iron confirm that the iron components of the age of wood were often locally made; and the types of iron indicate how it might be used with wood and with animals – such as for shoeing, wheels and other parts for wagons and sleighs, and hoops for barrels. Notwithstanding images of farmer self-sufficiency, the widespread presence of artisans demonstrates commercial engagement in the production of goods used by farmers. Whoever did the work, moreover, imports were only a small part of the ultimate value of these products.

Other hardware products for building included glass, screws, butts and other hinges, and locks, all purchased in every sample. In 1808–09, six people bought dogs (for holding logs during hewing and in a fireplace) and andirons; they were the most expensive hardware items purchased this year, costing $2.75 or $3.35 per pair.[35] Surprisingly, these are the only purchases of irons that might be used in a pioneer hearth; everything else there (cooking pots aside) must have been acquired in other ways. The 1828–29 sample adds one widely purchased building product, putty. Later samples add only three, none with all that many buyers: latches (1842), stove pipes and joints (1851), and plaster (1851).[36]

Glass for windows was imported by the box, and transactions were most commonly in "lights."[37] Purchases of one or a few lights might indicate repair of an existing window; if the buyer acquired enough glass for one or more windows, building or remodelling are implied. Because stories of backwoods isolation and transportation difficulties stress high costs and breakage, and many accounts of pioneer log houses imagine them as lacking window glass, it is important to emphasize its availability.[38] Indeed, the largest number of buyers in any sample was in 1808–09, when fifteen buyers bought more than 154 lights, transactions running from two or three who bought only a single light up to one who bought 36. Almost all were priced at 11.7 cents. Although glass could vary in qualities, dimensions, and thickness, all the glass imported in 1808 measured 7.5 by 8.5 inches.[39] Those were also the dimensions of the glass imported by Tett in the 1830s. In 1828–29, six buyers purchased a total of 63 lights, all priced at 8.7 cents. Later prices were lower still, with variations that indicate a growing choice of dimensions.[40] At Fowlds's in 1861, sizes ranged from 7 by 9 and 8 by 10 to 10 by 16 and 12 by 18; at Sherin's lights were 10 by 12, 10 by 14, and 12 by 16. Several 1861 transactions involving larger quantities than earlier also give a glimpse of the requirements of new houses and shops. One customer at Choate's in 1861 and two at Sherin's bought entire boxes (a standard measure, one hundred square feet, whatever the size of pane), from one to three at a time, priced at $3.00 or $3.50 per box. Scovil recorded purchases of 50 and 60 lights. Of the glass buyers, thirty-six also bought putty, almost always at the same time. On the other hand, the fifteen buyers in 1808–09 and thirty-one later glass buyers did not buy putty (although 1808 import invoices show that putty was stocked then).[41]

Screws were sold mainly by the dozen, for specialized purposes such as to install hinges.[42] They were quite varied, as was other building hardware: 1808 import invoices record a total of twelve "gross" of screws at eight different prices (from 35 to 75 cents); seven gross of butt hinges at six different prices (from 63 cents to $1.40); and two dozen hinges for chests (one at $1.20 and the other at $1.45). Invoices differentiate padlocks, cupboard locks, and chest locks.[43] Tett's imports in the 1830s show that variation in these products was often by size and that prices had fallen substantially since early in the century. He bought screws in seven lengths from one-half inch to two inches (at 15 to 60 cents per gross), cast butts in six sizes from two to three-and-a-half inches (at 33 to 75 cents per dozen), and four types of locks (the additional type was Banbury locks, at $1.90 per dozen the most expensive of locks).

We could multiply details but risk losing the larger pattern in doing so. Ordinary houses and other buildings required only a modest number of imported goods, and (as a book addressed to "the emigrant carpenter" advised) the tools to build them were likewise "few in number."[44] Construction, so important an activity in a developing economy, was otherwise very little reliant on long-distance trade.[45] There is considerable continuity in the list of products, with so many already visible in 1808. This does not mean that there were no changes across the period; everything we know about building suggests the opposite. Moreover, there was variation within categories of goods, visible to buyers; and as the wider range of pane sizes by 1861 confirms, choices grew over time. What is not on the list is also striking. Heating, for example, is visible only in a few andiron sets, some stove pipes, and three stoves purchased at Choate's in 1851 (see appendix B). Yet stoves were entering general use in this period, particularly around mid-century.[46]

Besides knives, more than twenty of the hardware products listed in appendix A were tools – for cultivating, harvesting, woods work, building, and maintenance of other tools. The 1808 list includes axes, files, rope, scythes, chains, awls, gimlets, hammers, saws, and sickles.[47] The others appear later, just two of them in 1861, however – points and landsides, both metal plough parts.[48] Many tools came in more than one type. For example, Darling's customers bought forks for hay, straw, and manure (each at a different price). Scythes were for grain and for grass.[49] Hammers for shoemaking differed from those for building; files had many purposes in woodwork and in sharpening and shaping metal (import invoices in 1808, for example, listed seven distinct kinds); rasps (a type of coarse file) were for horses' hooves, leather work, and blacksmiths' work; awls were for working with leather, wood, and fabrics (and were distinguished from gimlets).[50] These tools seem universal, required in virtually all rural households, and families must often have needed more than one, given the variety of most products and the likelihood that at times more than one person participated in a task. Tools were durable, however, and established settlers need not have bought them in the sample year.

After knives, the most frequently purchased tool was the ax, with fifty-one buyers at all ten stores. Axes were essential from the start of a farm's development, yet in the first three samples only five were purchased; clearly they could be bought elsewhere. In 1808 and 1828, prices were from $2.00 to $2.25. Prices dropped after that. For example, at Choate's in 1851, six buyers purchased eight axes, at from $1.25 to $1.60; and in 1861 at Darling's, nineteen buyers bought a total of thirty-one axes, paying from $1.00 for unwarranted axes to as much as $1.30 for "warranted."[51] Here, many customers supplied wood for the store's steamboat supply operation. As few of them were new to the trade in 1861, the implication of so many purchases is that tools in extensive use did not last forever. There was one exception to these prices in 1861: Fowlds recorded a broad ax at $3.00. This was the most expensive ax ever purchased. Such axes are always imagined as standard equipment, yet this was the only one purchased in any sample.[52]

Tool purchases were highly seasonal. Two-thirds of all axes (and every ax handle) were purchased between November and February, and most of the other axes were bought in October and March. A substantial majority of purchases of chains also fell in the winter. On the other hand, almost every scythe, cradle, snath (the shaft of a scythe), and whet (or scythe) stone was purchased in the six weeks from late June to early August.[53] These stones were portable, kept at hand while working. (By contrast, grindstones, which we have seen depicted as a farmer's alternative to using blacksmiths' services, were a different, very bulky product; sold by weight, they first appear on the list in 1851, and in all but one of the subsequent samples, but with only ten buyers.[54]) Nearly every fork (except for dung) and rake was purchased in the same six summer weeks. Other farm tools were rarely purchased in this period. Most hoes, land-sides, and plough points were purchased earlier, between April and June.[55]

If this list gives a sense of the normal tools in use, it does not by itself suggest why they were purchased. One way to consider this question is through combinations of tools. About half of those who bought a scythe also bought a sharpening stone; on the other hand, most stone buyers did not buy a scythe. Just seven bought a scythe, a stone, and a snath. And only one bought the principal tools for fieldwork visible in this list: Michael Hoolihan bought a hoe on 28 June 1854 (for 75 cents); a hay rake (20 cents), a scythe ($1.10), and a snath (65 cents) on 10 July; and a hay fork (75 cents) and another scythe and snath (at the same prices as before) on 19 July. These tools cost $5.20; an indication of relative costs is that this represented 4 percent of all his debits, or about as much as he spent on tobacco during the year.[56]

A total of eighty people bought a fork, hoe, rake, or scythe; adding other tools such as spades and shovels would increase this total further. On the other hand, there were only three purchases of ploughs and only one each of two other basic farm tools, potash and sugar kettles (both in 1851).[57] There were no purchases of tools needed for threshing and winnowing such as flails and fanning mills, or of the reapers that began to be introduced in Upper Canada after 1850. Evidently most farm tools were acquired through other channels (after mid-century, the more expensive equipment was likely sold by manufacturers and their agents).[58] The implication of our data is that a key role for the country store was convenience; a tool or a part (such as a handle for an ax or a scythe) could be obtained when something broke or an unexpected need arose.

Despite their limitations, the lists allow consideration of farm technology. If continuity is the strongest image, change is visible in the disappearance of sickles and the appearance of cradles, dung forks, and metal plough parts. Cradles are of particular interest; "a wooden-handled scythe, with a light wooden framework ... paralleling the steel blade" to "catch the grain as it was cut," cradles had (according to one authority) "been adopted about the time of the American Revolution."[59] If this chronology is accurate, the timing of their appearance on our list is problematic, because the first purchases were in 1851 (and they do not appear on import invoices at Yonge Mills and Tett's). They might have been used earlier and not caught in our samples, but it is also possible that their superiority was exaggerated by historians whose progressive interpretations have been based on their understanding of best practice. At a minimum, purchases of cradles show that farmers were aware of such tools; if some (or most) did not use them, the explanation must be choice, not cost or ignorance. Although cradles cost more than a standard scythe, if they saved effort and/or time they would very quickly have repaid the extra expense.[60]

Craftsmen required specialized tools, virtually none of which were found in our data.[61] For that matter, a number of other standard tools were scarcely visible. The 1808 import invoices include two blacksmiths' vices weighing 67 pounds priced at 22 cents per pound; two anvils weighing a total of 274 pounds and priced at 15 cents per pound; and one bellows pipe. The implication is that Jones was setting up – or supplying – a new blacksmith shop. These invoices recorded ten dozen chisels of four kinds, yet not one was purchased by members of that year's samples. Nor do they appear in appendix A, because in all ten samples only a single chisel was purchased. A similar story holds for planes; just one was purchased, although they too are imagined as both universal and varied.[62]

In her study of women as they appeared in a late eighteenth-century Nova Scotia store's accounts, Elizabeth Mancke provocatively contrasted men's and women's use of stores, writing that "women consumed to produce and men produced to consume."[63] Yet although some tools (hoes, rakes, awls, and knives, for example) likely were used by women, it is clear that these hardware products were purchased mainly for use by men. Almost the only hardware that we might think of as particularly for women is stoves. Many women's tools are included elsewhere in appendix A, however, notably in housewares (pails, pots, washboards, etc.) and among sewing supplies. A few are found elsewhere in appendix B, such as churns (four were purchased at Choate's and Scovil's in 1861, at four different prices ranging from $2.00 to $3.25) and a spinning wheel (a "wool wheel" bought at Scovil's for $3.00).[64]

HUNTING AND FISHING

Another basic pioneer tool that appears only in appendix B was the gun; just four were purchased in all the samples.[65] As durable, comparatively costly products involving craftsmanship, new guns might have been purchased in larger urban centres. That they were widely owned is evident from the ranking of gunpowder and gunshot in appendix A; with 111 and 87 buyers respectively, they were the third and fourth most commonly purchased goods on the hardware list. In total 155 buyers purchased a product indicating possession of a gun (table 21).[66]

Guns are essential in narratives of pioneering. Men are often depicted working with a gun at hand, for protection against the wolves and bears that appear so frequently in recollections; and hunting for sport and pleasure is a common theme. Through necessity and practice, men learned to fire quickly and accurately, bringing down large animals at considerable distances with a single shot.[67] Sometimes, shooting animals whose "depredations" threatened crops or people – bears, raccoons, squirrels, crows, blue jays, and woodpeckers – could itself be a sport, providing, in the words of one gentleman farmer, a "merry and joyous holiday."[68] Probably more important, as Richard Bonnycastle noted, "the universal rifle or fowling-piece" enabled a man to take advantage of the abundance of game to put food on the family's table.[69] Guns and hunting are thus closely associated with self-reliance, family, and a direct (if rather adversarial) relationship with nature.[70]

Another literature on the settlement era, derived from military history, offers a different sense of guns in pioneer society. Discussions of the militia suggest that although men were expected to bring guns to musters, not all did so; that others had guns that were so old or poorly maintained that they were unusable; and that skill with firearms varied widely. Despite a later mythology that depicted the militia of Upper Canada as the colony's main defenders during the War of 1812, trained British regular soldiers and aboriginal warriors were the core of the province's defence, supported by locally raised companies more than the general militia; all used guns issued by the army.[71] Twenty-five years later, when men from the countryside north of Toronto assembled to support William Lyon Mackenzie's attempt to overthrow the government of Upper Canada, many did not bring guns.[72]

All the stores sold the main products needed for shooting: gunpowder, shot, and flints or percussion caps. After the first sample, there were no purchases of balls, and although lead was very occasionally purchased later, it had other purposes besides making shot or cartridges. Flints were purchased in substantial quantities in 1808–09 and in 1842. By mid-century, percussion caps were becoming the standard means of firing a gun. There was one buyer in 1842 and thirty-four buyers after that, at all stores; this timing coincides exactly with the adoption of this system elsewhere, for example in the British army.[73] Converting to it required either purchase of a new gun or adaptation of a flintlock by installing a new firing mechanism. Gunpowder was also the principal general explosive: one 1842 purchase of four ounces was explicitly noted as "to blast cellar." Others probably were. In fact, six of the eleven largest powder purchases (involving two or more pounds at one time) were made by someone who made no other gun-related purchase during the year.[74] Nevertheless, to avoid underestimating gun use, we include all gunpowder purchases in our estimates.

Between the first and second samples, prices fell by around 50 percent: gunpowder was 70 to 90 cents per pound in 1808–09 and 30 to 40 cents in 1828–29; shot fell from 20 to 12.5 cents per pound. Two of three boxes of caps purchased in 1851 cost 25 cents, but most thereafter cost 12.5 cents.[75] The variation in prices within a single sample, such as when someone bought powder or shot at two prices in the same transaction, evidently represented differences in the quality or character of the product. For example, powder varied in quality; and, given the variety of guns and game, shot varied in size.[76]

On 1 September 1808, three men purchased powder and shot. Derick Hogeboom bought a half-pound of powder and one of shot, with a total value of 60 cents. Two weeks later, he purchased two flints (at 1.67 cents each). But although he visited eighteen more times from then until late April, he bought nothing else that was gun-related. Nathaniel Powers bought a quarter-pound of powder and one pound of ball, worth 40 cents. He visited another twelve times between December and August without making further gun-related purchases. Elias Tryan bought one pound of powder and two each of ball and shot, worth in total $1.60. He did make additional purchases, another quarter-pound of powder, two pounds of lead, and four flints on 26 December and a half-pound of powder on 1 May 1809. These men's purchases were among the more than twenty-one pounds of gunpowder, sixty-five pounds of shot and balls, and five pounds of lead purchased during the year, by thirty-five buyers (who included all but one of the largest accounts [table 25]).[77] Hogeboom, Powers, and Tryan, as it happens, did not have such large accounts. The proportion of the clientele making purchases confirms that in this Loyalist community along the American border gun ownership was common, and guns were used. This pattern fits what we would expect from literature on guns in colonial America, where hunting for food was important in the earliest phases of settlement and rural gun ownership continued to be normal thereafter.[78] At the same time, the variation in the scale and frequency of purchases may suggest variation in actual gun usage.

In the nine subsequent samples, there were 120 buyers. These included 36 who were among the stores' ten largest accounts; that is, 40 percent of the leading clients made at least one such purchase (table 25). Yet it is noteworthy, given the emphasis in the literature on high costs in the early stages of pioneering, that declining prices apparently coincided with diminished use of guns. Whether considered by volume, frequency, or number of buyers, later cases show substantially fewer gun-related purchases than in 1808–09. The next in all three terms were Tett's (thirty-five transactions including more than sixteen pounds of powder and thirty-five pounds of shot), Choate's in 1851 (thirty-one transactions including more than eight pounds of powder and nineteen of shot), and Darling's in 1861 (thirty transactions including nine pounds of powder and almost twenty of shot).

In all the transactions, there were just twenty-five occasions when someone bought one or more pounds of gunpowder at a time. Powder was normally bought in lots of one-quarter (fifty-five transactions) or one-half (sixty-one) pound, although twenty-three buyers made such purchases on more than one occasion in a year.[79] Including anything gun-related raises the number of those who made purchases on more than one day to fifty-seven (of whom twenty-two were in 1808–09). After 1808–09, not even one-quarter of buyers reached a threshold of 50 cents for gun-related purchases in a year. It was possible to buy powder, shot, and caps without reaching that threshold.

How much shooting did that allow? At one common figure, 110 grains per round, it was possible to fire 16 rounds per quarter-pound of powder. From about 200 to over 500 grains of shot might be required per round depending on the gun and the objective. If the average was 220 grains, 32 rounds could be fired per pound of shot.[80] These figures are used to estimate how many rounds each buyer could have fired, based on either powder or shot purchases, whichever yields the higher figure (table 26). The estimates range from sixteen people who could have fired about 16 rounds (they mostly purchased one-quarter pound of powder and/or one-half pound of shot) up to one buyer whose twenty-six pounds of shot might have allowed 832 rounds. In total, eighty-four buyers were like Hogeboom and Powers, buying enough to fire from 25 to 71 rounds. In 1808–09, twelve men bought enough to fire 72 or more rounds, including Tryan. If he used the lead he purchased to make shot, he could have fired close to 200 rounds.

The largest account, by a wide margin, was that of Peter Stevens; he bought six pounds of shot from Tett's store on 10 March 1842 and someone else (the name is illegible) bought three pounds of powder and twenty pounds of shot on his account on 4 April. We were unable to link Stevens to the census, but next to his name Tett noted "Indian." As the third party transaction indicates, he might have been buying for more than one person; but such purchases are reasonable for someone who hunted for food and likely for earnings.[81] Two other "Indians" also ranked among the six leading buyers at Tett's, John Hagar, who bought three pounds of shot, a half-pound of powder, and four flints on 15 February, and Little John, who bought a canister of powder on 12 December. Like Stevens and two other Indians (one of whom seems to have been Hagar's wife), they had small quantities of venison and skins credited to their accounts. Little John's credits also included a few pairs of moccasins and mitts. These three aboriginal men were among just twenty buyers at the nine later stores who could have fired seventy-two or more rounds. Of that twenty, moreover, four bought only gunpowder, raising the possibility that they were blasting, not shooting. It should be recalled also that these figures are for households. Even if shooting was a mainly male activity, brothers, sons, and even hired hands were potential gun users in many households.[82]

In 1861 there were relatively few buyers in the highest category in table 26 – no one at all at Scovil's, and just nine in the other four samples. At Fowlds's in 1861, there were nine gun-related transactions, and not many more at Scovil's and Sherin's. There was more activity at Darling's. The soil in the area was comparatively poor, and it is possible that the mix of activities in its rural economy was somewhat different from the province's agricultural heartland farther west.[83] Even so, just three buyers there could have fired seventy-two or more rounds. All were mature men with active farms and large households, with transactions on their accounts on many days throughout the year. Norman Landon had a family of ten; someone from his household made gun-related purchases on eight days, totalling 2.5 pounds of powder, 7.5 pounds of shot (enough, in our model, to fire 240 rounds), and two boxes of caps. John Wallace had sixteen in his household and the second largest account at this store; his family's purchases, made on seven days, totalled two pounds of powder (which would have fired 128 rounds), four pounds of shot, and two boxes of caps. Stephen Patterson had a household of eight (including two sons old enough to be recorded as labourers in the census); his farm, on Ash Island, had only thirteen acres under culture: transactions on this account included a pound of shot on 2 February and another two pounds of shot and a half-pound of powder on 15 November. This was enough shot for 96 rounds. On the other hand, six of the ten largest accounts at this store did not buy anything gun-related, although family members frequently visited the store. For example, Marsey Chismore and James Deer had transactions on 124 and 100 days respectively.

The timing of Patterson's purchases fits with sources that suggest winter was a season for hunting. For example, writing to family in Dublin from the wilderness of Erindale in January 1832, Thomas William Magrath described deer hunting then: "while the ground is covered with snow, and sealed up by frost, to the prevention of all farming operations ... we make it a point to provide abundantly for our larder."[84] Yet only about one-sixth of all the gun-related transactions occurred from December to March. There was a spring peak in April and another peak between August and November. It makes sense that the main shooting would be when animals were active and birds were migrating, even if these coincided with peak times of farm activity. In any case, winter had its own schedule of pressing activities in rural society.

Stocked by all the stores, powder and shot were evidently routinely available. Given the variety of ways in which people used any one store, we would not expect any product to be bought by all the main customers. Still, after the first sample, only a minority even of leading customers bought anything gun-related, and few of the buyers bought in quantities suggesting extensive shooting. Such evidence makes it difficult to argue for consistently high use of guns once the first phases of settlement were over. Indeed, if 60 percent of the largest accounts included no gun-related purchases, it seems possible that a substantial number might not have used a gun at all.

To test this argument, we can again use the Tables of Trade and Navigation as a benchmark. In 1861, $25,000 worth of "gunpowder and fireworks" was imported. To avoid underestimating what this meant in terms of volume, we assume that all of this was gunpowder and that the price at the point of import was 20 cents per pound (based on retail prices of from 30 to 40 cents at the stores in 1861); on this basis, imports in 1861 could have been as much as 125,000 pounds. Even if all of this went to civilian use, that was equivalent to less than five ounces per household in the Canadas.[85] In a mainly rural population, that rate does not suggest widespread and extensive shooting by most families. That this calculation overstates actual gunpowder imports is confirmed when the trade figures begin to report volumes; in 1868–69, when the value of gunpowder imports was also $25,000, the volume was 69,000 pounds.

Men like Tryan, Stevens, Landon, and Wallace (or members of their families) used their guns extensively, likely to put food on the table and perhaps to earn income. But they represent the extreme on the spectrum of shooting activity. At prevailing prices, the cost of powder and shot cannot have been a barrier to shooting. Numbers of large game animals in close proximity to settlement must have diminished over the years, but it seems improbable that in these areas, with their abundant water and extensive forests, depletion had reduced numbers of every kind of game to the point of severe scarcity. Rather, the generally modest powder and shot purchases in 1861 confirm the point of agriculture, which was to put food on the table reliably, without having to depend on hunting. This had also been the case in colonial America, where fish and game played a sharply diminishing role in the food supply after the earliest years.[86] It might prove necessary to shoot to protect stock and crops; hunting, on the other hand, was a choice, one that a substantial and growing proportion of rural Upper Canadians do not seem to have pursued.

This conclusion is reinforced by some of the anecdotal literature, which provides another explanation for the limited use of guns. "But little time was given to sport," one man recalled of his upbringing in the 1830s, "although there was plenty of large game. There was something of more importance always claiming attention."[87] This was the observation also of William Radcliff, an Irish gentleman in Adelaide Township, on the settlement frontier west of London. In 1832, he wrote home enthusing about the abundance of game not only in the woods but in the cleared fields as well: "You will be impatient to hear of the shooting ... [W]ould you believe? – I have not even had time to think about it."[88]

Fishing provided a second way of harvesting resources for food and a form of recreation, and all of the stores were on water. The relevant goods in appendix A are hooks, with thirty buyers at six stores, beginning in 1828, and line, with twenty-four buyers at seven stores, beginning in 1842.[89] Fully 80 percent of these transactions were at Tett's and Scovil's, both in the Rideau Lakes. Many hooks were explicitly for fishing, and most of those unspecified were similarly priced and often purchased by someone who also bought line. With the exception of three transactions at much higher prices, suggesting a tool or a building product, we have assumed all hooks were for fishing. Taking them and line together, a total of thirty-six people bought something indicating that they fished; half (including Hagar, Little John, and Norman Landon) also purchased shooting-related products. Of course someone might have had hooks and line without buying them in our sample years. Still, the timing of purchases reinforces a sense that fishing was not that common. More than half of all transactions in hooks and line were in June and July, good months for fishing – but very busy for other reasons in a farm economy. Eight of those buying hooks or lines were also among the thirty-five people who bought fish (see chapter 4); here too people supplying goods for themselves might also buy in the market – time, taste (i.e., type of fish), and season will all have entered into these choices. Together, the two types of purchase indicate more than sixty members of the sample who included fish in their diets. Whether that suggests fish was common or uncommon in everyday diets is a separate matter.

CHEMICALS

We have already noted William Cotton because of his large purchases of nails from Sherin's store in 1861. Among his other purchases were one-third of the thirty-three products we have grouped as chemicals. Made on twenty-two days during ten months, these included 7.75 gallons of oil costing $9.23, 5.5 quarts of turpentine ($1.58), and many modest transactions: 0.75 pound of alum (5 cents), one box of blacking (5 cents), a half-pound of blue (10 cents), 2 pounds of copperas (14 cents), thirty packets of washing crystals (87 cents), 2 pounds of washing soda (14 cents), 3.33 pounds of ochre (20 cents), two rolls of stove polish (20 cents), and 1 pound of saltpetre (26 cents). These and other chemical products and their uses would have been familiar to anyone in rural Upper Canada, but they pose interpretive challenges now. One is deciding how some products should be grouped. For example, three stores recorded sales of both sulphur and brimstone; we have combined them, however, based on price, dictionary definitions, and the Tables of Trade and Navigation, which listed them in the same category.[90] A larger challenge is that many nineteenth-century sources that provide extensive discussions of how such chemicals were produced take uses entirely for granted; when uses are addressed, they are often numerous and very diverse, in food preparation or preservation, personal care, dyeing, laundry, and other farm and craft work (tanning, for example). For example, the five most commonly purchased chemicals in appendix A are frequently found on lists of medical ingredients – we list them as chemicals because they had, or might have had, other uses.

Two examples illustrate the uncertainties. Sulphur was often recommended for fumigation, burned in a sealed room for twenty-four hours to rid it of infection or insect infestation. Guides suggested two pounds were required for a room ten feet square.[91] Yet only three of the ninety-nine transactions in sulphur were large enough to meet this specification; and seventy-three transactions were of a half-pound or less. One use for saltpetre was in meat packing; for pickling hams and pork shoulders, Catharine Parr Traill specified a half-pound of saltpetre for two hundred-weight (about one barrel), along with salt, molasses, and brown sugar.[92] But although meat preservation must have been common, purchases of molasses were infrequent, as we have seen; and only twenty of forty-four transactions in saltpetre were of a half-pound or more. It is of course possible that people used smaller quantities than was advised or that they bought these products elsewhere. But it is not clear why they would do so systematically for what appear to have been generic products.

In any case, total chemical purchases were relatively modest – in five samples they totalled less than twenty dollars. Only at Sherin's, where a few men, such as Cotton and Morrow, had extensive purchases, did their value exceed fifty dollars. Still, like the medicines discussed in the previous chapter, chemicals were of collective significance – many were purchased at numerous stores, and in total almost three hundred buyers purchased something on the list (table 21). Five of the six most frequently purchased appear in 1808–09: sulphur (with seventy-three buyers in all ten samples), indigo (discussed with dyestuffs in chapter 3), alum (also discussed in connection with dyeing), copperas (crystals of ferrous sulphate used in medicines, dyeing, ink, and other products),[93] and saltpetre. The others purchased then were chalk and lead; we include the latter here to have all entries involving lead on one list. (As noted above, it is possible that some was used for making shot in 1808, when three men bought a total of five pounds – two of the three also bought shot, however. There were only four later buyers, and lead had other uses too – in 1828 it was sold by the sheet, not by weight.)

Another twenty-six products are added later, twelve in 1842 alone. To distinguish among oils, we have relied on the unit, listing the oils sold in bottles and vials under medications and those sold by volume (pints, quarts, and gallons) as chemicals. We divide the latter into three groups, linseed and other paint-related oils (encompassing "raw," "boiled," and "paint" oils, with thirty-five buyers), oils for lighting (lamp, coal, and kerosene, twenty-four buyers), and a grouping of all others (a few listed as "machine oil," but most recorded just as "oil"; there were twenty-seven buyers, most of them in 1861).[94] Linseed oil and coal oil could, however, also be medications. So could madder, rosin, and turpentine. Another uncertain set of products includes "blue" as an operative description; "fig blue," purchased in small volumes in 1828–29 and 1842 (in total about 1.5 pounds among the eight buyers), was an indigo-based powder for whitening laundry.[95] Blue (which appears in 1851 and at most stores thereafter, with twenty-four buyers) and likely some of the other "blue" products were also for laundry, as were washing soda and crystals, which appear in 1861, with twelve buyers.[96] They were sold in modest quantities, measured in ounces or "papers." As only a few people made frequent purchases, there remains a degree of uncertainty as to how routinely they were used.

Were these products new, or old products that were not caught in the early samples? Two not purchased in 1808–09 were on import invoices then: fourteen pounds of fig blue and five dozen spirits of turpentine (the unit implying bottles, and a medical use). But many of the others likely were introduced later. Thus, oils for lighting first appear on the list in 1842, when Alexander Buist bought twenty-three gallons of "lamp oil," including two ten-gallon kegs, one explicitly noted as "for mill." This was the largest volume of such oils ever purchased. All but one of the remaining buyers of lamp oils were in 1861. This precisely coincides with the development of coal and petroleum-based illuminating oils that brought lamps into standard use by ordinary people.[97] On the other hand, only a modest proportion of sample members bought them.

Turpentine, black lead, rosin, and lamp black, all first listed in 1842, were sometimes associated with painting. So were many of the chemicals that appear in the 1850s, notably linseed oil, paint and varnish, white lead, red lead, Venetian red, blacking, and whitening. This is also when paint brushes appear (on the hardware list).[98] Although most had only modest numbers of buyers, more than eighty members of the seven samples beginning in 1851 made a purchase that was potentially paint-related.[99] To make sense of this timing, we refer to the work of Jeanne Minhinnick, whose *At Home in Upper Canada* is a standard source for those seeking to represent the province's past visually. Summing up her work on paints (in a later article), she saw painting, varnishing, and whitewashing as part of a timeless rural routine in Upper Canada. "The discovery, analysis, preservation or reproduction of original paint colours is an essential responsibility for those who hope to present a picture of this country's past." "Most respectable rural households 'kept things up' which meant repainting anything that was shabby or worn. In most cases only eccentricity, sentiment, or indifference and laziness left painted houses and furniture in their original condition. Like soap and water, paint was cheap. Housecleaning in the country ... meant painting."[100] For Upper Canada Village, in whose restoration she was deeply involved, nine colours were used, achieved with combinations of Venetian red, Prussian blue, chrome green, lamp black, raw sienna, raw umber, whiting, chrome yellow, and orange shellac.[101] Of these, our list includes three, lamp black (sixteen buyers), Venetian red (eight), and whitening (seven).

A key ingredient in paint was lead white. One expert notes that it was "used as a putty, primer, base color, and finishing color. Almost every painting job called for the use of lead white in one way or another."[102]

Purchases of lead white are thus a particularly good indicator of painting. It first appears in 1854 and at all but one store thereafter, with a total of seventeen buyers. Purchased by the pound in most cases, it was also sold by the can at Sherin's. At $3.50 per can, it was far from cheap: it was actually the most expensive chemical product purchased and accounted for 40 percent of Sherin's exceptionally large chemical sales. The leading buyer was Morrow, who was charged for six cans. Its appearance in the 1850s and the limited range of products purchased earlier that might have gone into paint suggest that Jeanne Minhinnick's vivid colours were only beginning to be used in rural Upper Canada at mid-century. This is also the implication of data on imports, which were relatively modest and began to be recorded after 1851.[103]

Of course such goods might have been purchased in larger towns, perhaps in drug stores that are said to have been an important channel for paint-related products. On the other hand, if some were stocked by village stores it is not clear why others would not have been if there had been general demand for them. A further consideration is that standard discussions of painting suggest that four or even five coats were needed to achieve a high quality finish, with all the usual steps between coats. If that much time was required in its application, does it make sense to call paint "cheap," whatever the cost of ingredients? Moreover, painting was skilled work, involving custom mixing of ingredients to get consistent colours and finishes and requiring a mastery of techniques in their application.[104] Yet the 1851 census reported only six hundred painters in Upper Canada, of whom one-third were in the five largest towns, making this one of the more urbanized crafts in the province.[105]

Minhinnick recognizes that painting was highly skilled and that many log and ordinary frame homes were not painted. Yet both explicitly and implicitly she discounts this idea; indeed, by systematically describing all possible finishes and colours, she represents them as being used. This way of presenting the settlement era is not, of course, unique to her.[106] Nor is another element of her account. As we saw in our discussion of fashion, a common tendency has been to read down from elite levels and back from later periods when more visual evidence is available. Thus, Minhinnick often cites sources from metropolitan centers and elite levels; many of her Upper Canadian written sources are from the colony's most prominent families; and many of her visual images are drawn from such untypical homes as Dundurn Castle and Whitehern (both in Hamilton) and even from the Victoria and Albert Museum in London.[107]

CONCLUSION

Writing in 1831 to a friend in Ireland, Thomas Magrath drew on his own family's recent experience to estimate that it would cost about $2,000 "for a gentleman and his family" to emigrate and start a farm in Upper Canada.[108] Although this was surely an impossible sum for most emigrants, Magrath's checklist of recommended tools can help to draw the ideas of this chapter together. It includes several implements mentioned by Traill in the passage quoted earlier (two axes, two spades, and two harrows), additional tools for fieldwork (a brush hook, a hatchet, two pitchforks, three iron wedges, and a pick axe), and various tools for working with wood (two screw augers with multiple bits, three planes, a hammer, a handsaw, a brace and set of bits, and a set of chisels). Curiously, two of the Traills' tools for farming, hoes and a hook for reaping (i.e., a scythe), were not mentioned. The field tools cost about sixteen dollars and the woodworking tools another eleven dollars. Compared to the other costs of starting a farm, these were very modest (e.g., together they cost about as much as two cows, or about half the price of a horse). Magrath recommended that tools be purchased in England, "where they are considerably cheaper than here." Perhaps the quality of tools he had in mind was exceptional; otherwise, prices in our accounts suggest that most of these tools could have been purchased for similar prices in Upper Canada.[109]

In fact local prices for most specific hardware items hardly seem to have been beyond the reach of rural buyers.[110] That suggests qualifying the idea, encountered earlier, that hardware was "more expensive" than alternatives, particularly as prices fell sharply after our first sample. Rather, as the modesty of hardware imports on a per capita basis also suggests, an economy and technology based on manual labour and on wood had limited and quite specific requirements for tools and other hardware.

Just eight of all the products considered in this chapter were purchased by seventy or more buyers (i.e., by about 10 percent of our sample). All appear on our list in 1808–09. This should be read not as an indication that the rural economy was timeless but as evidence of what worked in an Upper Canadian setting. Moreover, new developments during the period, such as the decline of hunting, the disappearance of sickles from the list of harvest tools, and the adoption of new products such as cut nails and gun caps, indicate rural readiness to change. The new goods, in fact, appear on our lists at much the same time as they were being adopted elsewhere. Purchases of glass in larger quantities and varied dimensions, of larger quantities of cut nails, and of paint all provide glimpses of what has been called the "massive rebuilding" that began in the 1850s.[111] If this represented a passage from the pioneer stage, it also reflected simultaneous developments elsewhere in North America, such as new techniques of framing and more widespread use of paint. This was, for example, exactly when commercial paints first became available in the United States. As one pioneer of the American paint industry recalled, "The first paints ready for use were made in 1852 by my house."[112]

Some of the craftsmen in our samples acquired key imports through these stores, but few if any can have bought all their requirements; and it is unlikely that country stores were the main distribution channel for specialized inputs. For goods that appear only occasionally on the lists and for tools and other inputs that do not appear at all, it is evident that there were other channels of commercial distribution. As we consider in the following chapter, the accounts suggest elements of the work and products of rural craftsmen, but do not provide a comprehensive overview. That is, we see craftsmen as autonomous participants in a wider market economy in which many kinds of locally produced goods and services were routinely bought and sold.

6

LOCAL GOODS: IMPORTERS AND THE
MARKET FOR LOCAL PRODUCTS

[T]he settlements ... [were] anything but simple, secure, homogeneous communities of independent households practising subsistence agriculture. Inequalities of material condition, social position, and economic prospects marked these complex places.

Bittermann, MacKinnon, and Wynn, 1993[1]

Although selling imported goods was the primary role of the general store, many local products appear in the accounts. To frame our reflection on these transactions, we begin with food, because it is often taken for granted in mainly rural societies. Those who did not farm had to buy food, of course, and so did a number of farmers – perhaps one-sixth of them in Upper Canada at the end of the settlement era and as many as one-third in Nova Scotia in the same period. This was just one element in the complexity of rural places that Bittermann, MacKinnon, and Wynn speak of.[2] For New France, the story was similar, demonstrated with particular clarity in a systematic exploration by Louise Dechêne of food production and distribution. If elements of that process were specific to New France (the seigneurial system, the obligation to pay tithes, and the frequency of wars), others (differentiation within rural society, the constraints and risks of agriculture in a cold climate, and the processes by which towns were fed) are equally relevant in rural Upper Canada. In her research, one key revelation was the importance of local exchange; as she writes, "Recent studies have shattered the image of an undifferentiated rural mass and, simultaneously, revealed the importance of local exchange."[3]

That kind of exchange has been almost entirely invisible in the history of Upper Canada, represented, if at all, as "carried on mostly by a system of barter," as Canniff Haight recalled.[4] That he could immediately go on to provide 1830 prices for twenty-four local products suggests a different story: that exchanges involved goods with a monetary value that must have been generally known. Transactions between people living in close proximity need not have involved a country store, however; and if they dealt directly with one another, they could avoid the costs of a middleman. Hence it is significant that more than sixty products and services are listed in the local sections of appendices A and B and that they were a major element in some customers' purchases – so much so that the total value of local goods at most stores was comparable to the main categories of imports. Nor does this category exhaust the local products on our lists: two other categories in the appendices (footwear and clothing) include many such goods, and other lists include several that might also have been local (e.g., pails, seed, and fish).

The products in appendix A – food for people and for animals, wood products, and hides and leather – are all easily imagined as timeless rural essentials.[5] More than half appear in 1808–09; and many of the others were produced then in Upper Canada, even if not found in our sample. For example, no one bought butter in 1808–09, but six people sold modest quantities to the store.[6] These goods were also widely produced, and none were purchased with the frequency of cotton, tea, and other leading imports. Yet in all the years we sampled more than four hundred people bought at least one of the products or services on our local lists, including ninety-three who bought postal services (the most prominent of the services) and fifty or more who bought boards, flour, pork, and butter, each purchased in nine samples (table 27).[7] As for the rarely purchased local products listed in appendix B, many were just as necessary to rural life as those in appendix A and undoubtedly were much more important in local markets than our data indicate. The few transactions in livestock, for example, illustrate what must have been an active market that did not normally involve a store. Animals – a pair of oxen at $65 and a cow at $17 (both in 1808) and horses at $35 and $50 (in 1854 and 1861) – were actually among the most costly of all purchases.[8]

One reason for local goods to appear in retail accounts is that local merchants often had multiple roles. As we have seen, Charles Jones, Thomas Choate, and the Fowlds brothers owned grist, saw, and woolen mills; and Benjamin Tett had a sawmill (and later a gristmill as well). Choate, Henry Fowlds, and Tett were also postmasters, as was Samuel Scovil. Because mills and post offices evidently kept separate accounts, store daybooks seldom provide a comprehensive view of these elements of their businesses. Nevertheless, we will see that some stores provide windows on these trades.

But merchants also sold goods that they did not produce, such as pork, butter, beef, oats, eggs, and apples. We can imagine a number of reasons for goods of this kind to appear in retail accounts. Barrels and tubs, for example, were occasionally priced as a distinct element in the purchase of their contents (but that was not the usual form of transaction). A few stores routinely stocked at least some produce for sale, such as whiskey in 1828 and a number of foods in Hastings and Lakefield; evidently some residents in and around these villages found it convenient to buy from the store. Other sales might be of goods the merchant accepted from customers as payments on their accounts; to take goods he would not use himself implies knowledge of who might buy them. Alternatively, sales might come from household stock, the most likely case being sales to an employee. A few products were not immediately local, but were brought from elsewhere in the province, perhaps as custom orders for specific customers. That could have been the case when two shoemakers, Robert Knox and A.P. Santry, shared in by far the largest transaction in leather in our study, 429 pounds of sole leather worth $107 purchased at Sherin's.[9] Sometimes the merchant may have had an interest in the transaction, as when pork was ordered for a timber shanty in which he was involved; depending on how the business was organized and accounts were structured, such goods might still be recorded as purchases by the foreman, partner, or artisan. Finally, local products appear in third-party transactions, exchanges between two customers recorded in store accounts as simultaneous debits and credits, with no difference between buying and selling prices.[10] Here and sometimes in other of these scenarios, the merchant did not profit directly from the sale. The transactions reflected relationships with his clientele that may not be directly visible in the account.

Our main objective is to see purchases from the buyer's perspective. To do so, we focus particularly on leading local accounts, those most likely to have been more than occasional buyers (tables 28, 29, and 31). Using selected examples, we consider standard situations – such as work, enterprise, and size of farm – that created demand for local goods. One often-imagined situation is not visible, however: no account suggests that markets were as centralized as stories of local monopoly imply. Nor is there evidence to support another tenet of the unequal exchange story, that prices of these goods varied systematically according to the customer's circumstances and bargaining power. For even the leading buyers, missing months, missing food products, and variation from month to month in quantities purchased reveal that they had other sources of supply. So, evidently, did non-farmers who bought few local goods from our stores. Many such families likely supplied some of their own food – eggs and poultry, milk if they kept a cow, pork if they kept pigs, and vegetables if they kept a garden. But they would still need to buy food (notably flour and meat); and unless they owned or rented pasture and woodland, they needed to buy fodder for any larger animals (especially if they were kept through the winter) and wood for heating and cooking. They also had to allocate time between these activities and earning an income, although responsibility for many of the former might fall to wives and older children.

In 1808–09, there were fourteen buyers of boards (worth almost $50), ten of flour (almost $100), and ten of pork (more than $150; see table 27). Together these products accounted for over half the value of local purchases.[11] More than three-quarters of the flour and pork were bought by the six customers included in table 28. Three evidently did not farm. Jeremiah Chichigran, for example, was a cooper; his local produce purchases included 654 pounds of flour ($22), in nine months, and 99 pounds of pork ($11), in eight months.[12] We do not know how many people were fed from these purchases, because he was not on the local census or tax roll, but this was ample flour to feed a small family or two adult men for a year. His meat purchases, on the other hand, fell well short of a man's annual consumption. The other non-farmers, Jabez and Stephen Andrews and Samuel Tollman, spent twice as much on local produce as Chichigran, but their purchases, concentrated in brief periods, were clearly not a year's supply. More than half the Andrews' purchases were on one day, 19 May 1809, when they were charged for almost 200 pounds of flour and 264 pounds of pork – along with 6 gallons of whiskey. As we have seen, buying alcohol in this quantity suggests collective activity, perhaps a large-scale work setting. Besides flour and pork, Tollman's purchases included feed for animals – 1.5 tons of hay (enough to feed a team of horses engaged in "severe" work for more than two months) and 3 to 6 bushels each of oats, corn, peas, and rye. All of the fodder was bought in February and early March. He bought pork slightly earlier (mostly in January) and flour later (in March and May). That he was engaged in commercial timber cutting, a winter activity, is suggested by subsequent credits to him and a partner for logs.[13]

The other three 1808–09 buyers in table 28 had small farms, with seven to ten acres in crop. They were perhaps just getting established, or their farms were complementary to other activities.[14] Peter Cronk's local debits were mainly for the oxen mentioned above, a capital investment useful both on a farm and in the woods.[15] Caleb Seaman Jr's main purchases were in November, when preparation for winter was a preoccupation; this was, for example, the usual season for slaughtering and preserving pork. He bought 1.5 barrels (about 300 pounds) of pork and 22 bushels of wheat. After allowing for the mill's toll, the latter, if for the six persons in his household, could have supplied flour for about six months.[16] We cannot know why John Cain began to make substantial flour purchases in May; it may be explanation enough that there were twelve people in this very large household and only 7 acres in crop on the family's 130-acre holding. For our purposes, this timing serves as a reminder of what must have been a standard scenario: by this late in the crop year, families might be running low on supplies they had produced the previous year and drawing on the commercial system until the next crop was harvested.[17]

Five of the ten largest accounts in 1808–09 bought little or no local produce. Four of these families had larger farms (with from sixteen to fifty acres in cultivation) that likely allowed producing most of their own food.[18] Years of work and investment were required to get a farm to that stage.

Each later sample includes buyers who did not farm or had only small farms. Some, such as Antoine Busea and Francis Russe in 1828–29, prove to have been employees (table 28). Neither was found in local census and tax records, but they were credited with wages for part or most of the year. Busea also received an allowance for board, in lieu of having that provided as part of his wage.[19] He bought 550 pounds of flour during the year, but only very modest quantities of pork and butter. Russe was briefly credited for "board of himself," the implication being that he otherwise did receive board.[20] Still, he purchased 112 pounds of flour in summer, some butter in autumn, and 81 pounds of pork in autumn and winter. Two customers in 1854 also proved to be employees; James and Thomas Brough were enumerated (with three of their brothers) on a substantial farm in 1852, but two years later they worked year-round for the Fowlds, Thomas as an apparently junior clerk and James, the oldest of the brothers, in unspecified employment at a considerably higher wage ($20 per month).[21] In the first half of the year, James bought $40 worth of flour and pork; otherwise, the Broughs mainly purchased lumber, $80 between them. As James had purchased a town lot from the Fowlds, we can imagine a house or other building under construction during the year.

Artisans were key participants in rural markets, as sellers of their services and products and as buyers of inputs for their work. Unless they combined a substantial farm with their trade, they must also have been buyers of produce. In 1842, John Hubbard, a blacksmith, was charged $86 for local purchases, accounting for 40 percent of the store's local produce debits.[22] He bought flour, pork, and butter, but not regularly and (as the modest values in table 28 indicate) not in anything like quantities sufficient for a year. His main purchases were almost 6,000 feet of lumber: clapboard, flooring, scantling, planks, and "seasoned" one-inch boards.[23] In 1854, two artisans were among the leading buyers. Robert Plunkett, a carpenter, made extensive lumber purchases, totalling about 13,000 feet.[24] From May onward, he bought flour at a rate averaging more than 140 pounds per month, ample for a seven person household. On the other hand his meat purchases represented a very small proportion of a family's requirements.[25] John Driscol, a shoemaker, bought 2,800 feet of lumber, almost all purchased in January, but no food and no leather.

Eb Heath, a cooper who accounted for half the local purchases at Scovil's, had the largest local account in table 28. The Heaths bought the most butter of anyone in the study (161 pounds, costing $22) and twelve cords of firewood (which might have been a year's supply). But their purchases of flour (720 pounds, costing $21) and pork (300 pounds, costing $25) were far from sufficient for a family of nine. Among their other purchases were thirty-three dozen eggs (bought mainly in April and May), ten bushels of oats, and one $13 transaction in barrel staves (obviously only a small proportion of his requirements).[26] They also rented their house from Scovil. On the credit side of his account, Heath earned $344 from coopering, supplying products that were often resold to other clients: twenty-three sample members bought a total of thirty-two butter tubs, twenty-seven pork barrels, two potash barrels, two butter churns (these are in appendix B because there were only four buyers in all samples), and one hundred sap buckets (counted as pails in appendix A). Almost all were debited at exactly the prices credited to Heath.[27] Modest further credits were earned by Heath's wife, Maria, and his fourteen-year old daughter Adelaide, the former by making clothing and the latter by work (7.5 weeks at 50 cents per week). Clearly there was a close association between Scovil and the Heaths, yet it is also evident that Scovil did not have a monopoly on their purchases – and probably not on Heath's sales of his products.

In addition to Heath, a number of customers at Scovil's earned credits with their produce, collectively supplying almost 100 cords of wood, almost 1,200 pounds of pork, almost 100 bushels of oats, and about 500 pounds of butter. When these were subsequently sold, it was nearly always at a higher price, giving the store a markup: thus, firewood was credited at $1.00 per cord and sold at $1.25; oats were credited at 25 cents and debited at 30 cents; and pork was credited at 5 or 5.8 cents per pound and sold at 8.5 and 10 cents. During the year, the price at which butter was credited fell from 13.3 cents per pound in January to 12.5 cents in June, then to 10 cents from July onward. Butter was sold at 15 cents until June and at 12.5 cents thereafter.[28] As we will see, this was a normal seasonal pattern. Scovil's ability to sustain these differentials suggests that direct buyer-seller exchanges might involve inconveniences and transaction costs sufficient to justify selling to and buying from the store. Benefits of the latter included not having to find a supplier for oneself and getting goods when needed and on credit.

Before leaving table 28, we note a puzzle regarding another large account, that of Edward Oakes. The 1851–52 census recorded him as a yeoman, with a household of twelve, thirty-five acres in crop, and output of ninety bushels of wheat. Yet between late January and mid-July 1854, he purchased $87 worth of flour (2,575 pounds). The timing is consistent with having had a limited wheat crop in 1853; it is also possible that he had a seasonal business and was supplying food to workers or that, like the Broughs, he was no longer farming.[29] In either of the latter cases, he would also have needed other produce that he did not buy from Fowlds.

WINDOWS ON SOME LOCAL TRADES

Several stores allow closer consideration of elements of local markets. Even if they are necessarily more illustrative than comprehensive, they provide a window on larger processes, in particular the forest economy, food supply, livestock feeding, and postal communications.

The forests were a vital element in the rural economy in all of our settings, and every business was in various ways connected to the wood economy. For example, in Samuel Tollman's case, the store sold goods to someone involved in cutting logs, who subsequently was credited by logs supplied; it is easy to imagine these being turned into boards at the sawmill for sale to other customers. At Darling's, the store required much wood for its sales to steamboats; indeed, more than 1,100 cords were credited to sample accounts in 1861. The demands on the local economy of a substantial commercial timber operation are most clearly exemplified in the 1842 account of Alexander Buist, although because of the exceptional scale of his debits, we omit their values from tables 27 and 28 and present them separately as table 29. We did not find him in the census, and we do not know his personal circumstances; but his account shows that he was an entrepreneurial associate of Benjamin Tett, responsible for one or two shanties, Tett's mill in Bedford Township, and rafting operations on the Rideau Canal.[30] To supply them, he bought 5,000 pounds each of pork and flour, 4.5 tons of hay, 462 bushels of oats, and 92 bushels of potatoes, these five products alone totalling $670. Reflecting the seasonal nature of shanty operations, all the hay, 90 percent of the oats, two-thirds of the pork, and almost half the flour were purchased between January and March.[31] Still, his purchases continued to be substantial during the rest of the year, averaging about 200 pounds of pork and over 300 pounds of flour per month. These seem unlikely to have been just for his personal consumption: provisions will have been required for men taking three rafts of lumber to Kingston during late spring and summer and working in off-season shanty-related operations or at the sawmill. On the other hand, he made only occasional (and much smaller) purchases of the other local products in the table. Either they were not usually consumed or they were acquired elsewhere, as seems probable for butter, more likely a routine than a rare element in men's diets. With the exception of pork (debited to him at 6 cents per pound rather than 7.5 cents), he was charged the same prices as other customers for these products.

We can explore food purchases through the two 1861 stores that had more than occasional local produce trades. This, of course, was particularly important for families who did not farm, as was the case for all but two of the leading accounts summarized in table 31. Fowlds's store provides our most comprehensive evidence on flour, in the form of monthly lists by volume transferred from the mill accounts, a total of about 15,000 pounds during the year, three-quarters of which was accounted for by the buyers in the table.[32] John Sherin, unlike the Fowlds, did not own a mill and almost no one bought flour at his store; but about a quarter of this sample bought pork, butter, eggs, and apples; and a number bought oats and cheese. Buyers here included the only farmers in table

31, Matthew Walton, who bought butter and a barrel of apples in January and cheese in two later months, and Charles Watley, who bought a total of 45 pounds of cheese.

The other eighteen families listed in table 31 all needed to acquire food. Most products were available at each store throughout the year (as indicated by the rows in the table for "total months"). Yet, when we look at the "months" columns for individual purchases of specific products, it is clear that there was wide variation in patterns. Sixteen bought pork, but only James Bush and James Phillips had transactions in more than three months.[33] Twelve bought butter, but only Robert Plunkett (by now listed as a millwright rather than a carpenter), Thomas Bolton, and William Cotton did so through most of the year. Only two of the leading customers at Fowlds's bought no flour. Two, Plunkett and Bush, bought flour throughout the year.

To interpret such purchases, we draw on estimates by Marvin McInnis, "based on fairly modest assumptions," for an average farm household's consumption in 1861: thirty-five bushels of wheat (equivalent to about 1,470 pounds of flour), sixty-nine bushels of potatoes, 1,282 pounds of meat (563 pounds of beef, 620 of pork, and 99 of mutton, all live weight), and dairy products equivalent to 258 pounds of butter (much actually in fluid milk).[34] Without going into the composition of households by age and sex (as we would if attempting a more detailed analysis of food requirements), we can nevertheless note that twelve of the households (seven at Fowlds's and five at Sherin's) exceeded the provincial average of six persons per household. But, of the eight flour buyers at Fowlds's, just the three largest accounts bought enough to reach McInnis's standard, and one of them, Pomeroy, had fifteen members. Only the Bush family bought enough meat to reach this standard. Potatoes are not included in the table because only seventeen bushels were purchased in these two samples (by five buyers). Just three households bought more than 100 pounds of butter and cheese. Clearly most had other sources of dairy products. Some perhaps kept one or more cows to supply fluid milk, which might help to explain why non-farmers bought mill byproducts from the Fowlds – some in very large volumes. Sherin also sold apples and eggs, products not visible in the census. A few customers bought these in as many as seven different months, but others less often and in more limited volumes.

Other than Buist, the Bush family had the largest local produce account in the entire study, almost $200. Their expenses were mainly for food and are a reminder of its importance in the budgets of non-farm households. It is striking also that someone described as a labourer could spend so much on food. James Bush was not, however, a single bread-winner: as we saw in chapter 3, he, his wife, two sons, and one or two daughters all earned income from the Fowlds, although none worked full-time (which makes it unlikely that the Fowlds were their only source of income). They purchased flour throughout the year, at a rate of about 200 pounds per month, and similar quantities of beef and/or pork (table 31). With nine members in this household, that was about twelve ounces of flour and meat per person per day, or slightly more than the rate suggested by McInnis. In a household with several adult children that was not an impossible amount (another possibility is that they were also feeding people in addition to the members of the household recorded in the census). Yet even they must have had other sources of food; for example, they bought much less meat in the summer than in other months, they did not buy butter after June, and they bought eggs only in May.[35]

If these accounts do not provide a complete view of anyone's food purchases and consumption, or of how these foods were prepared and served, they can nevertheless suggest some basic contours of rural diets in Upper Canada. Clearly, bread and other baking, pork, beef, milk, and butter need to be at the centre of our understanding of food ways there. These are not invisible in writings about the history of food in Canada, but their weight is not always clear in a genre that, because of its sources, can tend to elide vital differentiating factors such as period, place, occasion, and class. Systematic, routine evidence about specific people and places provides a sense of scale and probability to set alongside a literature based on reminiscences, elite writings, cook books, menus of special meals such as banquets and seasonal feasts, and the like.[36]

In addition to flour, grist mills earned supplementary revenue from byproducts (indeed, one successful miller considered these to be crucial to his profits).[37] We have combined several products into this category in appendix A. With forty-four buyers, they ranked just behind butter in terms of frequency of purchase (note that all eight buyers of flour at Fowlds's in table 31 bought byproducts as well). Bran (the hard outer layer of the wheat grain) was first recorded in 1808, with two buyers who purchased about 750 pounds (they paid 60 cents per 100 pounds – then and later, byproducts were priced at about one-sixth the price of flour). In 1828, Obid Robinson bought 912 pounds of cannel (canaille). He was also debited for 48 bushels of corn, 10 of rye, and 7.5 of a rye-corn mix – and credited for 224 gallons of whiskey. He was perhaps distilling all these grains and byproducts, but he might also have been feeding live-stock, an activity frequently associated with distilling.[38] A third byproduct, shorts, accounted for three-quarters of the purchases at Fowlds's in 1861. Although some sources indicate that Upper Canadians spoke of shorts and cannel as synonyms, the Fowlds recorded all three products in 1861, an indication that the province's more sophisticated mills produced three distinct byproducts.[39]

Almost half the buyers of these products were at Choate's store in 1851, when twenty buyers purchased more than 9,000 pounds of bran (two also bought shorts, as did one other buyer, among them a total of over 900 pounds).[40] Bran had several uses for human consumption, including in breads, curing meat, and producing starch. But for buyers of larger volumes, the main use was in feeding animals. Thus, the leading buyer at Choate's, Dennis Maloney, had a substantial farm, with thirty-six acres in cultivation, six head of cattle, four horses, and ten hogs. He purchased three-quarters of his 2,500 pounds of bran in January and February. Possibly it was coincidence, but in the same period he was teaming loads of lumber, flour, and plaster for Choate, at least once to "the front," likely Port Hope (seven others were also credited for such "drawing"). The next largest buyer was Con Shehan, a farmer whom we could not link because of duplication of names, whose purchases of about 1,700 pounds of bran were in an entirely different season, August and October.[41] Others bought more modest quantities, down to three who purchased less than 100 pounds. Unlike the non-farmers who dom-inated purchases of shorts at Fowlds's in 1861, most bran buyers at Choate's are known from the agricultural census to have had animals (and the census did not report poultry, which also might be fed these products). But farmers in apparently similar circumstances might buy much, some, or no bran. There was no consistent relationship between, or among, bran purchases and teaming credits; numbers of cattle, hogs, and horses; acreage cultivated; or butter output. The implication, perhaps not surprising but still important, is that farmers made choices in how they fed their stock, seasonally and in terms of their objectives for work output, rate of growth, quality of meat, and quantity of milk.

Of the four businesses that were the post offices in their villages (table 27), two have enough charges for postage to permit reflection on how customers used the mails.[42] Tett's accounts have ninety-eight entries for postage in 1842, by twenty-six customers. Among leading accounts, only Christopher Chant (the tailor, with twelve transactions totalling $1.87) and Alexander Buist made much use of the postal system. Otherwise, those with the most frequent charges had small accounts. The leader was Francis Baker, a merchant, whose $2.91 in charges (on twenty-one occasions in nine months) represented almost all his debits.[43] Others included the Reverend George Goodson, whose only debits were seven transactions for papers and pamphlets, and Aaron Chambers, a timber merchant with a small account. Most others had only one or two transactions. For example, Thomas Egan, an Irish-born farmer, was charged 27 cents for a letter to Ireland on 25 March and sent another on 8 August.[44]

In 1861, Fowlds's daybook recorded 175 postal transactions on thirty accounts and total debits amounting to $20.[45] Hastings was not on a railway but that would not preclude railway induced change in the intensity of use of the postal system. The most likely was that eleven customers were charged for newspaper subscriptions (recorded in the other goods category in appendix A). Otherwise, the pattern resembled Tett's. Here too a merchant was the principal user: John Sharpe accounted for one-third of all charges, in thirty-seven separate transactions. (The next largest user was a teacher, Miss Blanchard.) Of the other nine largest accounts (i.e., those in table 31), only three had transactions in as many as three months, and in each case their debits totalled less than $1. Only one of the twelve customers who had postal transactions this frequently was a farmer.[46]

We cannot know what share these charges represented of postal activity at these stores, but unless there was a systematic bias in charges, they permit speculation about the system and its users. This begins with the parallels between the two examples. Each reminds us that people whose work centrally involved communication had more reason than others to use the postal system. Whether or not they also complained more about the system, elite travellers, merchants, lawyers, and other bourgeois figures' writings are more likely to have survived – and to have shaped our core understanding of all aspects of colonial communications. Yet they were more able to afford postal costs than most people in the colony; and, as travellers and (in merchants' cases) shippers of goods, they could sometimes find other channels if they found postal services unreliable and expensive. By contrast, for emigrants, a pattern like Egan's might suffice. Because the expense of postage has been emphasized in the literature, it is worth noting that his letters and the paper they were written on could have been paid for with five pounds of butter or eight pounds of pork or a half-day of work at a labourer's wage. That was not a negligible cost, but it was not an absolute barrier to writing home, if it was a priority to do so. For many migrants, it evidently was.[47]

The continuity between our two samples has implications for the postal component of stories that make the 1850s a decade of dramatic change. For example, one account dates the beginning of a "Revolution in Postal Communications in Central Canada" precisely to 1851, "when the British government relinquished control to the ... provinces of the postal services in their territories." Besides policy, "the creation of railway systems was the most significant technological advance which facilitated the development of a mass postal network." The system before 1851 is described in starkly contrasting terms, with emphasis on "the high cost and limited availability of mail services and facilities," which created "walls of oblivion" for "people with limited means who moved substantial distances away from their kin." By removing these barriers, the postal revolution "must have made migration to Canada ... much less daunting than in earlier times ... and hence have facilitated the migration process." This is a puzzling conclusion, however, because 1851 marked virtually the end, not the beginning, of the mass migration that peopled Upper Canada. Indeed, as Egan's letters suggest, if there had ever been a "wall of oblivion," it was overcome before the changes of the 1850s.[48]

STORIES ABOUT PRICES

In table 32 we summarize the prices of four principal local products. From the range of prices within individual samples we are able to tell at least four stories about prices in the rural economy. One, visible in prices for flour, a major provincial export, is the influence of international trends. In the pre-1861 cases for which there are prices, there was a difference of from $1.00 to $1.80 between the lowest and highest price per hundredweight during the course of twelve months. In each, the difference reflected general trends in the market – Upper Canadian wheat prices rose from 1808 to 1809 and from 1828 to 1829, fell during 1842 and into 1843, and rose sharply during 1854.[49] A second, clearest in the prices for butter, is seasonality. In seven cases, butter prices varied by 2.5 cents per pound or more during the year. Except in 1854, when all prices surged during an inflationary boom, butter cost more in winter and early spring, then its price dropped in summer as local supplies increased. A third is that descriptions might cover distinct products. Whether that was true for butter (salted vs fresh) is not indicated in accounts. But for boards there are enough descriptive entries to show that distinct prices typically represented different products. Fourth, price differences could have represented variations in the quality of the product, visible to the buyer even if not explicitly recorded in the accounts.

Fresh pork and pickled pork were effectively distinct products, and (as the table indicates) pork was sold both by the barrel and by the pound. Converting the price of barrels of pork into a price per pound suggests that much of what was sold by the pound was also pickled. Thus, at Tett's in 1842, a barrel cost $12; if it contained the standard 208 pounds, that was equal to just under 6 cents per pound, the low end of the price range per pound there. In later samples, pork in the barrel was worth from 7 cents to 8.5 cents per pound.[50] It was common to slaughter hogs late in the year, which would have tended to make for seasonal fluctuations in pork supply. But there are few suggestions of a seasonal pattern for prices. A possible case is three pork purchases totalling over 500 pounds at Sherin's in November 1861, all at 4 cents per pound, the lowest price in any sample. A more likely explanation, however, is that these transactions involved fresh pork.[51]

A striking feature of the prices in table 32 is their long-term consistency. There are outlying prices, but the ranges at different stores generally overlap. This is in part a function of the years of our samples, which avoid extremes, such as the mid-1830s, when wheat prices were very low, and the two highest peaks of the century, during the War of 1812 and in 1855–56.[52] Still, the pattern contrasts with prices for imported goods, many of which, as we have seen in earlier chapters, cost substantially less in 1828–29 than in 1808–09. There was no such trend in local prices. In this and in the products themselves, in fact, the main story is long-term continuity.

CONCLUSION

To conclude, we return to our opening quotation on the complexity of rural places and to Dechêne's emphasis on the importance of local exchange. Many essential goods and services – including for food, warmth, shelter, and clothing – were produced and consumed everywhere.

Yet the processes by which they were acquired by people who did not produce them for themselves – and through which farmers and other local producers earned income – have largely been taken for granted in Upper Canada, both in and beyond rural settings.[53] In particular, how rural products got from farms and villages into larger towns and cities and then to individual households there has rarely been systematically considered, either taken for granted or not pursued for lack of appropriate evidence.[54]

Among them, our samples catch aspects of exchanges in boards, flour, pork, beef, artisans' products, bran and other gristmill byproducts, oats, butter, eggs, carding and fulling, and postal and other services. Products that appear more rarely – such as firewood, livestock, wool, hay, fruits, vegetables, and locally produced tools such as churns – surely were more extensively traded than store accounts imply. Although farmers did sometimes buy foods, the main buyers we have seen for these commodities were non-farmers.[55] Yet many of the latter bought few or no such goods at our stores, and no one bought a year's supply of all the principal routinely consumed foods.

That most of the channels through which buyers and sellers of local products and services met did not run through our stores suggests a very different pattern from the one imagined in stories that imagine merchants had local monopolies.[56] A better way of imagining the rural market for local goods is as a matrix with many points, structured by interactions among numerous participants and by routines and expectations.[57] On the buyers' side, people knew what could be bought and how (i.e., from whom, where, when – and how paid for). On the producers' side, it is often imagined that farms produced what they could and in "unusually favourable circumstances" might have a "surplus" to sell.[58] Of course natural variables such as frost, insects, heat, rainfall, and diseases of plants and animals affected yields, but what farms had to sell was also a function of the decisions and strategies of farm families, in the context of their specific settings. Surpluses reflected intention, not just luck, and families will have had an idea of what they might do with them – who might buy and what price they might expect. And if they had unexpected surpluses or shortfalls, the market provided an outlet or a source of supply.

HOUSEHOLD GOODS, FOOTWEAR, AND OTHER PURCHASES

From earliest times those who could afford it found no difficulty in finding suitable china for the dining room.

Jeanne Minhinnick, 1970[1]

The fork had triumphed, though knives and spoons continued to outsell forks until the early nineteenth century. The triumph of the knife and fork went along with the gradual transition to using china dinner plates.

Bee Wilson, 2012[2]

We have still to consider three categories in appendix A: goods for the home, footwear, and a residual group of "other" products. Together they represent about one-fifth of the entire list, including eleven products important enough that they were purchased by at least 10 percent of all customers. Eight of the latter appear in 1808, and a ninth, boots, was undoubtedly available then even if not found in our first sample. The others appear in 1842.

HOUSEHOLD GOODS

To consider products for use in the home, we begin with the serving and eating of food. In her reference to the "dining room," Jeanne Minhinnick speaks of houses grander than the log homes of many settlers; but in suggesting that the possession of china was essentially an economic question she opens the possibility that others too might have served food on china dishes. The second quotation links china to the utensils for dining, highlighting that eating from plates with a knife and fork was a relatively new practice in Western society, one that was just developing in the eighteenth century. Through our data we can explore whether rural Upper Canadians were part of this trend.

According to one standard image of pioneering, they were not: nine-teenth-century author William Canniff writes, "Many had but one or two dishes, often of wood ... and spoons of the same material. Knives and forks in many families were unknown. A few families had brought a very limited number of articles for eating, relics of other days, but these were exceedingly scarce. The wooden spoon was the most common article with which to carry food to the mouth."[3] Despite this story, it is clear from our list of household goods that Minhinnick is right; china was available, and from the earliest years. The list in appendix A is headed by cups and plates, and 20 percent of all buyers of both were in our 1808–09 sample. On the other hand, appendix A shows far fewer buyers of knives and forks, spoons, and dishes. Does that indicate that most rural families in Upper Canada ate without them – or that they did not buy such goods because they already possessed them? In the first case, we might expect the frequency of purchases to increase as settlement pro-gressed and the economy developed. But that was not the case. Many household products, including plates, knives and forks, were purchased at least as commonly in 1808–09 as in subsequent samples.

On 6 October 1808, Abel Fulford bought a half-dozen bowls, for 90 cents, and a single wine glass, for 17 cents. The latter was one of only two such purchases in the entire study.[4] The Fulfords were the kind of settlers Minhinnick speaks of. A well-established family of seven, they had one of the highest tax assessments among the clientele at Yonge Mills, a reflection of their land holdings, livestock, and residence.[5] At a time when most fam-ilies in the area had log dwellings, they lived in a two-storey frame house. It surely was equipped with basic necessities, which Fulford, his wife, and a daughter augmented throughout the year, purchasing household goods on eight more occasions. They were charged almost $7.00 for a cream cup (which we have counted as a cup, not a "creamer"),[6] a pair of shears,[7] a candlestick, a ball of candlewick, a total of thirteen plates (bought on three different days), a teapot, a set of cups and saucers, two tin cups, a sugar bowl, two other bowls, and over $2.00 worth of unspecified "crock-ery" (table 34). Other than the teapot (and perhaps some bowls), this list did not include products involved in preparing food.

Daybook entries seldom describe products in detail, but 1808 import invoices provide additional information. Notably, they confirm that vari-ations in retail prices generally reflected variation in the products themselves. Thus, the forty-three dozen bowls ordered by Charles Jones included three types, "C.C.," quart, and pint (each at more than one price); there were also forty-six dozen "large-size col[oure]d" sets of bowls and saucers, at three prices. The eighty dozen plates were "C.C. flat and soup" and "blue and green edge," with two or three prices for each.[8] "C.C." was cream-coloured ware. Developed in the second half of the eighteenth century, it was among the products that made the English potteries the Western world's leader in producing earthenware for everyday use. That Upper Canadians were buying it is a reminder both that English industrialization extended beyond the cotton industry and that for those sectors too colonial buyers were among the sources of demand for the new outputs.[9] Four dozen of the teapots Jones ordered cost $3.20 per dozen.[10] Another twenty-two, more precisely specified, were made of pewter, almost the only products so designated in all of our documents. They came in two sizes, three-pint and quart, and were much more expensive; at $17.40 and $13.00 per dozen, they cost four to five times as much as the everyday pots.[11] Other imports included seventeen dozen sets of cups and saucers (two prices); eighteen dozen sets of knives and forks (five prices); and generally smaller quantities of candle moulds, mugs, pitchers, iron candlesticks, scissors, and chamber pots. There were fifty iron pots with a total weight of 800 pounds and two dozen frying pans weighing 116 pounds. The only glasses were eight tumblers. The invoices also record products that appear in later years in appendix A or B, confirming that these were available in 1808–09, even if we found no buyers: spoons (three gross, at four prices, most specified as table spoons, primarily of "tin'd iron" – here and at other stores, cutlery sets did not include spoons), oval dishes, decanters, jugs, milk pots, basins, and six "pickling jars."[12]

Even if not all of these types of goods reached Charles Jones's country store, they still suggest richer domestic possibilities, for at least some Upper Canadians, than those presented in Canniff's story of pioneer dining. At the Yonge Mills store in 1808–09, in fact, household products accounted for 8 percent of customers' purchases and totalled almost $200, far more than at later stores. This relative prominence was not, however, attributable to the types of goods purchased by the Fulfords. Rather, it was because of products they did not buy: blankets and kettles, which accounted for more than half the value of household goods in 1808–09. For both, more than half the buyers in the entire study were at this store.[13]

Like other woolens, blankets (purchased by seven families in 1808–09) were costly, $7.50 per pair.[14] Import invoices record three- and four-point blankets; wholesale prices suggest purchases were the former.[15] Eleven people bought kettles in 1808–09, ranging from an unspecified kettle at $1.00 and tea kettles at $1.60 up to seven that cost $6.50.[16] If the latter were among the "iron pots" on the import invoices, they could easily have weighed fifty pounds. That seems heavy for household cooking, but there is no evident alternative: they cost far less than the prices Jones paid for twenty-five potash kettles that he imported (which ranged from $32 to $66), and most were bought in September, not the season for making maple sugar.[17] We recorded "bake" kettles and bake pans in a distinct category; they cost from $2.80 to $3.60 in 1808 and were purchased by five buyers.[18] Other purchases included two pots, several frying pans and skillets, and one "spider."[19] Altogether, eighteen customers here bought at least one of these cooking products. All were durable, and none seem to have been so expensive that settlers could not afford them if it was a priority to have a specific utensil; pots, for example, cost $2.25 to $2.80, and frying pans and skillets were $1.20 and $1.40. Although early cooking utensils are sometimes imagined as "primitive," there is no reason to think that women worked with kitchen tools that were anything other than standard products for the period.[20]

In 1828–29, purchases of household goods totalled less than $40. Yet thirty-three households bought something in this category, including five products added to appendix A and two to appendix B. Their purchases provide additional details that help to envisage the goods available: "patent" pails; "small" scissors; blue teapots and bowls; dishes described as oval, white, round, and sugar; two sizes of decanters; and three types of pitchers. A "large kettle" bought by Thomas Andrews cost $7.00, the most expensive kettle in any sample. Except for this, George Gardener was the leading buyer here, charged $4.38 on 13 December 1828 for dishes, plates, and other china, plus eight glass tumblers (table 34).

Like Fulford, Gardener was a well-established farmer.[21] So was John Cannon, the 1842 customer whose purchases are recorded in table 34.[22] Stephen Byington, the 1861 example in the table, had one of Scovil's largest accounts; he was a shoemaker with seven people in his household. That these families were leading buyers might suggest an association between relative affluence and the ability to buy such household products. But although they bought more than other customers, the goods they bought were typical. The Fulfords bought six of the first seven household products listed in appendix A. The Gardeners bought three, plus dishes, which head the list of goods added in 1828. Nor was any one product on either's list so expensive as to seem a luxury beyond the reach of other rural households.

To develop this argument, we can consider tea. With 390 buyers, it was among the most frequently purchased of all goods. Buyers clearly had the means to brew and serve it.[23] Yet only 36 people bought teapots (including four of the buyers in table 34). A few people bought creamers, sugar bowls (counted with bowls in appendix A), and mugs. Cups, as we have seen, were the most frequently purchased of all household products. Among the 98 buyers, at least 72 bought sets of cups and saucers; 16 of these buyers were in 1808–09. That 12 of them lived in round log homes and drank their tea from matching cups and saucers offers a very different view from Canniff's of life in such settings. Compared to the price of tea, moreover, cups and saucers were not expensive. The Fulfords were charged $1.27 on 2 January 1809 for a set of cups and saucers, a teapot, and a sugar bowl; but that winter and spring, in a span of less than five months, their tea purchases totalled $6. For all customers at this store, tea purchases totalled more than $150; their purchases of cups and saucers cost less than $8.[24]

This argument can be extended to other basic household goods that, like teapots, were purchased in modest quantities. For example, we saw earlier (table 20) that more than 120 families bought candles and/or wick. Yet only fifteen bought candlesticks, which in 1808 cost 23 cents. As for dining, although we cannot prove that no families ate in the manner Canniff described, we can say that, with 34 buyers (at eight stores), sets of knives and forks were purchased about as often as teapots, dishes, basins, spoons, chamber pots, pans, and pitchers, all goods that we can imagine in most homes. Knives and forks were sold in sets – evidently six of each – at a cost of between $1.00 and $1.30 in 1808–09.[25] That half of that year's sample spent this much or more on tea provides an indication of affordability. If there were families that resisted the trend to eating with knives and forks, it must have been a matter of priorities, taste, and manners, of what they ate and how; it was not an issue of cost.

A majority of the household products listed in appendix A appear in 1808, some of those added later were evidently available then, and none are added in 1861. For these goods, continuity is a central theme. If Tett's list of imports in the mid-1830s is indicative, however, many products likely came in greater variety as time went by.[26] For example, between September 1833 and the end of 1835, he placed three orders for a total of 140 teapots with more than a dozen distinct descriptions: common, fine, oval, and round; blue and black; glazed, painted, and "untin'd"; with various combinations of these (such as blue oval and black glazed).[27] Tett bought six dozen jugs, including lustre, coloured, and printed. His two spoon orders, totalling 3.5 gross, were mainly tea and tablespoons, which came in both iron and "BM" (Britannia metal, a polished metal substitute for silver).[28] Besides iron candlesticks, he also bought thirteen pairs of brass candlesticks. Such distinctions are an indication that customers could choose between basic and somewhat more luxurious products: BM spoons cost about twice what iron did; iron candlesticks cost Tett 85 cents per *dozen*, whereas brass cost 35 to 67 cents per *pair*.

As it happens, no one bought BM spoons or either kind of candlestick at his store in 1842. But people did buy seven products to be added to appendix A. Brooms are of particular interest: there were just two buyers in 1842, but ninety-one in subsequent samples (including Byington, who purchased three), reflecting the emergence at mid-century of broom manufacturing in the province, using imported broom corn.[29] Three others added this year were purchased in modest quantities at most or all stores thereafter. Jugs, as we have seen, were among the imports but not the purchases in 1808. Bed cords, used to support a mattress, were not a new product; our data do not allow deciding whether it was becoming more common to make beds this way in Upper Canada or just an accident that they do not appear earlier. Lamps and lamp glass may represent a trend; at least this timing coincides with our evidence (in chapter 5) on oils for lamps.

At Choate's store in 1851, forty-three customers bought household products (including eight who bought brooms). Three purchased crocks, two purchased strainers, and one bought a washboard, all found in most later samples, albeit with modest numbers of buyers. Crocks, used in dairying, were almost certainly another provincially manufactured product. In exactly these years, a domestic earthenware and stoneware industry was taking shape, with general stores as one of its key outlets; crocks, large jugs, and churns, all bulky products used for production and storage, were the principal outputs. This was a niche market; tableware continued to be imported from England.[30] Strainers may also have been used in the dairy. Washboards were a relatively new laundry aid; that we found just ten buyers in our samples leaves uncertainty about how widely rural women adopted them.[31] Cost cannot have been the issue if they did not: washboards cost 40 cents in 1851 and only 25 or 30 cents a decade later. The leading houseware buyers in 1851 were

Charles Davis and his wife (table 34).[32] Mrs Davis bought a crock in mid-April; three knives and forks, six plates, and an earthenware dish on 28 April; and a bake kettle, a teapot, a tea kettle, and two or three cups and saucers (along with a half-pound of tea, their first such purchase) on 16 May. Her final purchase, made on 30 December, was two tumblers. By then, they had purchased fourteen different products with a total value of $5.54, which represented about 10 percent of their overall account – and less than they spent just on tea.[33]

In this expanding society, new households were arriving or being established throughout our period. People might accumulate supplies before setting up a household, and immigrants might bring goods with them. Or, as with other goods, people might buy at more than one store; there must have been a more varied selection of household goods in larger towns than any one country store could stock. Thus it is not surprising that no one in all of our samples bought something like a complete household stock. The closest, perhaps, was the Davis family. We do not know their actual circumstances, but their purchases of many products in modest quantities allow reflection on the minimal requirements of a new household. What they bought, considered in relation to all the costs of setting up and operating a household, can hardly be seen as expensive. At the same time, their list did not include many goods that such a household might need: other than a bake kettle, for example, they bought nothing to cook with, and they also did not buy standard products like basins and chamber pots. Could they have done without these? Or is it likely they acquired them elsewhere?

These questions prompt reflection on other goods that we might imagine as standard but that do not appear in appendix A. A few textile products (bedding, counterpanes, and towels) and products of wood (bedsteads and chairs) are listed in appendix B; they were purchased so rarely that country stores cannot have been the usual source for them. Some, we might expect, were mainly produced within the household; others seem more likely to have been produced and sold within the local market and not to have needed the store as intermediary.[34] Other products, such as silver teaspoons, which Minhinnick imagines "most people" acquiring, were never purchased.[35] Such gaps and the limited purchases even of many standard goods make it impossible definitively to resolve the issue of styles of living in early log houses. But country store accounts do speak to the range of products needed for the home and the variety of available sizes and types (including new styles as they appeared). From the cost of such goods, it is clear that a basic repertoire was within reach for all but the poorest rural families. That we do not find more purchases is more likely to indicate that households already had them than that they were somehow doing without.

None of this is to suggest that houses could not be made much more comfortable and cooking and serving more refined over time. When families decided to do so, they might find it convenient to buy at the country store, which also could provide replacements for broken or worn products and an additional supply of standard products if a need arose. Most of these products were quite durable, however, and families did not need to buy them with anything like the frequency of groceries and textiles. Hence, although half of all sample members bought something in the household products category and there were many products to list in appendix A, these goods seldom represented more than a very modest proportion of anyone's account.

FOOTWEAR

Rural work was demanding, and Canadian winters were severe. Going barefoot in this setting was scarcely an option, unless perhaps for children at play in summer. Moccasins, purchased at five stores, were a distinctively Canadian possibility, but only fourteen sample members bought them.[36] Mainly, people wore shoes, bought at all ten stores, or boots, bought at nine. Many must have had both. These were durable (when well-made) and they could be repaired. But eventually they wore out; and footwear varied in function and style, as the distinction between boots and shoes reminds us. English estimates were that people required two pairs of shoes per year; boots were purchased by fewer people there and less frequently, but they became more common in the later eighteenth and early nineteenth centuries.[37] Hence it is not surprising that so many people – more than two hundred in all – bought footwear (table 33). There were just two buyers in the first sample, however, and only four in the second. By 1861, there had been a major change: at every store the value of purchases was higher than in earlier samples; at three, in fact, more than half the customers bought footwear, and they tended to buy many more pairs.

As with other clothing, almost all of what Upper Canadians wore on their feet was made in Canada. Shoemakers were among the most common craftsmen, found widely in rural areas, including all our communities (with the possible exception of 1808–09).[38] Their importance is confirmed by mid-century trade data, which record only very modest imports of footwear.[39] But shoemakers could deal directly with their clientele – and if shoes were custom-made they necessarily did. Hence the first question posed by our data is why someone might buy footwear from a merchant. For our early samples, one answer is a scenario considered in chapter 6, a worker's relationship with the business. Joseph Christmas (in 1808–09) and Antoine Busea and Francis Russe (in 1828–29) were paid wages. Another 1828–29 buyer, Isaac Desermo, resembled Busea and Russe in having a name that could be *Canadien* and in not appearing in local tax records; he could also have been an employee.[40] Why John Fields (charged $2.20 for a pair of shoes in 1809) and Ann Graham (who bought boots worth $1.50 in 1828) made their purchases is not evident.

There were many more transactions in 1842: sixteen customers bought a total of fourteen pairs of shoes, twenty-one pairs of boots, and three pairs of moccasins.[41] The shoes had six different prices, ranging from 90 cents to $2.75, and boots had nine, from 75 cents to $5.00 (table 35A). One buyer was Alexander Buist, whose relationship with Benjamin Tett was discussed in chapter 6; he was charged for two pairs of boots and three pairs of shoes (one pair noted as for his wife). Although many transactions were recorded just as boots or shoes, enough were specified to suggest that price variations generally represented variations in the actual products.[42] Thus, boots and shoes came in men's, women's, and children's (or boys' and girls') sizes. Most, presumably, were leather, but other materials were occasionally specified, such as the prunella boots charged to Ralph Barker for Hester, a daughter or servant. (Prunella, a worsted fabric, was used for the uppers of women's footwear.)[43] Other variations involved quality (such as a pair of "fine" boots) and style (a pair of "women's lace boots"). Prunella boots cost $1.50, fine cost $2.75, and "lace" cost $2.50 (as did the other boots specified as for women). Besides Buist, six of the buyers in 1842 were among the ten leading accounts. They do not seem to have purchased enough to represent all that a family would need during a year, however; that they sometimes bought from Tett evidently was a function of their wider commercial relationship with the store.

Of the three largest accounts that did not buy footwear from Tett, two were themselves shoemakers, Richard Leach and Timothy Cavanagh.

Each earned modest credits from repairs (in one case specifically of Tett's boots), and each was explicitly mentioned as the supplier of a few of the boots and shoes purchased. Where our sample catches both sides of such transactions, the selling price and the price credited to the shoemaker were the same; that is, these were third-party transactions settled through Tett's accounts. The shoemakers also bought a few inputs from Tett (thread, for example, and one small piece of leather for Leach). But obviously most of their income came direct from customers and most of their inputs from other sources.

In his first years in business, Tett bought modest quantities of footwear from outside suppliers: on four occasions between January 1834 and February 1836, he bought a total of forty-eight pairs of men's, women's, and boys' boots and shoes from Horace Billings, a merchant in Brockville; and he once bought two dozen pairs of moccasins from an unknown supplier in Montreal. The timing of the Brockville purchases, made during the winter, might suggest that he used Billings, his principal nearby supplier, for convenience, except that he did not buy any boots and shoes in Montreal. It is not clear where Billings's stock came from; one possibility, suggested by his location on the St Lawrence, is New England, where industrial shoemaking was expanding rapidly in the 1830s.[44] That Tett stocked some footwear is suggested also by an 1851 inventory, which counted fourteen pairs of men's boots (valued at $2.00 each). But it also recorded many shoemaking supplies: assorted awls, 5 pounds of shoe thread, closing thread, pegs by the quart, and several kinds of leather, notably 119 pounds of sole leather.[45] Taking into account the modesty of Tett's imports in the 1830s, the limited purchases by sample members in 1842, and the character of his stock in 1851, it is reasonable to conclude that most of the footwear worn by his clientele was locally made.

Choate's store in 1851 adds "half" boots, slippers, and India rubber shoes to the footwear types specified at Tett's. The timing of the appearance of the latter fits precisely with the development of this product in England, where the first workable process had been patented in 1843.[46] This sample includes at least two shoemakers, Thomas Riggs and George Tucker. They had very modest accounts, and there are no credits to them in the daybook for work. Even so, one of Choate's daybooks, like those discussed in chapter 6, provides a window into a local trade. An unnamed "shoemaker's account," separate from the usual daily flow of entries and running from 29 August 1850 until early May 1851, records

104 pairs of boots and shoes, their cost and selling prices, and the buyers' names.[47] The list includes all 6 pairs of boots and shoes debited to sample members in the first months of 1851, which suggests that Choate's footwear sales were of locally made products. Because credits to the shoemaker's account were dated almost simultaneously with debits to customers, it seems possible that Choate did not actually stock footwear.[48] Except for a few pairs for the Choate family, every pair was sold at a higher price than that credited to the shoemaker, markups ranging from 16 to more than 80 percent, with a mean of about 54 percent. Even so, Choate's selling prices were in line with or modestly lower than earlier samples (table 35A).

We cannot be sure how Choate sustained these margins when shoemakers and customers could meet directly. Whatever advantage there was to the customer in buying on credit and to the shoemaker in not having to extend credit, such substantial markups would have given each an incentive to bypass the middleman. More likely the shoemaker had a relationship with Choate that justified – or required – selling to the store at a discount.[49] One possibility is that Choate took shoes on consignment, crediting the shoemaker when a sale was made. Another is that the shoemaker's association with Choate was like that often encountered in rural settings, in which a craftsman, while appearing autonomous in the accounts, was in some respects an employee, paid with a share of the income or on a piece rate. In the latter case, Choate might have supplied work space and perhaps other inputs. During eight months, 104 pairs of boots and shoes were recorded, about one pair every second day, and credits to the shoemaker totalled $143 (less than $18 per month).[50] That was not much to live on if he also had to cover the cost of materials and other inputs. The implication is either that Choate supplied those inputs or that the shoemaker had other income from selling footwear directly. In any case, the modesty of purchases by sample members demonstrates that Choate cannot have been their main source of footwear.

A decade later, although there were several shoemakers in the community (and in the 1861 Choate sample), things were very different. Now 60 percent (forty-two of seventy) sample members at this store bought footwear, a total of 115 pairs, worth almost $200, five times the value of 1851 purchases.[51] These included 62 pairs of shoes (at twenty different prices), 49 pairs of boots (at twenty-one prices), 1 pair of moccasins, 1 pair of slippers, and 2 pairs of India rubbers. As the many prices indicate, Choate sold a wide variety of footwear. Entries often did not specify types, but even so, ten different kinds of boots and eight kinds of shoes were recorded (table 35B). For shoes, carpet, children's, junior, rubber, and small were at the low end of the price range and calf (at $2.25) was the highest; boots ranged from as low as 85 cents for small up to $3.50 and $4.00 for kip (a fine leather), $3.75 for strong, and $5.00 for fine.

This very sharp increase in footwear purchases was not unique to Choate's. In all our 1861 samples, footwear purchases were high, exceeding $100 in each case; and at Darling's and Sherin's, as at Choate's, more than half the sample bought footwear. Because this development occurred simultaneously in separate rural locations, it cannot have represented local circumstances or an extension of the arrangements documented in the 1851 accounts. Rather, it coincides with the first phases of the industrialization of boot and shoe making in Canada, as sewing machines and then pegging machines made it increasingly economical during the 1850s for entrepreneurs to concentrate production in industrial establishments. The footwear purchased in 1861 need not all have been factory-made, but a good deal of it must have been.

As historians have eloquently documented, factory competition deeply challenged shoemakers' skills, identity, independence, and culture.[52] Our evidence represents another perspective on this story, inviting reflection on why rural buyers would turn from a local maker, a near neighbour, to products made in a remote, impersonal factory. The answer must be that for many products factory-made shoes and boots were perceived as better value. Selection, style, quality, and other factors could all have entered into that decision. Price obviously mattered too, although the evidence on prices is complex. For example, the range in 1861 closely overlaps 1842 and 1851; the highest prices for boots in 1861 were the same as had been paid at Tett's in 1842; and the most expensive shoes in 1861 cost as much as shoes in our earliest samples (table 35A). On the other hand, average prices for shoes were lower at all five stores in 1861. But the mean encompasses prices for very different products (some of which may not have been factory-made), and the mix of those products could have varied among samples. Comparing prices for specific types is therefore preferable, but complicated because so many entries for footwear are not specific and because there was variation even within types. Women's boots serve as an example (table 35C). The highest 1861 price was $1.75 or $1.80, considerably lower than the $2.50 paid for three pairs in 1842.[53] But the women's boots purchased in 1851 had also cost $1.80, and that preceded industrialization. The most that can be said from this evidence, therefore, is that industrialization probably lowered prices for equivalent products, even after allowing for the storekeeper's margin. It is striking how quickly this happened. Footwear was an essentially new line of goods for the country retailer, and among the first lines of goods to come from Canadian manufacturers (brooms and crockery, as we have seen, were others). The pace at which manufacturing grew in part reflected that a distribution network already existed.

OTHER GOODS

After all the products we have considered, thirty-five remain in the "other" category in appendix A. Appendix B lists fifty more. Of these, combs (for grooming and for women to wear) were the most commonly purchased, with 184 buyers. In 1808–09, there were 21 buyers, whose purchases totalled $5.60. Import invoices show that these were "horn" combs; Charles Jones bought a total of nine gross of them. They came at three slightly different prices, a reminder of variance in even such everyday objects. More than half the combs purchased by our sample cost 10 cents, but customers also bought six much costlier "fine" or "hair" combs (at 40 or 46.7 cents). Twenty years later, almost all purchases were of the two latter kinds, at prices that still ranged up to 40 cents. In 1842, by contrast, Tett sold both for 10 cents, also the standard price for dressing and wood combs. A third of the sixty-nine transactions at his store were side combs (at 5 or 6.7 cents per pair).[54] That was more of the latter than at all other stores combined. Puzzlingly, he recorded no sales of back combs, yet in the 1830s he had imported them in substantial quantities. They do appear at other stores, as do some "coarse" combs, which seem to confirm that "fine" described the spacing of teeth. The range of prices for fine combs at every store indicates that they varied in style or quality. For example, Darling's sold twenty-one fine combs at six prices, ranging from 10 to 20 cents; here, as we have seen with other products, multiple purchases by the same customer confirm that variation was in the product, not by customer.

The lists include a variety of other products related to personal grooming, purchased far less frequently than combs. As they were durable and not expensive, it is not unreasonable to think that limited purchases indicate that many people already owned them. Thus, in 1842 James Rogers bought a looking glass, a razor, and a case (presumably for the razor, because bought at the same time as the other products) for 78 cents; and William Tremayne bought all three of these products plus a shaving brush and a shaving box, for 86 cents. Four others bought looking glasses in 1842, and two bought razors. Each of these products was bought at most subsequent stores in modest quantities. It is difficult to know how to interpret the rarity of purchases of brushes, which do not appear on the list until 1851 (and that year's purchase was a "scrubbing" brush). The first brushes explicitly for hair appear only in 1861. That is also when "hair oil" appears, purchased by sixteen buyers at all five stores; hair pins, purchased by nine buyers at four; and hair nets (on the clothing list) with thirteen buyers at all five stores – in total, thirty-three people bought at least one of these products.[55]

After combs, the next most common purchase was writing paper, bought in every sample, by a total of 128 people. Again the first was representative, in both volumes purchased and number of buyers. Sixteen people bought a total of fifteen quires of paper in 1808–09 (a quire was either twenty-four or twenty-five sheets), priced at 40 or 50 cents per quire. The difference, judging from import invoices, reflected size of sheet – Jones bought writing paper in Ogdensburg, New York, and foolscap in Montreal.[56] He also bought wrapping paper in Montreal, presumably for his own use. Twenty years later, paper cost 30 cents per quire. That was the upper end of the price range at most subsequent stores; the lower end was usually 20 cents. For example, that was the price for most purchases at Tett's.[57] He also sold individual sheets of paper (at 0.83 or 1.63 cents). Besides paper, the lists include several other products for writing: in 1808–09, four people bought ink powder (one of them also bought paper). Pencils, pens, and pen holders appear later on the list (in 1828, 1851, and 1861 respectively). Each had much smaller numbers of buyers than paper but was purchased at many or most stores. So were slates, in modest quantities beginning in 1842, and envelopes, which first appear in 1861.[58]

All of these products speak to writing. Reading is visible in the form of books (with 96 buyers at all ten stores), almanacs (with 29 buyers at six stores), and newspaper subscriptions (12 buyers, 11 of whom were at Fowlds's in 1861).[59] Combining all of these products related to reading and writing, more than 220 members of the samples bought something to indicate literacy. For example, in about six weeks in late 1808 and early 1809, 9 Yonge Mills customers bought almanacs, at a price of 13.3 cents. Twenty years later, there were 8 buyers of almanacs, which now cost 10 cents. By 1842, the price had fallen to just 5 cents (table 36). These seem to have been printed in Upper Canada – at least Tett's orders in the 1830s were from Kingston or Brockville.[60] Virtually all the other books purchased were textbooks. In the first two samples, there were two purchases of spelling books – possibly Mavor's spelling book, which was what Tett stocked in the 1830s. He also purchased six Bibles, paying 85 cents each, which made them much the most expensive books encountered; in 1842 he sold the only Bible in the entire sample, at just over $1.00. If many Upper Canadian households had a "family" Bible, passed from one generation to the next, only one child could inherit it. Hence there must have been a market for Bibles, even if we found only this faint trace of it.[61]

Reflecting the contemporary expansion of the provincial school system, the number and variety of book purchases increased substantially at mid-century. The leading buyer, Thomas Barrie, was not found in the census but seems to have been a teacher: in February 1851, he was charged $6.60 for a dozen First Books, a dozen Second Books, eighteen Third Books, and eight Arithmetics. These were the most commonly purchased books; there were at least ten more buyers in each case, from several stores. There were, of course, other channels of book distribution to families, teachers, and schools, including booksellers in larger centres and the provincial Educational Depository. Given that the latter was said to sell books "at prices well below what the commercial book trade in Upper Canada could sustain," it is significant that anyone bought school books in other ways.[62] In fact, if the average of more than twenty books per store in our 1861 samples is typical of all country stores, the total sold through them across the province might bear comparison with quantities supplied by the Depository.

One other paper product appears in 1808–09, purchased by six buyers then and by thirty more at later stores. Pasteboard was sold by the sheet and used in making women's hats.[63] Finally, among 1808–09 transactions, we note Catherine Leach's purchase of a pair of spectacles (for 56 cents). She was the only buyer (although Charles Jones had imported four dozen pairs that year, at four different prices, ranging from $1.30 to $7.80 per dozen).[64] Another nine people bought spectacles at three later stores. For this presumably widely needed product, it seems evident that there were other sources besides country stores.

One puzzling product is pipes. The Yonge Mills store sold more than 140 pounds of tobacco in 1808–09, and Jones imported ten gross of pipes, yet no one in this sample bought a pipe. Some men evidently chewed tobacco, but sales by the plug accounted for only a small proportion of all tobacco purchases – and none in 1808–09. Pipes were purchased by members of all but one later sample, but buyers were few compared to the number who bought tobacco. They were not expensive: in 1828–29, most cost 1.67 cents; and in 1842 they cost 0.83 or 1.67 cents. These two samples accounted for more than half of all buyers.[65] Several bought substantial quantities, as if buying for others as well as themselves (e.g., for workers or a logging camp). For example, Louis Vodra, another unlinked Yonge Mills customer with a francophone name, bought thirteen pipes in early October 1828. At Tett's, Peter Hassen bought fifty-four pipes and James Rogers bought thirty-eight, often a half-dozen at a time. Two other leading 1842 customers, Alexander Buist and Christopher Chant, each bought about twenty pipes.[66]

As well as tobacco, some Upper Canadians used snuff, bought at six stores by a modest number of buyers (two-thirds of them in the two earliest samples – and very few in 1861, just five buyers at two stores). Charles Jones purchased almost five dozen snuff boxes in 1808, at five prices, suggesting considerable variation in this product. Five customers purchased snuff boxes at Yonge Mills then (as it happens, only two of them bought snuff); we found only one such purchase in all later samples.[67]

On 12 July 1828, William Judd, a farmer with thirteen acres in cultivation, bought 6.25 pounds of seeds (not further specified), paying 7.5 cents per pound. He was the first of sixty seed buyers in seven samples, more than half of them farmers. Not knowing where these seeds came from and thinking it possible that some were imported, we chose not to include them with local produce. In subsequent samples, there were only a few purchases of seed in such volume: 74 pounds of clover seed purchased by seven customers in 1842 and another 37 pounds of clover by three buyers in 1851.[68] Seeds for the main farm crops are almost entirely invisible in these accounts: some grass seed in 1842 and one bushel of seed wheat and two pounds of flax in 1861. The most common purchases were "garden" seeds, sold by the packet or paper (with thirteen buyers), and turnips, sold by the pound though usually purchased in smaller quantities (with ten buyers); both appear in 1851 and at three stores in 1861. Seven other kinds of seeds (onion, swede, beet, cabbage, tomato, carrot, and watermelon) were purchased at one or two stores, often in packets or papers at a cost of 5 to 10 cents. With the exception of Judd's purchase and of two turnip seed purchases at Fowlds's in 1861, also made in early July, seeds were purchased between late March and mid-June. Because every farmer and gardener needed seed, and many must have had reasons to look beyond their own production for at least some of the seeds they planted each year, it is clear that our samples hardly begin to represent all that we can imagine growing even on a pioneer's farm or in a household garden. They do, however, serve as a reminder that there must have been other networks through which seeds were bought, sold, and exchanged.

Across all our goods categories, almost fifty products were purchased by at least 10 percent of all customers. The last of these for us to consider was matches, with 78 buyers. A new product developed during the 1830s, they were purchased by three buyers in 1842. Clearly, Upper Canadians were just beginning to discover their utility; as a box of matches cost 6.7 cents, price seems unlikely to have been a deterrent to their use. After that, the number of buyers indicates that matches were becoming more widely used, and almost half of those who bought them made more than one purchase in a year. How many fires, pipes, candles, and lamps could have been lit with the matches purchased at our stores is uncertain, however, in part because packages evidently varied: in 1861, a box cost 25 cents at Scovil's, 40 cents at Fowlds's, and up to 50 cents at Darling's.[69]

Animals were ubiquitous in a rural society, yet visible in only limited and partial ways in the store accounts. Among "other" goods, the most common product for them was horse blankets, which first appear in 1842, purchased by three people. They were relatively costly, at $1.40 for a single blanket or $3.00 for a pair, prices found also in three 1861 samples.[70] There was a seasonal pattern to these purchases, all being made between November and early February. Because such blankets were relatively durable, it is possible that many more horses were protected by blankets than our modest number of buyers suggests. In 1851, cow bells and strings of bells appear on the list, but with just a few buyers each. Finally, two or three products related to oxen (nobs, balls, and boes [sic]) appear in 1861, all in appendix B. It is intriguing that the latter appear so late, when the relative role of oxen in provincial agriculture was diminishing.

Parasols and umbrellas both appear in 1851. One of the purchases then was a silk umbrella, costing $1.90. Otherwise, umbrellas cost from 50 to 90 cents; size was an element in this variation, but there doubtless were other factors as well.[71] By contrast, most parasols cost from $1.40

to $2.25. The last, bought at Scovil's, was among the most expensive products purchased there; on the other hand, the cheapest parasols were also bought there, three cotton parasols at just 37.5 cents. The function of parasols was protection from the sun, but fashion was also involved, as the wide price range indicates. As it happens, nine of the ten buyers were women.

We have already addressed the other items appearing in 1861 in appendix A except fiddle strings, purchased by eight buyers at two stores.[72] They are almost the only indicator of musical activity in the entire study, other than two Jew's harps purchased by one buyer at Choate's in 1861 (at 2 cents each). That Tett had imported eleven dozen iron and brass Jew's harps in the 1830s suggests they were in common use; certainly they were always cheap. The more striking feature of 1861 purchases is the number of products appearing then in appendix B. Space does not permit consideration of them all, but buffalo robes warrant attention because they confirm that rural Upper Canadians were among those on the demand side of the market as supply increased massively in just this period. Our examples varied widely in price, from $6.00 for a robe at Scovil's to $8.00 each for two at Sherin's up to $16.50 each for two purchased by the Latimers, a farm-family customer at Darling's. Even at the lowest price, they were among the most expensive individual products ever purchased (indeed, the robe was the most expensive at Scovil's). It is possible that the many other 1861 products in appendix B indicate a sharp increase in the range and variety of goods that Upper Canadians had to choose among; that would fit Béatrice Craig's argument for dramatic change in rural consumption in New Brunswick at precisely this time.[73] Alternatively, these products may be just a reflection of the relative weight of 1861 evidence in our sample.

To complete our view of sample accounts, we note three further types of transactions whose values are included in table 33. One was for unspecified goods, such as the "sundries" that accounted for about $4.50 in purchases in 1808–09. These entries were modest except at Fowlds's store, where transfers from a "goods book" represented almost one-third of the value of all purchases in 1854 and 6 percent in 1861.[74] These must mainly have been the products we have considered, even if we have no way of identifying them. Second, every store had some entries expressed as "balance on" a purchase. This was most common in 1808–09 when there were 67 such entries, out of about 2,500 debit transactions, with a value of about twenty-five dollars; over half were for alcohol (thirty, totalling eleven dollars, were for "balance on rum"). Although these debits were for standard goods, we do not know the actual value and volume of the original transaction, just the residue to be paid. The original payment, not recorded, was likely in cash. The trace left by these entries suggests the possibility of other cash purchases; any made entirely in cash will have left no trace in the accounts. Third, there were a few product entries that resisted all our efforts to decipher them; we nevertheless include their value in table 33.

CONCLUSION

The products considered in this chapter allow us to imagine a wide range of everyday scenarios. Some products – blankets, the best boots, large cooking pots, or the finest parasols, for example – were relatively costly, yet clearly within the means of many rural households. Because many were infrequently purchased, our data are necessarily suggestive. Still, they represent, and invite consideration of, many routine scenarios: for example, household activities such as preparation of food and drink, eating, sleeping, lighting fires, cleaning and doing laundry; personal grooming; seasonal concerns including winter's cold, spring planting of household gardens, and protecting oneself from summer sun; teaching and learning; communicating and record-keeping. Every one of these routines involved goods purchased in the market, many of them already found in our first sample. Other products are known to have been available then, and very few were added in 1861. Change was nevertheless visible, in lower prices, books prescribed for the province's schools, new products such as brooms and matches, greater variation within familiar products such as china, and the appearance of goods produced by Upper Canadian manufacturers – most notably footwear, a new industry whose rapid growth was dramatically reflected in customer purchases in 1861.

CONCLUSION: "ESSENTIALS" AND EVERYDAY LIFE

The problem [is] ... how to speak of the grounded and rich particularities of social lives in a world of ... large abstractions.

Bruce Curtis, 2001[1]

This is a book about goods that some Upper Canadians bought. To conclude, we reflect on the stories that they can help us to tell about the people, their lives, and their economy and society. One, to which we have returned often because of its importance, is that these goods had prices. Although negotiation must have been part of many exchanges in this economy, that clearly was not the norm at country stores. Had bargaining been involved in individual transactions, as is often imagined, we might have expected prices to vary according to the identity of the buyer, but the price of standard goods was the same for customers in varying circumstances and whether the buyer was the head of household or a wife, child, servant, or third party. Where we found price differences for particular goods, they are nearly always explicable in other ways: at a single store by qualitative and functional differentiation within a product category and by seasonal price movements.[2] In the longer term, the most important change was the real decline in prices for many imported goods (woolens being a notable exception); particularly marked between our first two samples, that trend continued for many goods.

We can choose to call these goods necessities, but if so need to recognize that not all were needed in the same way. Consumption involved preference and taste. Even the most frequently purchased goods, such as tea, tobacco, sugar, and cotton, were not requirements of life in some absolute sense: after all, Europeans had lived without them for millennia. As it happens, we have seen no luxuries of the kind some images present, silk for dresses, chocolate for breakfast, or silver teaspoons. But we have identified goods like ribbons and trim that could have been luxuries for their buyers and products that introduced new possibilities, such as new fabrics and paint. For these and a number of others, buyers' choices involved decisions about appearance and quality as well as function and cost. A key finding is the wide variation in numbers of buyers and (among those buyers) in the quantities and frequency of purchases. These complicate stories about consumption in a society often seen as simple, relatively homogeneous, and having a uniform set of preferences. Among the complexities are variation in occupation, taste, and purchasing power; and buying from other suppliers, with the implication that rural Upper Canadian men and women routinely participated in the marketplace at multiple locations and through numerous points of access.

One genre of commodity history speaks of specific products that "changed the world."[3] Here we have instead used the hundreds of commodities listed in the appendixes as a way to look at rural Upper Canada.[4] Many of these goods were themselves varied. Had all the uses of the goods in appendix A been incorporated, it would have been very much longer. Products such as brushes, nails, knives, and oils – and even humble needles and pins – could have very different characters and purposes. Even for goods whose uses seem clear, there was much variation, exemplified in the fourteen types of buttons and eighteen kinds of thread imported by Charles Jones in 1808, the dozen varieties of teapot imported by Benjamin Tett in the mid-1830s, or the six different newspapers subscribed to through Fowlds's store in 1861. These goods allow us to begin to consider the "grounded and rich particularities" evoked in our quotation from Bruce Curtis: the routines, tastes, culture, knowledge, and practice that constituted the material world of rural Upper Canadians. From the relative frequency of purchase, some clearly were more important than others. It is the most commonly purchased that seem best to qualify as "essentials." Yet even they involved choice. It seems possible that not everyone drank tea; it is evident that not every man drank alcohol or hunted.

In total, about one-third of the products in appendix A appear on the list in 1808–09, including more than three-quarters of those purchased by at least 10 percent of all sample members. Another third of the list is added by the next two samples. Just 10 percent of the list consists of goods added in 1861, despite the fact that half of all our buyers were from that year. There was substantial change across the period, but the pattern is of evolution, not of a sudden and comprehensive transition. Because the 1850s are generally understood as "a decade of transformation," it is particularly significant that so many goods had appeared on the list by 1842, including all but two of the products bought by at least 10 percent of sample members (the exceptions are soda and rice, both added in 1851).[5] Upper Canadians were on the edge of the expanding world economy, but the timing of the appearance of new goods reminds us that they need to be seen within, not outside, it.[6]

As for the seldom-purchased goods found in appendix B, their presence indicates at least that they were available. Some, notably local goods, point to what clearly were substantial markets, but ones that mainly did not run through the general store. Others, perhaps especially the many that first appear in 1861, suggest nuances of choice and changes in fashion.[7]

Although there were variations among the stores, for example in the proportions of purchases attributable to the different lines of goods, all the stores sold goods in all categories (except medicines and drugs, which were not on the list in 1808–09). Because one common story of economic development focuses on specialization, stores' lack of specialization might seem to suggest simplicity and underdevelopment.[8] That would be misleading, however. What the pattern suggests is the value to the clientele of time and convenience. Many products came from specialized industrial producers, but for their markets the latter relied on a general distribution network. Department stores, when they appeared, continued this pattern. They gained economies of scale as urbanization and changing communications created very much larger markets, but they did not transform all shopping and they certainly did not eliminate smaller scale retailing. Indeed, one popular account extends the "golden age for general stores" well beyond the nineteenth century.[9]

One of our earliest findings was that almost no one bought everything from a single store. The only possible exceptions were a few people living near the store and having very tight relationships with the merchant as worker, supplier, or associate. Yet in almost every case, even these accounts prove, on close examination, not to have included all that such people likely bought. That merchants did not have monopolies confirms that the fundamental role of stores was to sell goods customers wanted.[10] As their long-term survival demonstrates, our stores were good at that, and well integrated in their settings. Of the seven stores, only Yonge Mills and Darling's had no immediately adjacent competition; the others were in villages large enough to sustain other retailers. Competition was, in any case, more than local; people could travel longer distances and shop in larger centres.

That customers were not confined to local stores is only one element in our argument that the frequent invocation of the difficulty and high costs of transportation as an explanatory strand in settlement history needs to be qualified. If the goods on our lists could get to the countryside, others could have done so too. The issue is not that physical constraints made goods unavailable; it is which goods were most worth having. A second issue is how they were to be brought to rural families – whether by a local merchant bringing them almost to the farm gate and artisan's shop door, or by the buyer going into (or ordering from) a larger town. Judging by the modesty of the accounts of those who might have been expected to be the largest consumers, the bourgeois families in our samples, the attractions of the latter were substantial.

Throughout the book we have drawn on accounts of many kinds for stories about goods and consumption in rural society. In the process, we have sometimes been led to question the emigrant guides, descriptions of colonial life, policy documents, and reminiscences that have shaped understandings of this society. For example, accounts from a metropolitan perspective or from hindsight may emphasize what was lacking. Others represent an elite perspective that is inappropriate for ordinary members of society. Read alongside such descriptive evidence, our lists suggest which stories are most likely to document actual experience. The lists also help us to see goods and processes that are invisible or incompletely captured in sources of other kinds, such as inventories and artifacts: the vast majority of the goods on the lists were transformed or disappeared in consumption.

Another source of information on imports is the trade figures that began to be published in 1850. Our data give a longer history to these official figures, a much more precise list of goods than the relatively undifferentiated categories used in the customs records, and a more specific sense of who bought what.[11] In turn, the import data serve as a check on the quality and implications of our data, allowing estimates of average per capita Canadian consumption and demonstrating that key products such as tea and tobacco were purchased in quantities that justify calling them goods of mass consumption (appendix C). At the same time, not many of our buyers exceeded the provincial averages, at least in what they bought from these stores.[12] Nor do these averages (less than

$4.00 per capita for all textiles and less than $1.50 for all iron and hardware in the early 1850s) seem especially high in terms of wage rates, prices for farm outputs, and indicators of per capita income in the period.

According to the best estimate, imports were equivalent to about one-quarter of Upper Canadian GDP, a proportion similar to that in colonial America.[13] As we saw in chapter 1, that rate can be construed in sharply contrasting ways. Our data suggest a balance among those interpretations. Upper Canada's reliance on the British economy for many everyday goods was at once substantial and not problematically costly. Imported fabrics, metal goods, sewing supplies, and crockery were important, as were a host of groceries, chemicals, and medications. Still, a key implication from a close focus on imports is that a great deal of what went into material life was locally produced. If much of this was produced within households for their own consumption, that was equally characteristic of the household economy of the rural world from which many emigrants came. Introducing the accounts of "a small-scale yeoman farmer" in eighteenth-century England, a participant in the most developed agricultural economy in the world in the midst of de Vries's "industrious revolution," Lorna Weatherill writes, "One of the most striking things about this household, and in this it was typical of others at the time, was the enormous amount of hard physical labour required to clothe, feed and maintain the family. This work was not done by an army of servants but by the family themselves with a little outside help."[14] At the same time, the place of artisans and mills in our communities demonstrates that households participated in and were sustained by many kinds of local market exchanges. We have caught glimpses of these processes; systematic study of documents focused on the local economy would reveal much more.

As the main chronological focus of Canadian historical research shifts ever farther forward in time, the settlement era can easily recede in historians' field of vision, becoming an abstract, timeless world "before" (for example, before markets or industrial capitalism or modernity).[15] This book offers a different perspective. By drawing on documents that directly recorded the purchases of some ordinary Upper Canadians, we have sought to see something of what Ian McKay has called (in another rural setting) their "complicated, difficult, interesting lives."[16] Like farm diaries, which historians have also begun to engage more deeply, country store accounts provide "rich details of everyday lives."[17] Without underestimating the contrast between rural Upper Canada and leading urban centres in and beyond the province, or between then and now, we can use these details to show that Upper Canadian men and women were consumers of goods that were modern in the context of their times. To do that, of course, they needed incomes.[18] Hence the importance of banishing Robinson Crusoe from Upper Canada.

Removing him does not, however, remove household production from the story of a developing farm and forest economy. Nothing in our findings calls its importance into question; as historians have shown, even as urbanization provided new possibilities for rural families to augment their incomes, it would be fundamental in rural Ontario (and elsewhere in Canada) far into the twentieth century. But as our long list of goods makes clear, household production should not be contrasted with market involvement.[19] It was wholly compatible with – in fact at all times required – deep engagement in the international world of goods.

TABLES

NOTE ON CURRENCY CONVERSION IN TABLES

Values at all stores until 1854, and for Darling's and Scovil's in 1861, are converted from Halifax currency (£1 = $4.00).

ABBREVIATIONS USED IN TABLES

STORES AND SAMPLES

YM08	Yonge Mills, 1808–09
YM28	Yonge Mills, 1828–29
T42	Tett, 1842
C51	Choate, 1851
F54	Fowlds, 1854
C61	Choate, 1861
F61	Fowlds, 1861
Sh61	Sherin, 1861
D61	Darling, 1861
Sc61	Scovil, 1861

OTHER ABBREVIATIONS

bbl	barrel
btl	bottle
bu	bushel
cult	cultivated
cwt	hundredweight (112 lbs)
dz	dozen
ft	foot
gal	gallon
hhold	household size
lb	pound
mo	month
n	number
oz	ounce
pc	piece
pkt	packet
ppr	paper
pr	pair
pt	pint
qt	quart
sk	skein
trans	transactions
val	value
vol	volume
yd	yard

Table 1
List of stores

Place	Township(s)	County(ies)	Proprietor	Period(s) studied
Yonge Mills	Yonge	Leeds	Charles Jones	1 Sept. 1808 – 31 Aug. 1809* 1 July 1828 – 30 June 1829
Newboro	North/South Crosby	Leeds	Benjamin Tett	1842
Warsaw	Dummer	Peterborough	Thomas Choate	1851*, 1861
Hastings	Asphodel Percy	Peterborough Northumberland	Fowlds Bros	1854 28 Jan. – 31 Dec. 1861*
Lakefield	Douro Smith	Peterborough	John Sherin	1861
Darlingside	Front of Leeds and Lansdowne	Leeds	Thomas Darling	1861
Portland	Bastard	Leeds	Samuel Scovil	1861

*Less than 12 months of data; see appendix D.

Table 2
Land occupation in principal sample townships, 1842, 1861

	Sample members in township					1842			1861		
	1808	1828	1842	1851/54	1861	Total area (000 acres)	Taken up (000 acres)	Proportion under culture	Occupied (000 acres)	Proportion under culture	Occupiers 50 or more acres N
Upper Canada							6,213	28%	13,355	45%	
Leeds County											
Yonge	41	45			1	60.6	38.2	39%	50.2	46%	341
Lansdowne & Leeds front					28	107.0	27.5	21%	46.2	39%	314
Escott					19	25.3	n/a		22.8	38%	158
Bastard			12		63	57.1	40.4	26%	48.1	50%	328
Crosby S			17		2	70.7	17.3	23%	28.0	34%	183
Crosby N			28		2	50.2	10.7	19%	27.6	32%	183
Northumberland County											
Percy				24	20	55.0	21.3	20%	46.8	44%	322
Peterborough County											
Asphodel				36	38	39.6	18.4	18%	35.0	47%	201
Dummer				44	47	73.0	21.3	23%	29.3	39%	199
Douro				15	62	41.0	24.0	18%	29.7	51%	244
Smith					21	61.2	32.5	30%	29.8	52%	182
Proportion of linked sample	87%	92%	100%	98%	92%	a	b	b	c	c	c

Sources:
(a) Armstrong, *Handbook of Upper Canadian Chronology*, 141–8.
(b) W.H. Smith, *Smith's Canadian Gazetteer*, 7, 10, 40, 46–9, 96, 144, 173, 224–5.
(c) Canada, *Census of 1860–1*, vol. 2. Land under culture = total of acreage in crops, pasture, and gardens.

Table 3
Aspects of samples and linkage

	Yonge Mills 1808		Yonge Mills 1828		Tett 1842		Choate 1851		Fowlds 1854		Choate 1861	
	Customers	Sample	Customers	Sample	Customers	Sample	Customers	Sample	Customers	Sample	Customers	Sample
Total	202	70	218	76	448	112	229	80	361	90	332	70
Linked	139	47	143	49	178	58	159	55	195	66	222	68
Unlinked	59	21	71	25	265	54	50	17	141	18	83	2
Unresolved duplicate names	4	2	4	2	5		23	8	25	6	27	2
Proportion linked	0.69		0.66		0.40		0.69		0.54		0.67	
Farm	86	29	89	37	124	30	125	35	125	32	149	38
Artisans					21	14	10	10	18	11	17	7
Labourers					8	2	13	4	33	13	22	7
Other nonfarm					10	6	6	4	14	7	16	7
No occupation					15	6	5	2	5	3	18	9
Total debits, sample customers		$2,565		$943		$1,589		$970		$3,377		$1,382
Top 10 accounts' share of debits		47%		41%		49%		40%		57%		49%
Unlinked in top 10		2		4		3		0		0		na
Farmers in top 10		5		5		2		8		5		6
Women with own accounts	4	1	5	2	42	23	16	16	4	4	16	6
Women in top half of sample (by value of purchases)						6		4		1		2
Largest account		$223		$53		$177		$56		$491		$151
10th largest account		$65		$23		$42		$27		$93		$41
Median account		$22		$9		$6		$8		$12		$12
25th percentile account		$9		$3		$1		$2		$4		$3
% in households of 7 or more	28%	30%	43%	41%	43%	42%	43%	41%	32%	36%	42%	35%
% farmers with 20 acres in crop	66%	59%	53%	54%	63%	67%	54%	51%	54%	42%		79%
	a		a		b, c				d, e			

Table 3 (cont'd)

	Fowlds 1861 Customers	Fowlds 1861 Sample	Sherin 1861 Customers	Sherin 1861 Sample	Darling 1861 Customers	Darling 1861 Sample	Scovil 1861 Customers	Scovil 1861 Sample
Total	715	74	206	59	166	57	491	107
Linked	424	71	138	59	124	47	351	85
Unlinked	250	3	41	0	31	7	82	14
Unresolved duplicate names	41		27		11	3	58	8
Proportion linked	0.59		0.67		0.75		0.71	
Farm	152	28	71	23	65	27	205	45
Artisans	59	23	16	12	9	5	33	16
Labourers	66	9	13	4	29	7	50	8
Other nonfarm	35	11	20	12	4	3	22	7
No occupation	112	0	18	8	17	5	41	9
Total debits, sample customers		$2,685		$2,265		$1,838		$1,915
Top 10 accounts' share of debits		66%		67%		59%		46%
Unlinked in top 10		na		na		0		0
Farmers in top 10		0		3		9		4
Women with own accounts	6	0	22	12	19	9	50	20
Women in top half of sample (by value of purchases)				3		2		8
Largest account		$310		$471		$202		$327
10th largest account		$85		$71		$65		$36
Median account		$6		$15		$14		$9
25th percentile account		$1		$3		$4		$2
% in households of 7 or more	46%	54%	37%	41%	52%	62%	45%	45%
% farmers with 20 acres in crop	75%	75%	66%	64%	83%	89%	82%	84%
	f, g, h, i		j		k			

Notes

See also discussion in appendix D.

No occupational data before 1842.

na = not applicable; see appendix D.

(a) For first two samples, farmers are defined as those with five or more acres cultivated.

(b) Lower linkage rate reflects lack of census manuscripts for Frontenac County.

(c) If 1842 census did not give any occupation and yet reported land in culture, we defined farmers as for 1808 and 1828.

(d) Count includes six sample customers at F54 who were found on agricultural census, although personal census with occupational designation is missing.

(e) Denominators exclude those with occupation of farmer or yeoman for whom we did not have information from agricultural schedules.

(f) See appendix D for explanation of very large number of customers.

(g) No agricultural census data available for three farmer customers; we count as farmers people with no occupation given but at least five acres in cultivation.

(h) Other occupations include two women who were reported as servants.

(i) Our sample actually included many more women but most proved to be part of household accounts. The unlinked accounts in the sample were all women.

(j) All eight with no occupation are women; for consistency with other samples, we treated occupational designations "wife," "widow," and "lady" as equivalent to no occupation.

(k) All nineteen women were included in the sample, but ten proved to be part of a family; see appendix D.

Table 4

Textile and related products purchases, ten sample summary

	YM08	YM28	T42	C51	F 54	C61
Buyers of any textile product (N)	61	58	80	57	56	53
Buyers of fabrics (N)	50	49	69	48	50	44
Buyers of 40 or more yds (N)	7	1	22	4	10	10
Varieties of fabrics bought (N)	19	23	38	26	30	32
Total yards bought by sample	952	525	2,071	679	1,314	979
Maximum yards by one buyer	73	40	139	54	259	84
Yards by 10 leading buyers	472	263	894	375	857	570
Median yards, buyers only	15	7	21	10	12	13
Most varieties by one buyer	10	8	16	9	14	12
Total value of fabrics bought	$684	$189	$565	$136	$436	$217
Maximum value, one buyer	$63	$26	$33	$12	$72	$21
Median value	$11	$2	$6	$2	$5	$3
Cotton as % of fabric values	46%	42%	53%	73%	39%	63%
Woolens as % of fabric values	38%	34%	33%	3%	39%	19%
All fabrics as % of all purchases	27%	20%	36%	14%	20%	16%
Buyers of ready-made clothing (N)	42	24	51	41	40	38
Total value of clothing bought	$101	$36	$90	$55	$228	$111
Buyers of notions (N)	54	46	67	50	43	43
Total value of notions bought	$84	$28	$93	$39	$63	$38
Buyers of dyes (N)	17	1	17	22	8	13
Total value all textile related	$869	$253	$748	$230	$727	$366
These values as % of all purchases	34%	27%	47%	24%	31%	26%

Notes:
Yardage includes estimates for some pieces.
Medians are according to distinct rankings by yardage, value.
Value of dyes excluded from total value because included in chemicals (table 21).
Denominator in calculating percentage of total values at F54 & F61 excludes debits from goods book.
See text for additional explanation.
Denominator for Scovil excludes storage and freight charges, mainly to one commercial customer, not a retail client.

Table 4 (cont'd)

	F61	Sh 61	D61	Sc61	totals
Buyers of any textile product (N)	46	48	52	74	585
Buyers of fabrics (N)	41	42	44	66	503
Buyers of 40 or more yds (N)	19	11	21	13	118
Varieties of fabrics bought (N)	44	33	32	31	
Total yards bought by sample	2,778	1,180	2,210	1,734	14,422
Maximum yards by one buyer	299	152	198	251	
Yards by 10 leading buyers	1,868	864	1,368	956	8,487
Median yards, buyers only	38	9	37	14	
Most varieties by one buyer	26	15	20	17	
Total value of fabrics bought	$877	$288	$411	$349	
Maximum value, one buyer	$90	$34	$42	$41	
Median value	$14	$3	$6	$3	
Cotton as % of fabric values	35%	45%	56%	52%	
Woolens as % of fabric values	46%	35%	22%	20%	
All fabrics as % of all purchases	35%	13%	22%	18%	
Buyers of ready-made clothing (N)	34	33	37	46	386
Total value of clothing bought	$205	$121	$144	$108	
Buyers of notions (N)	39	40	47	64	493
Total value of notions bought	$90	$56	$66	$72	
Buyers of dyes (N)	2	9	11	24	124
Total value all textile related	$1,172	$465	$621	$529	
These values as % of all purchases	47%	21%	34%	28%	

Table 5
Thomas Freel's textile and related purchases, September 1808 to May 1809

Date	Fabric	Yards	Val	Other product	Vol	Unit	Val
1 Sep.	cotton	5.00	$2.50				
	imitation	4.50	$3.15				
16 Sep.				shawl	2.00		$1.15
19 Sep.				thread	3.00	sk	$0.05
6 Oct.	flannel, red	10.00	$5.50	thread	1.00	bunch	$0.17
1 Nov.	cloth	3.50	$11.55	hat	1.00		$3.50
	sheeting, lancashire	1.50	$1.00	buttons	1.33	dz	$0.40
	sheeting, Russia	7.00	$6.30	needle & thread			$0.12
	velvet	0.75	$1.13	pins	1.00	ppr	$0.30
				silk	5.00	sk	$0.50
				twist	1.00		$0.08
				indigo	1.00	lb	$3.20
14 Nov.	cotton	3.13	$1.57				
28 Nov.	calico	1.00	$0.53	handkerchief	1.00		$2.50
				handkerchief	1.00		$1.10
				thread	4.00	sk	$0.08
1 Dec.	calico	0.50	$0.27	thread			$0.15
				blanket	1.00		$3.75
19 Dec.	calico (2 pieces)	10.25	$6.17	thread			$0.10
	cambric	1.00	$1.30				
	cotton	8.00	$3.20				
	linen	1.00	$0.95				
20 Dec.	cambric	0.75	$0.98	thread	4.00	sk	$0.10
	divinity	4.00	$2.93				
25 Dec.				needles			$0.03
27 Dec.				ribbon	1.50	yd	$0.20
				silk & thread			$0.17
31 Dec.	cambric	1.00	$1.30	gloves	1.00	pr	$0.60
	cotton	5.00	$2.00	hat	1.00		$0.45
				shawl, muslin	1.00		$1.00
4 Jan.	cloth	3.00	$8.40	buttons	1.00	dz	$0.33
	linen	1.00	$0.65	silk & twist			$0.40
9 Jan.				thimble			$0.03
10 Jan.	flannel	1.50	$1.20				
19 Jan.				thread			$0.13
21 Jan.				ribbon	3.50	yd	$3.97
30 Mar.				thread & needle			$0.12
10 May				carding for 1808			$0.46
Total		73.38	$62.57				$25.14
Total, all purchases on this account			$129.36				
Proportion of purchases, these goods			68%				

Table 6
Purchases of "luxury" fabrics at Yonge Mills, 1828–29

Buyer	Fabric	Date	Yards	Price	Value
James Avery	muslin	28 Feb.	0.50	$0.50	$0.25
Archibald Beaty	bombasine	27 Jun.	9.00	$0.47	$4.20
Bunel Burnham	bombtte	1 Jun.	7.25	$0.33	$2.42
	crape	1 Jun.	0.50	$1.50	$0.75
	silk, black	1 Jun.	1.00	$1.00	$1.00
Ann Graham	bombtte bomb.	12 Nov.	6.00	$0.33	$2.00
	bombarell	13 Nov.	0.75	$0.33	$0.25
	muslin	5 Mar.	0.50	$0.67	$0.33
Elisha Mallory	silk	22 Dec.	0.63	$1.00	$0.63
Phebe Murray	muslin	28 Mar.	0.50	$0.67	$0.33
James Redman	satinette	23 Feb.	1.00	$0.75	$0.75
Francis Russe	muslin	4 Jul.	0.25	$0.45	$0.12
	silk	23 Jul.	1.25	$1.40	$1.75
John Shipman	muslin	22 Dec.	0.75	$0.67	$0.50
	muslin	16 Feb.	1.00	$0.67	$0.67
Isaac Smith	silk, black	5 Dec.	2.00	$1.00	$2.00
	silk cloth	16 Feb.	0.50	$1.50	$0.75
William Webster	bombasine	22 Dec.	8.00	$0.45	$3.60
Totals			41.38		$22.30
Totals as percentage of all textiles purchased			8%		12%

Table 7
Purchases of textiles by three buyers, Tett's store, 1842

		Christopher Chant			Timothy Cavanagh			Richard & Robert Leach		
Product	Unit	Vol	Trans	Val	Vol	Trans	Val	Vol	Trans	Val
Textiles										
bagging	yd	4.0	1	$1.20						
canvas	yd				1.0	2	$0.30			
cloth	yd				1.5	1	$3.45	0.4	1	$1.93
cloth, H.M.	yd	1.8	1	$1.75						
cotton	yd	37.3	6	$6.01	69.8	7	$11.75	75.1	10	$10.78
flannel	yd	0.5	1	$0.20				7.0	2	$2.88
merino	yd	5.5	1	$2.57	1.5	1	$0.70			
moleskin	yd	5.5	3	$2.18						
muslin	yd	7.0	2	$3.60				1.0	1	$0.33
nett	yd				0.5	1	$0.13			
osnaburg	yd	1.3	1	$0.23				1.3	1	$0.23
print	yd	38.0	8	$6.98	4.0	1	$0.43			
shirting	yd	15.5	7	$2.19	0.5	1	$0.06	5.5	2	$1.00
Silesia lining	yd	4.0	1	$0.50						
silk, black	yd				1.0	1	$1.10			
stripe	yd	7.8	3	$2.33				3.5	1	$0.78
velvet	yd	1.0	1	$0.50	0.3	1	$0.13			
vesting	yd	9.5	2	$2.85	0.8	1	$0.23			
saxony	yd							2.5	2	$1.00
Total	yd	138.5		$33.09	80.8		$18.28	96.3		$18.93
Total days (all products)			30			11			13	

Table 7 (cont'd)

Product	Unit	Christopher Chant			Timothy Cavanagh			Richard & Robert Leach		
		Vol	Trans	Val	Vol	Trans	Val	Vol	Trans	Val
Other sewing supplies										
binding	yd, pc		4	$0.80		1	$0.05		1	$0.20
bobbins	bunch	1	1	$0.03						
button	dz	2.5	2	$0.25	3.3	3	$0.45	8.0	3	$0.85
cord	sk	1	1	$0.05						
cotton	ball	25	4	$0.21				6.0	2	$0.05
cotton	spool	1	1	$0.03						
darner	n	4	2	$0.03						
edging	yd	6	1	$0.15				4.0	1	$0.10
hook & eye	box, dz		5	$0.22		1	$0.04		.	
insertion	yd	1	1	$0.07	2	1	$0.13	3.0	1	$0.10
lace	yd	7.5	2	$0.75		1	$0.60	2.0	1	$0.20
lace, stay	n	5	3	$0.04						
laces	pr	3	3	$0.10		1	$0.03		3	$0.40.
lining	yd	1.5	1	$0.19						
needle	n, ppr		2	$0.27					1	$0.03
padding	yd				2	3	$0.60			
pins	oz, sheet, row		6	$0.25					1	$0.08
quilling	yd	5	2	$0.27				6.0	1	$0.25
ribbon	yd	4.25	2	$0.16	1	1	$0.05	10.0	5	$0.37
silk	sk				4	2	$0.27			
size stick	n				1	1	$0.40			
spool	n	11	10	$0.53	5	4	$0.27	8.0	5	$0.45
tape	yd, pc		6	$0.42	1.5	1	$0.02			
thimble	n	5	5	$0.15						
thread	oz, sk, ball, hank	2		$0.13		7	$0.85		4	$0.46
twist	yd				4.5	3	$0.30			
yarn, cotton	lb				2.9	1	$0.96			
Total				$5.10			$5.02			$3.54
Total days (all products)			58			22			25	

Table 8
Wool cloth making and buying, eight samples

	T42	C51	F54	C61	F61	Sh61	D61	Sc61	Totals
Landowners in sample (N)	42	40	37	49	31	26	35	52	312
Those owning sheep (%)	81	90	59	80	87	77	74	63	76
Sheep owners making cloth (%)	85	86	86	64	70	55	88	88	78
Others making wool cloth (N)	2	1	4	2	0	0	1	6	16
All woolen makers (N)	31	32	23	27	19	11	24	35	202
Cloth makers buying fabrics (%)	81	75	52	59	37	55	88	69	73
Makers of 40 + yards (N)	11	15	9	11	8	2	9	16	81
Makers buying 40 + yards (N)	7	1	4	3	3	2	12	3	35
Makers buying 10 - 39 yards (N)	12	13	5	8	1	1	7	9	56
Total sheep owned (N)	460	468	223	499	400	262	292	395	2,999
Total yards of wool cloth produced	1,098	1,245	832	876	785	282	779	1,613	7,510
Average yards/maker	35	39	36	32	41	26	32	46	37
Total yards purchased by makers	664	383	623	350	209	121	1,407	459	4,216

Notes: a   b, c

Data on textiles made and sheep owned are not available for 1808, 1828 samples.
Based on agricultural census schedules landowners include people whose census occupation was not farmer.
Very small landholdings omitted.
Linen making (very small quantities only) omitted.
(a) Two makers, discussed in text, account for 64% of yards bought.
(b) Accounts include carding and fulling for five clients not reported as makers in agricultural census.
(c) Six makers have debits for carding and fulling.

Table 9
Purchases of textiles by two leading buyers, Fowlds's store, 1854

		Edward Oakes			Michael Hoolihan		
		Vol yd	Trans	Val	Vol yd	Trans	Val
Cambric		10.5	3	$1.53	1.0	1	$0.10
Canvas					0.5	1	$0.15
Cloth		20.8	6	$17.28	7.8	2	$7.63
Cotton	*	105.0	12	$15.28	50.5	11	$5.20
Drill	**	2.5	1	$0.50	8.0	3	$3.01
Flannel		6.5	2	$3.55			
Linen		5.0	1	$1.25			
Moleskin	*	15.0	1	$9.00			
Muslin	*	2.0	1	$0.60	2.0	1	$0.60
Nett					0.5	1	$0.15
Orleans		7.0	1	$2.63			
Plaid					1.5	1	$0.80
Print	*	34.5	9	$6.70	38.0	5	$6.90
Satinette		3.0	1	$3.75	3.3	2	$4.07
Steam loom	*	6.0	1	$1.11			
Stripe	*	36.0	4	$7.20	39.0	6	$7.80
Ticking	*	5.0	1	$1.25			
Total		258.8	25	$71.63	152.0	22	$36.41
Total cotton		203.5		$41.14	129.5		$20.50
Total varieties		14			11		

Notes:
* Indicates cotton fabric.
** In each case some or perhaps all drill was explicitly cotton.
For consistency with appendix A, however, drill is not included in cotton count.
Total transactions counts multiple purchases on a single day as one transaction.

Table 10
Purchases of principal dyes at Scovil's store, 1861

	Unit	Vol	Buyers
Indigo	oz	37	13
Madder	lb	12	9
Logwood	lb	9	12
Total buyers, these 3 products			24
Total value of these dyes		$8.45	
Textiles purchased by these buyers	yds	895	23
Cloth made by these buyers	yds	553	
Number of buyers who made cloth			11

Table 11
Piece sizes of fabrics purchased

	Total pieces	
Yards	cotton	other
<1	200	239
1 @ 2.9	998	675
3 @ 4.9	441	235
5 @ 8.9	500	184
9 @ 11.9	127	33
12 @ 14.9	42	14
15 or more	84	6
Unknown	9	9
Total	2,401	1,395
Share under 3 yds	50%	66%

Notes:
Judging by values, unknown pieces were generally small.

Table 12
Grocery purchases (including medicines), ten-sample summary

	YM08	YM28	T42	C51	F54	C61	F61	Sh61	D61	Sc61	Total buyers
Tea											
volume (lbs)	99	101	56	136	214	112	321	174	169	194	
buyers	48	48	17	52	36	37	35	28	33	56	390
buyers in 4 or more months	11	16	4	17	15	12	16	11	13	23	
transactions of 2 or more lbs	5	0	1	2	16	5	22	19	11	4	
value	$153	$100	$56	$101	$174	$107	$286	$154	$140	$166	
Tobacco											
volume (lbs)	142	91	130	85	167	112	255	82	131	120	
buyers	34	48	42	42	41	29	35	19	30	52	372
buyers in 4 or more months	8	12	14	7	11	15	17	7	12	18	
transactions of 2 or more lbs	21	2	4	2	16	7	21	7	4	7	
value	$70	$23	$34	$29	$58	$36	$111	$26	$43	$45	
Sugar											
volume (lbs)	212	152	130	104	257	398	165	438	1064	356	
buyers	33	13	16	20	29	33	19	29	35	36	263
buyers in 4 or more months	5	0	3	4	4	12	0	8	13	3	
transactions of 5 or more lbs	10	5	5	1	18	17	11	20	86	14	
value	$42	$16	$17	$13	$31	$43	$21	$48	$101	$41	
Value of these 3 groceries	$265	$139	$107	$143	$263	$186	$418	$228	$284	$252	
These 3 as proportion of all groceries	41%	62%	58%	69%	74%	70%	80%	63%	71%	61%	

Table 12 (cont'd)

	YM08	YM28	T42	C51	F54	C61	F61	Sb61	D61	Sc61	Total buyers
Salt											
buyers	18	20	12	20	9	16	9	16	19	39	178
value	$35	$23	$9	$17	$15	$8	$5	$9	$22	$67	
Medical products											
buyers	0	23	47	43	26	36	32	20	10	46	283
value		$8	$26	$22	$20	$39	$39	$13	$5	$41	
Total, all groceries	$653	$223	$186	$208	$357	$269	$521	$363	$399	$410	
Groceries as share of all debits	25%	24%	12%	22%	15%	19%	21%	16%	22%	21%	
					a	b	a, c				

Notes:

Medical products are those listed as "Groceries: drugs and medicines" in appendices A and B.

Sugar volumes and buyers include maple sugar at YM28, T42, C51, D61, and Sc61; values of maple sugar are included in table 27.

Tobacco values and transactions include plugs (not counted in volumes however).

Whiskey is not included in grocery totals; as a local product it is reported in table 27.

(a) Denominator for excludes "goods book" debits.

(b) Includes estimates of values when volumes are known.

(c) Sugar purchases were very limited at F61; also, many transactions were not extended and only some values could be estimated.

Table 13
Imports of principal groceries, two Jones stores, 1808

Commodity	Variety	Vol lbs	Price	Note
Sugar				
	muscovado	1,700	$0.08	
	bright raw	325	$0.12	
	loaf	878	$0.14	
	total	2,903		
Tea				
	single	234	$0.90	
	souchong	71	$0.90	
	green	71	$0.95	
	hyson skin	467	$0.95	a
	unspecified	69	$0.95	
	total	912		
Tobacco				
	plug	531	$0.20	b
	pigtail	439	$0.13	
	total	970		

Source: 1808 import invoices; see appendix D.
Notes:
(a) 1 chest $1.05
(b) Some @ $0.26

Table 14
Alcohol purchases at Yonge Mills, 1808–09 and 1828–29, by product

	1808-09			1828-29		
	Buyers	Vol qts	Val	Buyers	Vol qts	Val
Brandy	11	31	$16	16	28	$13
Rum	49	560	$236	25	89	$22
Spirits	29	157	$71	1	4	$1
Wine	7	11	$7	8	9	$7
Whiskey	10	69	$29	50	685	$90
Total	54	828	$359	56	815	$133
Alcohol's share of all purchases		14%			14%	

Notes:
Many buyers bought more than one kind of alcohol.
Volumes in other units converted to quarts.

Table 15
Alcohol purchases at Yonge Mills, 1808–09 and 1828–29, by month

	1808–09						1828–29					
	≥ 8 qts		4 @ 6 qts	1 @ 3 qts	Total	Proportion	≥ 8 qts		4 @ 6 qts	1 @ 3 qts	Total	Proportion
	trans N	vol qts	vol qts	vol qts	vol qts	8 or more	trans N	vol qts	vol qts	vol qts	vol qts	8 or more
July	na						7	66	16	50	132	50%
Aug	na						3	28	38	55	121	23%
Sept	3	41	44	86	171	24%	3	47	32	22	101	47%
Oct	1	12	13	58	83	14%	–		4	21	25	0%
Nov	2	18	9	68	95	19%	1	16	22	23	61	26%
Dec	3	32	18	42	92	35%	2	16	24	17	57	28%
Jan	–		10	22	32	0%	–		12	25	37	0%
Feb	1	8	4	34	46	17%	1	12	8	30	50	24%
Mar	–		12	41	53	0%	–		18	34	52	0%
Apr	1	10	14	38	62	16%	1	8	8	8	24	33%
May	1	24	8	23	55	44%	6	70	12	40	122	57%
June	–			27	27	0%	–		18	15	33	0%
July	–		4	9	13	0%	na					
Aug	1	12	30	57	99	12%	na					
Total	13	157	166	505	828	19%	24	263	212	340	815	32%

Table 16
Alcohol purchases by leading customers, 1808–09 and 1828–29, weekly pattern

	Acres cult	Rank	Total debits	Alcohol debits	Kinds	Total vol	Vol in purchases of 2 gal +	Buy 2+ qts in weeks	Total alcohol weeks	Total weeks	Note
					N	qt	qt	N	N	N	
1808–09											
J & S Andrews	2	1	$220.40	$34.00	5	78	24	13	26	44	
Peter Cronk	10	2	$198.40	$28.00	4	62	22	9	17	25	
Henry Jones	nl	15	$52.40	$21.00	3	55	20	9	11	25	
Jeremiah Chichigran	nl	5	$106.80	$18.00	3	40	0	7	28	38	e
Samuel Tollman	0	3	$137.40	$17.60	4	37	8	7	11	18	
Daniel Patterson	0	27	$35.60	$15.20	3	36	0	10	21	29	e
Henry Plum	5	14	$55.20	$15.80	4	36	0	10	19	25	e
Caleb Seaman Jr	7	6	$104.40	$12.80	2	35	29	3	4	9	
Silah Robins	16	9	$72.80	$13.60	2	33	8	7	10	17	e
Calvin Patterson	nl	7	$96.80	$13.00	3	29	0	8	13	27	e
Joseph Christmas	nl	16	$50.40	$13.20	3	29	0	6	16	18	e
Total			$1,130.60	$202.20		470	111				

Table 16 (cont'd)

	Acres cult	Rank	Total debits	Alcohol debits	Kinds	Total vol	Vol in purchases of 2 gal +	Buy 2+ qts in weeks	Total alcohol weeks	Total weeks	Note
					N	qt	qt	N	N	N	
1828–29											
James Adams	na	9	$28.20	$9.60	5	53	32	6	12	19	
Antoine Busea	nl	2	$52.00	$7.40	2	45	16	4	6	21	
Benjamin Warren	pl	5	$21.20	$5.40	2	37	8	7	12	15	e
Francis Russe	nl	12	$38.00	$5.40	2	37	8	6	18	35	
A. Thomson	na	38	$9.20	$4.20	1	34	8	6	7	7	
Harmon Guild	0	23	$14.80	$4.20	2	31	24	5	6	13	
Elisha Mallory	6	3	$46.00	$5.00	3	31	8	7	11	28	
Peter Trickey	92	30	$11.40	$5.20	2	31	27	2	2	6	
Bunel Burnham	10	18	$18.60	$5.20	3	30	0	8	11	17	
James Brown	0	32	$11.00	$4.00	3	27	0	10	16	28	e
Total	a	b	$250.40	$55.60	c	356	131			d	

Notes:

In 1808–09, there were four other purchases of 2+ gallons, by three further buyers.
In 1828–29, there were eleven other purchases of 2 + gallons, by ten other buyers.
(a) na = not applicable, nl = not linked, pl = uncertain linkage (more than one of same name in the documents).
(b) Rank is by total debits.
(c) Kinds = rum, spirits, whiskey, brandy, wine.
(d) Total weeks excludes weeks with only financial or credit transactions.
(e) Customers with one or a few weeks with debits for "balance on" alcohol, volume unknown. Because full value of the purchase is not known, we do not include the value of these transactions in column for alcohol debits.

Table 17

Large volume grocery purchases, selected, 1861

Buyer	Store	Product	Vol lbs	Date	Price per lb	Total val
David Rose	F61	tea	60.0	9 Feb.	$0.80	$48.00
		tea	10.0	13 May	$0.80	$8.00
		tobacco	20.0	28 Jan.	$0.30	$6.00
		tobacco	14.0	18 Feb.	$0.30	$4.20
		sugar	20.0	9 Feb.	$0.13	$2.50
Andy Orr	F61	tobacco	32.0	9 Feb.	$0.30	$9.60
		tobacco	13.5	25 Feb.	$0.40	$5.40
		tobacco	13.5	26 Feb.	$0.40	$5.40
George Shields	Sh61	tea	14.0	1 Mar.	$0.80	$11.20
		tea	12.0	19 Oct.	$1.10	$13.20
		sugar	36.0	6 Sep.	$0.08	$3.00
		sugar	15.0	12 Sep.	$0.10	$1.50
Charles Watley	Sh61	tea	10.0	26 Jan.	$0.80	$8.00
		tea	4.0	2 Aug.	$0.80	$3.20
		tea	4.0	7 Aug.	$1.00	$4.00
Percy Warren	Sh61	coffee	6.0	1 Nov.	$0.25	$1.50
		coffee	30.0	3 Dec.	$0.25	$7.50

Table 18

"Branded" medications, selected, 1828–61

	Stores N
Pills	
Ayres	3
Brandrith's	2
Clarke's	1
Coit's	1
Cooper's	3
Lees	1
Moffat's	2
Morse's	1
Radway's	1
Other	
Bryant's wafers	1
Brockway's salve	1
Godfrey's cordial	4
Moffat's bitters	1
RRR (Radway's Ready Relief)	3
Turlington's balsam	2

Note:.
Most entries for pills, balsam, etc. did not specify a "brand."

Table 19
Repeat purchases of medications, selected, 1851, 1861

Buyer	Store	Product	Quantity	Unit	Date
James Kidd	C51	pills	1	box	16 Jan.
		pills (Brandrith's)	1	box	5 Feb.
		pills (Brandrith's)	4	box	7 Feb.
		pills (Brandrith's)	2	box	21 Aug.
		pain extractor	1	box	13 Sep.
James Quinn	C61	pills	1	box	29 Jan.
		pills	1	box	21 Mar.
		pills	1	box	28 Jun.
		pills	1	box	13 Jul.
		pills	1	box	25 Jul.
		pills	1	box	10 Aug.
		pills	1	box	30 Aug.
		pills, ayres	1	box	16 Sep.
Robert Gutridge	Sc61	Balsam Life	2	vial	14 Mar.
		Balsam	6	vial	5 Jul.
		Balsam, Turlington's	2	vial	9 Jul.
		Balsam, Turlington's	6	vial	20 Jul.
		Balsam, Turlington's	4	vial	22 Aug.
		Balsam life, large	1	btl	21 Nov.
Eb Heath	Sc61	Balsam	1	vial	23 Jan.
		Balsam, Turlington's	1	vial	2 Mar.
		Balsam, Turlington's	2	vial	7 Mar
		Balsam, Turlington's	2	vial	3 Oct.
		Balsam, Turlington's	2	vial	16 Oct.
		Balsam, Turlington's	2	vial	22 Nov.
		Balsam, Turlington's	1	vial	10 Dec.
		Balsam, Turlington's	2	vial	13 Dec.
Note on prices:					
		pills	$0.25		
		balsam in vials	$0.13		
		balsam, bottle	$1.40		

Table 20
Grocery buying and making, some indicators, ten sample summary

	YM08	YM28	T42	C51	F54	C61	F61	Sh61	D61	Sc61	Totals
Sugar											
Makers (N)	na	na	25	21	19	24	18	10	13	31	161
% of farmers making	na	na	63%	49%	45%	45%	61%	42%	41%	63%	51%
Total made (lbs)	na	na	2,454	1,307	1,510	3,615	3,547	832	1,113	3,365	17,743
Makers buying (N)			4	2	4	11	3	7	9	12	52
Total bought (lbs)			12	17	88	84	32	37	478	62	810
Other buyers (N)			12	18	25	22	16	23	26	24	166
Total bought (lbs)			118	83	169	314	133	401	586	296	2,100
Total bought by all	212	146	130	100	257	398	165	438	1,064	354	3,264
Candles											
Buyers of wick (N)	2	2	5	9	4	10	3	11	13	16	75
Buyers of candles (N)	0	1	6	2	8	2	11	14	11	12	67
Buyers of both (N)	0	0	2	0	2	0	2	3	5	5	19
Farmer buyers (N)	0	0	2	1	3	0	0	2	9	3	20
Soap											
Buyers (N)	0	9	24	12	16	17	17	19	10	16	140
Farmer buyers (N)		5	6	8	11	9	3	8	9	5	64
	a	a	a					a	a		

Notes:

Not all makers were listed as farmers in census.

(a) At these stores, some sugar purchases were explicitly recorded as maple sugar.

Table 21
Hardware and chemical purchases, ten sample summary

	YM08	YM28	T42	C51	F54	C61	F61	Sb61	D61	Sc61	Total
Values											
all hardware	$174	$80	$141	$199	$137	$226	$173	$568	$236	$265	
all chemicals	$34	$3	$37	$17	$13	$28	$10	$87	$8	$46	
Buyers (N)											
of any hardware product	54	48	61	55	50	47	40	37	37	59	488
of any chemical product	34	10	44	39	18	29	19	31	22	47	293
Buyers of selected products (N)											
gunshot, gunpowder, other gun	35	15	22	22	11	12	8	8	12	10	155
nails	23	29	36	33	30	28	25	24	21	29	278
glass	15	6	4	10	4	12	7	8	5	11	82
Hardware and chemicals as % of total debits	8%	9%	11%	22%	6%	18%	7%	29%	13%	16%	
Proportion buying hardware &/or chemicals	81%	64%	68%	71%	62%	69%	55%	68%	67%	61%	
Proportion buying something gun-related	50%	20%	22%	28%	13%	17%	11%	14%	21%	9%	
			a		b		b				

Notes:

(a) Denominator is the 102 who bought something; another 10 did not.
(b) Denominator for share of total debits excludes goods book debits.

Table 22
Varieties of nails and iron

Product	1st year	Stores (N)
Nails		
nails	1808	10
shingle	1808	8
cut	1828	8
brass	1828	2
horse	1842	8
wrought	1842	7
rose	1842	1
pressed	1854	4
clout	1861	2
boat	1861	1
Iron		
iron	1808	10
english	1828	1
cutter/sleigh	1851	2
horse shoe	1851	3
round	1861	2
hoop	1861	2
swedish	1861	2
stirrup	1861	1
tire	1861	1
bar	1861	1
scotch	1861	1
band	1861	1
wagon	1861	1

Table 23
Leading nail buyers, selected, 1842–61

Name	Occupation	Store	Type	Vol lbs	Trans	Other vol	Other trans	Total vol	Total trans	Total value	Other type(s)
Stephen McCathron	tanner	T42	cut	68	3	16	2	84	3	$7.27	a
Robert Plunkett	carpenter	F54	cut	71	4			71	4	$5.88	
James Brough	employee	F54	cut	70	7	1	1	71	7	$5.92	b
Thomas Brough	clerk	F54	cut	73	1			73	1	$6.08	
John Driscol	shoemaker	F54	cut	54	2			54	2	$4.50	
John Sharpe	merchant	F61	cut	160	18			160	18	$9.50	
Thomas Hunt	farmer	D61	cut	50	1	1	1	51	2	$2.63	c
Isaac Errott	farmer	D61	cut	50	2			50	2	$2.50	
William Kyle	sawyer/framer	Sc61	cut	60	2	20	1	80	2	$4.00	d
William Cotton	carpenter	Sh61	cut	806	6			806	6	$40.47	
A. Morrow	merchant	Sh61	cut	800	30	50	1	850	31	$42.47	d
Kenneth Urquhart	tailor	Sh61	cut	292	7	21	2	313	8	$15.66	d
John Hubbard	blacksmith	T42	horseshoe	9	4	76	5	85	9	$8.71	e
Thomas Pomeroy	blacksmith	F54	horseshoe	29	1			29	1	$7.23	
Thomas Pomeroy	blacksmith	F61	horseshoe	92	6	45	10	137	16	$31.40	f
Daniel Dwyer	blacksmith	C61	horseshoe	43	41	2	1	45	42	$11.68	g
John Grant	blacksmith	Sc61	horseshoe	6	2	39	12	45	14	$4.60	h
George Shields	blacksmith	Sh61	horseshoe	150	2	41	11	191	13	$35.53	i

Notes:

Trans = number of days with transactions in this product; often more than one type was purchased at same time.

Many transactions in nails at Sherin's were recorded simply as "nails"; for most, cut is assumed, on basis of standard price.

Many transactions at F61 are incompletely entered; some types, volumes, or values are estimated based on standard prices.

One entry for Thomas Pomeroy in 1861 is incorrect in terms either of volume or value; to avoid overestimating volume, we assumed value was correct.

Notes on "other" types:

(a) shingle (11 lbs), rose (5 lbs)

(b) unspecified (more expensive than cut)

(c) pressed

(d) shingle

(e) cut (72 lb), rose (0.5 lb), and shingle (3 lb)

(f) cut (c 34 lb), wrought (c 9 lb), and clout (c 2 lb) (see note)

(g) unspecified (likely cut)

(h) cut (27 lb), wrought (5 lb), clout (4 lb), shingle (3 lb)

(i) unspecified (likely cut) (38 lbs), pressed (2 lb) and wrought (1 lb).

Table 24
Leading iron buyers, selected, 1851–61

Name	Occupation	Store	Vol	Trans	Total	Note
			lbs		value	
Edward Kennedy	blacksmith	C51	312	7	na	a
Daniel Dwyer	blacksmith	C61	113	19	$5.64	b
George Shields	blacksmith	Sh61	6,359	5	$259.29	
Thomas Pomeroy	blacksmith	F61	1,100	6	$61.00	c,d
David Latimer	farmer	D61	1,800	2	$89.86	e
John Grant	blacksmith	Sc61	2,341	36	$108.07	f
Eb Heath	cooper	Sc61	175	4	$8.70	
James Ireland	blacksmith	Sc61	141	1	$6.97	
Miles Lockwood	blacksmith	Sc61	114	1	$5.13	

Notes:

(a) Values not given for Kennedy; others here paid 4¢ or 5¢ per pound.

(b) Dwyer volumes estimated from values and vice versa, based on standard price of 5¢/lb.

(c) Pomeroy was the only iron buyer from Fowlds in 1854, a single purchase of 48 pounds, worth $4.50.

(d) In 1861 Pomeroy also bought two bars of iron, weight not recorded. Other volumes estimated from values or vice versa.

(e) Value for Latimer is for invoice from Montreal supplier; volume estimate assumes a price of 5¢ per pound.

(f) Grant's purchases included the following (lbs):

"iron"	746
tire	575
scotch	281
horseshoe	200
round	173
band	130
Swede	118
sleigh	59
Scot square	50
hoop	9

Table 25
Purchases of gun related products, ten sample summary

	Trans all	Powder lbs	canisters	Shot lbs	Balls lbs	Flints N	Caps box	Other products	Buyers in 10 largest accounts
YM08	68	21.50		54.8	10.5	53		lead	9
YM28	17	4.25	1	8.0		1		lead, gun lock	3
T42	35	15.00	1	35.0		29	2	lead	5
C51	31	7.50		19.5		2	4	gun	5
F54	14	6.00		3.0			8		4
C61	17	3.50	1	12.0			5	guns, lead	4
F61	9	1.50		11.0			5		2
Sh61	12	4.50	1	5.3			8	powder flask	3
D61	30	9.00		19.5			8	gun	4
Sc61	11	3.50		5.0			6		5
Total, 4 main stores	164	53.00	1	128.8	10.5	84	14		23
Proportion at 4 main	67%	70%	25%	74%	100%	99%	30%		52%
Total, all stores	244	76.25	4	173.1	10.5	85	46		44

Notes:
Italicized entries signify principal stores for gun-related sales; see text.
Some volumes estimated on basis of values.
Purchases of more than one product by a customer on one day
counted as one transaction.

Table 26
Estimated rounds fired (number of buyers in each range)

	Unknown	1 @ 24	25 @ 47	48 @ 71	72 or more	Total	Unknown purchased
YM08	1	1	9	12	12	35	flint
YM28	2	3	7	2	1	15 a	flint, gun lock
T42	6	1	7	2	6	22 a	flints, caps
C51	3	2	11	4	2	22	flints, caps
F54	3	3	1	3	1	11 a	caps
C61	1	3	4	2	2	12	gun
F61	1	1	4	0	2	8	caps
Sh61	2	0	2	1	3	8 a	caps
D61	1	2	4	2	3	12	caps
Sc61	3	0	5	2	0	10	caps
Totals	23	16	54	30	32	155	

Notes:
Maximum rounds per customer estimated by volume of powder and/or shot.
  0.25 lb powder = 1,750 grains or about 16 rounds of 110 grains.
  1 lb shot = 7,000 grains or about 32 rounds of 220 grains.
If shot and powder estimates differ, the higher is used here.
Most estimates are multiples of 16: thus, ranges focus on 16, 32, 64, 96.
Unknown includes eight who bought only flints, twelve only caps.
To ensure that gun use is not underestimated, lead purchases in 1808–09 are assumed to have been used for shot.
(a) Includes purchasers of 2 lbs or 1 canister of powder but no other product.
      (two at Tett & Sherin, one at YM28 and F54)

Table 27
Local goods and services purchases, ten sample summary

	YM08	YM28	T42	C51	F54	C61	F61	Sb61	D61	Sc61	Totals
Value of all local produce and services	$553	$300	$230	$161	$870	$63	$327	$488	$220	$327	
Buyers of any product or service (N)	39	63	43	45	46	20	44	30	21	52	403
Buyers, selected products (N)											
boards	14	6	9	17	30	5	7	4		1	93
flour	10	15	5	2	14		21	3	3	5	78
pork	10	3	6		6	1	13	14	4	6	63
butter		2	4	4	4	3	7	15	4	7	50
whiskey	10	50	4								64
Buyers, selected services (N)											
carding &/or fulling	13	1		30			12				56
postage			26	2	6	1	30			28	93
All local as % of total debits	22%	32%	14%	17%	37%	5%	13%	22%	12%	17%	
Proportion of sample buying something local	56%	83%	42%	56%	46%	29%	59%	51%	37%	49%	
	a	a, b	a, b, c, d	b, e	f		f, g, h		b	b	

Notes:

These figures exclude fish (see chapter 4).
(a) Includes N of buyers and value of whiskey (discussed in chapter 4).
(b) Includes maple sugar (see also table 12).
(c) Includes one buyer (Buist) in the counts but excludes the value of his transactions from total values (see text and table 29).
(d) Includes produce lent transactions for three customers (see text for discussion).
(e) Includes eighteen buyers for whom value of transactions was unknown; other values are incomplete. Thus total value is low.
(f) Denominator for proportion of value excludes goods book debits.
(g) Includes ten buyers for whom value of transactions is entirely unknown; for many others, values are incomplete (see text).
(h) Total value does not include estimates for transactions recorded only by volume; if they were valued, local debits would exceed 25 percent.

Table 28

Local goods purchases, principal buyers, five samples
(total account and selected products)

	Occupation	Hhold	Acres cult	Account rank	Produce % of acc't	Produce (all)	Boards
YM08							
J. & S. Andrews		5	2	1	43%	$94	$3
Peter Cronk		5	10	2	39%	$77	
Samuel Tollman		5	0	3	67%	$91	
Jeremiah Chichigran	cooper	nl*		5	40%	$42	$1
Caleb Seaman Jr		6	7	6	53%	$55	
John Cain		12	7	11	49%	$31	$3
YM28							
Antoine Busea		nl*		2	50%	$29	
James Avery		7	30	4	27%	$12	
Francis Russe		nl*		5	47%	$18	
Benjamin James		nl*		6	75%	$28	$10
John Shipman		7	30	7	82%	$29	$7
James Adams		5		9	48%	$13	$1
T42							
John Hubbard	blacksmith	7		2	50%	$86	$47
F54							
Robert Plunkett	carpenter	7		1	31%	$153	$80
Edward Oakes	yeoman	12	35	2	35%	$111	$2
William Lobb	farmer	8	30	4	16%	$34	$32
John Driscol	shoemaker	4		5	35%	$47	$41
James Brough	employee	**		6	50%	$76	$29
John Plunkett	labourer	1		9	37%	$35	
Thomas Brough	clerk	**		10	59%	$55	$51
Sc61							
Eb Heath	cooper	9		1	48%	$157	

Notes:
*nl = not linked.   **See text for discussion of Broughs.

Table 28 (cont'd)

	Flour mo	Flour val	Pork mo	Pork val	Butter mo	Butter val	Main other product	val
YM08								
J. & S. Andrews	1	$8	3	$45			cow	$17
Peter Cronk	1	$2	1	$4			oxen	$65
Samuel Tollman	2	$18	2	$33			hay	$12
Jeremiah Chichigran	9	$22	8	$11			beef	$2
Caleb Seaman Jr			1	$30			wheat	$22
John Cain	3	$25					carding	$2
YM28								
Antoine Busea	4	$18	2	$2	2	$1	whiskey	$4
James Avery			1	$9			whiskey	$2
Francis Russe	2	$3	5	$8	2	$1	whiskey	$4
Benjamin James	4	$14					eggs	$2
John Shipman	1	$19					blacksmith	$2
James Adams	2	$4					whiskey	$6
T42								
John Hubbard	4	$12	2	$14	4	$6	oats	$3
F54								
Robert Plunkett	9	$49	1	$16			beef	$4
Edward Oakes	7	$87	3	$18	1		beef	$3
William Lobb								
John Driscol							freight	$6
James Brough	5	$16	4	$25	2	$1		
John Plunkett							horse	$35
Thomas Brough	1	$4			1			
Sc61								
Eb Heath	9	$21	8	$25	8	$22	house rental	$30

Table 29
Local goods charged to Alexander Buist, 1842

Commodity	Mo	Val	Vol	Unit
Pork	11	$287.40	24	bbl
Flour	12	$168.57	5,053	lb
Oats	5	$139.49	462	bu
Hay	2	$46.40	5	ton
Potatoes	5	$27.75	93	bu
Peas	7	$5.40		bu, lb, gal
Whiskey	5	$3.00	6	gal
Beans	2	$2.70		bu, lb
Butter	2	$2.08	19	lb
Tallow	2	$2.02	15	lb
Apples	1	$1.40	3	bu
Keg	1	$1.00		
Boards	1	$0.72	119	ft
Bran	1	$0.22	60	lb
Total		$688.15		

Table 30
Estimated values, unpriced produce purchases, Fowlds's store, 1861

Product	Volume	Unit	Standard price	Total value
Flour	150	hundred pounds	$3.00	$450
Pork	11.5	barrels	$14.00	$161
Pork	1,124	pounds	7.8¢	$88
Beef	1,858	pounds	6.3¢	$115
Butter	272	pounds	13¢	$36
Total				$850

Table 31
Volume and frequency of individual produce purchases, two stores, 1861
Selected products, ten leading customers (listed in descending order by value of whole account)

F61 Customer	Occupation	Hold	Flour		Mill byproducts		Butter		Pork		Beef		Value of all local (estimated)*	Local share of total debits
			lb	mo	lb	mo	lb	mo	lb	mo	lb	mo		
Thomas Pomeroy	blacksmith	15	1,620	8	926	3			294	3			$82	22%
James Bush	labourer	9	2,466	10	500	5	44	3	1,430	10	490	4	$196	47%
Robert Plunkett	millwright	7	2,670	11	3,570	6	133	9	452	3	100	2	$139	45%
Andrew Orr	labourer	6	950	9	200	2	36	5	251	3	305	4	$66	28%
Baptiste Touro	cooper	12	1,145	6	625	3			208	1			$52	25%
Stephen D. Griffis	carriage mkr	10							26	1	64	2	$8	5%
David Rose	lumberer	7												0%
John Sharpe	merchant	5	209	2	710	.2	57	1	11	1	25	1	$20	16%
D.C. Clement	carpenter	6	850	7	850	4	2	1	104	1	38	2	$46	37%
James M. Phillips	painter	7	1,300	9	102	2			177	5	202	4	$62	51%
Total, these customers			11,210		7,483		272		2,953		1,224		$671	
Proportion of total sample purchases			74%		75%		98%		84%		64%			
Buyers in ten largest accounts (N)			8		8		5		9		7			
Other buyers, this product (N)			13		7		2		4		5			
Total months, this product			11		11		9		10		6			

Note:
* Missing values are estimated for leading F61 customers only, based on volumes (see text for discussion).

Table 31 (cont'd)

Sb61

Customer	Occupation	Hold	Apples lb	Apples mo	Cheese lb	Cheese mo	Butter lb	Butter mo	Pork lb	Pork mo	Oats bu	Oats mo	Eggs dz	Eggs mo	Value of all local	Local share of total debits
George Shields	blacksmith	8	3	1	7	2	42	7	209	1	4	2	18	2	$21	4%
Wm. Cotton	carpenter	5	23	4	37	4	79	9	208	1	2	1	67	7	$47	26%
George Bolton	teamster	3	2	1	25	4	38	7	60	1	119	6	21	4	$53	32%
A. Morrow	merchant	8	12	1			14	4			63	7			$41	29%
Charles Watley	farmer	9			45	2									$10	8%
Thomas Bolton	sawyer	4	13	7	36	7	77	11	100	1			40	7	$32	28%
Kenneth Urquhart	tailor	1			8	2	18	5	201	2			15	4	$21	22%
Matthew Walton	farmer	7	30	2	15	2	11	1							$15	18%
Thomas Fitzgerald	sadler	4	8	2			12	3	103	1					$9	11%
Robert Knox	shoemaker	9							208	1					$70	98%
Total, these customers			91		173		291		1,089		188		161		$318	
Proportion of total sample purchases			79%		92%		77%		57%		95%		53%		66%	
Buyers in ten largest accounts (N)			7		7		8		7		4		5			
Other buyers, this product (N)			7		2		7		7		4		8			
Total months, this product			11		11		12		9		8		10			

Table 32
Price ranges of four principal local products, 1808–61
(prices in cents)

	Boards per 100 ft range		Flour per 100 lbs or cwt range		Pork per lb range		Pork per bbl range		Butter per lb range	
	low	high	low	high	low	high	low	high	low	high
YM08	60	180	340	500	5.0	14.0				
YM28	70	80	280	460	8.3	10.0			10.0	12.5
T42		80	250	350	6.0	7.5	1200		12.5	15.0
Ch51	50	90							12.5	
F54	45	80	300	400	5.0	8.3	1400	1600	13.3	16.7
Ch61	60	160			7.0				12.0	12.5
F61	80	100		300	6.0	10.0	1400		12.0	17.0
Sh61		100		300	4.0	12.5	1450	1600	12.5	18.0
D61			250	300		12.5	1400	1700	12.5	20.0
Sc61				300	8.5	10.0			12.5	15.0

Notes:
Blank cells: either no transactions or no usable prices.
Where there was only one price, it is aligned in either low or high column, depending on patterns of other stores.

Table 33
Other goods purchases, ten sample summary

		YM08	YM28	T42	C51	F54*	C61	F61*	Sb61	D61	Sc61	Totals
Footwear	buyers	2	4	16	13	26	42	23	34	30	25	215
	pairs	2	6	38	21	51	115	85	123	87	59	587
	value	$4	$11	$88	$37	$112	$196	$125	$170	$187	$118	
Housewares	buyers	42	33	42	43	30	30	29	31	29	52	361
	value	$194	$39	$84	$60	$46	$35	$64	$56	$42	$72	
Other	buyers	50	41	70	51	49	49	37	37	37	62	483
	value	$85	$35	$76	$58	$82	$198	$130	$70	$124	$148	
Total value, these products		$283	$85	$248	$155	$240	$429	$319	$296	$353	$338	
These products as proportion of all purchases		11%	9%	16%	16%	10%	31%	13%	13%	19%	18%	
"goods book"*						$1,032		$165				

Note:
*See text for discussion of these debits; they are not included in the denominator in calculating percentages for F54 and F61.

Table 34
Household products purchased by five buyers, 1808–61

Product	Unit	Abel Fulford YM08		George Gardener YM28		John Cannon T42		Charles Davis C51		Stephen Byington Sc61	
		Vol	Val	Vol	Val	Vol	Val	Vol	Val	Vol	Val
Transactions		9		1		3		9		14	
Total value			$7.83		$4.38		$4.96		$5.54		$7.28
Buyers include		self, wife, daughter		self		self, wife		self, wife		self, wife, girl, boy	
Basin										1	$0.15
Basket						2	$0.80				
Bottle										1	$0.10
Bowls	dz	0.75	$1.70							0.58	$0.88
Broom										3	$0.85
Candle stick	n	1	$0.23								
Chamber pot										2	$0.70
Cream cup	n	1	$0.10								
Crock								1	$0.40		
Crockery			$2.17								
Cups & saucers	set	1	$0.70	1	$0.40	0.5 dz	$0.30		$0.17	1.5	$0.38
Cups, tea or tin	n	2	$0.33								
Dishes	n			7	$1.08	5	$1.28	1	$0.33		

Table 34 (cont'd)

Product	Unit	Abel Fulford YM08		George Gardener YM28		John Cannon T42		Charles Davis C51		Stephen Byington Sc61	
Transactions		9		1		3		9		14	
Total value		$7.83		$4.38		$4.96		$5.54		$7.28	
Buyers include		self, wife, daughter		self		self, wife		self, wife		self, wife, girl, boy	
		Vol	Val	Vol	Val	Vol	Val	Vol	Val	Vol	Val
Glass	n	1	$0.17								
Jug								1	$0.33		
Kettle, bake								1	$1.00		
Kettle, tea								1	$0.85		
Knife & fork	dz					0.5	$1.00	0.25	$0.65		
Milk pot	n			1	$0.10						
Mill, pepper										1	$0.45
Pail								1	$0.30	1	$1.20
Pan								2	$0.40		
Pitcher	n			1	$0.45						
Plates	dz	1.08	$1.53	1	$0.75	0.5	$0.90	0.5	$0.38	1.25	$1.50
Shears	pr	1	$0.20					1	$0.20		
Teapot	n	1	$0.40	1	$0.60	1	$0.38	1	$0.30		
Tumblers	n			8	$1.00	3	$0.30	2	$0.15	2	$0.25
Wick, candle	ball	1	$0.30					1	$0.08	4	$0.22
Window rope										4	$0.60

Table 35
Prices of boots and shoes, 1808–61

A. All stores

	Shoes					Boots					Other footwear
	pr N	prices N	lowest	highest	mean	pr N	prices N	lowest	highest	mean	see list below
YM08	2	2	$2.00	$2.20	$2.10	1	1	$1.50			
YM28	5	2	$1.70	$2.00	$1.94	21	9	$0.75	$5.00	$2.93	a
T42	14	6	$0.90	$2.75	$1.65	10	5	$1.60	$3.75	$2.46	b
C51	9	6	$0.35	$1.90	$1.42						
F54	24	10	$0.40	$2.25	$1.40	27	13	$0.90	$4.25	$3.07	
C61	62	20	$0.40	$2.25	$1.36	49	21	$0.75	$5.00	$2.20	a,b,c
F61	10	4	$0.90	$2.00	$1.28	52	14	$0.50	$5.00	$1.83	a,b,c,d,e
Sh61	83	23	$0.40	$2.25	$1.05	24	12	$0.85	$4.75	$2.67	a,c,e
D61	6	5	$0.30	$1.60	$1.14	78	22	$0.80	$3.60	$2.29	b
Sc61	22	12	$0.40	$1.60	$0.96	34	9	$0.90	$4.00	$2.75	a,c
	237					296					Other types
											(a) moccasins
Total to 1854	54					59					(b) slippers
Total in 1861	183					237					(c) rubbers
Proportion in 1861	77%					80%					(d) overshoes
											(e) shoepacks

Note:
Where total boots and shoes do not equal total pairs in table 33, the difference is represented by other footwear types.

Table 35 (cont'd)

B. Price range for specific types of footwear, C61

Shoes	Low	High		Boots	Low	High
carpet	$0.40			small	$0.85	$1.30
small	$0.50	$0.95		girls	$1.15	$1.30
junior	$0.75			women's	$1.30	$1.75
rubber	$0.75			boys	$1.60	$3.00
children's	$0.95			prunella	$2.00	
women's	$1.25	$1.35		congress	$3.00	
boys brogans	$1.50			men's	$3.00	
calf	$2.00	$2.25		kip	$3.50	$4.00
				strong	$3.75	
				fine	$5.00	

C. Prices for women's boots, 7 samples

YM28 (1 pair)			$1.50			
T42 (all 3 pairs)						$2.50
C51 (both pairs)					$1.80	
C61	$1.30	$1.40	$1.50		$1.75	
D61		$1.40	$1.50	$1.60	$1.75	
F61			$1.50		$1.80	
Sh61			$1.50		$1.75	

Table 36
Book purchases by sample members, 1808–61

Product	First sold	Total stores	Stores in 1861 N	Books bought N	Buyers (all stores) N	Price 1808 cents	Price 1842 cents	Price 1851 cents	Prices 1861 cents	Note
Almanac	1808	6	3	31	29	13.3	5	na	5	a
Book, spelling	1808	5	3	19	14	40	23.3		12.5, 25	b
Bible	1842	1	0	1	1		103.4			
Book, reader	1842	1	0	1	1		40			c
Books, Sunday school	1842	1	0	na	1		na			d
Testament	1842	1	0	2	2		30			
Geography	1851	2	1	3	3			75	75	
Book, 1st	1851	5	4	28	13			4.2	3.3, 4, 5	e
Book, 2nd	1851	5	4	34	19			13.3	10, 12.5, 13	e
Book, 3rd	1851	4	3	28	11			25	17.5, 20, 25	e
Book, 4th	1851	4	3	5	5			30	30	
Book, 5th	1854	3	2	4	4				25, 30, 40	
Arithmetic	1861	3	3	24	16				12.5, 30, 75	f
Book, prayer	1861	1	1	1	1				2.5	
Grammar	1861	1	1	2	2				11.6, 12.5	
History	1861	2	2	6	6				15, 75	g

Notes:
(a) In 1861, all but two at lower price.
(b) Said to be at cost price.
(c) Entry is $1.00 no volume given.
(d) Unclear if this is a Bible or a form for a will.
(e) See text for large volume purchase by one buyer at C51.
(f) Eight at 12.5¢, twelve at 30¢, four at 75¢.
(g) Three at each price.

APPENDICES

Goods purchased by five or more sample members, 1808–61

Commodity	Usual unit	First year	Stores (N)	Buyers (N)	Note
Section A: Textiles					
(1) Cottons					
cotton	yd	1808	10	321	
calico	yd	1808	4	101	
muslin	yd	1808	10	83	
ticking	yd	1808	10	47	
check	yd	1808	6	34	
jean	yd	1808	7	31	
fustian	yd	1808	3	12	
shirting	yd	1828	8	63	
turkey	yd	1828	4	5	
print	yd	1842	7	190	
stripe	yd	1842	7	66	
moleskin	yd	1842	6	34	
gingham	yd	1842	6	28	
steam loom	yd	1851	6	59	includes "s loom"
factory	yd	1861	2	31	
denim	yd	1861	3	8	
(2) Linens					several might also refer to cotton (see text)
cambric	yd	1808	9	78	
linen	yd	1808	10	77	
sheeting	yd	1808	6	38	
osnaburg	yd	1828	2	9	
drill	yd	1842	8	52	
silesia	yd	1842	7	27	
holland	yd	1842	4	13	
towelling	yd	1842	4	11	
derry	yd	1861	4	26	
(3) Luxury					
velvet	yd	1808	8	31	
satinette	yd	1828	8	22	
silk	yd	1828	4	19	
crepe	yd	1828	8	15	
alpaca	yd	1851	3	8	
luster	yd	1854	3	10	

(4) Woolens

cloth	yd	1808	9	123	includes buyers of specifically named cloths (see chap. 3)
flannel	yd	1808	10	98	
baize	yd	1808	2	8	
merino	yd	1842	2	14	
home made	yd	1842	1	7	includes one buyer of home made flannel; others are hm cloth
saxony	yd	1842	1	7	
serge	yd	1842	2	5	
delaine	yd	1851	5	23	
tweed	yd	1854	4	43	
fulled	yd	1861	2	6	

(5) Mixed and other

net	yd	1808	9	25	also netting
imitation	yd	1808	1	5	
plaid	yd	1828	8	29	
canvas	yd	1842	8	43	
bagging	yd	1842	2	11	
vesting	yd	1842	2	7	
orleans	yd	1851	7	31	
cobourg	yd	1854	5	32	

Section B: Clothing and footwear
(1) Clothing and related items

handkerchief		1808	10	159	
hat		1808	10	92	
gloves	pr	1808	9	73	also gauntlets
socks	pr	1808	9	68	
shawl		1808	10	60	
mittens	pr	1808	10	55	
stockings	pr	1808	8	32	
vest		1808	8	25	
braces	pr	1828	9	62	
cap		1828	9	62	
pants	pr	1828	8	22	also trousers, pantaloons
shirt		1842	6	21	
dress		1842	4	6	
bonnet		1842	3	6	includes straw
neck tie		1851	6	37	
comforter		1851	3	5	possibly not clothing?
coat		1854	6	40	
hose		1854	4	23	Some stores sold hose, socks and stockings
collar		1854	5	16	
muffler		1854	3	6	
belt		1861	5	29	
hair net		1861	5	13	
cape		1861	2	7	
scarf		1861	3	6	

(2) Footwear

shoes	pr	1808	10	113	
boots	pr	1828	9	140	
moccasins	pr	1842	5	14	
slippers	pr	1851	4	7	
shoepacks	pr	1861	2	11	
rubbers	pr	1861	4	9	

Section C: Groceries (see also E, Chemicals)

(1) General

tea	lb	1808	10	390	
tobacco	lb	1808	10	373	some sales in plugs
sugar	lb	1808	10	259	buyers of maple sugar included (see chaps 4 & 6)
salt	bu	1808	10	184	other units: bags, bbl, qt, lb
pepper	lb	1808	10	140	
rum	qt	1808	2	74	
coffee	lb	1808	8	58	
allspice	lb	1808	10	49	
ginger	lb	1808	9	41	also vial (ginger essence), ppr
snuff	lb	1808	6	35	
spirits	qt	1808	2	30	
cinnamon	oz	1808	9	28	includes cinnamon essence, sold by bottle
brandy	qt	1808	3	28	
wine	qt	1808	4	18	
soap	lb	1828	9	141	also bar
candle	lb	1828	9	67	
molasses	qt	1828	7	21	
vinegar	qt	1828	6	15	
currants	lb	1842	7	78	
raisins	lb	1842	7	73	
saleratus	lb	1842	5	69	
starch	lb	1842	8	63	
mustard	lb	1842	7	42	
peppermint	btl	1842	7	40	includes essence; unit sometimes vial. also stick
liquorice	oz	1842	6	22	
cloves	oz	1842	6	16	
cayenne	oz	1842	2	13	
nutmeg	oz	1842	5	10	
caraway seeds	lb	1842	3	5	
soda	lb	1851	7	123	includes baking soda (one store)
rice	lb	1851	7	76	
candy		1851	5	44	includes bulls eye, sweets, gum drops
lemon essence	btl	1851	4	12	
fish	lb, dz, bbl	1854	5	35	includes cod, herring, white, fresh, and "fish"

syrup	qt	1861	4	46	could be a medication (see chap. 4)
hops	lb	1861	1	6	

(2) Medicines and drugs

pills	box	1828	9	75	
oil, castor	btl	1828	9	63	If "c" oil is included, 8 additional buyers.
salts	lb	1828	6	38	includes Epsom salts
camphor	oz	1828	5	22	
oil, b…	btl	1828	8	19	includes black, British, "b" (latter when sold by btl)
calomel & jalap	dose, grain	1828	4	14	includes a few transactions in calomel or jalap alone
opodeldoc	btl	1828	5	13	
paregoric	btl	1828	7	12	
bark	oz	1828	4	11	
cream of tartar	oz	1842	6	27	
senna	oz	1842	6	22	
aloes	oz	1842	4	18	
quinine	grain	1842	6	16	
plaster	oz	1842	7	14	
ointment	box	1842	5	14	includes "magnetic" ointment and diachylon
balsam	btl	1842	4	13	
oil, spike	btl	1842	3	13	
cordial	vial	1842	6	12	
pink root	oz	1842	4	11	
squills syrup	oz	1842	3	11	
emetic	n	1842	2	9	includes tartar emetic
wafers	box	1842	5	9	
magnesia	oz	1842	5	6	
laudanum	oz	1842	3	5	also by vial
pain extractor	box	1851	6	30	also pain killer, pain destroyer
vermifuge	btl	1851	5	21	includes worm candy (sold by stick)
lozenges	box	1851	3	16	includes worm lozenges
salve		1851	6	14	
linament	btl	1851	5	6	
burgundy pitch	oz	1851	3	5	
"medicine"	vial	1851	4	5	actual product not specified
conditioning powder	ppr	1854	5	21	
oil, gargling	btl	1861	5	14	
R.R.R.	btl	1861	3	13	Radway's Ready Relief

pectoral	btl	1861	3	12	includes cherry pectoral
worm tea	ppr	1861	4	10	other unit: pkt
asophoetida	oz	1861	1	5	
essences	vial	1861	2	5	

Section D. Hardware

nails	lb	1808	10	276	sold by count in 1808–09
knife		1808	10	127	includes pocket, jack, butcher, shoe, pen
gunpowder	lb	1808	10	111	also sold by the canister
shot	lb	1808	10	87	also includes "ball" in 1808
glass	pane, box	1808	10	81	panes also called lights
screws	dz	1808	10	79	
iron	lb	1808	10	58	
butts	pr	1808	10	53	
lock		1808	10	53	
axe		1808	10	51	
file		1808	10	50	
rope		1808	10	43	units include lb, yd, pc
scythe		1808	8	34	
tacks	dz	1808	9	34	includes shoe tacks; other units paper and gross
chain	lb, pr, n	1808	9	30	includes halter and trace
wire		1808	6	29	includes bonnet and cap wire
hinges	pr	1808	9	27	
awl		1808	7	25	
flint	dz, n	1808	3	20	
gimlet		1808	8	20	
steel	lb	1808	6	16	
saw		1808	9	15	
twine		1808	8	15	
axe handle		1808	7	14	also helve, halve
hammer		1808	7	13	
dogs	pr	1808	1	6	includes andirons; similar price and use.
sickle		1808	1	5	
whips		1828	9	59	includes lash, whiplash, whip stalk
putty	lb	1828	9	51	
rake		1828	6	35	
hooks		1828	6	30	most are fish hooks (see chapter 5)
auger		1828	8	21	includes 4 buyers of auger bits
sand paper	sheet	1828	6	16	

hoe		1828	6	11	
bolts		1828	4	10	
stone		1842	7	45	includes scythe, whet
caps	box, dz	1842	8	35	
shovel, spade		1842	8	30	
line, fish		1842	7	24	
scythe snath		1842	5	19	
comb, curry		1842	6	18	
latch		1842	7	15	
rasp		1842	4	7	two kinds, for horses, shoes
chalkline		1842	4	7	
brad		1842	3	6	units include 100, paper, packet
sprigs		1851	3	13	
brush, paint		1851	4	12	also whitewash brush
pipes, stove		1851	5	11	
grindstone		1851	6	10	sometimes sold by weight
cradle		1851	4	7	
plaster	bbl	1851	3	6	
square		1851	3	6	
fork		1854	5	20	includes hay, manure, straw forks
plough point		1861	3	16	
landside		1861	2	8	
glue	lb	1861	3	6	
horse card		1861	3	5	includes one "horse brush"
line, deepsea		1861	2	5	
zinc	lb	1861	1	5	

Section E. Chemicals

sulphur	lb	1808	10	84	includes brimstone, sold at 3 stores (which also sold sulphur)
indigo	lb	1808	9	75	
alum	lb	1808	8	52	
copperas	lb	1808	9	40	
saltpetre	lb	1808	9	40	
chalk	lb, oz	1808	6	17	includes, white, red, and plain
lead	lb	1808	4	7	sold also by sheet; see also black, red, white lead, below
blue, fig	lb	1828	2	8	
rosin	lb	1842	8	41	
turpentine	btl, qt, pt	1842	7	36	
oil (other)	gal, qt, pt	1842	7	27	includes unspecified oil sold in these units, also machine oil

logwood	lb	1842	6	26	
oil, lighting	gal	1842	6	24	lamp, coal, kerosene; other units qt, pt
redwood	lb	1842	7	21	
madder	lb	1842	4	16	
vitriol	oz	1842	3	16	
lamp black	lb	1842	6	16	also sold in paper
lead, black	ppr	1842	7	13	
borax	lb	1842	5	8	
lead, sugar	oz	1842	4	7	included here to have all lead entries together; likely a medicine
blue stone	oz	1842	3	6	other unit: lb
oil, linseed	qt, pt	1851	6	35	includes oil (paint), raw, boiled, and "b" (if sold in these units)
blue	oz	1851	5	24	other unit: lb; includes bluing
paint & varnish	varies	1851	4	11	units include pt, btl
venetian red	lb	1851	3	8	
blue, button	oz	1851	2	5	kept separate from "blue" because price differs
lead, white	lb, can	1854	5	17	
lead, red	lb	1854	4	15	
blacking	box	1854	4	12	other units: roll, packet; includes stove blacking, stove polish
whitening		1854	3	7	also whiting
yellow ochre	lb	1861	4	13	
soda, washing	ppr	1861	2	12	other unit: lb. Includes washing crystals
tar	qt, pt	1861	1	10	

Section F. Housewares

cups (and saucers)	n, set, dz	1808	10	98	includes tin
plates	n, dz	1808	10	85	
wick, candle	ball	1808	10	77	
bowls		1808	10	70	
pail		1808	9	66	includes tin, patent, and wooden
teapot		1808	9	36	
scissors and shears		1808	8	35	
knife & fork	n, set, dz	1808	8	34	
chamber pot		1808	9	33	
pan		1808	8	33	includes tin, milk, iron, round, frying
pitcher		1808	7	28	
tumblers	n, dz	1808	7	24	
kettle		1808	4	19	
candle stick		1808	5	15	

blankets	pr	1808	5	13	
mug		1808	2	11	
bake kettle, bake pan		1808	5	10	
pot		1808	4	10	
crockery		1808	2	10	not specified
dipper		1808	5	8	
lantern		1808	3	5	
creamer		1808	1	5	
spoons	n, dz, set	1828	9	36	includes teaspoons, table spoons, other spoons
dishes		1828	9	30	
basin		1828	7	21	includes wash basin, wash bowl
basket		1828	4	12	includes bushel basket
pepper box		1828	4	7	also pepper castor
broom		1842	8	93	
jug		1842	6	26	
bed cord		1842	7	23	
lamp, lamp glass		1842	6	15	includes lamps and parts of lamps
iron, flat etc		1842	4	9	includes smoothing (in pairs), roller irons
baker		1842	1	6	
salt cellar		1842	2	5	also salt dish, salt stand
crock		1851	6	12	
washboard		1851	4	10	
sieves and strainers		1851	5	7	
table cover, table cloth		1851	2	6	
bottle		1851	2	5	
jar		1854	4	6	

Section G. Notions

thread	sk, bunch	1808	10	265	
buttons	dz, n	1808	10	217	
ribbon	yd	1808	10	181	
pins	ppr, oz	1808	10	120	other units bunch, "row"
needles	dz, n	1808	10	106	
silk	sk, bunch	1808	8	85	
tape	yd, pc	1808	10	64	
twist	stick, yd	1808	8	60	
lace	yd	1808	9	56	
thimble		1808	10	48	
binding	yd	1808	8	35	
edging	yd	1808	9	34	
needle, knitting	pr, set	1808	8	24	includes knitting "pins"
cotton	ball	1808	4	26	
needle, darning	n	1808	4	13	
quality	yd	1808	1	10	
pattern		1808	5	9	vest, frock, dress, apron
lining	yd	1828	9	67	

warp or yarn, cotton	lb	1828	8	40	
slack	ball	1828	2	30	
cord	bunch, yd	1828	6	16	
spool		1842	8	184	
trimming		1842	7	56	
hook & eye	dz, n	1842	8	54	
braid	bunch	1842	7	45	
laces	pr, n	1842	7	31	excludes stay laces (3 buyers)
padding	yd	1842	2	12	
quilling	yd	1842	1	12	
insertion	yd	1842	2	9	
crepe	yd	1842	2	5	most for "hat band"
batting		1851	6	31	
hemp	ball	1851	4	31	
wadding	yd, sheet, lb	1851	5	18	
bonnet-related		1851	5	6	border, shape, front
border		1854	3	11	
whalebone		1854	3	5	
hoops	set, n	1861	4	30	
elastic	yd	1861	4	11	
blonde	yd	1861	3	7	
feathers		1861	5	6	also plume

Section H. Other goods

comb	n, pr	1808	10	184	
paper	quire, sheet	1808	10	128	
book		1808	10	96	includes a few blank books
ink		1808	9	40	powder and bottle
pasteboard	sheet	1808	6	36	
almanac		1808	6	29	
bags		1808	7	25	includes sack
spectacles	pr	1808	4	10	
pocket book		1808	4	7	
snuff box		1808	2	6	
pipe		1828	8	64	
seed	lb, ppr, pkt	1828	7	60	some may be local
pencil		1828	8	29	
lines, "hambro"		1828	2	5	
matches	box	1842	8	78	
looking glass		1842	6	26	includes mirrors
blanket, horse		1842	5	17	includes 1 "horse rug"
slate		1842	6	15	
razor		1842	6	13	
newspapers		1842	2	12	subscription to out-of-town newspaper
shoe bills	lb	1842	1	12	
box		1842	5	10	
quills	bunch, oz, n	1842	1	5	distinguished from quilling by unit
pen		1851	6	16	
brush		1851	5	13	includes cloth, scrubbing, hair

parasol		1851	4	10	
umbrella		1851	6	9	
bell, cow		1851	4	6	
broach		1851	3	6	
bells	string	1851	2	5	
hair oil	btl	1861	5	16	
pen holder		1861	5	14	
envelope		1861	4	11	
hair pins	box	1861	4	9	
fiddle string		1861	2	8	

Section I. Local goods and services
  (1) Goods

boards (all kinds)	100 ft	1808	9	92	other units ft & 1000 ft
flour	cwt, lb	1808	9	78	includes middlings
whiskey	qt, gal	1808	3	64	
pork	lb, bbl	1808	9	63	excludes ham
mill by products	cwt, lb	1808	6	44	bran, cannel, screenings, shorts
oats	bu	1808	7	33	
eggs	dz	1808	7	29	
barrels (all kinds)		1808	6	26	includes cask, potash barrels
beef	lb	1808	5	25	
leather	lb, side	1808	6	18	
firkin		1808	4	15	
corn	bu	1808	2	15	
peas	bu	1808	5	12	
wheat	bu	1808	5	12	
hides, skins		1808	4	9	includes calf, deer
potatoes	bu	1808	3	7	
lard	lb	1808	3	6	
butter	lb	1828	9	50	
maple sugar	lb	1828	5	15	
cheese	lb	1842	6	21	
tallow	lb	1842	4	9	
mutton	lb	1842	2	6	
apples	lb, bu, bbl	1851	3	17	includes dried
shingles	bunch	1851	3	5	
wood	cord	1854	4	10	
tubs		1861	3	27	for butter, except 3 "wash" tubs
oat meal	lb	1861	1	5	

  (2) Selected services

carding or fulling	1808	4	56	
blacksmith account	1828	2	15	
mending and making	1828	5	10	of clothing, shoes
postage	1842	6	93	
cartage, "drawing," freight	1842	6	19	
sawing	1851	2	13	

Select list of goods with four or fewer buyers, 1808–61
(Year is first year the product was found in samples)

A. Textiles (unit is yards in all cases)			elastic	1861
(1) cottons			hornet proof	1861
corduroy	1808		Linsey Woolsey	1861
beaverton	1828		Oil Baize	1861
nankeen	1828		pants stuff	1861
regatta	1854			
jaconet	1861		B. Clothing & footwear	
tarlatan	1861		(1) clothing and related	
			frock	1828
(2) linens			tippet	1828
diaper	1842		drawers	1842
oil cloth	1854		apron	1851
duck	1861		stays	1851
			head dress	1854
(3) luxury			suit	1854
bombasine	1808		armlets	1861
mohair	1854		corsets	1861
satin	1854		cravats	1861
cashmere	1861		crinoline	1861
damask	1861		cuffs	1861
sarcenet	1861		garters	1861
			helmet	1861
(4) woolens			hood	1861
coating	1808		mantel	1861
durant	1808		overalls	1861
russell	1808		sash	1861
fearnought	1828		skirt	1861
forrest, br	1842		turban	1861
kerseymere	1842		undershirts	1861
lambskin	1861		veil	1861
swanskin	1861		victorine	1861
(5) mixed, other, and uncertain			(2) footwear	
divinity	1808		overshoes	1861
buckram	1828			
doeskin	1842		C. Groceries	
cheesecloth	1851		(1) general	
woolen substitute	1851		shrub	1828
carpeting	1854		gin	1842
cassinette	1861		nuts	1842
crinoline	1861		orange	1842

rhubarb	1842		wheel head	1851
corn starch	1854		studs	1854
biscuit	1861		bridle	1861
chicory	1861		cleaner, lamp	1861
crackers	1861		drier	1861
figs	1861		elbows	1861
oil, olive	1861		flask, powder	1861
			grease	1861
(2) medicines and drugs			horse shoe	1861
antimony	1842		nuts, w	1861
basilicon	1842		oil can	1861
bitters	1842		powder flask	1861
ether	1842		pulleys	1861
hartshorn, s	1842		rule	1861
myrrh, gum	1842		screw driver	1861
nitre, spirits	1842		screw plate	1861
opium	1842		spring	1861
precipitate, red	1842		spurs	1861
salamoniac	1842		steelyards	1861
blister salve	1851		trap, rat	1861
tartaric acid	1851		trowel	1861
strawberry, wild	1854		wagon	1861
tooth drops	1854		wheel	1861
wild cherry	1854			
arrowroot	1861		E. Chemicals	
balm	1861		lime	1828
camomile fl	1861		varnish	1851
columba root	1861		chrome yellow	1861
drops, cold	1861		Spanish brown	1861
drops, hot	1861		ultramarine	1861
drops, ear	1861		umber, turkey	1861
eye water	1861			
galvanic fluid	1861		F. Housewares	
gum	1861		glasses	1808
oil, sweet	1861		moulds (candle,etc)	1808
pitch	1861		platter	1808
quick silver	1861		skillet	1808
tincture	1861		spider	1808
wine, forest	1861		decanter	1828
wintergreen ext	1861		milk pot	1828
			bed clothes,	1842
D. Hardware			covers	
bit, tapering	1808		pincers	1842
compasses	1808		tin	1842
cards,wool	1828		whisk	1842
chisel	1828		chairs	1851
grid iron	1828		clock	1851
gun lock	1828		coffee pot	1851
rivets	1828		counter panes	1851
plough	1842		ladle	1851
brace & bitts	1851		towels	1854
clippers	1851		bedstead	1861
crank	1851		clothes line	1861
drag teeth	1851		clothespins	1861
gun	1851		ewer	1861
plane	1851		mill, pepper	1861
stove	1851		mop	1861

mop stick	1861
paper blinds	1861
rugs	1861
sniffer, brass	1861
tray	1861
window paper	1861

G. Notions

cap pattern	1808
feretting	1828
webbing	1828
bobbins	1842
laces, stay	1842
piping	1842
shalloon	1842
size	1842
twilling	1842
beads	1851
gimp	1851
buckle	1861
floss	1861
fringe	1861
stuffing	1861
tassels	1861
wool, Berlin	1861

H. Other goods

taps	1808
trunk	1808
wrapper	1808
coal	1828
floats	1828
ink stand	1828
tobacco box, steel	1828
brush, shaving	1842
case	1842
vial	1842
box, band	1851
cooler	1851
lasts	1851
bag, carpet	1854
cane	1854
corks	1854
key ring	1854
aromatic	1861
ball mould	1861
beeswax	1861
bracelets	1861
bristles	1861
buckles	1861
buffalo robe	1861
bureau	1861
chair, rocking	1861
doll	1861
face salt	1861
flower pot	1861
fly killer	1861

foil	1861
furs	1861
hair cord	1861
Jews harp	1861
measures	1861
mouse trap	1861
needle case	1861
ox bow	1861
ox nob, ball	1861
pearls	1861
perfume	1861
razor strop	1861
snuffs	1861
table	1861
tassel	1861
tins	1861
toy tea set	1861
watch guard	1861
watch key	1861
wheel, wool	1861
woods	1861

I. Local goods and services

(1) goods)

cow	1808
hay	1808
hog	1808
hogs head	1808
oxen&yoke	1808
rib	1808
rye	1808
wool	1808
ashes	1828
buckwheat	1828
veal	1828
poles	1828
ham	1842
keg	1842
logs	1842
venison	1842
barley	1854
high wines	1854
horse	1854
berries	1861
churn	1861
corn meal	1861
fence pickets	1861
flour, buckwheat	1861
honey	1861
onions	1861
staves	1861
suet	1861
turkey	1861

(2) services

coopering	1861
drawing (document)	1861

Selected principal imports, Province of Canada, 1850–52, 1860–62 (annual and per capita averages)

	1850–52		1860–62	
	Annual average	*Per capita*	*Annual average*	*Per capita*
Values	($000)		($000)	
iron and manufactures of iron and hardware	$2,749	$1.49	$3,042	$1.21
cottons	$3,543		$5,298	
woolens	$2,731		$4,124	
silks, satins and velvets	$712		$865	
linens	$355		$309	
total fabrics	$7,341	$3.98	$10,596	$4.23
Volumes	(000 lbs)	(lbs)	(000 lbs)	(lbs)
tea	3,909	2.1	5,022	2.0
tobacco	3,298	1.8	5,877	2.3
sugar	18,331	10.0	39,365	15.7
Population of the Canadas (000)				
Upper Canada	952		1,396	
Lower Canada	890		1,112	
	1,842		2,508	

Sources:

1850–52 from Province of Canada, Legislative Assembly, Journals, 1853, Appendix A, Tables of Trade and Navigation for 1852, schedule 18.

1860 from Province of Canada, Legislative Assembly, Sessional Papers, 1862, #2, Tables of Trade and Navigation, schedule 3.

1861–62 from Province of Canada, Legislative Assembly, Sessional Papers, 1864, #3, Tables of Trade and Navigation, schedule 3.

Notes:

To avoid underestimating iron in 1860–62, the duty-free category, "pig iron, pig lead, and pig copper," is included under iron.

On a per capita basis, these duty-free metals equaled about 10 cents.

A sharp upsurge in unmanufactured tobacco imports in 1862 has an impact on 1860–62 average for tobacco.

APPENDIX D

SOURCES AND SAMPLES

As explained in chapter 2, this study is based on structured samples drawn from the customers listed in country store accounts for the relevant year. Here we extend that discussion, listing the documentary sources on which we have drawn for this work and describing the selection of the samples. The counts in table 3 incorporate minor variations that proved necessary as the research went forward. As a result, there are very slight variations from the data that appeared in earlier publications from this project. For example, a few people proved not actually to have had an independent account, and several people we had thought were distinct proved not to be. Explanations for the latter include name variations, inconsistent spelling, and difficult-to-decipher handwriting. Thus, after close work with the 1808–09 data, we established that "Widow," Nabby, and Abigail Comstock were the same person; similar cases were John Cronk or Cronkright, Peter Cronk or Cronkwright, and Jeremiah (or Jerry) Chichigran or Coughran.

The linked samples were structured rather than random, drawn by taking names at regular intervals from the complete linked customer list at each store, sorted by the occupation reported in the census and by household size (two variables we thought could be of particular relevance to buying patterns). As discussed below, our first pilot project (Choate's in 1861) also included birthplace in the sort, and we lacked occupational data for Yonge Mills. A number of people with other occupational designations were recorded in the agricultural schedules of the census, but we do not count them in the "farm" category in table 3. We do count a handful of widows with land who were designated as "farmers" and men reported as farmers even if we did not find them in the agricultural schedule.

Usually transactions were entered in daybooks in the name of the account holder (generally the household head), although also indicating who actually made a purchase. But at three stores in 1861 (Fowlds's, Darling's, and Scovil's), the accounts normally recorded the name of the person making the purchase. In these cases, as we discuss below, a final step in preparing the sample was to add other names from the household of anyone who was part of the initial sample selection, the aim being to ensure as full a view as possible of the household's purchases. In these cases, the sample summary in table 3 is a count of households, with occupations based on that of the household head.

YONGE MILLS 1808–09

Archives of Ontario, Toronto [AO], Charles Jones Fonds (F180), Yonge Mills Records, Daybook no. 3, 1808–09, MU 3165. Sample data were checked against entries in Ledger 1, April 1807 to 1811, MU 3155. In the chapters on goods we also draw on an import invoice book, 1802–08, series E 1, MU 3184. The names in the daybook were linked to AO, Johnstown District Fonds (F1721); Yonge Township census, 1808 and 1810, MS 2554; and assessments, 1808 and 1809, MS 2555; and Elizabethtown census, 1808 and 1809, MS 2550; and assessments, 1808 and 1809, MS 2557. Not all of those linked were found in all four possible lists for a township. The daybook begins on 1 September 1808; we recorded transactions to 31 August 1809. But note that there were only twelve transactions (on only four days) between the end of June and 9 August 1809. As the ledger confirms, the store was evidently inactive in this period.

Our sample was based on a sort by township, household size, and total assessment. Unlinked and duplicates were listed alphabetically. We took every third name. The four women were added. Much detail on the Elizabethtown assessments is illegible in the original. Because tax assessments do not indicate lot and concession numbers, they do not permit locating customers within a township.

YONGE MILLS 1828–29

AO, Charles Jones Fonds (F180), Yonge Mills Records, Daybooks, 1828 and 1828–9, MU 3171–2. These were linked to AO, Johnstown District Fonds (F1721); Yonge Township Census, 1828 and 1829, MS 2554; and assessments, 1828, MS 2556, and 1829, MS2555; and Elizabethtown census and assessment, 1828 and 1829, MS2556. A few of those linked were not found in all four possible lists for their township. Data are for the twelve months from 1 July 1828 to 30 June 1829.

Our sample took one in three of both linked and unlinked customers. For the linked population, we sorted by household size, then by assessed value of property. For the unlinked (and for duplicate names), we listed alphabetically. Three women not caught in this process were added. Although it is doubtful that anyone farmed more than one piece of land, in the row for farm size in table 3 we total arable acreage for thirteen people in the population and two in the sample whose assessments reported arable acres on more than one holding. In ten such cases, there was at least one farm with twenty acres in culture, but we do not know if it, or any, of these holdings was actually occupied and farmed by the customer.

TETT 1842

Queen's University Archives, Kingston, Ontario [QUA], Tett Papers (no. 2247): vol. 27, Daybook, 17 September 1841 to 23 July 1842, and vol. 28, Daybook, 23 July 1842 to 2 February 1844. We recorded data for all of 1842. These were checked against vol. 58, the ledger for 1838–44. The chapters on goods also make extensive use of vol. 67, an invoice book, 1833–36, and an inventory from 1851 found in vol. 73. Linkage was to Library and Archives Canada [LAC], census microfilm reel M5908, 1842 manuscript census for North Crosby, South Crosby, and Bastard Townships (latter includes Burgess Township as well). Census manuscripts for Frontenac County have not survived; hence the low rate of linkage here. Tett's sawmill, for example, was in Frontenac, in Bedford Township.

The 1842 census lists heads of household but not the names of other family members; moreover, the daybook often referred to women just as "Mrs" or "Miss," in many cases with reference not to the main ledger but to "small accounts." Hence we often could not infer a relationship with a man of the same surname. The census tabulated information in columns for the entire household not individual members; for example, the age columns provided a count in ranges by gender. There are also some inconsistencies in form among the townships. For example, the census in North and South Crosby lacks lot and concession numbers, and the Bastard Township census often does not give occupations. In the latter case, for landholders with no occupation given, we use the same definition of "farmer" in table 3 as for Yonge Mills: five or more acres in cultivation.

To keep the total sample manageable, we decided to have about equal numbers of unlinked and linked. For the linked, we sought a full range of artisan and other non-farm occupations, then took one in four of other groups (farmer, labourer, and no occupation). The unlinked sample was also structured: we took all seven identified by Tett as Indians (including three women), two of the three unlinked whose accounts had occupational designations (one of the two doctors and the only clergyman), and half of all women. We then took one in every eight of the other unlinked men.

CHOATE 1851

Trent University Archives, Peterborough, Ontario [TUA], Choate Family Papers (B-77-026/1), Daybooks 1 and 2, 21 June 1850 to 11 June 1851; 1 August 1851 to 17 July 1852. We sampled data for 1851, but have no information for the period of summer 1851 between these two books. We linked to the 1852 census for Douro and Dummer Townships, LAC census microfilm reel C11748.

The basic sample was one in four, except that we included all the artisans, the only professional (a clergyman), and all the women. Their inclusion increases the proportions in several of the occupational categories: thus, two widows were recorded as having farms and are counted among the farmers, and "housekeepers" account for three of the four "other" occupations.

FOWLDS 1854

TUA, Fowlds Papers (B-72-001), Accounts, vol. 3, Ledger, 1853–5. Besides providing an earlier sample from a store we had studied in 1861, these accounts serve as a pilot project based on a ledger. It provided full detail on more than two-thirds of transactions (the rest, as we discuss in the text, were charges transferred from a "goods book"). Because the ledger began during 1853 and did not comprehensively cover the year, we chose to record each account holder's transactions during 1854. The ledger generally indicated the township or village in which the customer lived. Even so (despite having a location for 75 percent of those we were unable to link), we found only 54 percent of customers in the 1852 census for eight townships: LAC, Census microfilm, reels C11748, for Asphodel, Belmont,

Dummer, and Otonabee, all in Peterborough County; C11739, for Percy, Haldimand, and Alnwick, and C11740, for Hamilton, all in Northumberland County. The village of Hastings was on the border between Asphodel and Percy; 93 percent of linked customers were found in these two townships (as were 87 percent of those for whom the ledger gave a location but whom we could not find in the census). There are a number of gaps in the manuscripts for Northumberland; the loss of part of the agricultural census for Percy is the most significant for us.

For artisans, we took at least one of each craft represented, and two for the more common trades; for "other" occupations, we likewise took at least one of each. For farmers (or yeomen, as the Percy census reported them) and labourers we took a sample of one in five. Once this was done, we added others in sample members' households, with the objective of seeing if there were larger household patterns that would have been missed with single individuals. We also selected an unlinked customer said to have been resident at the Indian village at Alnwick; all four women with accounts (two of them unlinked); and one unlinked doctor. Finally, we took one of every ten unlinked customers.

More than 40 percent of the linked customers were also customers in 1861. On the whole we treat the two samples as independent in our analysis, but it should be noted that ten from the 1861 sample (which we took first) were included in the 1854 sample. A few of these required a slight variation in the selection routine (i.e., if the next name to someone who would have been in the 1854 sample was in the 1861 sample, we chose the latter instead).

CHOATE 1861

TUA, Choate Family Papers (B-77-026/1), Daybook 3, 1 January to 31 December 1861. We linked to the census manuscripts for Douro and Dummer townships: LAC census microfilm, reels C1066–7.

This was our first sample and we did several things differently from our later procedures. For example, we initially linked to the personal schedule of the census and recorded data from the agricultural census only for members of the sample. We also included birthplace in our sort, after occupation, and before household size. At this stage, we had not yet discovered that few if any families bought all their goods at one store, and we imagined that origin might be a relevant variable. In subsequent samples, we recorded birthplace, religion, and the other available identifiers in the census manuscripts, but we no longer expected to find (and indeed did not find) any indication that these were of specific importance in purchasing. This is not to say that ethnicity, birthplace, etc. could not have had an influence via occupation, extent of land in cultivation, and other variables. The sample includes one in every four farmers, one in three labourers, and at least one of each of the other non-farm occupations. We include the six women we were able to link, all of whom were recorded as not having an occupation. Although we did not intend to have unlinked or duplicate names in the sample, we later found that two of the names were duplicates.

FOWLDS 1861

TUA, Fowlds Papers (B-72-001), Accounts, vol. 6, Daybook, 28 January to 31 December 1861. This is the only full daybook in the Fowlds papers, and, as the dates indicate, we lack information for the first four weeks of the year. We searched the same townships as in 1854 plus Seymour (in Northumberland): LAC Census microfilm reels C1066–7 for Peterborough County and C1054–6 for Northumberland County.

This source recorded transactions in the name of the buyer rather than the head of household. Thus, far more names appeared than in most of our other sources. Perhaps because of the rapid growth of Hastings in the period, we found more craftsmen here than in any other sample, representing seventeen different trades; we took at least one of most, except one in four of the two most common, blacksmiths and carpenters. We also took one in four of other occupations. For farmers and labourers we took one in six. Once this had been done, we added others in the households of sample members (thirty-one of whom were women), using the census and common ledger references as cues. Although we generally excluded unlinked customers at this stage of our research, we did include three women whom we could not locate in the census.

SHERIN 1861

TUA, Sherin Papers (B-71-002), Daybooks 1 and 2 (6 June 1860 to 12 November 1861; 13 November 1861 to 23 December 1862); we took all transactions in 1861. We linked to the census manuscripts for Smith and

Douro townships: LAC census microfilm, reels C1066–7.

This was our second sample, and we still focused exclusively on linked customers. We sorted by occupation and household size, further sorting farmers (or yeomen, as the Smith census-taker termed them) by value of farm in order to get a range of farm types. We then took one in three farmers, one in three labourers, one each of craft and commercial or professional occupations (except we took two coopers and shoemakers), and all the women. The latter included four "serving maids" (in the households of two men also in the sample, Rev. Percy Warren and Robert Strickland). Here, as in other samples, we counted people with different surnames found in a household when considering household size but otherwise tracked their purchases separately, treating them as distinct members of the sample. Two farmers, Sam Curtis and William Sherwood, were also in the Choate 1861 sample. Their combined purchases at the two stores (forty and twenty dollars respectively) were modest enough to suggest that these were not the only two stores they patronized.

DARLING 1861

QUA, Darling Family Papers (no. 2303.28), Daybooks, vols 4 and 5, 1857–61, 1861–64. We recorded transactions for all of 1861. The daybooks were linked to census manuscripts for the Front of Escott and of Leeds & Lansdowne and then to Yonge Township, LAC, Census microfilm, 1861, reels C1044–5. We also checked customer names in the index of vol. 25-A, a ledger spanning 1857–75. More than half the names in the daybooks for 1861 were not in this ledger, however; their entries were marked as transferred to "small accounts," to a "small ledger," or "paid." Our discussion also draws on the following volumes in box 6: an inventory book, 1 April 1858; a small notebook (undated) of comments on types of goods to stock; and a series of books (covering 1844 to 1883) recording wood received and sold.

The daybooks recorded transactions in the name of the actual buyer. For our sample, we took all nineteen women whose names appeared (four of whom were not linked to the census); one of each artisan and other non-farm occupation (including an unlinked clergyman, designated "Rev." in the accounts); and one of every four farmers and labourers. Almost all of those for whom no occupation was recorded were women. We then took one in four of the other unlinked accounts and those for whom we found duplicated names in the census. After this was done, we added other members of the same family so as to get all of the household's purchases. As can be seen by the final number of farmers in table 3, many of those added in this process were heads of farm households, and the overall effect of the procedure was also to increase the weighting of large households in the sample by comparison with the longer linked list.

SCOVIL 1861

QUA, Scovil General Store Accounts (A.Arch 2217), series I, vols 21 and 22, Daybooks, 1861–62. Portland is in Bastard Township. Three-quarters of our linked customers and of our sample were found there, but we also searched census manuscripts for Kitley, South Elmsley, North & South Crosby, and North & South Burgess, LAC, Census microfilms, reels C1042–5.

These daybooks recorded transactions in the name of the person making a purchase rather than the account holder or household head. Our sample consisted of one in six farmers and labourers, half of the women (most of whom had no occupation listed; but there were two women "tailors" who were included, and counted among the artisans), at least one of each craft (and one in three for blacksmiths and shoemakers), and one in three for other non-farm occupations. For the unlinked, we took one in ten (plus five women recorded in the accounts as widows) and one in eight of the duplicate names. Finally, we added other members of the households of those selected in the sampling process; this procedure had implications for the household count of the sample in table 3, increasing the number of farmers and decreasing the number of labourers and women.

NOTES

PREAMBLE

1   Caption introducing part of the Design section at the Stedelijk Museum, Amsterdam, seen 22 April 2013.

2   See appendix D. The store's ledger begins in April 1807, but the mill might already have been open. Daybook 3 is the first to survive. An invoice book for shipments to the business begins in April 1802, but these likely were initially to the Brockville store. Its first surviving daybook [daybook A no. 4] begins 30 December 1803. Yonge was surveyed in 1794 and its first legal settler was recorded in 1796. Armstrong, *Handbook of Upper Canadian Chronology*, 148.

3   McIlwraith, "Charles Jones," DCB.

4   The household census did not list occupations in this period, but we have defined someone with five or more acres in cultivation as a farmer. Robins was one of the twenty-nine people (out of seventy we studied at this store) who qualified. That so large a proportion of the group had little or no land in cultivation is a measure of the early stage of settlement in Yonge; that they could make a living suggests more complex patterns of local exchange than many stories of settlement society in Upper Canada provide for.

5   For consistency and clarity to a modern reader, values throughout the book are given in dollars and cents. In fact, seven of the accounts (including two in 1861, after the province's official conversion to decimal currency) were kept in Halifax currency. One shilling Halifax currency (usually abbreviated cy) equalled 20 cents, there were twelve pence in a shilling, and twenty shillings in a pound. Thus £1 cy = $4.00. Cronk's initial purchases were 1 shilling, 9 pence (1/9) for rum and 5/6 per yard for ticking.

6   Later in the day, his account would be charged for a bandana handkerchief worth $1.10 and needles worth 5 cents.

7   This count includes vest as a fabric, not a finished product.

8   The books used here are AO, Charles Jones Fonds, F180, MU 3155 (daybook) and MU 3165 (ledger). See appendix D.

9   Wien, "Introduction: Habitants, marchands, historiens," 6 (his emphasis).

10 Shammas, "Changes in English and Anglo-American Consumption," 177 (her emphasis).

11 Haydon, *Pioneer Sketches*, 205.

12 By 1842, the two principal local villages, Fitzroy Harbour and Pakenham village, each had four stores and one gristmill. Smith, *Canadian Gazetteer*, 59, 141.

13 Cohen, *Women's Work, Markets, and Economic Development*, 73. The story is

also used in Houston and Prentice, *Schooling and Scholars*, 5, where Haydon is described as a "commentator of the period." Actually, he was born in 1867 and his story was published a century after settlement began in Fitzroy.

CHAPTER ONE

1   *The Backwoods of Canada*, 123. Traill had used the Crusoe theme before coming to Upper Canada and returned to it in *Canadian Crusoes: A Tale of the Rice Lake Plains* (1852). See Peterman, "Catharine Parr Strickland (Traill)."

2   *The Backwoods of Canada*, 1.

3   *The Backwoods of Canada*, 124.

4   Lewis and Urquhart, "Growth and the Standard of Living in a Pioneer Economy," 161, 180. That was about one shop for every sixty families; as we will see, each of our stores dealt with many more families than that. For their discussion of imports, see 166–8. Drawing on the work of Robert Gourlay, Wood, *Making Ontario*, 52–3, suggests an even greater intensity of stores in about 1817: one store for every 200 people in western Upper Canada and for every 123 in some well-developed waterfront townships in eastern Upper Canada.

5   Examples include Widdis, *With Scarcely a Ripple*, 51: "farm households were largely self-sufficient during the pioneer period"; Norrie, Owram, and Emery, *A History of the Canadian Economy*, 100: "even small sums of cash were important to largely self-sufficient farmers"; Conrad and Finkel, *History of the Canadian Peoples*, vol. 2, 90: "a majority of" families in "pre-industrial British North America … rel[ied] only peripherally on … the marketplace"; Baskerville, *Ontario: Image, Identity, and Power*, 72: "most [farms] produced just about enough for their own needs"; Harris, *The Reluctant Land*, 338 "small farmers … supplied their own needs as much as possible"; Parr, *Domestic Goods*, 199: "there was, of course, a time when no one, either female or male, shopped – when necessaries were found or chased or made or traded." For a penetrating critique of this mythology, see Bittermann, "Farm Households and Wage Labour," 13–21.

6   Belisle, *Retail Nation*, 28; Conrad and Finkel, *History of the Canadian Peoples* vol. 1, 267.

7   Weaver, "Making Place on the Canadian Periphery," Chapter 3, provides a rich discussion of this theme in modern settings.

8   Belisle, *Retail Nation*, 15; Bliss, *Northern Enterprise*, 289. See also Wermuth, *Rip Van Winkle's Neighbors*, 92.

9   Wermuth, *Rip Van Winkle's Neighbors*, 8. Even sources denying self-sufficiency may still use it as the basic reference point. See, e.g., Larkin, *The Reshaping of Everyday Life*, 36: "American rural households were almost never completely self-sufficient."

10 Fellman, *Little House, Long Shadow*, 67.

11 Conrad and Finkel, *History of the Canadian Peoples*, vol. 1, 232, 275; see also 306. Unequal exchange is fundamental to many representations of rural Upper Canada. Recent examples include Schrauwers, *Union Is Strength*, 35, 122; and Romney, *Getting It Wrong*, 33. For critical views of this understanding in other

Canadian colonial contexts, see Cadigan, "Power and Agency in Newfoundland and Labrador's History"; and Dépatie, "Commerce et crédit à l'Île Jésus, 1734–75," e.g., 152, 167. Ommer, ed., *Merchant Credit and Labour Strategies*, provides extensive consideration of the issues in numerous settings.

12 Ulrich, *The Age of* Homespun, 39.

13 Innis, *The Fur Trade in Canada*, 383–4.

14 Piva, *The Borrowing Process*, xiii.

15 Russell, *How Agriculture Made Canada*, 16.

16 Greer, *Peasant, Lord, and Merchant*, 156. Greer reconciles an account based on peasant self-sufficiency with the presence of merchants by imagining (157) that many sales (for example, textiles) were to "a minority of village dignitaries and rich peasants." This is not an issue just for historians. The concept of real or basic needs runs throughout discussions of welfare policy and consumption (see, e.g., Shammas, "Standard of Living, Consumption, and Political Economy," 212). In Canada, it has also been the explicit basis of judicial decision-making in aboriginal treaty rights cases (see Wicken, *Mi'kmaq Treaties on Trial*, 227, 235).

17 Quoted terms are from Bruegel, *Farm, Shop, Landing*, 97; Clark, *The Roots of Rural Capitalism*, 27, 31–4, 164, 167; Merrill, "Putting 'Capitalism' in Its Place," 315, 321; Greer, *Peasant, Lord, and Merchant*, 158; Appadurai. "Introduction: Commodities and the Politics of Value," 6–9. Similar dichotomies can be found in Matson, "A House of Many Mansions," 57, which contrasts "customary pricing and local reciprocity" with "regularized patterns of production and exchange"; Wermuth, *Rip Van Winkle's Neighbors*, 9, which contrasts "community values" and "commercial market development"; and Samson, *The Spirit of Industry and Improvement*, 53, which distinguishes between "plainly communitarian" and "driven largely by economic calculations."

18 Brewer and Porter, *Consumption and the World of Goods*, 2.

19 Note Parr, *The Gender of Breadwinners*, 8, which, in another context, eloquently calls on historians to "problematize and unmake the chain of binary oppositions."

20 Compare Shammas, *The Pre-industrial Consumer*, 68, 73–5, 292; T.H. Breen, *The Marketplace of Revolution*, 62; and Clark, *The Roots of Rural Capitalism*, 28. See also Smith, "The Market for Manufactures in the Thirteen Continental Colonies."

21 See the thoughtful discussion in Samson, "Introduction: Situating the Rural in Atlantic Canada" and "Afterword: Capitalism and Modernization in the Atlantic Canada Countryside," 29–30, 260–5.

22 For the ways in which stores and shopping could support and reinforce practices of making things, see, e.g., Ulrich, *The Age of Homespun*, 298–9, 308; Craig, *Backwoods Consumers and Homespun Capitalists*, 183–6.

23 Mancke, "At the Counter of the General Store," 169.

24 Haskell and Teichgraeber, "Introduction: The Culture of the Market," 14, discussing the work of Fernand Braudel. See also Benson and Ugolini, "Introduction: Historians and the Nation of Shopkeepers," 1–2.

25 Brewer and Trentmann, "Introduction: Space, Time and Value in Consuming Cultures," 4.

26 Benson, *Counter Cultures*.
27 Conrad and Finkel, *History of the Canadian Peoples*, vol. 2, 423.
28 Livingston, "Modern Subjectivity and Consumer Culture," 419–20.
29 Lemire, *Fashion's Favourite*, 3. There are rich accounts of seventeenth-century consumption patterns in, e.g., Pennell, "Material Culture in Seventeenth-Century 'Britain,'" and Pope, *Fish into Wine*, 350–93. The latter, an account of seventeenth-century Newfoundland, is notable for taking imports seriously.
30 McKendrick, "Introduction: The Birth of a Consumer Society," 1.
31 Weatherill, *Consumer Behaviour and Material Culture in Britain*, 98, 193, 199. There is a similar emphasis on the "middling sort" in Carson, "The Consumer Revolution in Colonial British America: Why Demand?" 619.
32 de Vries, "Between Purchasing Power and the World of Goods," 107.
33 de Vries, *The Industrious Revolution*. Our phrasing reflects his definition (10) of a household as "usually a family, or with a family at its core." For this idea in North American context, see Craig, "Y-eut-il une 'révolution industrieuse' en Amérique du Nord?"
34 Clemens, "The Consumer Culture of the Middle Atlantic, 1760–1820," 577; Carson, "The Consumer Revolution in Colonial British America: Why Demand?"
35 Breen, *The Marketplace of Revolution*, xvii.
36 Cf. Hood, *The Weaver's Craft*, 112; Main, "The Standard of Living in Southern New England," 128–9. Contrast Kulikoff, *From British Peasants to Colonial American Farmers*, 241, "[T]he modest purchases of middling farm families hardly presaged the start of a consumer society, much less a consumer revolution."
37 Main, *Peoples of a Spacious Land*, 210–11.
38 Ulrich, *The Age of Homespun*, e.g., 102–5, 385–9, 413.
39 Sellers, *The Market Revolution: Jacksonian America*. An example of a work framed by this idea is Wermuth, *Rip Van Winkle's Neighbors*, 9.
40 See, e.g., Osterud, *Bonds of Community*, 206–7; Merchant, *Ecological Revolutions*, 149, 172–4, 308–10.
41 Kulikoff, *From British Peasants to Colonial American Farmers*, 292. See also Stokes, "Introduction," 7–8; and Merrill, "Putting 'Capitalism' in Its Place," 324, which contrasts "the capitalism of the moneyed few and the democratic political economy favored by many … farmers, mechanics, and laborers." On the importance of the land market, see, e.g., Paquet and Wallot, "Stratégie foncière de l'habitant: Québec," 556.
42 Clark, *The Roots of Rural Capitalism*, 11.
43 Sylvester, *The Limits of Rural Capitalism*, 4. See also discussion of "the commercial farmer or profit maximizer" in Russell, *How Agriculture Made Canada*, 17.
44 Maynard, "Between Farm and Factory," 81. Under capitalism, Samson, *The Spirit of Industry and Improvement*, 6, writes, "poor and middling settlers" would be left in "complete reliance on the market."
45 Clark, *The Roots of Rural Capitalism*, 14, 16–17.
46 "[L]e passage d'une société essentiellement de subsistence … à une société transformée par le marché," "une discontinuité importante [qui] transforme la socio-économie québécoise au tournant du XIXe siècle[,] la modernisation et l'instauration d'un régime de capitalisme commercial." Paquet and Wallot, "Structures sociales et niveaux de richesse dans les campagnes du Québec,"

248. On changes in housing in rural Quebec in this period, see Martin, *À la façon du temps présent*, 103. On merchant competition and activity in the countryside, see also St-Georges, "Commerce, crédit et transactions foncières."

47 Courville, *Entre Ville et Campagne*, 26.

48 Livingston, "Modern Subjectivity and Consumer Culture," 416.

49 Fraser, *The Coming of the Mass Market*, 239.

50 Belisle, "Toward a Canadian Consumer History," 181. Her *Retail Nation*, 28, speaks of "a growing propensity to consume among populations that had previously lived at or near subsistence levels."

51 Walden, *Becoming Modern in Toronto*, 334; see also 198.

52 Benson, *Counter Cultures*, 81.

53 "[D]e nombreux citoyens ... ont pu se permettre, pour la première fois, d'acheter des biens au-delà du strict nécessaire." Fahrni, "Explorer la consommation dans une perspective historique," 466. That is also the implication of standard textbooks. Conrad and Finkel, *History of the Canadian Peoples*, Vol. 2, has a chapter titled "Mass Consumer Society and the Search for Identity, 1919–1939," and other index entries for "consumerism" all lead to topics in the twentieth century. Similarly, entries in the index of Norrie, Owram, and Emery, *A History of the Canadian Economy*, that somehow relate to core elements of daily economic life (such as "consumer spending") almost all lead to twentieth-century topics.

54 See Strasser, McGovern, and Judt, "Introduction," to *Getting and Spending*, 3–5.

55 Cohen, *A Consumers' Republic*, 10.

56 Conrad and Finkel, *History of the Canadian Peoples*, Vol. 2, 345. Christie and Gauvreau, "Introduction: Recasting Canada's Post-war Decade," 4.

57 de Vries, *The Industrious Revolution*, 4–5.

58 As is evident when proponents of a particular revolution attempt to connect it to the longer history. See, for example, Cohen, *A Consumers' Republic*, 20–1: "Almost from its initial European settlement, America participated in an economy of commercial exchange, and gradually over the centuries a market revolution increased the amount of goods that Americans purchased rather than made at home (or did without)."

59 Pennell, "Material Culture in Seventeenth-Century 'Britain,'" 83.

60 Shammas, *The Pre-industrial Consumer*, 113n4.

61 Bruegel, *Farm, Shop, Landing*, 160.

62 de Vries, *The Industrious Revolution*, 154.

63 McDonald, "Transatlantic Consumption," 122, discussing the work of Sidney Mintz.

64 McCalla, *The Upper Canada Trade* and *Planting the Province*. For rural marketing as seen through store accounts, see the latter work, 76–81.

65 Brewer and Trentmann, "Introduction: Space, Time and Value in Consuming Cultures," 13.

66 *Consumption and the World of Goods*, 6.

67 The difficulty would be compounded if we sought to consider the implications of goods we might have expected to find but did not. On goods not purchased, see, e.g., Ommer, "Merchant Credit and the Informal Economy," 180.

68 This understanding of the complexity of interpreting even standard goods is much influenced by Pocius, *A Place to Belong*, 280–96.

69 Gerber, *Authors of Their Lives*, 97, 132.

70 See the rich discussion of genre in men's diaries in Vickery, *Behind Closed Doors*, 53–5. Of course, routinely generated quantitative sources also have their own standard forms and conventions; see, e.g., McGaw, "'So Much Depends upon a Red Wheelbarrow,'" 341–3.

71 See the thoughtful discussion in Welch, *Shopping in the Renaissance*, 3–4, 14.

72 For example, Belisle, *Retail Nation*, 15–21, sums up our period – and indeed the longer history of consumption – as "Beginnings." See Russell, *How Agriculture Made Canada*, 21–2, 294n34, for reflection on the issue of "timeless tradition" and rural society.

73 Shammas, *The Pre-industrial Consumer in England and America*, 78.

74 Cf. O'Brien, "Imperialism and the Rise and Decline of the British Economy," 51–5. See also McCalla, "Economy and Empire."

75 Harley, "The Antebellum Tariff: Different Products or Competing Sources?" 799–805. There was still some scope for transborder trade: some American products were better suited to the colonial market, and for a few products American prices were sometimes lower than in Britain. For example, until Britain stopped protecting the East India Company's monopoly, tea was sometimes sufficiently cheaper to warrant the risk and effort of smuggling it across a relatively open border.

76 Breen, *The Marketplace of Revolution*, 35. Breen also does not mention diaries and household accounts, which Laurel Thatcher Ulrich and others have used to excellent effect.

77 Appadurai, "Introduction: Commodities and the Politics of Value," 57.

78 See Rothenberg, *From Market-Places to a Market Economy*, 57–62.

79 Inwood and Wagg, "Wealth and Prosperity in Nova Scotian Agriculture," 254. For uses of inventories as a way to measure wealth inequality in two Canadian jurisdictions, see Gwyn and Siddiq, "Wealth Distribution in Nova Scotia during the Confederation Era," and di Matteo and George, "Canadian Wealth Inequality in the Late Nineteenth Century." In the latter, see 456n7 on earlier probate records. Paquet and Wallot, "Structures sociales et niveaux de richesse dans les campagnes du Québec," 240, make the case for prioritizing stocks over flows.

80 See, e.g., Osborne, "Wills and Inventories: Records of Life and Death in a Developing Society." The extent of coverage is suggested by the fact that, for the three counties of the Midland District, Osborne found only 129 usable inventories in Surrogate Court records covering a period of more than sixty years, from 1795 to 1858. Confirming analyses for other jurisdictions, he shows that clothing and groceries, among the main goods in this study, were not at all well represented. On the variability and limitations of inventories, see also Michel, "Le livre de compte (1784–1792) de Gaspard Massue," 375–6.

81 Mancke, "At the Counter of the General Store," 172, 178.

82 Craig, Rygiel, and Turcotte, "The Homespun Paradox," 49; Craig, *Backwoods Consumers and Homespun Capitalists*, 181–98. For a discussion of accounting sources, see Craig, Rygiel, and Turcotte, "Survival or Adaptation? Domestic Rural Textile Production in Eastern Canada," 154n51.

83 Craig, *Backwoods Consumers and Homespun Capitalists*, 219. The quotation is the subtitle of this book.

84 For example, Michel, "Le livre de compte (1784–1792) de Gaspard Massue"; "Endettement et société rurale dans la région de Montréal," 173–8; "Un marchand rural en Nouvelle-France."

85 Sweeny, "Accounting for Change," 121; see also Sweeny with Bradley and Hong, "Movement, Options and Costs," which demonstrates how much can be learned just from the indexes to the ledgers. Templeman accounts are drawn on also in Ommer, "Merchant Credit and the Informal Economy." Thorp, "Doing Business in the Backcountry," provides a colonial American example.

86 Desrosiers, "Un aperçu des habitudes de consommation de la clientèle de Joseph Cartier"; and "La clientèle d'un marchand général en milieu rural."

87 Sweeny with Bradley and Hong, "Movement, Options and Costs," 112.

88 For example, in her excellent account of the Kentucky frontier, Elizabeth Perkins used one firm's daybook over four months and another's ledger for nine months; even so, she chose to draw small samples from each. Perkins, "The Consumer Frontier," 494.

89 Selecting a few years from a massive set of accounts is also the strategy of Wermuth, *Rip Van Winkle's Neighbors*, 94.

90 Craig, *Backwoods Consumers and Homespun Capitalists*, 121.

91 Bittermann, MacKinnon, and Wynn, "Of Inequality and Interdependence," 34. Dépatie, "Commerce et crédit à l'Île Jésus, 1734–75," 152; Sweeny with Bradley and Hong, "Movement, Options and Costs," 114n8, 119–20; and Pronovost, *La bourgeoisie marchande en milieu rural*, 199, all demonstrate that competition was normal.

92 Cf. Belisle, *Retail Nation*, 13, which sees the department store as representing "retail's transformation from local economies to international economies."

93 McInnis, "The Economy of Canada in the Nineteenth Century," 75.

94 Belich, *Replenishing the Earth*, 51–5, 58–62.

95 Darroch and Soltow, *Property and Inequality in Victorian Ontario*, 13. See also Darroch, "Scanty Fortunes and Rural Middle Class Formation."

96 Examples of other categorizations include Greer, *Peasant, Lord, and Merchant*, 156; and Craig, *Backwoods Consumers and Homespun Capitalists*, 261

97 Our findings also tend to confirm Howard, "'The Biggest Small-Town Store in America,'" 458–9, that "[s]tudies of rural consumers challenge the notion of a homogeneous, urban-focused consumer society."

CHAPTER TWO

1 www.uppercanadavillage.com/index.cfm/en/about-the-village/tour-the-village/crysler-store/ (accessed 1 September 2013).

2 Graham, "Darlingside," 681–6, has modern photographs of the by-now empty store's interior, including the attic, used for storage. (It also has one of the interior of Scovil's store.) Fleming, *General Stores of Canada*, provides photographs of store interiors, necessarily from later than our period.

3 QUA, Darling Papers, box 6, stock inventory, 1 April 1858. For products that varied substantially, a number of lines might be required. For example, it required four lines to record different sizes of augers with a total value of less than four dollars.

4 QUA, Tett Papers, vol. 73, inventory, 30 October 1851.

5 So as not to exaggerate the contrast, we made generous assumptions about equivalents and categories. For example, nails are a single category, although there was some variation in the types of nails recorded at the two stores;

similarly, we treated the many kinds of books found at Darling's, but not Tett's, as a single category. More than eighty products were common to the two lists; but more than sixty listed by Tett were not on Darling's list, and more than seventy on the latter were not on the former.

6   QUA, Tett Papers, vol. 1, letterbook, 1833–49, 1 and 5–6, Tett to Macintosh & Co, 11 November 1833 and 30 August 1834.

7   For example, Adam Hope's store in St Thomas, a larger town than those we consider, initially required four people: Hope and Thomas Hodge, his partner; plus a labourer and a young man to help around the store. See Hope to Robert Hope, 11 November 1838, in Crerar, *Letters of Adam Hope*, 314.

8   McCalla, *Planting the Province*, 219–31. See also Darroch and Soltow, *Property and Inequality in Victorian Ontario*, 6; and Darroch, "Scanty Fortunes and Rural Middle Class Formation," 635.

9   McInnis, "The Economy of Canada in the Nineteenth Century," 68.

10 Of course others might have engaged in these activities without involving our specific store.

11 Smith, *Smith's Canadian Gazetteer*, 21; see also Wood, *Making Ontario*, 37.

12 McGaughey, "Ephraim Jones," and McIlwraith, "Charles Jones."

13 McIlwraith, "The Logistical Geography of the Great Lakes Grain Trade," 275–6.

14 McCalla, *Planting the Province*, 94–9. Data on local deliveries to the mill for each month in 1834 are shown in Norrie, Owram, and Emery, *A History of the Canadian Economy*, 107.

15 Mackay, *The Canada Directory 1851*, 472.

16 See Akenson, *The Irish in Ontario*, 62–3.

17 Graham, "Darlingside." The site was designated as a National Historic Site in 2000, and the store was still standing in 2008. See www.ltihistoricalsociety.org/darlingside.html (accessed 23 August 2012), which includes images of the property. The latter gives Darling's birth and death dates as 1813–82; dates in the text are from the finding aid to the Darling Papers, QUA.

18 QUA, Darling Family Papers, 2303.28, box 6, Wood Accounts, 1864–76; Wood Book a/c of Steamers, 1876–83. In the 1860s, his selling price was $1.50 per cord for softwood and $2.50 for hardwood.

19 Schurman, "Benjamin Tett of Newboro, 1820–1843"; Patterson, "Benjamin Tett and Bedford Mills."

20 For images of this property, see www.ghosttownpix.com/ontario/imgNW/bedimg.html (accessed 23 August 2012).

21 My reading of the Scovil papers at Queen's University Archives is that the accounts are Wing's until May 1846 and Scovil's thereafter. The finding aid to AO, F 4280, Samuel S. Scovil Fonds, says Scovil worked for Wing from 1841 to 1849 and acquired the business in the latter year. See www.archeion.ca/samuel-s-scovil-fonds;rad, accessed 21 August 2012. Scovil's house and store were still standing in 2006. See *"My Own Four Walls" Heritage Buildings in Bastard and South Burgess Township*, by Diane Haskins, edited by Pamela Fry, 214–18, as quoted at archiver.rootsweb. ancestry.com/th/read/ONT-LEEDS-GRENVILLE/2006-06/1149603729 (accessed 21 August 2012).

22 Cole, *Illustrated Historical Atlas of Peterborough County*, 87, says there were "nearly 700 heads of family" in Dummer alone in 1835; this seems high, considering that in 1861 there were only 229 occupiers of land in this almost entirely rural township. On Thomas Choate, see 89–90.

23 TUA, Choate Papers and Additions, B77-026, Preliminary Inventory. By now Warsaw's population was about 150. *Directory of United Counties of Peterborough and Victoria*, 30, lists another store, a grocer, and a tavern. See also Cole, *Origins: The History of Dummer Township*, 192–6 and (for pictures of Choate, the store, and the mill) 41, 68, and 75.

24 See TUA, Fowlds Papers, B72-001, Preliminary Inventory, 1–2. See also Ennals, "Zacheus Burnham"; Jones, "John Gilchrist"; Ouellette, "James Crooks"; and Brunger, "Richard Birdsall."

25 Cole, *Illustrated Historical Atlas of Peterborough County*, 74; *Directory of United Counties of Peterborough and Victoria for 1858*, 29. There were four other stores and two inns in the village, which by 1858 had a population of 430.

26 TUA, Fowlds Papers, box 14, file 1, [?] Fowlds to Hugh Lock, 20 July 1863; [?] Fowlds to N.Y. Paterson, 4 February 1869 (copy). Fires are stressed in Cole, *Illustrated Historical Atlas of Peterborough County*, 74.

27 Lovell, *Province of Ontario Directory* (1871), 453, lists Fowlds Brothers as "storekeepers and lumber merchants," Henry Fowlds as postmaster, Henry M. Fowlds as a "lumber merchant," James S. Fowlds, of "Fowlds Brothers," as reeve of Percy, and William as another member of Fowlds Brothers.

28 See Ennals, "Zacheus Burnham."

29 *Directory of United Counties of Peterborough and Victoria* (1858), 32, lists two stores, but not Sherin's, and gives a population of "about 80." By contrast, Sherin's is the only local store listed in Lovell, *Canada Directory for 1857–8*, 253.

30 See TUA, Sherin Papers, B71-002, Finding Aid, Introduction. The collection includes accounts from as early as 1856, confirming that the business was in existence before 1858. Business description from *Fuller's Counties of Peterborough and Victoria Directory for 1865 & 1866*, 86; this gives a population of "about 300." Despite this description, hardware and chemicals, as we will see, were more prominent than either dry goods or groceries in Sherin's sales.

31 Smith, *Smith's Canadian Gazetteer*, 88, 151, 205. Mackay, *The Canada Directory 1851*, 255, 281, 462, gives the same number of stores.

32 For comment on customers' travel to Brockville, see, e.g., QUA, Tett Papers, vol. 1, letterbook, 1833–49, 31, Tett to Thomas McKay, 28 February 1840.

33 Otherwise, we anticipated that the collection, management, and interpretation of all the data in even a single daybook could be overwhelming. The constraints included the capacity of the spreadsheet software available when the project began, the time required to enter and check data, and the time needed subsequently to investigate and resolve the many nuances, variations, and ambiguities encountered within the data. In any case, sampling generated appropriate and much more than sufficient data for our project's aims and requirements.

34 As we note in appendix D, the ledger for Fowlds's in 1854 gave locations for

most customers; 90 percent were in the two immediate townships. In our pilot projects, we also looked beyond the adjacent townships but found almost none of those we had not linked even as we increased the likelihood of finding duplicate names. In general, as we argue below, it seems unlikely that people would have travelled considerable distances on a regular basis, passing closer stores, to patronize a specific country store.

35   Wermuth, *Rip Van Winkle's Neighbors*, reports a similar linkage rate; he also selects single years for study; see 94, 99.

36   Craig, *Backwoods Consumers and Homespun Capitalists*, 296n65, uses this threshold too.

37   Note that households organized the key dimensions of food and shelter; and people working for wages, such as servants and labourers, were often "found," that is had board, room, and sometimes other goods as part of their wages. See de Vries, *The Industrious Revolution*, 10–12, 29; also useful is Riello, *A Foot in the Past*, 186.

38   At various points we use a threshold of the ten leading buyers as a convenience, intended to explore those for whom we might have a large proportion of purchases during the year (as opposed to an occasional purchase whose relationship to overall consumption patterns would be difficult to estimate). Because accounts could be large for various reasons, the ten leaders in specific product categories may not coincide exactly with the ten largest accounts overall; and the rank-order within the group of large accounts could also vary from one category to another.

39   Two examples: among the ten leading buyers were men who made only one or two purchases, such as a large quantity of leather or a horse.

CHAPTER THREE

1   Brett, "Clothing Worn in Canada: Changing Fashions in the Nineteenth Century." This chapter incorporates material from McCalla, "Textile Purchases by Some Ordinary Upper Canadians," reprinted with the permission of the publisher, Cape Breton University Press. Variations from data reported there result from a comprehensive review of all data sets and of additional work on fabrics and definitions.

2   For cotton in Lower Canada, see Hood and Ruddel, "Artifacts and Documents in the History of Quebec Textiles," 65; and Vallières and Desloges, "Les échanges commerciaux de la colonie laurentienne avec la Grande Bretagne," 448. The latter covers imports to both Canadas.

3   Her Canada's Visual History study has been described as "pivotal in the literature on Canadian costumer history." See Beaudoin-Ross and Blackstock, "Costume in Canada: An Annotated Bibliography," 67.

4   For a similar emphasis on silk, lace, velvet, etc., see, e.g., Bates, "'Beauty Unadorned.'"

5   Burnham and Burnham, *"Keep me warm one night,"* 13; also, e.g., 85, 143, 179. Severin, "Muslin Gowns and Moccasins," 140.

6   Hood and Ruddel, "Artifacts and Documents in the History of Quebec Textiles," 88.

7   The speaker was Adams George Archibald, quoted in Creighton, *British North America at Confederation*, 27. Archibald's relationship to everyday

rural life is suggested by his biographer's description of his family as "long ... prominent politically, economically, and socially." See Pryke, "Sir Adams George Archibald."

8   "La plupart des femmes s'habillent en étoffe du pays qu'elles filent, tissent, teignent et coupent." Le collectif Clio, *L'histoire des femmes au Québec*, 120.

9   Brett, *Women's Costume in Early Ontario*, 4.

10 Brett, "Country Clothing in Nineteenth-Century Ontario," 40.

11 Brett, *Women's Costume in Early Ontario*, 3.

12 Brett, "Clothing Worn in Canada: Changing Fashions in the Nineteenth Century."

13 Cohen, *Women's Work, Markets, and Economic Development*, 75–82; quote at 82.

14 Duplessis, "Was There a Consumer Revolution in Eighteenth-Century New France?" 150–1, 153.

15 Ruddel, "Consumer Trends, Clothing, Textiles and Equipment in the Montreal Area," 53.

16 Craig, *Backwoods Consumers and Homespun Capitalists*, 181–98.

17 Inwood and Wagg, "The Survival of Handloom Weaving in Rural Canada"; Roelens and Inwood, "'Labouring at the Loom.'" The 1851 census recorded 1,700 weavers in Upper Canada, and the 1871 census reported 2,600; see McCalla, *Planting the Province*, 280. Our samples include four whose occupations were "weaver," three of whom proved to have only tiny accounts. The fourth is discussed below. Obviously many more people wove than were caught by the occupational descriptions in the census.

18 Craig, *Backwoods Consumers and Homespun Capitalists*, 189, 216.

19 Errington, *Wives and Mothers, School Mistresses and Scullery Maids*, 200. See also discussion of homespun at 99–100.

20 Skelton, *The Backwoodswoman*, 204–5, recognizes that "the culture of flax and hemp was never widespread in Canada," then explains the linen-making process anyway. On the actual history of flax in Upper Canada, and its emergence in the 1850s as a locally important industrial fibre, see MacFadyen, "Fashioning Flax."

21 Craig, *Backwoods Consumers and Homespun Capitalists*, 196; Hood, *The Weaver's Craft*, 120–3. For a set of bed curtains, valances, covers, and window curtains, fifty yards of fabric might be needed.

22 The latter usage is dated 1837 in the OED, but some sources, including Inwood and Wagg, "The Survival of Handloom Weaving in Rural Canada," 347, attest to its being produced in American mills from about 1820. On the problems of textile terminology, see, for example, Hood, 136–7, 159; also Cox, "Objects of Worth, Objects of Desire."

23 Farnie, "The Role of Merchants as Prime Movers in the Expansion of the Cotton Industry," 29.

24 Shipments to Charles Jones's stores in 1808 were mainly of yellow fancy calico but also included nine pieces of "printed calico"; and Tett's 1834 purchases in Montreal included both calico and print. Buchanan, *The Dictionary of Science and Technical Terms*, 183, says that "In England, unprinted cotton cloth is called calico; in America, the cloth is called calico after it is printed." The OED also makes this distinction. But, as all such fabrics sold at our stores were from Britain, this does not resolve our puzzle.

25 As a result, the data for some of the specific cottons are lower-bounded. The

object of the table is, in any case, to identify fabrics and provide orders of magnitude.

26 The others were corduroy (one buyer, four yards), divinity (two buyers, five yards), and imitation (five buyers, sixteen yards). Russell (one buyer, nine yards) and durant (one buyer, six yards) have been included with woolen cloth. Another product sold by the yard was "quality," for which I have not discovered a definition. Its price (an average of about 10 cents per yard) was too low for any fabric; I have assumed it belongs in the category of notions.

27 The length of six large "pieces" of cotton is estimated in this total, on the basis of price.

28 On Russian sheeting, see Minhinnick, *At Home in Upper Canada*, 82. Divinity might have been dimity; one twenty-nine-yard piece of it was imported by Jones in 1808; but in the daybook it does not seem to be spelled that way.

29 We discuss blankets further in chapter 7. Although Freel owned a total of 300 acres of land, at this stage of settlement that was not necessarily an indicator of unusual wealth; like most of their neighbours, the family lived in a round log home.

30 As an example of the interpretive challenge, consider the cross-references in the entry for calico in the *Dictionary of Traded Goods*, which says it was "used to make apron, bed gown, breeches, cap, caul, coat, coif, counterpane, coverlet, cupboard cloth, curtain, frock, gown, head cloth, head roll, hood, lining, mantua, neck cloth, night gown, petticoat, pillow bere, polonaise, quilt, sheet, shift, shirt, stockings, suit, table cloth, tester, valance, waistcoat (for women and children), window curtain," www.british-history.ac.uk/report.aspx?compid=58713 (accessed 2 May 2009).

31 He was charged just over 40 cents on "clothing account" (i.e., for fulling) on 9 May 1809, enough for only a few yards of cloth. A number of accounts, including one other sample member, had similar entries transferred from the mill books that day.

32 These volumes, intended not to underestimate domestic production, are based on standard rates later in the province's history, when carding generally cost 6.7 cents per pound at the province's mills. Cohen, *Women's Work, Markets, and Economic Development*, 77, gives a price of 12.5 cents per pound, but this was during the War of 1812, a period of high inflation. Gourlay, *Statistical Account of Upper Canada*, 259 and 277, has examples from this region in 1817–18 of carding at 8.3 cents and 10 cents per pound. At these prices, the charge to Seaman would have represented 46 or 38 pounds.

33 AO, F180, MU3184, Charles Jones Papers, invoice book, E-1, 1802–08. For 300 pieces, actual lengths are recorded, a total of over 7,200 yards. We estimate remaining yardage based on prices per piece.

34 These were calamancoe, camblet, "capl," carpeting, chambrays, damask, duffle, Florentine, gauze, green & blue, molton, mazurin, nankeen, Pomeranian, Silesia, stripe, stroud, taffeta, velveteen, and vesting. Four of these appear in appendix A in later years.

35 Purchases in September 1808 account for almost one-third of the total yardage in table 4, but that is partly a reflection of very limited activity at this store in summer 1809. Monthly volumes were roughly equivalent in October, March, and April (which together accounted for another third of yardage).

The same monthly pattern holds in purchases of other sewing supplies. Even if they were not buying fabrics at this store, people might also have travelled farther to buy during the winter, when travel was easier on frozen roads. Seasonal patterns were visible in later samples but not to this extent or with this precise periodization.

36   The prices of calico, fustian, jean, muslin, and cambric were half or slightly over half; cotton, ticking, check, and linen were one-third or slightly higher; and sheeting was just one-quarter its earlier price. Most fabrics came in a range of qualities and prices, however. Thus, the 1808 import invoices give three distinct values for calicos; most were valued at 31.7 cents, but there were smaller quantities at 38.3 cents and 58.3 cents. With a few higher and lower exceptions, calico purchases were priced between 47 cents and 53 cents. By comparison, calico sold at Yonge Mills in 1828–29 for 15 cents to 40 cents (with 20 cents the most common price and just four transactions at more than 25 cents); cotton cost 12 cents to 25 cents. By contrast, Irwin and Temin, "The Antebellum Tariff on Cotton Textiles Revisited," 778–80, claim that goods worth less than 25 cents per yard "were not typical of British products" in the period after 1816. The British price indexes for this period found in Mitchell and Deane, *Abstract of British Historical Statistics,* 469–71, are not quite right for our purposes, but generally indicate that much of the fall in prices had happened by 1822–23. The most systematic overview of prices in Canada in the period does not include manufactured goods in its price index; see Paquet et Wallot, *Un Québec moderne, 1760– 1840,* 176.

37   In this area, oats, potatoes, butter, beef, and pork were one-third lower than twenty years earlier; and wheat, peas, and hay were between 10 and 20 percent lower. See McCalla, *Planting the Province,* 336–9. Many of these products are included in Paquet and Wallot, *Un Québec moderne, 1760–1840,* 176–9: their index indicates that prices at Quebec in 1828 were 90 percent of those in 1808; and at Montreal were 83 percent.

38   During the year they also bought sixteen sewing or pegging awls and 7.5 pounds of shoe bills (a type of nail); they were also credited for making and repairing shoes.

39   Another example of making and buying was John Cannon (not shown in the table), who had twenty sheep and reported production of sixty pounds of wool, thirty yards of fulled cloth, and twenty yards of flannel. He also purchased sixty-two yards of ten different fabrics, none of them woolens. In a nine-person household, cloth made and bought equalled twelve yards per person.

40   On the complexity of this apparently simple term in the eighteenth century, see Hood, *The Weaver's Craft,* 136.

41   Earlier and later sources from this firm provide additional context for our evidence from 1842. Tett's imports in 1834–35, as he began the business, confirm that woolens and cottons were the main fabrics, together accounting for 5/6ths of textile values and yardage in each year. A comprehensive inventory at 30 October 1851 recorded about five thousand yards of fabric, over four thousand of which were cotton. In terms of value the approximately 230 yards of woolen cloth ranked next behind cottons; linens were also around 200 yards but much lower in value; and the only luxury fabric was about 130

yards of satinette. QUA, Tett Papers (2247), vol. 67, invoice book, 1833–38; vol. 73, business inventory.

42 Cole, *Origins: The History of Dummer Township*, 69–71.

43 These included John Biset and Charles Peters, who, besides making thirty and fifty yards of flannel respectively, were also among the five buyers of flannel.

44 On warp, see Craig, *Backwoods Consumers and Homespun Capitalists*, 184–6.

45 Most were farmers. The exceptions were two women who did not appear on the agricultural census, one person not linked, one labourer, and one weaver.

46 The most likely explanation for these patterns is that we see only a part of the total mill output; for example, the mill might have had its own accounts, or buyers could have paid the mill directly in cash or with a share of the product. Other possibilities for the variation are that people had only one part of processing done at this mill (doing other work by hand or using some other mill), that markets and exchanges diverted some of the flow between stages of production (e.g., if carded wool was sold), or that production was focused in July (for which we do not have accounts). The census, taken early in 1852, reported 1851 production.

47 This was the case for one weaver whose accounts survive and have been analyzed with great sophistication in Livingston-Lowe, "Counting on Customers."

48 Because a number of pieces were involved, this is an order of magnitude, sensitive to the price used in estimating lengths.

49 And outranked by only two 1861 Fowlds's customers in the entire sample group.

50 Craig, *Backwoods Consumers and Homespun Capitalists*, 219.

51 Allowing for eighteen who bought both at Fowlds's in 1861, this makes a total of 274 buyers of one or both of these fabrics, ranking them as among the most commonly purchased of all goods. The OED makes gingham either cotton or linen; but the *Dictionary of Traded Goods* confirms cotton and says it was "not common in the shops."

52 Jensen, "Needlework as Art, Craft, and Livelihood," 3.

53 QUA, Tett Papers, vol. 73, Store inventory, 30 October 1851, lists 100 and 200 yard spools.

54 Despite the range of prices for sales, the 1808 invoices for imports give just five prices for ribbon (satin [three different prices], narrow, and stamped); possibly the "velvet" was also ribbon. This level of variation is confirmed by Tett's inventory in 1851; for example, it included buttons at twelve different prices.

55 Martin, "Ribbons of Desire: Gendered Stories in the World of Goods," 183.

56 As we will see in chapter 5, "caps" could also be for guns; they can be distinguished from wearing apparel by the unit, the "box."

57 Neck ties could be and belts normally were for women. About one-third of buyers of the former (in six samples) and three-quarters of buyers of the latter (at all five 1861 stores) were definitely women. Two of the men who bought belts (both at Darling's) are recorded as having bought ladies' and silk belts.

58 For example, at Tett's store, four customers were credited with homemade cloth (from 2.5 to 9 yards), two with mitts (three and four pairs), and one with socks (eighteen pairs). See also discussion of the Bush family, below.

59 See Craig, *Backwoods Consumers and Homespun Capitalists*, 210.

60   And in fact, of the almost one hundred transactions in indigo at all stores, over 60 percent were of just one or two ounces; only five exceeded a half-pound.

61   Minhinnick, *At Home in Upper Canada,* 112, says indigo was used routinely for laundry bluing.

62   Adrosko, *Natural Dyes and Home Dyeing,* 17, 68–9, 88–95; Bemiss, *The Dyer's Companion,* 9–13. Moreover, some recipes required both madder and indigo. Total purchases from all samples of the other main dyestuffs were nineteen pounds of madder, thirteen pounds of logwood, twenty-seven pounds of redwood, and twenty-five pounds of ochre. A few volumes are missing in these transactions, but even if we imagine one hundred pounds of the four dyes and halve the standard recipe to four ounces per pound of wool, these would have allowed dyeing at most four hundred yards of fabrics. This can be compared to the over 7,500 yards of wool cloth produced just by the people in the eight samples for which this information is available.

63   Traill, *Canadian Settler's Guide,* 173–6.

64   Alum is a sulphate of potassium and aluminum, and copperas a sulphate of iron. S.D. Smith, "The Market for Manufactures in the Thirteen Continental Colonies," 690–1, uses alum imports as an indicator of the colonial wool economy, but notes that "it does not seem possible to arrive at a reliable multiplier" from volumes to total colonial output of dyed fabric, because formulas varied and alum had other uses, notably in leather tanning. In our samples, where alum and a dye were purchased at the same time, volumes ranged from one part alum to four of the dye up to equal parts. See also Hood, *The Weaver's Craft,* 107–8.

65   Robertson, *Guide to Dressmaking and Fancy Work,* 13. The specified length is for cloth thirty-two inches wide. For the figure of five to nine yards, see Weatherill, *The Account Book of Richard Latham,* xxvi. See also Rothstein, *Barbara Johnson's Album of Fashions and Fabrics,* for variation in yardage requirements for dresses in early nineteenth-century England, from six to fourteen yards; only some of the variation was a function of fabric widths. My thanks to Dr Alexandra Palmer for this reference and for her advice on the complexities of dress and fashion.

66   Craig, *Backwoods Consumers and Homespun Capitalists,* 200. See also Taylor, "Fabric in Women's Costume from 1860 to 1880," 26–7.

67   See Bara, "Cradled in Furs," 44; and illustration in Cunnington et al, *A Dictionary of English Costume,* 229.

68   Robertson, *Guide to Dressmaking and Fancy Work,* 14, speaks of whalebone as among the supplies that "must not be forgotten" when planning a dress.

69   With less than 7 percent of provincial population, Johnstown accounted for more than 11 percent of linen output in 1842; across the province, per capita linen output was one-third of a yard.

70   For the sheep economy in Johnstown District c. 1817, see Gourlay, *Statistical Account of Upper Canada,* 263–68, 277–8; for 1842, see Akenson, *The Irish in Ontario,* 394–5.

71   On the provincial wool economy in this period, see Inwood and Wagg, "The Survival of Handloom Weaving in Rural Canada"; and McCalla, *Planting the Province,* 322–5.

72   See, e.g., Perkins, "The Consumer Frontier," 507.

73 The leading Fowlds's buyers purchased over three hundred yards of woolens, compared to about one hundred at Darling's.

74 In fact, only sixteen of the forty-one exceeding four dollars were households of four or more; they included Oakes and ten customers at Fowlds's in 1861. "Leading" relates to ranking by yardage purchased, as in table 4.

75 See Cole, *Origins: The History of Dummer Township*, 217–18. On someTett invoices from the 1830s for goods supplied by wholesalers, a few hats and gloves stand out at the high end of prices for these goods; in every case they are identified as being for members of the Tett family, not resale.

76 Just six reached even twenty dollars and the only one to reach thirty dollars was Widow Comstock, discussed in the text above.

77 For Leeds, see his *Statistical Account of Upper Canada*, 262–70, 284–5. On domestic service, see Errington, *Wives and Mothers, School Mistresses and Scullery Maids*, 85–130.

78 Cf Ruddel, "Consumer Trends, Clothing, Textiles and Equipment in the Montreal Area," 59.

79 Such as Peter Ewing's purchases on 17 August 1842 for himself and for George Thurlow: 1 yard each of black ribbon, 1 yard each of black crepe, and 0.75 yard each of black silk. All of the silk purchased at this store was black, a total of 12 yards bought by eight buyers in eleven pieces ranging from 0.5 yard to 2.5 yards. Another example was the charges to John Crea's account at Darling's on 1 April 1861, which included 9 yards of black orleans, 3 yards of black crepe, and 1.5 yards of black cambric. Other purchases on that day included hooks and eyes (which typically were used for dress-making) and three kinds of thread.

CHAPTER FOUR

1 Chase, *Dr Chase's Recipes*, 176. I owe this reference to Bernadine Dodge. Origanum was marjoram. Variations on this formula can be found in other sources, for example the OED, which includes Steers's recipe and cites the Edinburgh and British *Pharmacopoeia*. This chapter, a revised version of McCalla, "A World without Chocolate," is reprinted with the permission of the publisher, the Agricultural History Society. It also draws on McCalla, *Consumption Stories: Customer Purchases of Alcohol*, reprinted by permission of CIEQ. Any variations from data published in these sources result from a complete recheck of data and from continuing close editorial scrutiny of the data in subsequent years. My thanks to Kris Inwood for the chapter title.

2 Chavasse, *Advice to a Mother*, 69. On Chavasse, a popular Birmingham obstetrician, see Adams, *Architecture in the Family Way*, 104.

3 Jefferis, *Search Lights on Health*, 81; note its warning of the importance of "taking care not to drink the lotion by mistake."

4 Gough, *The Journal of Alexander Henry the Younger*, vol. 2, 737.

5 The stores are Yonge Mills in 1828–29, Tett in 1842, Choate in 1851, Fowlds in 1854, and Scovil in 1861. Invoices to the two Jones stores in 1808 include three dozen bottles of Steers opodeldoc at $4.00 per dozen. Opodeldoc also appears in an inventory at Darling's, but no one in the 1861 sample bought any there.

6 On "the primacy of chocolate" in the early stages of this story, see Norton, "Tasting Empire," 666.

7   See, for example, A Thorough Housewife, *The Dominion Home Cook-Book*,
     121–2; Driver, *The Home Cook Book*, 220, 224, 230, 261–2, 298, 312–13,
     323, 330–1, 340, 343. Chocolate can sometimes be found in lists of prices
     of beverages and in other forms of description; see, for example, Hart,
     Pioneering in North York, 148.

8   Frances Brooke, *The History of Emily Montague*, vol. 1, 134. For another
     genteel woman consumer, see extracts from the diary of Elizabeth Russell,
     1806, in Firth, *The Town of York, 1793–1815*, 257, 265.

9   Campbell, *Travels in the Interior Inhabited Parts of North America*, 299.
     Campbell was writing here of a scheme to produce kelp in the New World
     and the context is the high cost of labour.

10   Lambert, *Travels through Canada, and the United* States, vol. 1, 102.

11   Thomas G. Ridout to his father, 15 July 1811, in Edgar, ed., *Ten Years of
     Upper Canada in Peace and War*, 41.

12   Dunlop, ed., *Our Forest Home*, 90.

13   Invoices to the two Jones stores in 1808 do, however, include twenty-eight
     pounds of chocolate, at a value of 40 cents per pound. This made it one of
     the most modest of all grocery imports. Tett's import invoices do not include
     chocolate, nor do later inventories from Tett's and Darling's stores.

14   Province of Canada, Legislative Assembly, *Sessional Papers*, 1862, no. 2, TTN,
     schedule 2. The value of imports was three thousand dollars (about 12 cents per
     pound). Annual imports averaged just over one thousand dollars in 1850–52.

15   Shammas, *The Pre-industrial Consumer in England and America*, 235.

16   Shammas, *The Pre-industrial Consumer in England and America*, 78–84.

17   Jones and Spang, "Sans-culottes, sans café, sans tabac," 40.

18   E.g., Traill, *The Canadian Settler's Guide*, 133–4.

19   For goods consumed by adults only, actual per capita consumption was, of
     course, much higher. For example, enough tobacco was imported to the
     Canadas in 1860–62 to permit annual consumption of almost 8 pounds per
     adult male. Oddly enough, suitable data on provincial tobacco outputs are
     available only for 1851, when a reported 777,000 pounds were produced,
     almost all in the westernmost counties, Essex and Kent. If it was consumed
     within the province, it was equivalent to another 0.75 pound per capita (or
     about 3 pounds per male over fifteen).

20   In the 1830s, according to his import invoices, Benjamin Tett bought salt in
     barrels of 280 pounds. A minot was a unit of volume (about 92 percent of a
     Winchester bushel); see Paquet and Wallot, "Some Price Indexes for Quebec
     and Montreal," 311.

21   There were also five buyers of snuff boxes, three of whom are not recorded as
     having bought snuff.

22   Among them they accounted for 38 percent of all tea purchased, 44 percent
     of tobacco, and 56 percent of sugar. Groceries represented between one-fifth
     and one-third of total debits to these accounts.

23   There were no sugar sales between early May and late August; after the end
     of April there were just two small tea transactions, both in May; and there
     were just three transactions in tobacco after late June (all in August).

24   Seaman was the only leading customer not to buy tea.

25   There were five who bought tea, four who bought tobacco, and three who

bought sugar (i.e., one customer bought two of these that frequently: Stephen Bisnet's modest purchases of tea and sugar occurred in four months, and he bought tobacco in three).

26　For the whole 1808–09 sample, there were four purchases of two pounds of tea, twenty-one of two or more pounds of tobacco, and ten of five or more pounds of sugar.

27　Actually, import invoices record all rum as spirits; the latter term in the daybook presumably refers to "Jamaica spirits," which were more expensive than "Grenada spirits."

28　Per gallon, rum was $1.30 in September, $1.40 then $1.60 in November, and $2.10 from February to May.

29　The price per gallon was exactly four times the price per quart; thus 50 cents or 60 cents.

30　Larkin, *The Reshaping of Everyday Life*, 286.

31　Merritt, "Early Inns and Taverns," 206.

32　Lockwood, "Temperance in Upper Canada as Ethnic Subterfuge," 46.

33　Akenson, *The Irish in Ontario*, 218.

34　E.g., Greer, *The Patriots and the People*, 54–5.

35　Noel, *Canada Dry*, 222.

36　Greer, *Peasant, Lord, and Merchant*, 158–9.

37　Moreira, "Rum in the Atlantic Provinces," 22.

38　For social drinking, the context might be reciprocal treating; thus it may not be unreasonable to estimate individual consumption on the basis of purchases.

39　Wilson, "Reciprocal Work Bees and the Meaning of Neighbourhood," 433–4n5. See 443 for writers who suggested 5 gallons of whiskey for a bee with sixteen men, an amount equal to 2.5 pints per man, five times the daily rate suggested by Moreira!

40　Among the twenty leading accounts by total debits in each of these samples, just three bought no alcohol, the fifteenth, seventeenth, and twentieth ranked buyers in 1828–29. On the other hand, two of the leading accounts in 1808–09 bought two gallons or less; and two of the leading accounts in 1828–29 bought just three quarts each.

41　And his rate (1.25 gallons per week) was far below the "half a gallon per person per day" (in logging bees) cited by Clarke, *The Ordinary People of Essex*, 407. Clarke's source is Guillet, *The Pioneer Farmer and Backwoodsman*, vol. 1, 338. As usual for these extraordinary rates, Guillet's source is a temperance advocate, here an 1898 recollection that claimed this rate of individual consumption was often sustained "over a period of months." Guillet is skeptical, but as is common with stories of alcohol in pioneer society, he includes the story anyway. We cite it as an indication of how improbable consumption stories can persist even in serious scholarly work.

42　Some examples can help extend this argument. The longest gap in purchasing for the Andrews was a three-week span (in which there were transactions on nine days) from 27 November to 17 December 1808. Calvin Patterson bought no alcohol between 25 December 1808 and 18 February 1809, yet there were transactions on his account on thirteen days in this period. The leading 1828–29 buyer, James Adams, had charges on his account in eight of the weeks between 6 July and 20 September 1828, yet the only alcohol he bought then was a quart of wine, on 30 August. Francis Russe bought eight quarts of whiskey and four of rum in two days, 4–5 July 1828, and another sixteen quarts in the next ten weeks. After that, there were transactions on his account in fifteen of the next seventeen weeks, but he bought alcohol in only six weeks, a total of six quarts of whiskey. Elisha Mallory bought fourteen quarts in a four-week span from 10 August to 6 September 1828. Subsequently there were periods when he bought goods, but little or no alcohol, for example a single quart of whiskey in the five weeks from 14 December to 17 January. Or, if the two gallons he purchased on 4 December are counted, his purchases were nine quarts in eight weeks. James Brown bought five quarts in the three weeks from 2 to 22 November; and four quarts in the two weeks 25 January to 7 February 1829. In the three weeks from 4 to 24 January and the four weeks from 5 April to 2 May, there were transactions on his account but no purchases of alcohol.

43 Comstock was the thirty-fourth ranked alcohol buyer in 1808–09. In 1828–09, Ann Graham (seventeenth ranked in terms of overall debits) and Phebe Murray (thirty-third ranked) had accounts as large as several of the leading buyers, but neither bought any alcohol.

44 As a way of assessing leading buyers' consumption, we can think of their purchases in relation to wage rates or agricultural earning power. A reasonable daily wage was $1.00 in 1808–09 and 50 cents in 1828–29; a bushel of wheat at Yonge Mills was worth $1.00 in 1808 and 90 cents in 1828–29. In 1808–09, Christmas bought $13.20 of alcohol in sixteen weeks, about 80 cents per week; Daniel Patterson, $15.20 in twenty-one weeks, about 70 cents per week; and Peter Cronk, $28 in seventeen weeks, $1.65 per week. In 1828–29, Bunel Burnham spent $5.20 in eleven weeks, 47 cents per week; Benjamin Warren, $5.40 in twelve weeks, 45 cents per week; and A. Thomson, $4.20 in seven weeks, 60 cents per week.

45 In 1808–09, seventeen of the twenty leading buyers of alcohol bought tea, and all twenty leaders in 1828–29 did so. T.H. Breen, *The Marketplace of Revolution*, 283–4, argues for a gender distinction in discourse in the later eighteenth century, with tea represented as for women and alcohol for men. In nineteenth-century Canada, tea was clearly also a man's drink; it was, for example, the standard drink in timber shanties.

46 Although brandy and wine were also medical products, for brandy the seasonal pattern in 1808–09 does not suggest an occasional purchase to treat illness. Wine was not purchased in large enough quantities to allow an argument one way or the other.

47 Roberts, *In Mixed Company*.

48 See Roberts, *In Mixed Company*, 59; Gagan and Gagan, "Working Class Standards of Living in Late-Victorian Urban Ontario," 178–80; and McCalla, *Planting the Province*, 279.

49 Maple sugar, listed as a local product in appendix A, is combined for analysis with imported sugar in the data in table 12, and its (very modest) value is included in grocery totals.

50 One explanation is that purchases of tea were relatively limited at this store, perhaps because another local merchant (McDonald) seems to have been

primarily a grocer. In the thirty months from September 1833 to February 1836, Tett's import invoices show that he purchased about six hundred pounds of tea, considerably less than Charles Jones's purchases just in 1808 (albeit intended for two stores).

51 See also Minhinnick, *At Home in Upper Canada*, 60, for pearlash "used in place of baking powder. It was called saleratus and could be produced at home, and eventually it could be bought." Peppermint includes peppermint essence.

52 The OED reports "soda" as soda water (1842) and sodium bicarbonate for baking and cooking (1851).

53 E.g., Scovil credited William Ready by $5.00 worth of fish on 18 November 1861. Tett's 1830s import invoices show codfish bought by the barrel in Montreal.

54 QUA, Darling Papers, box 6, stock inventory, 1 April 1858, records a forty gallon cask of syrup, valued at 70 cents per gallon; sales in 1861 were at 80 and 90 cents per gallon.

55 This seems not to have been corn syrup, whose development, according to a standard authority, dates from later in the 1860s; see Harold McGee, *On Food and Cooking*, 677. On medicinal syrup, see, e.g., Soeurs de la Providence, *Traité élémentaire de matière médicale*, 6–7, where Syr. Simplex is a standard ingredient in various mixtures. See Chase, *Dr Chase's Recipes*, 135, for "simple syrup of molasses" as a base for a recommended cure for rheumatism; another example of simple syrup is at 139. He very much opposed the use of something called "Soothing Syrup" (134), however.

56 Minhinnick, *At Home in Upper Canada*, speaks, for example (61–2), of the "generous additions of nutmeg and allspice" in Canadian apple pies. But there were just ten buyers of nutmeg, from five samples beginning in 1842, and quantities were very modest. Even allspice (forty-nine buyers in all ten samples) was not purchased on a scale to match the probable consumption of apples in Upper Canada.

57 For brandy as medication, see Chavasse, *Advice to a Mother*, 247. For madder used as an emmenagogue, see Klepp, "Lost, Hidden, Obstructed, and Repressed," 83, 86–7; other products used here included aloes and gum guaiacum.

58 Armstrong, *Sulphur & Molasses*. My thanks to Catharine Wilson for this reference.

59 It is not clear exactly how the new foods were used. Recipes for fruitcakes, for example, often called for both currants and raisins, as in the recipe for Old English Plum Pudding in *The Canadian Housewife's Manual of Cookery*, 217, which specified both, plus several other imported groceries, lemon peel, mace, ginger, and brandy. It did, however, recognize (39) that some recommended ingredients "are not always available in this country." A total of 124 families bought currants and/or raisins, but there were only seventeen occasions (most at Sherin's store) when someone bought both at the same time.

60 Donald Fyson, "Du Pain au Madère," 80–1, nicely describes such goods as "essential luxuries" ("produits de luxe essentiels"). Harris, *The Reluctant Land*, 110, speaks of the "pleasurable and addictive qualities" of tobacco and alcohol.

61 Later, he bought another 17 pounds of tea (in May, June, September, and

December) and 5 pounds of sugar. According to the census, his family also made 125 pounds of sugar that year.

62   See entry for 8 November 1861. Whether this was the same shanty as Rose's is not clear. Altogether, Orr bought seventy-five pounds of tobacco during the year.

63   See Minhinnick, *At Home in Upper Canada*, 47, for a conflicting view.

64   In fact at Sherin's a few paid less, likely for a different quality of tea. Interpreting such price variations is complicated because they might represent differences in quality or type that are only occasionally explicit in entries (such as Bolton's occasional purchase of "best" tobacco, at a higher price). As with tea, prices for some products also rose during 1861, as the onset of the Civil War began to have an inflationary impact.

65   It would, in fact, be twice as long if the many medications purchased by four or fewer people were included.

66   Duffin, *Langstaff: A Nineteenth-Century Medical Life*, 76–7, 85–8.

67   Soeurs de la Providence, *Traité élémentaire de matière médicale*, 638–9.

68   E.g., Minhinnick, *At Home in Upper Canada*, 106, speaks of it as a common mouthwash. Purchases in our samples were too modest to make this seem likely.

69   The flyer on Merchant's Gargling Oil was found in the Choate records for 1861.

70   On the use of opium, see Duffin, *Langstaff*, 75.

71   Chase, *Dr Chase's Recipes*, 133–4; he also has some pectorals that included opium.

72   Chase, *Dr Chase's Recipes*, 190–2, has three recipes for balsams: one based on rosin and turpentine, for coughs, internal pains and strains; another based on alcohol, for cuts, bruises, and abrasions; and a third based on oil of turpentine, sulphuric acid, and alcohol for internal and external bleeding, including excessive menstrual bleeding. None of these are the kinds found in our samples, however.

73   The only other doctors among the ten samples were Dr Ebenezer Hartwell, recorded at Tett's store with a small account but not found in the 1842 census for the area, and Dr David Copway, a customer at Fowlds's store in 1861, listed in the census as "Indian Reserve Doctor." His account was also small and included no groceries.

74   Armstrong, *Sulphur & Molasses*, 87.

75   Borax was used in welding; see Chase, *Dr Chase's Recipes*, 235, 240. Many of the uses in advice books were for women, such as for treating tenderness of nipples during a first pregnancy. See Napheys, *The Physical Life of Woman*, 168–9.

76   But note the possibility that these were different qualities of wick. The Tett import invoices show two grades, fine at 40 cents per pound in Montreal, and common, at 25 cents. The weight of the "ball" sold at retail is not known.

77   At Sherin's store in 1861, six customers bought tallow, which we classify with provisions; five of them also bought candles.

78   According to the 1842 Census, maple sugar output in the Johnstown District was 214,000 pounds, or about seven pounds per person; in the Colborne District, output of 130,000 pounds was equal to more than nine pounds per person. The 1861 Census reported 258,000 pounds of output in Leeds, about

seven pounds per person, and 114,000 pounds in Peterborough, slightly below five pounds per person.

79 Not all the sugar sold at 10 cents per pound was specified as "maple." The pattern was similar at the later stores where occasional transactions in maple sugar were recorded. At Tett's, much sugar was "m," which could be muscovado or maple: the price range for sugar described as "maple" ranged from 10 cents to 12.5 cents. Scovil credited maple sugar at 10 cents when buying and sold it at the same price as most other sugar. In 1851, the Choate store recorded just one sale of maple sugar, at 8.5 cents. The only maple sugar bought at Darling's cost 12.5 cents, higher than the main sugar price here, 10 cents.

80 The others known to have had a sufficient supply to consume this much sugar were some of those who made sugar.

81 In total, Upper Canadian production was equal to 7.6 pounds per capita in 1842 and about 5 pounds per capita in 1861. For 1851, the data on maple sugar production are improbably low (with per capita output of just over 2 pounds). If we add Canadian per capita imports of around 16 pounds in 1861, average consumption was about 21 pounds per capita, almost the English level.

82 For the importance of this pattern, see Shammas, *The Pre-industrial Consumer in England and America*, 243.

83 Duncan, *Canadians at Table*, 61.

84 For this theme in bourgeois life, see, Noël, *Family Life and Sociability*.

CHAPTER FIVE

1   Hindle, "Introduction: The Span of the Wooden Age," 7. Cf. Fossier, *The Axe and the Oath*, 180: "It can be said that the Middle Ages was the 'age of wood'…"

2   See Inwood, "The Iron and Steel Industry," 186. For the expansion of the metal trades in this period, see, e.g., Kristofferson, *Craft Capitalism*.

3   Traill, *The Backwoods of Canada*, 194 (2 November 1833).

4   Wylie, "The Blacksmith in Upper Canada," 35.

5   Wylie, "The Blacksmith in Upper Canada," 182.

6   Wylie, "The Blacksmith in Upper Canada," 35, 33.

7   Norrie, Owram, and Emery, *A History of the Canadian Economy*, 97.

8   McCalla, *Planting the Province*, 280. Contrast Wylie, "The Blacksmith in Upper Canada," 183, on the blacksmith's world after 1850: "The rural smith survived but within an ever-contracting circle of work possibilities."

9   Wylie, "The Blacksmith in Upper Canada," 154.

10 The census reported 7,600 carpenters in Upper Canada in 1851, 3,900 boot and shoemakers, 1,900 coopers, 1,500 masons, 900 saddlers and harness makers, 900 wagon makers, and 600 tanners. See McCalla, *Planting the Province*, 280. Wylie, "Nebulous Substance: The Portrayal of Iron and Steel Employment," 129–30, addresses complexities and uncertainties in census counts of the metal trades; blacksmiths are not a problematic category, however.

11 For example, the focus of the standard text by Norrie, Owram, and Emery, *A History of the Canadian Economy*, is on external markets; its index has no entries for construction, housing, lumber, land, or wood. Wood, *Making*

Ontario, addresses environmental transformation and adds the use of wood for fuel (14), but otherwise tends to frame the subject in terms of exports; see, e.g., 6 and the discussion of sawmilling at 102–6. Baskerville, *Ontario: Image, Identity and Power*, pays more attention to the domestic wood economy, e.g., at 71–2.

12 Pocket knives ranged from $11.00 to $16.40 per "gross"; shoe knives from 45 cents to 90 cents per dozen; and pen knives from 97 cents to $1.57 per dozen. Later, a few drawing knives were recorded at Choate's in 1851; as well, Tett imported very modest quantities of them in the 1830s. For their uses, see Tunis, *Colonial Craftsmen and the Beginnings of American Industry*, 22, and Sloane, *A Museum of Early American Tools*, 38–9. The latter writes that "there are probably more drawknives extant than any other tool." Knives for the dinner table, generally sold in sets with forks, are listed under housewares in appendix A.

13 Sloane, *A Museum of Early American Tools*, 92. For American nail production as a manufacturing process, see Hazen, *The Panorama of Professions and Trades*, 285. Although Wylie, "The Blacksmith in Upper Canada," 132–4, provides a full account of how smiths made nails, he recognizes that nails actually were mainly imported.

14 Hebert, *The Engineer's and Mechanic's Encyclopaedia*, vol. 2, 181, says someone in the nail trade would know some 3,000 distinct terms, because of variation in purpose, head, point, length, thickness, etc. In its purchasing specifications in 1813 (i.e., before cut nails came on the scene), the ordnance department of the British Army described more than 160 different nails; see Weaver and Buggey, "A Most Significant Reference Document: A List of Nails and Spikes." For later variation in nails, see the 1884 price list of Frothingham & Workman of Montreal in McNally, "Technical Advance and Stagnation," 42.

15 Almost half of the 80,000 nails imported to the two Jones stores in 1808 were fourteen-penny nails. Tunis, *Colonial Craftsmen and the Beginnings of American Industry*, 58, says that this measurement system originally reflected "the cost of a hundred of that size." At Yonge Mills in 1808–09, fourteen-penny nails cost 33 cents and sixteen-penny were 35 cents per hundred.

16 As well, although no brass nails were purchased at Tett's in 1842, they had been among his imports in the 1830s.

17 Rosenberg, "America's Rise to Woodworking Leadership," 43. In 1861, 5 cents was standard, except prices were 6 and 7 cents at Choate's and 6 cents at Fowlds's.

18 A total of fifty-eight pounds were purchased by twenty-seven customers, at 10 cents per pound for most of the year (i.e., slightly more than most cut nails). For images of rose and other nails, see Wylie, "The Blacksmith in Upper Canada," 133; Hebert, *The Engineer's and Mechanic's Encyclopaedia*, vol. 2, 182; and Weaver and Buggey, "A Most Significant Reference Document: A List of Nails and Spikes," 95–118.

19 Although Hebert, *The Engineer's and Mechanic's Encyclopaedia*, vol. 2, 184–7, speaks of cut and pressed as synonyms, our data suggest otherwise, because pressed were substantially more expensive than cut: 10 to 12 cents per pound at Sherin's, 12.5 cents at Darling's, and 17.5 cents at Scovil's.

20 Definition from *OED*. At Scovil's, there were two purchases of boat nails and

one of clout nails, all at 25 cents per pound. Fowlds sold clout nails at 30 cents per pound. Bolts also tended to be for carriages. Except for one small purchase in 1828, they appear only in 1861, almost all of the transactions then being explicitly for carriages. Shields, the blacksmith who was a prominent customer at Sherin's, was the leading buyer, with 700 bolts for $29 (and another hundred cheaper ones whose type was not specified).

21 About one-quarter of the ten largest accounts at each store did not.

22 After that, his account had only a few transactions in hardware: a paint brush and some paint drier in August (the latter not in appendix A because there were only two buyers at this one store), packets of brads in September and November, and six pounds of zinc and two files in November. During the summer he made a few purchases of nails on others' accounts, however. He bought soap in six of the months from May to November, tobacco in October and November and tea in May, August, and December. That he did not buy tea and tobacco consistently may indicate that he had other sources of supply; and that may have been true also for hardware. Or he may have been doing other work altogether.

23 Buchanan, *The Dictionary of Science and Technical Terms*, 158; Sloane, *A Museum of Early American Tools*, 92.

24 In 1808 shoe tacks were the only kind of tacks imported. Later, other kinds of tacks with other uses (e.g., for carpets) were also recorded, but most often the type of tack was not specified. Some shoemakers' tools were also recorded; for example, Francis Charland bought four shoe knives and two awls from Scovil's. "Sprig" could also designated a small headless nail used in glazing (see Weaver and Buggey, "A Most Significant Reference Document: A List of Nails and Spikes," 118); possibly some of our transactions were of this kind, but they were purchased from only a few stores, and far less often than glass.

25 For the range of horseshoe nails, see McNally, "Technical Advance and Stagnation," 45, citing a 1909 catalogue that specified ten lengths, ranging up to 3.25 inches.

26 Shields paid the lowest unit price of any buyer, 22 cents per pound; Pomeroy paid the highest price, 30 cents in 1861. They were the largest accounts in their samples. Note that all but three blacksmiths in the samples (all at Fowlds's in 1861) are represented in tables 23 and/or 24.

27 Some sample farmers did not report draft animals, but most had horses and/or oxen. Wylie, "The Blacksmith in Upper Canada," suggests that oxen commonly were not shod (149), and he doubts that horses were reshod as frequently as experts (e.g., the British army) advised. In fact, he wonders if even horses were all shod (49). Each shoe required eight nails (142).

28 One customer bought a bridle and spurs at Choate's in 1861, the only purchase of either in our samples.

29 Most iron was purchased by weight, although there were some purchases by the sheet. Very modest quantities of steel were also purchased at six stores (appendix A). Seven of the sixteen buyers were in the first sample, their purchases totalling about 40 pounds. Among later steel buyers, Kennedy, Shields, and Pomeroy, listed in table 24, purchased about 50 pounds in total. The 1808 import invoices for Jones's two stores included 341 pounds of Crowley and 127 of blistered steel, both in "bundles." The important point is that steel was available.

30   Sheets of iron cost 43 cents in 1808 and 35 cents in and after 1828. Most of the iron purchases in 1861 were at 4–5 cents per pound (Shields paid 4 cents for most of his). Swedish iron (bought by Grant and Shields) was 7 cents.

31   For the forms in which iron was available and the timing of the decline in prices, see Wylie, "The Blacksmith in Upper Canada," 77–8. For Swedish iron, see 32; its use in making shoeing nails is discussed in Tunis, *Colonial Craftsmen and the Beginnings of American Industry*, 21. The Tables of Trade and Navigation reported the following categories in the early 1850s: bar, rod, and sheet; boiler plate and railroad bars; pig, scrap and old; and hoop.

32   This was also the case for Alexander Buist, the main iron buyer at Tett's. Tett seems to have had little engagement in the iron trade, in fact, with just one other small purchase, by Hubbard.

33   Note that this was comparable to the volume imported by Charles Jones in 1808; as we note below, his imports suggest setting up, or supplying, a new smithy.

34   Other than by craftsmen, iron was often bought in autumn or winter, but that was as true at mid-century as it had been in 1808 and 1828, and there were other strong reasons for such seasonal patterns.

35   Dogs are combined with andirons in appendix A based on common price and overlapping definitions. For dogs in hewing, see, e.g., Meehan, "Demonstrating the Use of Log House Building Tools," 41.

36   Plaster for building can be distinguished from medical plasters because it was purchased in barrels. Although bolts could be used in building, the identity of the principal buyers suggests that those purchased from these stores were for carriage making.

37   "Pane" was a synonym; and a few entries were in squares or feet. Mirrors ("looking glasses") and glasses for drinking are listed in housewares. For box sizes, see Pacey, "A History of Window Glass Manufacture in Canada," 36.

38   For breakage, see, e.g., Pacey, "A History of Window Glass Manufacture in Canada," 33.

39   Rempel, *Building with Wood*, 59, says 7 by 9 was the basic size in early Upper Canada, with six panes per window, or twelve for a standard double-hung window. Of the fifteen buyers at Yonge Mills in 1808–09, eight bought in multiples of six (two bought six, three twelve, two eighteen, and one thirty-six). Three bought odd numbers (five, nine, and fifteen) and the others bought from one to four panes.

40   Buyers in 1842 all paid 5 cents; those in 1851 paid 5 cents or 5.8 cents. At Choate's and Scovil's in 1861, the range was 4 to 6 cents. At Darling's, prices ranged from 3.3 to 8.3 cents. Transactions at Sherin's make it clear that higher unit prices were for larger panes. For example, 10 by 14 panes cost 10 cents and 12 by 16 cost 13 cents, a difference exactly proportionate to the difference in size.

41   A total of fourteen bladders were imported, each of fourteen pounds. Other 1808 imports include one dozen japanned latches. Purchases of both putty and glass had something of a seasonal pattern: in the ten samples, 60 percent of transactions in both were between October and December.

42   In all the samples, however, there was only one purchase of a screwdriver, at Sherin's. See also Rempel, *Building with Wood*, 102, on screws required for butts.

43   There was also one "fine drawback lock" at $2.80, worth more than a dozen of any other locks (chest locks were $2.45, cupboard $2.30, and padlocks $1.70 per dozen).

44   Burn, *The Colonist's and Emigrant's Hand Book*, 62. He listed saws, axes, adzes, augers, hammers, chisels, a plumb-rule, and a square. Rempel, *Building with Wood*, 371, would add planes to this list.

45   See Doucet and Weaver, *Housing the North American City*, 54–5, quoting Donald Adams's work on Philadelphia to the effect that, in the 1850s and for the next century, labour represented 56 percent of a balloon frame house's costs and materials 44 percent. Timber framing had a higher proportion of labour costs. Rempel, *Building with Wood*, also stresses the economies of the frame house, noting (123) that a principal requirement was "lots of nails."

46   See Moussette, *Le chauffage domestique au Canada*, 124, 231–75. The prices at Choate's ($15, $20, and $28) confirm those given by Moussette. Two buyers at Choate's were also debited for stove pipes.

47   Craig, *Upper Canada: The Formative Years*, 7–8, quotes Sir John Johnson, 31 January 1785, on Loyalist requirements for tools: "Nails, hammers, gimlets, plains [sic], chizzels, gouges, ...handsaws, X cut saws, broad axes, adzes, rub stones, whipsaws, ...carpenter tools, blacksmiths tools, carpenter squares and compasses, hoes, spades, pick axes, plow shares, twine." Rempel, *Building with Wood*, 370–1, provides a similar list from 1784.

48   Five people bought both plough points and landsides (thus a total of nineteen buyers). The largest volume of both plough parts was at Scovil's, where the cost of a plough point was 50 cents, and a landside was 17.5 cents. These products perhaps represented a new development in ploughing or possibly just that stores could now supply standardized metal plough components that might otherwise have been supplied by a smith.

49   Grass scythes are explicitly mentioned at Fowlds's in 1854 and Darlings, and grain at Choate's in 1851.

50   For example, among the eleven files charged to Alexander Buist's account at Tett's were handsaw, millsaw, and X-cut files.

51   Prices were much the same at Scovil's, except a warranted axe cost $1.35. See also Wylie, "The Blacksmith in Upper Canada," 156–7.

52   Tett's imports in the 1830s included six broad axes (at $2.00 each), however, plus a "box" of "Kings" axes.

53   It is not clear from our data whether purchases of snaths imply that a "scythe" was just the blade.

54   For example, an eighty-five pound grindstone was purchased at Choate's in 1861 for $2.55 (3 cents per pound).

55   None of these products were purchased between November and March.

56   Hoolihan was an established farmer so surely must have already owned these basic tools. Unless he was very unfortunate in terms of breakage, the implication is that additional hands were being put to work.

57   Ploughs are listed in appendix B; two were purchased at Tett's in 1842 at a cost of $10 and one at Darling's for $11. The potash kettle, purchased in February 1851, cost $25, and the sugar kettle, purchased in March, was noted as 73.5 pounds at 5 cents per pound (thus $3.675). All kettles are listed in housewares in appendix A. Judging by price ($6.50), the "large" kettles

recorded in the Yonge Mills daybook in 1808 could have been "5 pail" kettles (priced in that year's import invoices at $4.50). Jones also imported twenty-five potash kettles in 1808; evidently they were much larger, as they cost from $32 to $66, but we found no retail purchases.

58 This reflection draws on research by Jordan Baker for an unpublished BA essay that explored the accounts of a substantial implement maker, Frost and Wood, held in the University of Guelph Archives.

59 Rasmussen, "Wood on the Farm," 30, and see image at 32.

60 Cradles were more expensive than scythes: one purchased in 1851 cost $3.50; two at Choate's in 1861 were $4.50; they were $4.25 at Sherin's, and $2.50 or $3.00 at Fowlds's in 1861.

61 A cooper, for example, might require as many as fifty different tools. See Kealey, *Toronto Workers Respond to Industrial Capitalism*, 53.

62 Rempel, *Building with Wood*, 375–88; he emphasizes (386) that these were mainly factory made. Yonge Mills's 1808 import invoices included 3.5 dozen "plane irons." Tett's imports between 1833 and 1836 included just two planes (jack and worthington), bought in November 1834.

63 Mancke, "At the Counter of the General Store," 171; at 170, however, she recognizes men's productive purchases.

64 Buxton-Keenlyside, *Selected Canadian Spinning Wheels*, 273, speaks of stores as one of the channels of distribution. She recognizes that they required substantial and diverse skills and tools to build, yet pictures another channel as homemade.

65 One gun, at Choate's store in 1851, cost $4.50, two at the same store in 1861 were a double gun for $18.00 and a single for $7.50, and one at Darling's store in 1861 cost $6.50. It is not known if these were new, however. The 1808 import invoices include two guns, worth $7.50 each. One customer at Yonge Mills in 1828 bought a gunlock for $1.50. Of the communities in which these stores were located, only Warsaw is known to have had a resident gunsmith (Stephen Payne) in our period; see *Directory of the United Counties of Peterborough and Victoria for 1858*, 30. Lakefield and Newboro later had resident gunsmiths, but not for long; see Gooding, *The Canadian Gunsmiths 1608 to 1900*, 83, 147.

66 This section draws upon material from McCalla, "Upper Canadians and Their Guns," reprinted with the permission of *Ontario History*. Minor discrepancies in totals reflect comprehensive revisiting of the data set in the course of preparing this book. Gun maintenance required oil, and shooting required paper or cloth to make cartridges, but it is not possible to identify any specifically gun-related materials among sales of these products.

67 See, e.g., Galt, *The Canadas, as They at Present Commend Themselves*, 235; and Hilts, *Among the Forest Trees*, 18, 27, 202.

68 Abbott, *Memoranda of a Settler in Lower Canada*, 34–5. For critical perspective on this source, see Gerber, *Authors of Their Lives*, 10.

69 Bonnycastle, *Canada and the Canadians*, vol. 1, 68. For game, fowl, and fish as food, see, e.g., Traill, *The Canadian Settler's Guide*, 153–9.

70 Note, e.g., the centrality of the gun and hearth in "Scenes from the 'New England Kitchen,'" *Harper's Illustrated Weekly*, 15 July 1876, reproduced in Ulrich, *The Age of Homespun*, 28. On the other hand, some images of

contemporary Canadian hearths did not show guns; see, e.g., Hardy, *La vie quotidienne dans la vallée du Saint-Laurent*, 25, 31, 58, 81 (and colour reproductions of three of these between 96 and 97); and Baskerville, *Ontario: Image, Identity, and Power*, 81, 82, and (facing) 90.

71 Sheppard, *Plunder, Profit, and Paroles*, 41; Taylor, *The Civil War of 1812*, 113, 150, 232, 307; and Benn, *The Iroquois in the War of 1812*, 68–75. On the militia myth, see Granatstein, *Canada's Army*, 3–23.

72 Read and Stagg *The Rebellion of 1837 in Upper Canada*, xlii–xliv, 115–16, 121. For Lower Canada, see Greer, *The Patriots and the People*, 301, 303–4, 307–8, 327.

73 See, e.g., Upper Canada Historical Arms Society, *The Military Arms of Canada*, 18–19, 24–5.

74 For this use of gunpowder, see, e.g., Moodie, *Roughing It in the Bush*, 195; and Russell, *Everyday Life in Colonial Canada*, 31. Flints also could be used for fire-lighting; eight buyers in the four samples from 1808 to 1851 bought flints but no powder or shot.

75 The size of boxes might have varied. Thus, two boxes of caps were sold at Darling's store for 12.5 cents and five at 10 cents; and at Sherin's, three boxes were purchased at 13 cents, two at 20 cents, and one at 25 cents.

76 See Hamilton, *Firearms on the Frontier*, 35, for various sizes of shot. Russell, *Firearms, Traps, & Tools of the Mountain Men*, 48, identifies four standard grades of powder.

77 Although it is obviously difficult to compare directly, given the differences in circumstances, the volume of purchases at Yonge Mills in 1808–09 can be related to those at contemporary Hudson's Bay Company posts. In 1810–14, at three western posts, powder sales ranged from 150 to almost 900 pounds per year, and shot from 240 to 850. Such volumes vastly exceeded purchases by members of our samples, but are comparable when expressed as a rate per family: they equalled about one pound of powder per family per year at Brandon, one-half pound at Carlton, and six pounds at Cumberland. Cumberland, unlike the other two, was a woodland post, whose clientele did far more hunting. Ray, *Indians in the Fur Trade*, 149–53, 163n24.

78 See Miller, "An Archaeological Perspective on the Evolution of Diet in the Colonial Chesapeake, 1620–1745"; and Main, "Many Things Forgotten," 213–14.

79 When shot and powder were purchased simultaneously, transactions at Yonge Mills in 1808–09 tended to be at a ratio of four to one. Later, there were about equal numbers of purchases with ratios of four to one and two to one.

80 For some examples of powder and shot requirements in these ranges, see Russell, *Firearms, Traps & Tools*, 36, 86–92; and Given, *A Most Pernicious Thing*, 97–9. For a gun that used balls thirty-six to the pound, see Galt, *The Canadas, as They at Present Commend Themselves*, 235.

81 For the hunting of an avid English sportsman in the Kettle Creek and later Long Point areas of Upper Canada, which involved firing 500 to 1,000 or more rounds per year, see Barrett, *The 19th-Century Journals & Paintings of William Pope*, 32, 146–67. I am grateful to Mr Barrett for drawing the relevance of this work to my attention.

82 Of course the women buyers also may have had men (e.g., sons, brothers) in

their households; in one case, a son was the actual purchaser, on his mother's account. Women are sometimes recorded as buyers on accounts in their husband's or father's names as well; the most common buyer if not the customer himself was a son.

83 See Akenson, *The Irish in Ontario*, 51, 62, 216, 242.

84 Thomas William Magrath to Thomas Radcliff, January 1832, in Radcliff, *Authentic Letters from Upper Canada*, 144. For another example, see Kirby, *The U.E.: A Tale of Upper Canada*, 108.

85 Based on an average of six persons per household. Data for 1861 are from Province of Canada, Legislative Assembly, *Sessional Papers*, 1862 no. 2, TTN, schedules 2 and 3. For the five-year period 1859–63, the value of such imports averaged about $22,000 per year, with a range from $12,000 in 1858 to $32,000 in 1863. Canada's imports in 1868–69 were valued at just over $25,000, equal to almost 37 cents per pound; see Canada, Parliament, House of Commons, *Sessional Papers*, 1870, no. 1, TTN, schedule 4.

86 See Miller, "An Archaeological Perspective on the Evolution of Diet," 183–7, 193. Also relevant is Merchant, *Ecological Revolutions*, 62–8. For the importance of wild meat in early settlement on the Canadian prairies, see Colpitts, *Game in the Garden*, 75–81.

87 Haight, *Country Life in Canada Fifty Years Ago*, 41.

88 William Radcliff to Arthur Radcliff, December 1832, in Radcliff, *Authentic Letters from Upper Canada*, 106–7. See also 144, Thomas William Magrath to Thomas Radcliff, January 1832: "I have known the most devoted sportsmen, when once settled on their own property … to have abandoned the fowling piece altogether, during the busy season." On the other hand, William Pope, an English gentleman settler in the same area, did hunt and fish extensively in summer (e.g., on more than half the days each month in summer 1842); see Barrett, *The 19th-Century Journals & Paintings of William Pope*, 34.

89 Deepsea line, purchased at Darling's and Scovil's, was a device for taking soundings (i.e., a different product entirely). Both stores were located on navigable waterways.

90 In the early 1860s, the total value of Canadian imports was modest, $3,000 to $4,000 per year. Most standard works treat them as synonyms. For example, see Buchanan, *The Dictionary of Science and Technical Terms*, 691.

91 See *Sanitary and Preventive Measures*, 4; and *Useful Household Helps Hints and Receipts*, 258–9. I am grateful to Catharine Wilson for the latter reference. For sulphur as a fire lighter, see Russell, *Everyday Life in Colonial Canada*, 74. Hebert, *The Engineer's and Mechanic's Encyclopaedia*, vol. 2, 760, stresses flammability, adding "its great utility in the arts is too well known to need specifying." For its use in various kinds of skin care and for syphilis, see Jefferis, *Search Lights on Health, Light on Dark Corners*.

92 Traill, *The Canadian Settler's Guide*, 150–3.

93 From: "Grana germanica – Green flax," *Dictionary of Traded Goods*, www.british-history.ac.uk/report.aspx?compid=58778&strquery=copperas (accessed 14 October 2008).

94 Taking all three categories, there were a total of sixty-five buyers of one or more of these oils.

95 See *A Dictionary of Traded Goods*, www.british-history.ac.uk/report.aspx?

compid=58763&strquery=fig%20blue#s3 (accessed 14 October 2008).

96 See discussion of blue for laundry in Minhinnick, *At Home in Upper Canada*, 112.

97 Russell, *Everyday Life in Colonial Canada*, 81–3; see also his *Lighting the Pioneer Ontario Home*, 14–15. Although he suggests a price of 25 cents per gallon for kerosene from petroleum, the price at the 1861 stores in this sample was $1.20 to $1.28.

98 Another (blue vitriol, used to tint whitewash) appears in 1861 (though it could evidently be used also as a sheep dip). See Minhinnick *At Home in Upper Canada*, 134.

99 This count omits rosin and spirits of turpentine, which were the most commonly purchased but had numerous uses. Some twenty-three buyers from 1851 onward bought three or more of the other paint-related products, and another fifteen bought lead white, paint, varnish, or a brush, all products explicitly for painting.

100 Minhinnick, "Some Personal Observations on the Use of Paint," quotes from 13, 14, 16.

101 See Minhinnick, *At Home in Upper Canada*, 125, for a longer list of twenty advertised ingredients before 1820 – white and red lead and yellow ochre are also on it. Note the particular emphasis on white lead and lamp black, which "gave some tone to these pigments..." Minhinnick indicates whiting might also be used, like blacking, for stove polishing.

102 Penn, "Decorative and Protective Finishes, 1750–1850," 8.

103 "Paints and Colors" appear in 1852, with imports valued at $132,000, 80 percent of this from Britain. Province of Canada, Legislative Assembly, *Journals*, 1853, appendix A, TTN, schedule 17.

104 Russell, *Everyday Life in Colonial Canada*, 62.

105 We found no painters among customers at our stores. In addition to Cotton, at Sherin's, carpenters were among the leading buyers of paint-related products at Choate's in 1851 and 1861 and at Fowlds's in 1854; that suggests the possibility that their work extended to painting. Because people might buy goods that others would work on, buyer identity does not permit certainty on the identity of those actually doing the work, however.

106 Thus, Wylie, "The Blacksmith in Upper Canada," 48, provides a table, based on systematic use of evidence from account books, of what smiths *usually* did. But he also comprehensively describes and illustrates techniques for making all the things a smith *could* produce, which might imply that it was normal actually to do so. For example, after showing all the kinds of manufactured files that could be purchased, Wylie describes (130) how smiths might make them (though he does not say why they would).

107 See, e.g., the chapter on painting and decorating, 123–41. Because Upper Canada Village aimed to represent the 1860s, the restorations that she supervised there fit with our chronology.

108 Magrath to Rev. Thomas Radcliff, November 1831, in Radcliff, *Authentic Letters from Upper Canada*, 1–11; quotes at 6. We have assumed that all prices are quoted in sterling. Other elements in the calculation were passage in the best cabins, subsistence for the first year, one hundred acres of well-situated land, a house and basic furnishings, clearing ten acres, and basic farm

stock (two cows, one horse, a yoke of oxen with chains), a wagon, and seed wheat.

109 To the extent our data allow comparison with Magrath's figures, the advantage in buying at home and paying to ship such goods is unclear. For example, axes were about $2.50 on his list, but no more than $2.25 in our 1828–29 sample; he priced a handsaw at about $1.60 and handsaws were just $1.00 in our 1842 sample; and the various augers found in our 1842 data all cost less than the $1.80 he indicated (but his price included multiple bits). On the other hand, he gave a price of about 60 cents for a spade, as compared to the 90 cents found in our 1842 sample. It is, of course, possible that qualitative differences in products were involved. A second source of comparison is the cost to Benjamin Tett of such tools in 1833–36; for example, he paid about $1.40 for axes, 50 cents for spades, and 80 cents for handsaws.

110 Thus, in 1808, when the price of wheat at Yonge Mills was one dollar per bushel, a scythe represented 1.5 bushels and an ax 2 bushels.

111 Ennals and Holdsworth, *Homeplace*, 89.

112 Tiemann, "The Paint, Oil, and Varnish Trade," 622–3. My thanks to Josh MacFadyen for this reference.

CHAPTER SIX

1 Bittermann, MacKinnon, and Wynn, "Of Inequality and Interdependence in the Nova Scotian Countryside," 35.

2 McInnis, "Marketable Surpluses in Ontario Farming." In New Brunswick in the same period, about one-sixth of farms "were able to provide no more than a dwelling and a few basic commodities." See Acheson, "New Brunswick Agriculture at the End of the Colonial Era," 52–7

3 "Les travaux récents ont fait voler en éclat l'image d'une masse rurale indifférenciée et, du même coup, révélé l'importance de la circulation locale." Dechêne, *Le partage des subsistances au Canada*, 23.

4 Haight, *Country Life in Canada Fifty Years Ago*, 105–7. This is an account of life along the Bay of Quinte a full fifty years after settlement began. For a similar view of early trade, see Russell, *How Agriculture Made Canada*, 17. All twenty-four of the local products for which Haight gives 1830 prices can be found on the local lists in appendix A or B. We do not consider credits to customers' accounts made in kind as "barter" because the goods involved had prices and their value was credited to a continuing account rather than their being exchanged immediately for goods of equal value.

5 Some hides and leather were also imported, but quantities were not sufficient to meet a large share of Canadian demand. Annual imports to the Canadas of tanned leather averaged about $175,000 per year in 1850–52 and about $300,000 per year in 1859–61; imports of hides averaged almost $225,000 per year in 1850–52 and over $600,000 per year in 1859–61. See Province of Canada, Legislative Assembly, *Journals*, 1853, appendix A, TTN, schedule 18; and *Sessional Papers*, 1862, no. 2, TTN, schedule 3. Some manufactures of leather (boots and shoes and other) were also imported.

6 A total of fifty-one pounds worth about eight dollars was credited to six

customers. One 1861 product, butter tubs, probably was just another name for firkins, there in 1808.

7   The frequency of debits for boards and carding or fulling suggests these were often purchased, but they might also be paid for in kind, with a share of the output that the mill could sell. There was a standard grist mill toll of one-twelfth of flour output. The other product with more than fifty buyers was whiskey, addressed in chapter 4.

8   Three of these transactions are visible in table 28. The other was at Darling's in 1861, a horse costing $50 debited to Edward Nalty. Compare Haight, *Country Life in Canada Fifty Years Ago*, 106, which gives an 1830 price for a "good horse," $80; a yoke of oxen, $75; and a milch cow, $16. Note also a debit of $10 to John Poole at Tett's in January 1842, "part payment" for a cow.

9   Both transactions were on 30 April, Santry taking 210 pounds at 26 cents per pound and Knox 219 pounds at 24 cents. They also shared in the purchase of a calf skin worth $6.25. Knox actually paid cash for most of his share, which suggests that the lower price for his share represented a discount. These purchases meant they had the tenth and eleventh ranked accounts at Sherin's; other than leather, they bought very little.

10 Note that we only see both sides of these transactions if each party was a member of our sample.

11 In total, there were twenty-one buyers of boards, flour, and pork. The lumber consisted of almost 4,000 feet of lath; about 2,000 feet of other boards; and about 300 feet of planks: lath cost 60 cents per 100 feet; other boards cost from 60 cents to $1.00 per 100 feet; and planks cost $1.50 and $1.80 per 100 feet. This much higher price may indicate that the planks were measured in linear rather than board feet. The flour totalled 21 hundredweight [cwt]. At this store a hundredweight had its usual meaning, a unit of 112 pounds; some later stores seem to have used this word to refer to units of 100 pounds.

12 We identified him by credits for barrels and "coopering" (the latter a service listed in appendix B). The highs for flour were 164 pounds in October and 127 pounds in April; in three months he bought between 60 and 80 pounds, and in four just 30 to 40 pounds. In April 1809, he bought 16 pounds of pork and 57 of beef but in May only a single pound of pork and a hogs head weighing 13 pounds. John Gorman, credited fifty dollars for one hundred barrels, may also have been a cooper; the only local product among his modest debits was a charge for carding.

13 See Scribner, *Scribner's Lumber & Log Book*, 144, for the figure of 40 pounds of hay for a span of horses per day. Thus, Tollman's hay would have sustained a team for seventy-five days. He bought a small amount of pork in October and 286 pounds in January and substantial quantities of flour in early March and May. Credits on his account include $74 in logs in May (and a cow credited at $15 on 29 November, possibly the cow purchased by the Andrews two weeks later). The phrasing of the credit for logs suggests that there had also been credits to the business of Tollman and Hubbell. The assessment roll did not report Tollman's having horses or oxen, but he might have hired someone with a team. His business associate, Etnathan Hubbell, was assessed as having two horses and one ox. Hubbell had a huge holding of land (1,500 acres), none of it in cultivation.

14 Note, e.g., the requirement in the Talbot settlement to have ten acres fenced
    and in crop as a condition for a settler to receive title to his lot. "Every settler,
    said Talbot, needed that quantity of land for the support of his family." Gates,
    Land Policies of Upper Canada, 128. Clarke, *The Ordinary People of Essex*,
    205, suggests that a family could be sustained on as little as three acres; but
    later (264) he reports a man cropping more than six acres who was "proba-
    bly the poorest in the county."

15 According to the assessment roll, Cronk also had a pair of horses, which sug-
    gests a more complex operation than simple clearing of land might require.

16 Although early winter was the main time to slaughter hogs, the point of pre-
    serving in barrels was to have pork at other seasons, and there were
    purchases of pork in most months. Seaman was one of six wheat buyers in
    this sample. A hypothetical calculation suggests that at prevailing prices he
    would have come out ahead. At a standard rate of five bushels (300 pounds)
    of wheat = one barrel (196 pounds) of flour, his 1,300 pounds of wheat
    would have yielded about 850 pounds of flour. After paying one-twelfth of
    the flour in toll he would have 780 pounds (c. seven hundredweight), which,
    at $3.40 would have been worth $23.80. This was about 140 pounds per
    person in his household. But he might also have been equipping a shanty; he
    was the only customer besides Tollman whose accounts included credits for
    logs ($30 on the same day as the wheat and pork purchases).

17 Note Cain was credited $4.50 in November by "work to Montreal." There
    were transactions on his account in other months in fall and winter. He had
    been in the area long enough to have had a carding account from 1807. He
    was assessed as having three head of cattle (including two cows) but no
    horses, oxen, or swine. Although we have no evidence of these in 1808–09, it
    is worth noting other scenarios that might lead farmers, even well-established
    ones, to need to supplement their own production: the arrival of extra people
    in the household (as must have been common in an immigrant society) and
    unexpected circumstances, such as spoilage, livestock disease, insect infesta-
    tion, and crop failure.

18 Thomas Freel had twenty acres in cultivation, Silah Robins had sixteen, Abel
    Fulford had thirty, and William Avery had fifty acres. Avery's was among the
    largest farms in this sample.

19 His main credits were by four months and one day of work at $12 per
    month, and by board for an equivalent period (seventeen weeks and three
    days) at $1.50 per week. These credits preceded the debits, coming in early
    July 1828; judging by the subsequent flow of transactions, it seems that the
    working relationship continued.

20 Six months at $11 per month and two months and 4.5 days at $8 per month
    (a total of $83.50); his credit for board was also $1.50 per week.

21 James, the eldest, twenty-eight in 1852, was one of three recorded as a farmer.
    Thomas, then nineteen, was a labourer. At sixty cultivated acres, this was one
    of the largest farms encountered in our samples. James was credited $240 for
    a year of work on 31 October. Thomas was a clerk, credited $145 on 2 June
    for two years work. Thomas's modest wage and his age might indicate a com-
    mercial apprenticeship, which typically involved living at the business and
    receiving room and board. Or he might have lived with family.

22 By contrast, Christopher Chant (a tailor), who had the third largest account, made hardly any local purchases, the main one being twenty-one pounds of butter between April and July.

23 The lumber was purchased between July and December: 3,000 feet of clap-board, 1,300 of flooring, 326 of scantling, 314 of planks, and 526 of "seasoned" 1-inch boards. Hubbard bought 33 pounds of butter in late February and March, a barrel of pork in June, and a barrel of flour in November. At other times in the year he made modest purchases of butter, beef, mutton, pork, oats (nine bushels in four transactions, all in February), and cheese. Twice he was recorded as having been "lent" flour, in smaller quantities, presumably to be repaid in kind later. This form of transaction arose also with five other customers at this store, for beef, pork, oats, flour, and whiskey; since the accounts debited these, we recorded them as pur-chases, and in fact none was recorded as returned during 1842. On lending, see Dechêne, *Le partage des subsistances au Canada*, 25–6.

24 That was unlikely to be a year's supply for someone working as a builder; but clients would typically provide materials for their projects. More than half of the value of local purchases in this sample was accounted for by boards, with twenty-eight buyers. Many transactions in the ledger were recorded as a value of "lumber to date," evidently summaries of another account, likely kept at the saw mill. Occasional unit prices allow us to estimate volumes, however. At the most common price (60 cents per 100 feet), the total value of lumber deb-ited implies purchases of about 75,000 feet board measure. Note that even a modest log house, 20 by 16 feet, could require about 2,000 feet of boards for framing, flooring, roofing, etc. See specifications of lumber for several early log houses in Rempel, *Building with Wood*, 76–81.

25 Actually, he returned pork of equivalent value for credit within a week. We have left it in the total debits to be consistent with other entries for goods recorded as "lent," because the latter often were not returned, or at least not within our sample year.

26 He also bought over 500 "hoop poles" (for seven dollars).

27 Credits included 120 pork barrels ($1.00 each); six potash barrels ($1.25); one large barrel ($1.50); 140 buckets (20 cents); 22 churns ($3.00); at least nine pails (50 cents); 188 butter tubs (50 cents); and seven washtubs ($1.00 to $1.30 each).

28 Firewood included one credit for $1.25 for maple – that is, the price differ-ence here represented a quality difference.

29 This possibility of entrepreneurial activity is suggested also by some financial and third-party transactions on his account. He bought a barrel of pork in January and another in May, a modest volume by comparison with the flour. He continued to buy other goods regularly from the store after his flour buying stopped.

30 This is based on numerous transactions involving third parties, wage payments, sales of lumber rafts, and travel expenses. Usually, he was not the person in the store for these transactions; about twenty different men made purchases on his account. If Buist was based at the mill, which was in Bedford Township, our failure to link him to the census would be because the manu-script census has not survived for Frontenac County.

31 The potatoes, purchased between March and July, included 6 bushels of seed potatoes in early June. In 1848, William Stewart estimated requirements to get out 60,000 cubic feet of timber: eighteen men would be needed, working for six months to a year, depending on their tasks; and they would need 52 barrels (10,800 pounds) of pork and 60 barrels (11,800 pounds) of flour. Two yoke of oxen and six spans of horses, needed for four months, would require 1,170 bushels of oats. This document, intended for publication in a year of crisis, was unlikely to underestimate the requirements of the timber industry. See Reid, *The Upper Ottawa Valley to 1855*, 156. Another firm's private estimate of costs (in 1843 or 1844) to produce the same volume of timber reckoned on thirty barrels of pork and fifty of flour. See McCalla, *Planting the Province*, 54.

32 In table 27, for Fowlds's in 1861 we report the value of produce purchases as recorded in the daybook. An alternative would be to estimate the value of flour, pork, beef, and butter, including the many entries that were only by volume, using entries that were priced. On this basis, the value of 1861 purchases of local produce at Fowlds's would be more than twice the value recorded in table 27, these four products alone amounting to about $850. Because large accounts were among the main customers to have transactions recorded only by volume, valuing the latter would not change the relative ranking of accounts. Unusually high volumes in February suggest that entries for flour then included January's transactions (table 30).

33 The Plunketts bought two barrels of pork and more modest quantities of meat on other occasions. They seem also to have been feeding animals, judging by purchases of large amounts of mill byproducts between May and December (350 pounds of bran, 500 pounds of cannel, and 2720 pounds of shorts) and of 14 bushels of peas in February. Although they were the leading buyers of butter at this store, that would not rule out having a cow for milk.

34 McInnis, "Marketable Surpluses in Ontario Farming," quote at 93, figures at 100. He is uncertain of both mutton and potatoes, but bases these on farm stocks and reported outputs. Among buyers here, Orr did buy modest amounts of mutton.

35 Assuming six in a household, McInnis's figures are equivalent to eleven ounces of flour and nine ounces of meat per person per day (although the latter is based on live weight, so actual consumption would have been more modest). An indication that they kept one or more animals is their regular purchases of modest quantities of mill byproducts between June and December and of peas during the winter. There were also chronological and other gaps in food purchases on two other large accounts here. Andy Orr and his wife bought flour in nine different months; but meat in only six and butter in five. Among their other purchases were about fifty dozen eggs in the six months from April to September and three cords and two "loads" of wood, which would have provided only a small proportion of what would be needed for warmth and cooking. Baptiste Touro bought no flour after July; his pork was purchased in April; and his grist mill products (bran and shorts) between February and May. He and his family continued to buy other products such as textiles, tea, and tobacco throughout the year.

36 For example, Duncan, *Nothing More Comforting*, gives more attention to

minor foods than the staples of daily diets; this work hardly discusses meat, and then mainly to discuss preserving pork, not cooking it. Duncan's *Canadians at Table* gives appropriate priority to bread.

37 Leung, *Grist and Flour Mills in Ontario,* 106–7, 110–11, 234, 239, 241. She translates canaille as "carnel" (234); she also uses "offal" (239) to refer "to the less valuable products of flour milling, i.e., bran, shorts and screenings tailed out of the flour bolts and grain cleaners and fed to livestock."

38 The daybook records his transactions by date and volume (not value), tallying an ongoing relationship between the merchant and the local distiller. Another buyer here was John Shipman, a substantial farmer, with thirty acres of land in cultivation, whose account was dominated by local produce and services, notably 612 pounds of middlings (which we have included as flour because of the relatively high price, $3.50 per hundredweight). See Leung, *Grist and Flour Mills in Ontario,* 111.

39 For shorts and "canaille" as synonyms, see Traill, *The Canadian Settler's Guide,* 99. For uses of bran, see, e.g., 98, 150, 180, 190. In 1861 there was also one purchase of a fourth product, screenings, at Fowlds's. From transactions that were priced (at 80 cents per 100 pounds for shorts and 60 and 75 cents per 100 pounds for bran), we can estimate the value of such byproducts at Fowlds's in 1861 at more than $75.

40 Just a few transactions were priced, at 35 or 40 cents per 100 pounds. If they were representative, bran would have added more than $30 to the value of local purchases. But because almost all were listed only by volume, we did not include the few transactions that were priced in calculations of the value of accounts.

41 For another farmer, buying bran and shorts in large quantities in autumn 1890, see Loewen, *From the Inside Out,* 161–3.

42 Later, at least, regulations forbade extending credit on postal business, but some storekeeper-postmasters would still charge services to store accounts. See Amyot and Willis, *Country Post,* 110. My thanks to John Willis for his encouragement and helpful advice on postal matters over the years. There were a few postal charges at Scovil's, but it is clear that this was not the main record.

43 Of the store's ten largest accounts, three had no postal charges and five had only one or two. Chambers had 90 cents in charges in fourteen transactions, half of them explicitly for copies of the "Albion." He was one of two recipients of this publication.

44 Most newspapers and printed materials were charged 3.4 cents, and the cost of a letter ranged upward from 7 cents, depending on weight and destination. Seventeen cost 20 cents or more. Egan's second letter is known because he had a small charge for the "balance on" it. Including the cost of the sheets of paper that Egan purchased on 15 February and 23 July, the two letters would have cost him about 57 cents.

45 Subscriptions are recorded in other goods in appendix A; i.e., they are not recorded in postal totals here. Sharpe's charges were $6.34. Miss Blanchard and her mother were charged $2.53, with transactions in six months.

46 Charles Beamish's six transactions between March and October totalled 94 cents, one-third of his entire account.

NOTES TO PAGES 126–30   261

47 See the discussion in Cameron, Haines, and Maude, *English Immigrant Voices*, xxix–xxxv; and Gerber, *Authors of Their Lives*, 106, 161.

48 Osborne and Pike, "Lowering 'The Walls of Oblivion,'" quotations from 202, 220. The title comes from a celebratory later account by the daughter of a British postal reformer. See also Goheen, "Canadian Communications Circa 1845."

49 McCalla, *Planting the Province*, 336–41.

50 The standard for a barrel of pork was 208 pounds; Paquet and Wallot, "Some Price Indexes for Quebec and Montreal," 310, report a range of from 200 to 208 pounds.

51 A third explanation, that this represented a discounted price for a bulk transaction, is unlikely. We have found very few examples of what seem to be lower unit prices for large volume purchases for any product in any sample.

52 For overall trends in the period, see Paquet and Wallot, *Un Québec moderne, 1760–1840*, 137–92; and "Some Price Indexes for Quebec and Montreal," 297–9, 302, 314–20. Boards and pork are not included in their ten-product series.

53 For a penetrating exploration of such issues in another setting, see Dépatie, "Jardins et vergers à Montréal au XVIIIe siècle."

54 As its title indicates, Matthews, "Local Government and the Regulation of the Public Market in Upper Canada," addresses urban market regulation, but not how urban market stalls actually obtained their supplies. In discussing urban centres, Wood, *Making Ontario*, focuses on their role in "serving the agricultural economy" rather than as sources of demand for rural produce (141; see also 162). For farmer participation in local markets in another setting, see Morneau, *Petits pays et grands ensembles*, 131–3.

55 McInnis, "Marketable Surpluses in Ontario Farming, 1860," 106.

56 For a similar perspective, see Sylvie Dépatie, "Commerce et crédit à l'Île-Jésus," 174–6.

57 See, e.g., Courville, Robert, and Séguin, *Atlas historique du Québec : Le pays laurentien au XIXe siècle*, 61–3.

58 Russell, *How Agriculture Made Canada*, 19.

CHAPTER SEVEN

1 Minhinnick, *At Home in Upper Canada*, 41.

2 Wilson, *Consider the Fork*, 193.

3 Canniff, *The History of the Settlement of Upper Canada*, quoted in Minhinnick, *At Home in Upper Canada*, 64. Because Canniff's descriptions of early days often appear to be based on memory, it is worth noting that he had no direct experience of the pioneer era. The grandson of Loyalists, he was born in 1830 and grew up "in relative affluence." See MacDougall, "William Canniff."

4 The other wine glass was purchased in 1828. Tett's invoices from the 1830s include four dozen "wines" (likely wine glasses) at 55 cents per dozen. It seems possible that the purchase of individual glasses means that they were associated not with social use but for consumption of wine as a form of medicine.

5   They held two hundred acres, of which thirty were in culture, and had a pair of horses, a pair of oxen, three milk cows and two other cattle. Fulford also owned a half-share in a saw mill.

6   The analogy is with the sugar bowl that the Fulfords purchased on another day; we found no other purchases of cream cups. Creamers, according to the OED, were "a flat dish for skimming the cream off milk," which does not sound like a "cup." They were priced at 12, 13, and 17 cents (the latter for one "flowered" creamer). There are no cream cups or creamers on the import invoices for this year.

7   Shears were the usual term in the 1808–09 retail accounts, although one pair of scissors was recorded (at the same price); import invoices record scissors and do not mention shears.

8   See Minhinnick, *At Home in Upper Canada*, 41.

9   de Vries, *The Industrious Revolution*, 130–3. See also Berg, "In Pursuit of Luxury," 127–31, 141–2.

10   A few of the teapots purchased were described as "flowered."

11   Based on price, none of the teapots purchased at the Yonge Mills store can have been of pewter.

12   There were also one dozen corkscrews. Although Tett also imported them in the 1830s, we found no purchases in our samples. As we have seen, wine was not purchased that frequently. Here and later, the quantity in a "gross" is unknown.

13   For example, almost all buyers of mugs were at this store, and half of all buyers of bake kettles.

14   A pair was the standard unit; a single blanket cost exactly half the price of a pair. Traill, *The Backwoods of Canada*, 179, recommended that immigrants bring "good bedding, especially warm blankets; as you pay high for them here, and they are not as good as you would supply yourself with at a much lower rate at home."

15   Points were an indication of size. Import invoices record fifty-four pairs, including thirty-one three-point at $3.70 and twenty four-point at $6.40. There was only one price level for the blankets purchased at Yonge Mills. After allowing for a markup for retail sale, it seems likely that four-point blankets would have been more expensive than the price recorded in the day-book.

16   The total value of blanket purchases was forty-three dollars and the kettles totalled sixty-four dollars.

17   Minhinnick, *At Home in Upper Canada*, 60, says kettles and pots were synonyms. Pots were not individually specified in import invoices; like other heavy iron goods, they were priced by weight, in this case a total of over 800 pounds, for which Jones paid 6.7 cents per pound. To estimate a unit price at retail, we arbitrarily doubled this price. Four of the large kettles purchased at Yonge Mills in 1808 were bought in September; the other two were purchased in late December. Later, Benjamin Tett ordered a potash kettle weighing from eight to nine hundredweight, costing about $4.00 per hundredweight; see QUA, Tett Papers, vol. 1, letterbook, 35–6, Tett to William Tett, 3 June 1840. Many customers made potash, but none bought such pots. Years later, in February and March 1851 (that is, after the sharp fall in iron prices discussed

in chapter 6), Kim Tighe purchased two kettles. One cost $5.73; the second, specifically for sugar, weighed 73.5 pounds and was priced at 5 cents per pound (thus $3.67).

18 Note Traill, *The Backwoods of Canada*, 184, on the importance of the bake kettle in household cooking "for the making and baking of huge loaves." In later samples where they were purchased, they cost from $1.17 to $1.70. They were not equivalent to "bakers," purchased in 1842, which cost no more than 45 cents. Tett's invoices in the 1830s included 4.5 dozen bakers of at least two kinds and with several prices for each, ranging from 6.7 to 22.5 cents. These invoices clearly distinguish them from much heavier "bake pans," priced by weight (4 cents per pound), and recorded on the same line as "pots, bellied." Six of the latter weighed a total of 229 pounds.

19 For spiders (appendix B), see Minhinnick, *At Home in Upper Canada*, 57: "a short-handled frying pan with three legs (called a spider – a name eventually applied to all iron frying pans)." The average weight of the frying pans imported in 1808 was 4.8 pounds, but that does not indicate the distribution around the mean (i.e., the size and variety of pans). As a comparison, the cast iron frying pan in our kitchen today weighs almost 7 pounds.

20 Duncan, *Canadians at Table*, 68.

21 He had forty acres in cultivation, a frame house, a household of ten (of whom six were children under sixteen), and one of the highest assessments in the 1828–29 sample.

22 Cannon had nine people in his household and seventy acres improved.

23 Note Minhinnick, *At Home in Upper Canada*, 47: "The historian William Canniff, writing in 1869, said, 'Tea, now considered an indispensable luxury of every family, was quite beyond the reach of all for a long time because of its scarcity and high price.'"

24 The teapots bought by the Gardeners and Cannons cost about as much as a half-pound of tea in 1828 and 1842 – although as it happens, neither bought any tea from our stores.

25 Later, the usual unit for them and for cups and saucers was the dozen. But it was common for transactions to involve a half-dozen, which seems likely to have been the quantity in a "set." Two stores recorded both units for cups and saucers: at Darling's, sets cost from 20 to 45 cents and dozens were 50 cents, $1.00, and $1.20; at Scovil's, sets cost from 25 to 30 cents and dozens were 50 cents. That a half dozen knives and forks at Tett's in 1842 generally cost $1.10 or $1.30 (much the same range as earlier and in 1851) has implications for reading Minhinnick, *At Home in Upper Canada*, 49: "The backwoods settler used his own knife from pocket or sheath, plus a pewter spoon, and it was hardly likely that his children would grow up thinking that forks were essential."

26 Tett bought plates and bowls in generally smaller quantities than Jones, however.

27 In the same period he bought just thirteen coffee pots, along with six coffee mills.

28 See Minhinnick, *At Home in Upper Canada*, 43.

29 Annual Canadian imports of broom corn from the United States averaged more than $14,000 in the early 1850s and almost $50,000 a decade later. By comparison, imports of "brooms and brushes of all kinds" totalled about $14,000 per year in the early 1860s. Province of Canada, Legislative

Assembly, *Journals*, 1853, appendix A, TTN, schedule 18; and *Sessional Papers*, 1862 no. 2, TTN, schedule 3, and 1864, no. 3, TTN, schedule 3. See Clark, *The Roots of Rural Capitalism*, 236-7, on transitions in broom-making in New England.

30 For this timing, see Newlands, *Early Ontario* Potters, 3, 23-7.

31 Washboards were being patented and spoken of in the 1830s and 1840s. See "When were washboards invented?" www.oldandinteresting.com/washboards-history.aspx (accessed 5 March 2012).

32 The only Charles Davis we found in the census manuscripts for Douro and Dummer was single; given that so many purchases on this account were made by a wife, it is evident that our linkage was incorrect.

33 The 17 cents paid by Mrs Davis for cups and saucers was one-sixth of the cost of a dozen of the most expensive cup and saucer sets here or slightly over one-quarter of the cost of the least expensive. Their other purchases came in late autumn and early winter, which was also when Davis purchased a stove (for fifteen dollars).

34 Some products that were more frequently purchased might also be locally made. For example, imported pails were evidently made of metal, whereas wooden pails were produced locally by coopers, who must often have sold them directly rather than through stores.

35 Cf Minhinnick, *At Home in Upper Canada*, 42, "Once a home was established, most people could afford some silver, if only teaspoons."

36 Brett, "Clothing Worn in Canada," writes, "Many people resorted to the native moccasin, sometimes of necessity, but more often for practicality and comfort." She does not consider the production and distribution system that would have been required for this to be routine; the implication is of a widespread aboriginal supply system.

37 Riello, *A Foot in the Past*, 20-2.

38 We do not have occupational data for the first two samples. But in 1828-29 James Adams was credited for a pair of boots at $5.50 and for three pairs of shoes at $1.60. These boots were the most expensive footwear encountered in the entire sample. On another occasion, he was credited 20 cents for mending a pair of boots.

39 Imports of manufactures of leather of all kinds were valued at less than $200,000 in the early 1850s. In 1861, boot and shoe imports to the Province of Canada were valued at less than $160,000.

40 Joseph Christmas bought a pair of shoes for $2.00 on 20 April 1809; Busea was charged $2.00 for shoes on 17 July 1828 and again on 4 June 1829; Russe was charged $1.70 for shoes on 22 July and $2.00 for another pair on 31 December; Desermo was charged $2.00 for shoes in December.

41 One of the Indian clients noted earlier, Little John, was credited on 12 December with three pairs of moccasins at 60 cents each. Of the three pairs Tett sold, each had a different price. One was sold at 60 cents on 12 December, suggesting a third-party transaction. The other two were at higher prices, $1.25 and $1.00, and purchased before the credit to Little John.

42 Riello, *A Foot in the Past*, 35-8.

43 OED; the term dates from the seventeenth century.

44 Dawley, *Class and Community*, 73-6, 245.

45 The inventory also counted one pair each of buckskin moccasins, "half boots (coarse-small)," slippers, and boots in camp (valued at 40 cents, which suggests they were used).

46 Riello, *A Foot in the Past*, 85–7.

47 This need not have been a local shoemaker, although that seems very unlikely given the presence of two in our sample and several others in Douro and Dummer.

48 Four of the six transactions were on the same date; the others were two and four days apart.

49 If Choate supplied raw materials and other supplies, that is not visible in these accounts, however. With so many shoemakers in the area, there were perhaps competitive advantages in having the merchant as an ally. Making shoes to sell on consignment, for example, might sustain production when orders were short.

50 For an exactly contemporary comparison, see Laberge, "Un cordonnier de Kingston au milieu du XIXième siècle." In this case, the shoemaker, Richard Webb, handled more than 900 orders in 1851 and 1853, and over 700 in 1852 (although these seem to include repair orders as well as orders for new footwear). Webb's billings, mainly between late 1849 and early 1854, totalled almost $5,000, something like $80 per month in the core period of his accounts. My thanks to J.L. Granatstein for this reference.

51 At Fowlds's in 1854, there were more buyers (twenty-six) and pairs purchased (fifty-one) than in any previous sample. There were two shoemakers in the clientele, James Cuff and John Driscol, the latter with the fifth-largest account. Their shoemaking activities do not appear in the ledger, however.

52 Kealey, *Toronto Workers Respond to Industrial Capitalism*, 21–3.

53 Note also Ann Graham's purchase of boots at $1.50 in 1828. We do not know materials (e.g., prunella was less expensive), however, or if they were for her own wear. Table 35 assumes they were.

54 All of these varieties were among Tett's 1830s imports, as were back, pocket, horn, and ivory combs.

55 None were on Jones's import list. Tett bought a half-dozen hairbrushes and two dozen shaving brushes over the 1833–36 period for which we have import invoices. Shaving brushes are reported separately in the "other" section of appendix B; brushes for horses and for painting are on the hardware list. An 1858 inventory for Darling's store included eight hair brushes at 50 cents each (the most expensive brushes), along with nine other kinds: cloth, shaving, horse, scrubbing, shoe, stove, tooth, whitewash, and what seem to be "banister" brushes.

56 In total he bought twelve reams (about 6,000 sheets); eight from American suppliers and four of foolscap from Montreal.

57 "Ruled" paper cost 25 cents.

58 Ink stands (in appendix B) appear in 1828 but were on the 1808 import list. We have not ascertained what "quills" were; they were only found at Tett's in 1842 (although they were imported in substantial quantities in 1808).

59 These charges may have represented postage on subscriptions.

60 Tett's Kingston supplier for almanacs and other books (including Bibles) was James Macfarlane; see Errington, "James Macfarlane."

61 But the 1858 inventory for Darling's store included twelve "school bibles" at 40 cents each.

62   For the schoolbooks in use in Upper Canada, see Houston and Prentice, *Schooling and Scholars in Nineteenth-Century Ontario*, 76, 237–49, and 312–15; quotation at 312.

63   Craig, *Backwoods Consumers and Homespun Capitalists*, 210. We have combined entries for pasteboard with a few for bonnet paper. Jones's 1808 imports did not mention pasteboard but included two dozen sheets of "Bon't paper" at 83 cents per dozen. One purchase of bonnet paper was recorded, at 20 cents per sheet, and there were five of pasteboard (three at 20 and two at 10 cents).

64   The lowest price was for spectacles and cases; if the entry was incorrect and this was actually just cases, then the lowest priced spectacles were $1.80 per dozen. Retail prices at Tett's ranged from 25 to 75 cents per pair and at Darling's from 20 to 60 cents.

65   There were thirteen buyers at Yonge Mills and twenty-six at Tett's. On the early history of cheap clay pipes, see Pennell, "Material Culture in Seventeenth-Century 'Britain," 73–6.

66   Scovil's had only four buyers but there the standard purchase unit was the dozen, at 6.7 or 10 cents per dozen.

67   Tett imported two dozen boxes in 1833 but none subsequently, and no snuff boxes were purchased in 1842.

68   Clover cost 20 cents per pound in 1842 and just 10 cents a decade later.

69   At Sherin's, almost all purchases were of one-quarter of a "gross," at 13 or 15 cents; Choate in 1861 once sold a quarter gross at 30 cents. This is a large discrepancy for nearby stores. Four customers at Darling's and three at Scovil's spent 50 cents or more on matches during the year, presumably an indication of considerable use. Another seventeen, all in 1861, spent from 25 to 49 cents.

70   There were purchases in 1861 at $3.00, $3.10, and $3.20 per pair. In 1842, there was one purchase of a "horse rug," at 75 cents; we have counted it with blankets although the price makes clear that it was a distinct product. Another price puzzle were the two "horse blankets" purchased at Choate's in 1851 at 80 cents each. I am grateful to Deborah Livingston-Lowe (personal communication) for information on how horse blankets were used and also on their production by local weavers. We do not know the source of supply for our stores, but because five sold such blankets, an imported product seems more likely.

71   Tett's purchases in the 1830s included small quantities of umbrellas in two sizes, twenty-four and twenty-eight inches.

72   There were five buyers of thirteen fiddle strings at Scovil's and three buyers of fiddle and/or violin strings at Fowlds's; prices ranged from 5 to 10 cents. Darling's 1858 inventory included seventy-two Jew's harps, all at 3.3 cents.

73   Craig, *Backwoods Consumers and Homespun Capitalists*, 216–20.

74   There were thirty-two accounts with such debits in 1854; a number relate to people working with this business in some capacity, but not all fit this profile.

CONCLUSION

1   Curtis, *Politics of Population*, 309, drawing on the work of Raymond Williams.

2   On the importance of qualitative differences, see Berg, "In Pursuit of Luxury," 124.

3   For example, Kurlansky, *Cod: A Biography of the Fish that Changed the World*; or Farnie and Jeremy, eds, *The Fibre that Changed the World*.

4   For comparison, see the "liste des principaux produits pour lesquels des prix ont été trouvés" ("list of the principal products for which prices have been found") in Paquet and Wallot, *Un Québec moderne, 1760–1840*, 173–5, which includes about three hundred different goods purchased in Lower Canada in this period, with indications of numerous variations. Their indexes of consumer prices are oriented to the urban buyer. Of the twenty goods in their Quebec index, coffee, candles, lamp oil, molasses, rum, salt, and tobacco are the only ones farmers might have bought; all ten of the goods in their Montreal index were farm produce. See 192n31–2.

5   McInnis, "Marketable Surpluses in Ontario Farming, 1860," 88. Another example (from the authoritative DCB) is Nicholson and Moir, "Armand-François-Marie Charbonnel," which speaks of "a decade of revolutionary social, economic, political, demographic, educational, and technological changes in Upper Canada."

6   A point made eloquently by Bouchard, *Quelques arpents d'Amérique*, 128–9: "The concept of marginality does not really advance us much ... because it suggests an absence of relations between two communities (the 'marginal' society and the 'non-marginal'...) that are in fact interlocked ... and also because it tells us nothing of the content, of the structure, nor of the features of the society deemed marginal – and describes mostly what it is not." ["Au fond, le concept de marginalité ne nous avance guère ... parce qu'il suggère une absence de relations entre deux collectivités (la société 'marginale' et l'autre...) qui sont en fait imbriquées ... ensuite parce qu'il ne nous dit rien du contenu, de la structure, des traits de la société dite marginale, dont il désigne surtout ce qu'elle n'est pas."] See also Crerar, *Letters of Adam Hope*, xxi.

7   See Craig, *Backwoods Consumers and Homespun Capitalists*, 216.

8   See Bruegel, *Farm, Shop, Landing*, 164.

9   Fleming, *General Stores of Canada*, 25. For general discussion of retailing after our period, see Drummond, *Progress without Planning*, 275–6.

10   Craig, *Backwoods Consumers and Homespun Capitalists*, 223; Ommer, "Rosie's Cove," 25.

11   Note Riello, *A Foot in the Past*, 17, "[O]ne of the obvious gaps in present research on consumption [is that] ... [m]uch attention has been given to undifferentiated categories, rather than micro-studies on specific commodities."

12   The trade figures apply to the whole of the Province of Canada. If, as is often assumed, Lower Canadian living standards were not as high as those in Upper Canada, per capita figures for the latter are underestimated by this procedure.

13   Lewis and Urquhart, "Growth and the Standard of Living in a Pioneer Economy," 160–1, 166–8.

14   Weatherill, *The Account Book of Richard Latham*, xi, xxviii–ix.

15   "AHR Forum: Investigating the History in Prehistory," 708.

16   McKay, *The Quest of the Folk*, xvi.

17   Loewen, *From the Inside Out*, ix. See also Wilson, "Reciprocal Work Bees and the Meaning of Neighbourhood," 434n6; and Wood, *Making Ontario*, 87–93.

18   See McCalla, *Planting the Province*, 77–84, and passim. Modern-day back-to-

the-landers likewise encountered this reality; see the sophisticated account in Weaver, "Making Place on the Canadian Periphery," 103–63.

19 Nor do our lists support a common model of consumption in the period, in which the driving force was households beginning to buy goods they had previously made for themselves. See Bruegel, *Farm, Shop, Landing,* 185.

BIBLIOGRAPHY

ABBREVIATIONS

CIHM Canadian Institute for Historic Microreproductions
DCB *Dictionary of Canadian Biography* (www.biographi.ca)
OED *Oxford English Dictionary* (www.oed.com)
TTN Tables of Trade and Navigation (see Government Documents, below).

MANUSCRIPT SOURCES

For citations of the specific documents used from these collections, see appendix D.
Archives of Ontario, Toronto, Ontario [AO]
    Charles Jones Fonds, F180
    Johnstown District Fonds, F1721
Library and Archives Canada, Ottawa, Ontario [LAC]
    Census Manuscripts, Upper Canada / Canada West, 1842–61. See appendix D
    for reel numbers.
Queen's University Archives, Kingston, Ontario [QUA]
    Darling Family Papers, 2303.28
    Scovil General Store Accounts, A.Arch 2217
    Tett Papers, 2247
Trent University Archives, Peterborough, Ontario [TUA]
    Choate Papers and Additions, B77-026
    Fowlds Papers, B72-001
    Sherin Papers, B71-002

GOVERNMENT DOCUMENTS

Canada, Province of, *Census of 1860–1*, vol. 2 (Quebec: S.B. Foote, 1864).
Canada, Province of, Legislative Assembly, *Journals* and *Sessional Papers*, 1850–70,
    Tables of Trade and Navigation [TTN]. For specific references, see appendix C.

BOOKS AND ARTICLES

Abbott, Joseph. *Memoranda of a Settler in Lower Canada or the Emigrant to
    North America*. Montreal: Lovell and Gibson for the author, 1842 [CIHM
    21859].
Acheson, T.W. "New Brunswick Agriculture at the End of the Colonial Era: A
    Reassessment." In *Farm, Factory and Fortune: New Studies in the Economic*

History of the Maritime Provinces, edited by Kris Inwood, 37–60. Fredericton: Acadiensis Press, 1993.

Adams, Annmarie. *Architecture in the Family Way: Doctors, Houses, and Women, 1870–1900*. Montreal and Kingston: McGill-Queen's University Press, 1996.

Adrosko, Rita. *Natural Dyes and Home Dyeing: A Practical Guide with over 150 Recipes*. New York: Dover, 1971.

"AHR Forum: Investigating the History in Prehistory: Introduction." *American Historical Review* 118, no. 3 (June 2013): 708.

Akenson, Donald Harman. *The Irish in Ontario: A Study in Rural History*. Montreal and Kingston: McGill-Queen's University Press, 1984.

Amyot, Chantal, and John Willis. *Country Post: Rural Postal Service in Canada, 1880 to 1945*. Mercury Series, Canadian Postal Museum Paper, no. 1. Gatineau: Canadian Museum of Civilization, 2003.

Appadurai, Arjun. "Introduction: Commodities and the Politics of Value." In *The Social Life of Things: Commodities in Cultural Perspective*, edited by Arjun Appadurai, 3–63. Cambridge: Cambridge University Press, 1986.

Armstrong, Audrey. *Sulphur & Molasses: Home Remedies and Other Echoes of the Canadian Past*. Don Mills: Musson, 1977.

Armstrong, Frederick H. *Handbook of Upper Canadian Chronology*. Rev. ed. Toronto: Dundurn Press, 1985.

Bara, Jana. "Cradled in Furs: Winter Fashions in Montreal in the 1860s." *Dress* 16 (1990): 39–47.

Barrett, Harry B. *The 19th-Century Journals & Paintings of William Pope*. Toronto: M.F. Fehely, 1976.

Baskerville, Peter. *Ontario: Image, Identity, and Power*. Toronto: Oxford University Press, 2002.

Bates, Christina. "'Beauty Unadorned': Dressing Children in Late Nineteenth Century Ontario." *Material History Bulletin* 21 (spring 1985): 25–34.

Beaudoin-Ross, Jacqueline, and Pamela Blackstock. "Costume in Canada: An Annotated Bibliography." *Material History Bulletin* 19 (spring 1984): 59–92.

Belich, James. *Replenishing the Earth: The Settler Revolution and the Rise of the Anglo-World, 1783–1939*. Oxford: Oxford University Press, 2009.

Belisle, Donica. *Retail Nation: Department Stores and the Making of Modern Canada*. Vancouver: UBC Press, 2011.

– "Toward a Canadian Consumer History." *Labour / Le Travail* 52 (fall 2003): 181–206.

Bemiss, Elijah. *The Dyer's Companion*. 1815. Reprint of 3rd ed., edited by Rita Adrosko. New York: Dover, 1973.

Benn, Carl. *The Iroquois in the War of 1812*. Toronto: University of Toronto Press, 1998.

Benson, John, and Laura Ugolini. "Introduction: Historians and the Nation of Shopkeepers." In *A Nation of Shopkeepers: Five Centuries of British Retailing*, edited by John Benson and Laura Ugolini, 1–24. London and New York: I.B. Taurus, 2003.

Benson, Susan Porter. *Counter Cultures: Saleswomen, Managers, and Customers in American Department Stores, 1890–1940*. Urbana and Chicago: University of Illinois Press, 1986.

Berg, Maxine. "In Pursuit of Luxury: Global History and British Consumer Goods in the Eighteenth Century." *Past & Present* 182 (February 2004): 85–142.

Bittermann, Rusty. "Farm Households and Wage Labour in the Northeastern Maritimes in the Early Nineteenth Century." *Labour / Le Travail* 31 (spring 1993): 13–47.

Bittermann, Rusty, Robert A. MacKinnon, and Graeme Wynn, "Of Inequality and Interdependence in the Nova Scotian Countryside, 1850–70." *Canadian Historical Review* 74, no. 1 (March 1993): 1–43.

Bliss, Michael. *Northern Enterprise: Five Centuries of Canadian Business.* Toronto: McClelland & Stewart, 1987.

Bonnycastle, Sir Richard Henry. *Canada and the Canadians*, new edition. London: H. Colburn, 1849 [CIHM 32649].

Bouchard, Gérard. *Quelques arpents d'Amérique : Population, économie, famille au Saguenay 1838–1971.* Montreal: Boréal, 1996.

Breen, T.H. *The Marketplace of Revolution: How Consumer Politics Shaped American Independence.* New York: Oxford University Press, 2004.

Brett, Katharine B. "Clothing Worn in Canada: Changing Fashions in the Nineteenth Century." In *Canada's Visual History*, Set 41, CD-ROM. Ottawa: National Film Board of Canada, Canadian Heritage Information Network, Canadian Museum of Civilization, 1994 [1980] [unpaginated].

– "Country Clothing in Nineteenth-Century Ontario." In *Fourth Annual Agricultural History of Ontario Seminar Proceedings*, edited by Alan A. Brookes, 40–69. Guelph: University of Guelph, 1979.

– *Women's Costume in Early Ontario.* Toronto: Royal Ontario Museum, 1966.

Brewer, John, and Roy Porter, eds. *Consumption and the World of Goods.* London and New York: Routledge, 1993.

Brewer, John, and Frank Trentmann. "Introduction: Space, Time and Value in Consuming Cultures." In *Consuming Cultures, Global Perspectives: Historical Trajectories, Transnational Exchanges*, edited by John Brewer and Frank Trentmann, 1–17. Oxford: Berg, 2006.

Brooke, Frances. *The History of Emily Montague.* London: J. Dodsley 1769 [CIHM 28235].

Bruegel, Martin. *Farm, Shop, Landing: The Rise of a Market Society in the Hudson Valley, 1780–1860.* Durham, NC: Duke University Press, 2002.

Brunger, Alan G. "Richard Birdsall." DCB.

Buchanan, W.M. *The Dictionary of Science and Technical Terms Used in Philosophy, Literature, Professions, Commerce, Arts, and Trades* with *Supplement* edited by James A. Smith. London: George Bell & Sons, 1884.

Burn, Robert Scott. *The Colonist's and Emigrant's Hand Book of the Mechanical Arts.* Edinburgh: Blackwood, 1854.

Burnham, Harold B., and Dorothy K. Burnham. *"Keep me warm one night": Early Handweaving in Eastern Canada.* Toronto: University of Toronto Press, 1972.

Buxton-Keenlyside, Judith. *Selected Canadian Spinning Wheels in Perspective: An Analytical Approach.* Mercury Series, History Division Paper, no. 30. Ottawa: National Museums of Canada, 1980.

Cadigan, Sean. "Power and Agency in Newfoundland and Labrador's History." *Labour / Le Travail* 54 (fall 2004): 223–43.

Cameron, Wendy, Sheila Haines, and Mary McDougall Maude, eds. *English*

Immigrant Voices: Labourers' Letters from Upper Canada in the 1830s. Montreal and Kingston: McGill-Queen's University Press, 2000.

Campbell, Patrick. *Travels in the Interior Inhabited Parts of North America in the Years 1791 and 1792.* Edinburgh: printed for the author, 1793.

The Canadian Housewife's Manual of Cookery ... Especially Adapted to This Country. Hamilton: W. Gillespy, 1861 [CIHM 64026].

Canniff, William. *The History of the Settlement of Upper Canada (Ontario) with Special Reference to the Bay Quinte.* Toronto: Dudley and Burns, 1869.

Carlos, Ann M., and Frank D. Lewis. "Trade, Consumption, and the Native Economy: Lessons from York Factory, Hudson Bay." *Journal of Economic History* 61, no. 4 (December 2001): 1037–64.

Carson, Cary. "The Consumer Revolution in Colonial British America: Why Demand?" In *Of Consuming Interests: The Style of Life in the Eighteenth Century*, edited by Cary Carson, Ronald Hoffman, and Peter J. Albert, 483–697. Charlottesville: University Press of Virginia for the United States Capitol Historical Society, 1994.

Chase, A.W. *Dr Chase's Recipes; or ... about Eight Hundred Practical Recipes.* 2nd Canadian ed. London, ON: E.A. Taylor, 1867.

Chavasse, Pye Henry. *Advice to a Mother on the Management of Her Children and on the Treatment of Some of Their More Pressing Illnesses and Accidents.* Toronto: Willing and Williamson, 1880 [CIHM 26929].

Christie, Nancy, and Michael Gauvreau, "Introduction: Recasting Canada's Postwar Decade." In *Cultures of Citizenship in Postwar Canada, 1940–1955*, edited by Nancy Christie and Michael Gauvreau, 3–26. Montreal and Kingston: McGill-Queen's University Press, 2004.

Clark, Christopher. *The Roots of Rural Capitalism: Western Massachusetts, 1780–1860.* Ithaca: Cornell University Press, 1991.

Clarke, John. *The Ordinary People of Essex: Environment, Culture, and Economy on the Frontier of Upper Canada.* Montreal and Kingston: McGill-Queen's University Press, 2010.

Clemens, Paul G.E. "The Consumer Culture of the Middle Atlantic, 1760–1820." *William and Mary Quarterly* 3rd ser. 62, no. 4 (October 2005): 577–624.

Cohen, Lizabeth. *A Consumers' Republic: The Politics of Mass Consumption in Postwar America.* New York: Alfred A. Knopf, 2003.

Cohen, Marjorie Griffin. *Women's Work, Markets, and Economic Development in Nineteenth-Century Ontario.* Toronto: University of Toronto Press, 1988.

Cole, A.O.C., ed. *Illustrated Historical Atlas of Peterborough County 1825–1875.* Peterborough: Peterborough Historical Atlas Foundation, 1975.

Cole, Jean Murray. *Origins: The History of Dummer Township.* Township of Dummer, 1993.

Collectif Clio, le [Micheline Dumont et al]. *L'histoire des femmes au Québec depuis quatre siècles.* Montreal: Le Jour, 1992.

Colpitts, George. *Game in the Garden: A Human History of Wildlife in Western Canada to 1940.* Vancouver and Toronto: UBC Press, 2002.

Conrad, Margaret, and Alvin Finkel. *History of the Canadian Peoples.* 5th ed. Toronto: Pearson Longman, 2009.

Courville, Serge. *Entre ville et campagne: L'essor du village dans les seigneuries du Bas-Canada.* Sainte-Foy: Les Presses de l'Université Laval, 1990.

Courville, Serge, Jean-Claude Robert, and Normand Séguin. *Atlas historique du Québec : Le pays laurentien au XIXe siècle: Les morphologies de base.* Sainte-Foy: Les Presses de l'Université Laval, 1995.

Cox, Nancy. "Objects of Worth, Objects of Desire: Toward A *Dictionary of Traded Goods and Commodities, 1550–1800.*" *Material History Review* 39 (spring 1994): 24–41.

Craig, Béatrice. *Backwoods Consumers and Homespun Capitalists: The Rise of a Market Culture in Eastern Canada.* Toronto: University of Toronto Press, 2009.

– "Y-eut-il une « révolution industrieuse » en Amérique du Nord? (Et devrions-nous nous en préoccuper?)." In *Famille et marché XVIe-XXe siècles,* edited by Christian Dessureault, John A. Dickinson, and Joseph Goy, 33–48. Sillery: Septentrion, 2003.

Craig, Béatrice, Judith Rygiel, and Elizabeth Turcotte. "The Homespun Paradox: Market-Oriented Production of Cloth in Eastern Canada in the Nineteenth Century." *Agricultural History* 76, no. 1 (winter 2002): 28–57.

– "Survival or Adaptation? Domestic Rural Textile Production in Eastern Canada in the Later Nineteenth Century." *Agricultural History Review* 49, pt 2 (December 2001): 140–71.

Craig, Gerald. *Upper Canada: The Formative Years, 1784–1841.* Toronto: McClelland & Stewart, 1963.

Creighton, D.G. *British North America at Confederation: A Study Prepared for the Royal Commission on Dominion-Provincial Relations 1939.* Ottawa: Queen's Printer, 1963 [1939].

Crerar, Adam, ed. *Letters of Adam Hope, 1834–1845.* Toronto: The Champlain Society, 2007.

Cunnington, C. Willett, Phillis Cunnington, and Charles Beard. *A Dictionary of English Costume, 900–1900.* London: Adam & Charles Black, 1960.

Curtis, Bruce. *The Politics of Population: State Formation, Statistics, and the Census of Canada, 1840–1875.* Toronto: University of Toronto Press, 2001.

Darroch, Gordon, and Lee Soltow. *Property and Inequality in Victorian Ontario: Structural Patterns and Cultural Communities in the 1871 Census.* Toronto: University of Toronto Press, 1994.

Darroch, Gordon. "Scanty Fortunes and Rural Middle Class Formation in Nineteenth-Century Rural Ontario." *Canadian Historical Review* 79, no. 4 (December 1998): 621–59.

Dawley, Alan. *Class and Community: The Industrial Revolution in Lynn.* Cambridge, MA: Harvard University Press, 1976.

Dechêne, Louise. *Le partage des subsistances au Canada sous le régime français.* Montréal: Boréal, 1994.

Dépatie, Sylvie. "Commerce et crédit à l'Île Jésus, 1734–75 : Le rôle des marchands ruraux dans l'économie des campagnes montréalaises." *Canadian Historical Review* 84, no. 2 (June 2003): 147–76.

– "Jardins et vergers à Montréal au XVIIIe siècle." In *Vingt ans après Habitants et marchands : Lectures de l'histoire des XVIIe et XVIIIe siècles canadiens / Twenty Years Later: Reading the History of Seventeenth- and Eighteenth-Century Canada,* edited by Sylvie Dépatie, Catherine Desbarats, Danielle Gauvreau, Mario Lalancette, Thomas Wien, 226–53. Montreal and Kingston: McGill-Queen's University Press, 1998.

Dépatie, Sylvie, Catherine Desbarats, Danielle Gauvreau, Mario Lalancette, and Thomas Wien, eds. *Vingt ans après Habitants et marchands: Lectures de l'histoire des XVIIe et XVIIIe siècles canadiens / Twenty Years Later: Reading the History of Seventeenth- and Eighteenth-Century Canada.* Montreal and Kingston: McGill-Queen's University Press, 1998.

Desrosiers, Claude. "Un aperçu des habitudes de consommation de la clientèle de Joseph Cartier, marchand général à Saint-Hyacinthe à la fin du XVIIIe siècle." *Canadian Historical Association, Historical Papers-Communications historiques* (1984): 91–110.

– "La clientèle d'un marchand général en milieu rural à la fin du XVIIIe siècle : analyse des comportements de consommation." In *Sociétés villageoises et rapports villes-campagnes au Québec et dans la France de l'Ouest, XVIIe–XXe siècles*, edited by François Lebrun and Normand Séguin, 151–8. Trois-Rivières: Centre de Recherche en Études Québécoises, 1987.

de Vries, Jan "Between Purchasing Power and the World of Goods: Understanding the Household Economy in Early Modern Europe." In *Consumption and the World of Goods*, edited by John Brewer and Roy Porter, 85–132. London and New York: Routledge, 1993.

– *The Industrious Revolution: Consumer Behavior and the Household Economy, 1650 to the Present.* New York: Cambridge University Press, 2008.

Dictionary of Traded Goods and Commodities, 1550–1820. Nancy Cox and Karin Dannehl, compilers. University of Wolverhampton, 2007 (www.british-history.ac.uk/source.aspx?pubid=739).

di Matteo, Livio, and Peter George. "Canadian Wealth Inequality in the Late Nineteenth Century: A Study of Wentworth County, Ontario, 1871–1902." *Canadian Historical Review* 73, no. 4 (December 1992): 453–83.

Directory of the United Counties of Peterborough and Victoria for 1858. Peterborough: T & R White, 1858 [CIHM A00072].

Doucet, Michael, and John Weaver. *Housing the North American City.* Montreal and Kingston: McGill-Queen's University Press, 1991.

Driver, Elizabeth, ed. *The Home Cook Book, Compiled from Recipes Contributed by Ladies of Toronto.* Reprint edition. North Vancouver: Whitecap Books, 2002 [1878].

Drummond, Ian. *Progress without Planning: The Economic History of Ontario from Confederation to the Second World War.* Toronto: University of Toronto Press, 1987.

Duffin, Jacalyn. *Langstaff: A Nineteenth-Century Medical Life.* Toronto: University of Toronto Press, 1993.

Duncan, Dorothy. *Canadians at Table: Food, Fellowship, and Folklore: A Culinary History of Canada.* Toronto: Dundurn, 2006.

– *Nothing More Comforting: Canada's Heritage Food.* Toronto: Dundurn, 2003.

Dunlop, Eleanor S., ed. *Our Forest Home: Being Extracts from the Correspondence of the late Frances Stewart.* Toronto: Presbyterian Printing and Publishing, 1889 [CIHM 13970].

DuPlessis, Robert. "Was There a Consumer Revolution in Eighteenth-Century New France?" *French Colonial History* 1 (2002): 143–59.

Edgar, Matilda, ed. *Ten Years of Upper Canada in Peace and War, 1805–1815: Being the Ridout Letters.* Toronto: William Briggs, 1890 [CIHM 02885].

Ennals, Peter. "Zacheus Burnham." *DCB*.

Ennals, Peter, and Deryck W. Holdsworth. *Homeplace: The Making of the Canadian Dwelling over Three Centuries*. Toronto: University of Toronto Press, 1998.

Errington, Elizabeth Jane. *Wives and Mothers, School Mistresses and Scullery Maids: Working Women in Upper Canada 1790–1840*. Montreal and Kingston: McGill-Queen's University Press, 1995.

Errington, Jane. "James Macfarlane." *DCB*.

Fahrni, Magda. "Explorer la consommation dans une perspective historique." *Revue d'histoire de l'Amérique française* 58, no. 4 (spring 2005): 465–73.

Farnie, Douglas A. "The Role of Merchants as Prime Movers in the Expansion of the Cotton Industry, 1760–1990." In *The Fibre That Changed the World: The Cotton Industry in International Perspective, 1660–1990s*, edited by Douglas A. Farnie and David J. Jeremy, 15–55. Oxford: Pasold Research Fund: Oxford University Press, 2004.

Farnie, Douglas A. and David J. Jeremy, eds. *The Fibre That Changed the World: The Cotton Industry in International Perspective, 1660–1990s*. Oxford: Pasold Research Fund: Oxford University Press, 2004.

Fellman, Anita Clair. *Little House, Long Shadow: Laura Ingalls Wilder's Impact on American Culture*. Columbia: University of Missouri Press, 2008.

Firth, Edith, ed. *The Town of York, 1793–1815*. Toronto: The Champlain Society, 1962.

Fleming, Rae B. *General Stores of Canada: Merchants & Memories*. Toronto: Lynx Images, 2002.

Fossier, Robert, *The Axe and the Oath: Ordinary Life in the Middle Ages*. Princeton: Princeton University Press, 2010.

Fraser, W. Hamish. *The Coming of the Mass Market, 1850–1914*. London: Macmillan, 1981.

Fuller's Counties of Peterborough and Victoria Directory for 1865 & 1866. Toronto [1865?] [CIHM A00836].

Fyson, Donald. "Du pain au madère : L'alimentation à Montréal au début du XIXe siècle." *Revue d'Histoire de l'Amérique française* 46, no. 1 (summer 1992): 67–90.

Gagan, David, and Rosemary Gagan. "Working Class Standards of Living in Late-Victorian Urban Ontario: A Review of the Miscellaneous Evidence on the Quality of Material Life." *Journal of the Canadian Historical Association* 1 (1990): 171–93.

Galt, John. *The Canadas, as They at Present Commend Themselves ...* London, 1832 [CIHM 34101].

Gates, Lillian. *Land Policies of Upper Canada*. Toronto: University of Toronto Press, 1968.

Gerber, David A. *Authors of Their Lives: The Personal Correspondence of British Immigrants to North America in the Nineteenth Century*. New York: New York University Press, 2006.

Given, Brian J. *A Most Pernicious Thing: Gun Trading and Native Warfare in the Early Contact Period*. Ottawa: Carleton University Press, 1994.

Goheen, Peter G. "Canadian Communications Circa 1845." *Geographical Review* 77, no. 1 (January 1987): 35–51.

Gooding, S. James. *The Canadian Gunsmiths 1608 to 1900*. West Hill, ON: Museum Restoration Service, 1962.

Gough, Barry M. ed. *The Journal of Alexander Henry the Younger 1799–1814*. Toronto: The Champlain Society, 1992.

Gourlay, Robert. *Statistical Account of Upper Canada*. London: Simpkin and Marshall, 1822. Abridged and edited by S.R. Mealing. Toronto: McClelland & Stewart, 1974.

Graham, Fern. "Darlingside." Parks Canada Report, 1992-20: 661–94.

Granatstein, J.L. *Canada's Army: Waging the War and Keeping the Peace*. Toronto: University of Toronto Press, 2002.

Greer, Allan. *The Patriots and the People: The Rebellion of 1837 in Rural Lower Canada*. Toronto: University of Toronto Press, 1993.

– *Peasant, Lord, and Merchant: Rural Society in Three Quebec Parishes 1740–1840*. Toronto: University of Toronto Press, 1985.

Guillet, E.C. *The Pioneer Farmer and Backwoodsman*, vol. 1. Toronto: Ontario Publishing Company, 1963.

Gwyn, Julian, and Fazley Siddiq. "Wealth Distribution in Nova Scotia during the Confederation Era, 1851 and 1871." *Canadian Historical Review* 73, no. 4 (December 1992): 435–52.

Haight, Canniff. *Country Life in Canada Fifty Years Ago: Personal Recollections and Reminiscences of a Sexagenarian*. Toronto: Hunter Rose, 1885.

Hamilton, T.M. *Firearms on the Frontier: Guns at Fort Michilimackinac 1715–1781*. Reports in Mackinac History and Archaeology, no. 5. Mackinac Island: State Park Commission, 1976.

Hardy, Jean-Pierre. *La vie quotidienne dans la vallée du Saint-Laurent (1790–1835)*. Sillery: Septentrion, 2001.

Harley, C. Knick. "The Antebellum Tariff: Different Products or Competing Sources? A Comment on Irwin and Temin." *Journal of Economic History* 61, no. 3 (September 2001): 799–805.

Harris, Cole. *The Reluctant Land: Society, Space, and Environment in Canada before Confederation*. Vancouver: UBC Press, 2008.

Hart, Patricia W. *Pioneering in North York: A History of the Borough*. Don Mills: General Publishing, 1968.

Haskell, Thomas L., and Richard F. Teichgraeber III. "Introduction: The Culture of the Market." In *The Culture of the Market: Historical Essays*, edited by Thomas Haskell and Richard F. Teichgraeber III, 1–39. Cambridge: Cambridge University Press, 1993.

Haydon, Andrew. *Pioneer Sketches in the District of Bathurst*. Vol. 1. Toronto: Ryerson Press, 1925.

Hazen, Edward. *The Panorama of Professions and Trades; or Every Man's Book*. Philadelphia: U. Hunt, 1836.

Hebert, Luke. *The Engineer's and Mechanic's Encyclopaedia, Comprehending Practical Illustrations of the Machinery and Processes Employed in Every Description of Manufacture of the British Empire*. 2 vols. London: Thomas Kelly, 1836.

Hilts, Joseph. *Among the Forest Trees or How the Bushman Family Got Their Homes*. Toronto: W. Briggs, 1888 [CIHM 05620].

Hindle, Brooke. "Introduction: The Span of the Wooden Age." In *America's*

Wooden Age: Aspects of Its Early Technology, edited by Brooke Hindle, 3–12. Tarrytown, NY: Sleepy Hollow Restorations, 1975.

Hood, Adrienne Dora. *The Weaver's Craft: Cloth, Commerce, and Industry in Early Pennsylvania*. Philadelphia: University of Pennsylvania Press, 2003.

Hood, Adrienne Dora, and David-Thiery Ruddel, "Artifacts and Documents in the History of Quebec Textiles." In *Living in a Material World: Canadian and American Approaches to Material Culture*, edited by Gerald L. Pocius, 55–91. St John's: Institute of Social and Economic Research, Memorial University, 1991.

Houston, Susan, and Alison Prentice. *Schooling and Scholars in Nineteenth-Century Ontario*. Toronto: University of Toronto Press, 1988.

Howard, Vicki. "'The Biggest Small-Town Store in America': Independent Retailers and the Rise of Consumer Culture." *Enterprise & Society* 9, no. 3 (September 2008): 457–86.

Innis, Harold Adams. *The Fur Trade in Canada*. Rev. ed. Toronto: University of Toronto Press, 1956.

Inwood, Kris. "The Iron and Steel Industry." In Ian Drummond, *Progress without Planning: The Economic History of Ontario from Confederation to the Second World War*, 185–207. Toronto: University of Toronto Press, 1987.

Inwood, Kris, and Phyllis Wagg. "The Survival of Handloom Weaving in Rural Canada Circa 1870." *Journal of Economic History* 53, no. 2 (June 1993): 346–58.

– "Wealth and Prosperity in Nova Scotian Agriculture, 1851–71." *Canadian Historical Review* 75, no. 2 (June 1994): 239–64.

Irwin, Douglas A., and Peter Temin. "The Antebellum Tariff on Cotton Textiles Revisited." *Journal of Economic History* 61, no. 3 (September 2001): 777–98.

Jefferis, B.G. *Search Lights on Health, Light on Dark Corners: A Complete Sexual Science and a Guide to Purity*. 25th ed. Toronto: J.L. Nichols, 1894 [CIHM 29321].

Jensen, Joan M. "Needlework as Art, Craft, and Livelihood before 1900." In *A Needle, A Bobbin, A Strike: Women Needleworkers in America*, edited by Joan M. Jensen and Sue Davidson, 1–19. Philadelphia: Temple University Press, 1984.

Jones, Colin, and Rebecca Spang. "*Sans-culottes, sans café, sans tabac*: Shifting Realms of Necessity and Luxury in Eighteenth-Century France." In *Consumers and Luxury: Consumer Culture in Europe 1650–1850*, edited by Maxine Berg and Helen Clifford, 17–62. New York: Manchester University Press, 1999.

Jones, Elwood H. "John Gilchrist." DCB.

Kealey, Gregory S. *Toronto Workers Respond to Industrial Capitalism 1867–1892*. Toronto: University of Toronto Press, 1980.

Kirby, William. *The U.E.: A Tale of Upper Canada*. Niagara, 1859 [CIHM 36153].

Klepp, Susan E. "Lost, Hidden, Obstructed, and Repressed: Contraceptive and Abortive Technology in the Early Delaware Valley." In *Early American Technology: Making and Doing Things from the Colonial Era to 1850*, edited by Judith McGaw, 68–113. Chapel Hill and London: University of North Carolina Press, 1994.

Kristofferson, Robert B. *Craft Capitalism: Craftworkers and Early Industrialization in Hamilton, Ontario, 1840–1872*. Toronto: University of Toronto Press, 2007.

Kulikoff, Allan. *From British Peasants to Colonial American Farmers.* Chapel Hill and London: University of North Carolina Press, 2000.

Kurlansky, Mark. *Cod: A Biography of the Fish That Changed the World.* Toronto: Knopf Canada, 1997.

Laberge, Alain. "Un cordonnier de Kingston au milieu du XIXième siècle." Unpublished essay, York University [nd].

Lambert, John. *Travels through Canada, and the United States of North America, in the years 1806, 1807, & 1808,* 2nd ed. London: C. Cradock and W. Joy, 1813 [CIHM 36169].

Larkin, Jack. *The Reshaping of Everyday Life, 1790–1840.* New York: Harper & Row, 1988.

Lebrun, François, and Normand Séguin, editors. *Sociétés villageoises et rapports villes-campagnes au Québec et dans la France de l'Ouest, XVIIe–XXe siècles.* Trois-Rivières: Centre de Recherche en Études Québécoises, 1987.

Leung, Felicity L. *Grist and Flour Mills in Ontario: From Millstones to Rollers, 1780s–1880s,* History and Archaeology Series, no. 53. Ottawa: National Historic Parks and Sites Branch, Parks Canada, 1981.

Lewis, Frank D., and M.C. Urquhart. "Growth and the Standard of Living in a Pioneer Economy, Upper Canada, 1826 to 1851." *William and Mary Quarterly* 3rd ser. 56, no. 1 (January 1999): 151–81.

Livingston, James. "Modern Subjectivity and Consumer Culture." In *Getting and Spending: European and American Consumer Societies in the Twentieth Century,* edited by Susan Strasser, Charles McGovern, and Matthias Judt, 413–29. Cambridge: Cambridge University Press for the German Historical Institute, 1998.

Livingston-Lowe, Deborah. "Counting on Customers: John Campbell, 1806–1891, Middlesex County Handloom Weaver." MA thesis, University of Guelph, 2012.

Lockwood, Glenn J. "Temperance in Upper Canada as Ethnic Subterfuge." In *Drink in Canada: Historical Essays,* edited by Cheryl Krasnick Warsh, 43–69. Montreal and Kingston: McGill-Queen's University Press, 1993.

Loewen, Royden, ed. *From the Inside Out: The Rural World of Mennonite Diarists, 1863 to 1929.* Winnipeg: University of Manitoba Press and Manitoba Record Society, 1999.

Lovell, J. *The Canada Directory for 1857–8 Containing Names of Professional and Business Men and of the Other Principal Inhabitants.* Montreal: J. Lovell, 1857 [CIHM 29571].

– *Lovell's Province of Ontario Directory.* Montreal: J. Lovell, 1871 [CIHM A00583].

MacDougall, Heather. "William Canniff." DCB.

MacFadyen, Joshua D. "Fashioning Flax: Industry, Region, and Work in North American Fibre and Linseed Oil, 1850–1930." PhD thesis, University of Guelph, 2009.

Mackay, Robert W.S. *The Canada Directory ... 1851.* Montreal: J. Lovell, 1851 [CIHM 29570].

Main, Gloria L. "Many Things Forgotten: The Use of Probate Records in *Arming America.*" *William and Mary Quarterly* 3rd ser. 59, no. 1 (January 2002): 211–16.

– *Peoples of a Spacious Land: Families and Cultures in Colonial New England.* Cambridge, MA: Harvard University Press, 2001.

- "The Standard of Living in Southern New England, 1640–1773." *William and Mary Quarterly* 3rd ser. 45, no. 1 (January 1988): 124–34.

Mancke, Elizabeth. "At the Counter of the General Store: Women and the Economy in Eighteenth-Century Horton, Nova Scotia." In *Intimate Relations: Family and Community in Planter Nova Scotia 1759–1800*, edited by Margaret Conrad, 167–81. Fredericton: Acadiensis Press, 1995.

Martin, Ann Smart. "Ribbons of Desire: Gendered Stories in the World of Goods." In *Gender, Taste, and Material Culture in Britain and North America 1700–1830*, edited by John Styles and Amanda Vickery, 179–200. New Haven and London: Yale Center for British Art & The Paul Mellon Center for Studies in British Art, 2006.

Martin, Paul-Louis. *À la façon du temps présent : Trois siècles d'architecture populaire au Québec*. [Sainte-Foy]: Les Presses de l'Université Laval, 1999.

Matson, Cathy. "A House of Many Mansions: Some Thoughts on the Field of Economic History." In *The Economy of Early America: Historical Perspectives & New Directions*, edited by Cathy Matson, 1–70. University Park, PA: Pennsylvania State University Press, 2006.

Matthews, W. Thomas. "Local Government and the Regulation of the Public Market in Upper Canada, 1800–1860: The Moral Economy of the Poor." *Ontario History* 79, no. 4 (December 1987): 297–326.

Maynard, Steven. "Between Farm and Factory: The Productive Household and the Capitalist Transformation of the Maritime Countryside, Hopewell, Nova Scotia, 1869–1890." In *Contested Countryside: Rural Workers and Modern Society in Atlantic Canada, 1800–1950*, edited by Daniel Samson, 70–104. Fredericton: Acadiensis Press for the Gorsebrook Research Institute, 1994.

McCalla, Douglas. *Consumption Stories: Customer Purchases of Alcohol at an Upper Canadian Country Store in 1808–9 and 1828–9*. Québec: Centre interuniversitaire d'études québécoises, *Cheminements – Conférences* series, 1999.

- "Economy and Empire: Britain and Canadian Development, 1783–1971." In *Canada and the British Empire*, edited by Phillip A. Buckner, 235–53. Oxford: Oxford University Press, 2008.

- *Planting the Province: The Economic History of Upper Canada, 1784–1870*. Toronto: University of Toronto Press, 1993.

- "Textile Purchases by Some Ordinary Upper Canadians, 1808–1861." *Material History Review / Revue d'histoire de la culture matérielle* 53 (spring-summer 2001): 4–27.

- *The Upper Canada Trade 1834–1872: A Study of the Buchanans' Business*. Toronto: University of Toronto Press, 1979.

- "Upper Canadians and Their Guns: an Exploration via Country Store Accounts (1808–61)." *Ontario History* 97, no. 2 (autumn 2005): 121–37.

- "A World without Chocolate: Grocery Purchases at Some Upper Canadian Country Stores, 1808–61." *Agricultural History* 79, no. 2 (spring 2005): 147–72.

McDonald, Michelle Craig. "Transatlantic Consumption." In *The Oxford Handbook of the History of Consumption*, edited by Frank Trentmann, 111–26. Oxford: Oxford University Press, 2012.

McGaughey, Elva Richards. "Ephraim Jones." *DCB*.

McGaw, Judith, ed. *Early American Technology: Making and Doing Things from the Colonial Era to 1850*. Chapel Hill and London: University of North

Carolina Press, 1994.
– "'So Much Depends upon a Red Wheelbarrow': Agricultural Tool Ownership
in the Eighteenth-Century Mid-Atlantic." In *Early American Technology:
Making and Doing Things from the Colonial Era to 1850*, edited by Judith
McGaw, 328–57. Chapel Hill: University of North Carolina Press, 1994.
McGee, Harold. *On Food and Cooking: The Science and Lore of the Kitchen.*
Rev. ed. New York: Scribner, 2004.
McIlwraith, Thomas F. "Charles Jones." *DCB.*
– "The Logistical Geography of the Great Lakes Grain Trade, 1820–1850." PhD
thesis, University of Wisconsin, 1973.
McInnis, Marvin. "The Economy of Canada in the Nineteenth Century." In *The
Cambridge Economic History of the United States, Vol. 2: The Long
Nineteenth Century*, edited by Stanley L. Engerman and Robert E. Gallman,
57–106. Cambridge: Cambridge University Press, 2000.
– "Marketable Surpluses in Ontario Farming, 1860." Reprinted in *Perspectives on
Canadian Economic History*, edited by Douglas McCalla and Michael
Huberman, 2nd ed., 87–108. Toronto: Copp Clark Longman, 1994.
McKay, Ian. *The Quest of the Folk: Antimodernism and Cultural Selection in
Twentieth-Century Nova Scotia.* Montreal and Kingston: McGill-Queen's
University Press, 1994.
McKendrick, Neil. "Introduction: The Birth of a Consumer Society: The
Commercialization of Eighteenth-Century England." In *The Birth of a Consumer
Society: The Commercialization of Eighteenth-Century England*, by Neil
McKendrick, John Brewer, and J.H. Plumb, 1–6. London: Europa, 1982.
McNally, Larry. "Technical Advance and Stagnation: The Case of Nail Production in
Nineteenth-Century Montreal." *Material History Bulletin* 36 (fall 1992): 38–48.
Meehan, James. "Demonstrating the Use of Log House Building Tools at the New
Windsor Cantonment." *APT: Bulletin of the Association for Preservation
Technology* 12, no. 4 (1980): 39–44.
Merchant, Carolyn. *Ecological Revolutions: Nature, Gender, and Science in New
England.* Chapel Hill & London: University of North Carolina Press, 1989.
Merrill, Michael. "Putting 'Capitalism' in Its Place: A Review of Recent Literature."
William and Mary Quarterly 3rd ser., 52, no. 2 (April 1995): 315–26.
Merritt, Richard D. "Early Inns and Taverns: Accommodation, Fellowship, and
Good Cheer." In *The Capital Years: Niagara-on-the-Lake, 1792–1796*, edited by
Richard Merritt, Nancy Butler, and Michael Power, 187–222. Toronto and
Oxford: Dundurn, 1991.
Michel, Louis. "Endettement et société rurale dans la région de Montréal au dix-
huitième siècle : Premières approches et éléments de réflexion." In *Sociétés
villageoises et rapports villes-campagnes au Québec et dans la France de l'Ouest
XVIIe–XXe siècles*, edited by François Lebrun and Normand Séguin, 171–81.
Trois-Rivières: Centre de Recherche en Études Québécoises, 1987.
– "Le livre de compte (1784–1792) de Gaspard Massue, marchand à Varennes."
Histoire sociale / Social History 13, no. 26 (novembre 1980): 369–98.
– " Un marchand rural en Nouvelle-France : F.A. Bailly de Messein, 1709–1771."
Revue d'histoire de l'Amérique française 33 no. 2 (septembre 1979): 215–62.
Miller, Henry M. "An Archaeological Perspective on the Evolution of Diet in the
Colonial Chesapeake, 1620–1745." In *Colonial Chesapeake Society*, edited by

Lois Green Carr, Philip D. Morgan, and Jean B. Russo, 176–99. Chapel Hill: University of North Carolina Press for The Institute of Early American History and Culture, 1988.

Minhinnick, Jeanne. *At Home in Upper Canada*. Toronto: Clarke, Irwin, 1970.

– "Some Personal Observations on the Use of Paint in Early Ontario." *APT: Bulletin of the Association for Preservation Technology* 7, no. 2 (1975): 13–31.

Mitchell, B.R., and Phyllis Deane, *Abstract of British Historical Statistics*. Cambridge: Cambridge University Press, 1971.

Moodie, Susanna. *Roughing It in the Bush*. London: Richard Bentley, 1852. New Canadian Library, no. 31, edited by Carl F. Klinck. Toronto: McClelland & Stewart, 1962.

Moreira, James. "Rum in the Atlantic Provinces." In *Tempered by Rum: Rum in the History of the Maritime Provinces*, edited by James H. Morrison and James Moreira, 15–30. Porters Lake, NS: Pottersfield Press, 1988.

Morneau, Jocelyn. *Petits pays et grands ensembles : Les articulations du monde rural au XIXe siècle : L'exemple du lac Saint-Pierre*. Sainte-Foy: Les Presses de l'Université Laval, 1999.

Moussette, Marcel. *Le Chauffage domestique au Canada : Des origines à l'industrialisation*. Québec: Les Presses de l'Université Laval, 1983.

Napheys, George Henry. *The Physical Life of Woman: Advice to the Maiden, Wife, and Mother*. Toronto: MacLear, 1871 [CIHM 11355].

Newlands, David. *Early Ontario Potters: Their Craft and Trade*. Toronto: McGraw-Hill Ryerson, 1979.

Nicholson, Murray W., and John S. Moir. "Armand-François-Marie Charbonnel." *DCB*.

Noël, Françoise. *Family Life and Sociability in Upper and Lower Canada, 1780–1870*. Montreal and Kingston: McGill-Queen's University Press, 2003.

Noel, Jan. *Canada Dry: Temperance Crusades before Confederation*. Toronto: University of Toronto Press, 1995.

Norrie, Kenneth, Douglas Owram, and J.C. Herbert Emery. *A History of the Canadian Economy*. 4th ed. Toronto: Thomson, Nelson, 2008.

Norton, Marcy. "Tasting Empire: Chocolate and the European Internalization of Mesoamerican Aesthetics." *American Historical Review* 111, no. 3 (June 2006): 660–91.

O'Brien, Patrick. "Imperialism and the Rise and Decline of the British Economy, 1688–1989." *New Left Review* 238 (November-December 1999): 48–80.

Ommer, Rosemary E. "Merchant Credit and the Informal Economy: Newfoundland 1918–1929." Canadian Historical Association, *Historical Papers* (1989): 167–89.

– ed. *Merchant Credit and Labour Strategies in Historical Perspective*. Fredericton: Acadiensis Press, 1990.

– "Rosie's Cove: Settlement Morphology, History, Economy, and Culture in a Newfoundland Outport." In *Fishing Places, Fishing People: Traditions and Issues in Canadian Small-Scale Fisheries*, edited by Dianne Newell and Rosemary E. Ommer, 17–31. Toronto: University of Toronto Press, 1999.

Osborne, Brian, and Robert Pike. "Lowering 'The Walls of Oblivion': The Revolution in Postal Communications in Central Canada, 1851–1911." *Canadian Papers in Rural History* 4 (1984): 200–25.

Osborne, Brian S. "Wills and Inventories: Records of Life and Death in a Developing Society." *Families* 19, no. 4 (1980): 235–47.

Osterud, Nancy Grey. *Bonds of Community: The Lives of Farm Women in Nineteenth-Century New York*. Ithaca: Cornell University Press, 1991.

Ouellette, David. "James Crooks." *DCB*.

Pacey, Antony. "A History of Window Glass Manufacture in Canada." *Bulletin of the Association for Preservation Technology* 13, no. 3 (1981): 33–47.

Paquet, Gilles, and Jean-Pierre Wallot. *Un Québec moderne, 1760–1840 : Essai d'histoire économique et sociale*. Montreal: Hurtubise, 2007.

– "Some Price Indexes for Quebec and Montreal (1760–1913)." *Histoire sociale / Social History* 31, no. 62 (November 1998): 281–320.

– "Stratégie foncière de l'habitant: Québec (1790–1835)." *Revue d'histoire de l'Amérique française* 39, no. 4 (spring 1986): 551–81.

– "Structures sociales et niveaux de richesse dans les campagnes du Québec 1792–1812." In *Évolution et éclatement du monde rural : Structures, fonctionnement et évolution des sociétés rurales françaises et québécoises XVIIe–XXe siècles*, edited by Joseph Goy et Jean-Pierre Wallot, 239–58. Paris and Montreal: Éditions de l'École des Hautes Études en Sciences Sociales et Presses de l'Université de Montréal, 1986.

Parr, Joy. *Domestic Goods: The Material, the Moral, and the Economic in the Postwar Years*. Toronto: University of Toronto Press, 1999.

– *The Gender of Breadwinners: Women, Men, and Change in Two Industrial Towns 1880–1950*. Toronto: University of Toronto Press, 1990.

Patterson, Neil A. "Benjamin Tett and Bedford Mills." *Historic Kingston* 25 (March 1977): 60–2.

Penn, Theodore Zuk. "Decorative and Protective Finishes, 1750–1850: Materials, Process, and Craft." *APT: Bulletin of the Association for Preservation Technology* 16, no. 1 (1984): 3–46.

Pennell, Sara. "Material Culture in Seventeenth-Century 'Britain': The Matter of Domestic Consumption." In *The Oxford Handbook of the History of Consumption*, edited by Frank Trentmann, 64–84. Oxford: Oxford University Press, 2012.

Perkins, Elizabeth A. "The Consumer Frontier: Household Consumption in Early Kentucky." *Journal of American History* 78, no. 2 (September 1991): 486–510.

Peterman, Michael. "Catharine Parr Strickland (Traill)." *DCB*.

Piva, Michael. *The Borrowing Process: Public Finance in the Province of Canada, 1840–1867*. Ottawa: University of Ottawa Press, 1992.

Pocius, Gerald. *A Place to Belong: Community Order and Everyday Space in Calvert, Newfoundland*. Montreal and Kingston: McGill-Queen's University Press, 2000.

Pope, Peter E. *Fish into Wine: The Newfoundland Plantation in the Seventeenth Century*. Chapel Hill and London: University of North Carolina Press for the Omohundro Institute of Early American History and Culture, 2004.

Pronovost, Claude. *La bourgeoisie marchande en milieu rural (1720–1840)*. Sainte-Foy: Les Presses de l'Université Laval, 1998.

Pryke, K.G. "Sir Adams George Archibald." *DCB*.

Radcliff, Thomas, ed. *Authentic Letters from Upper Canada*. Dublin: William Curry, 1833. Toronto: Macmillan, 1952.

Rasmussen, Wayne D. "Wood on the Farm." In *Material Culture of the Wooden Age*, edited by Brooke Hindle, 15–34. Tarrytown: Sleepy Hollow Press, 1981.

Ray, A.J. *Indians in the Fur Trade: Their Role as Hunters, Trappers and Middlemen in the Lands Southwest of Hudson Bay 1660–1870*. Toronto: University of Toronto Press, 1974.

Read, Colin, and Ronald Stagg, eds. *The Rebellion of 1837 in Upper Canada: A Collection of Documents*. Toronto: The Champlain Society, 1985.

Reid, Richard, ed. *The Upper Ottawa Valley to 1855: A Collection of Documents*. Toronto: The Champlain Society, 1990.

Rempel, John I. *Building with Wood and Other Aspects of Nineteenth-Century Building in Central Canada*. Rev. ed. Toronto: University of Toronto Press, 1980.

Riello, Giorgio. *A Foot in the Past: Consumers, Producers and Footwear in the Long Eighteenth Century*. Oxford: Oxford University Press, 2006.

Roberts, Julia. *In Mixed Company: Taverns and Public Life in Upper Canada*. Vancouver: UBC Press, 2009.

Robertson, J.S. *Guide to Dressmaking and Fancy Work*. c. 1876, ed. Eileen Collard. Burlington: Eileen Collard, 1977.

Roelens, Janine, and Kris Inwood, "'Labouring at the Loom': A Case Study of Rural Manufacturing in Leeds County, Ontario, 1870." *Canadian Papers in Rural History* 7 (1990): 215–35.

Romney, Paul. *Getting It Wrong: How Canadians Forgot Their Past and Imperilled Confederation*. Toronto: University of Toronto Press, 1999.

Rosenberg, Nathan. "America's Rise to Woodworking Leadership." In *America's Wooden Age: Aspects of its Early Technology*, edited by Brooke Hindle, 37–62. Tarrytown, NY: Sleepy Hollow Restorations, 1975.

Rothenberg, Winifred Barr. *From Market-Places to a Market Economy: The Transformation of Rural Massachusetts 1750–1850*. Chicago: University of Chicago Press, 1992.

Rothstein, Nathalie, ed. *Barbara Johnson's Album of Fashions and Fabrics*. London: Thames & Hudson, 1987.

Ruddel, David-Thiery. "Consumer Trends, Clothing, Textiles and Equipment in the Montreal Area, 1792–1835." *Material History Bulletin* 32 (fall 1990): 45–64.

Russell, Carl P. *Firearms, Traps, & Tools of the Mountain Men*. New York: Knopf, 1967.

Russell, Loris. *Everyday Life in Colonial Canada*. Toronto: Copp Clark, 1973.

– *Lighting the Pioneer Ontario Home*. Toronto: Royal Ontario Museum, 1966.

Russell, Peter A. *How Agriculture Made Canada: Farming in the Nineteenth Century*. Montreal and Kingston: McGill-Queen's University Press, 2012.

St-Georges, Lise. "Commerce, crédit et transactions foncières: Pratiques de la communauté marchande du bourg de l'Assomption, 1748–1791." *Revue d'histoire de l'Amérique française* 39, no. 3 (winter 1986): 323–43.

Samson, Daniel. "Introduction: Situating the Rural in Atlantic Canada" and "Afterword: Capitalism and Modernization in the Atlantic Canada Countryside." In *Contested Countryside: Rural Workers and Modern Society in Atlantic Canada, 1800–1950*, edited by Daniel Samson, 1–33, 257–72. Fredericton: Acadiensis Press for the Gorsebrook Research Institute, 1994.

– *The Spirit of Industry and Improvement: Liberal Government and Rural Industrial Society, Nova Scotia, 1790–1862*. Montreal and Kingston: McGill-Queen's

University Press, 2008.

Sanitary and Preventive Measures, Disinfectants and How to Use Them. Halifax, 1885 [CIHM 08201].

Schrauwers, Albert. *Union Is Strength: The Children of Peace and the Emergence of Joint Stock Democracy in Upper Canada.* Toronto: University of Toronto Press, 2009.

Schurman, D.M. "Benjamin Tett of Newboro, 1820–1843." *Historic Kingston* 10 (January 1962): 3–14.

Scribner, J.M., assisted by Daniel Marsh. *Scribner's Lumber & Log Book ... Being a Correct Measurement of Scantling, Boards, Plank, Cubical Contents of Square and Round Timber, Saw-Logs, by Doyle's Rule.* Rev. ed. Rochester, 1887.

Sellers, Charles. *The Market Revolution: Jacksonian America, 1815–1846.* New York: Oxford University Press, 1991.

Severin, Elizabeth. "Muslin Gowns and Moccasins." In *The Capital Years: Niagara-on-the-Lake, 1792–1796*, edited by Richard Merritt, Nancy Butler, and Michael Power, 131–41. Toronto: Dundurn, 1991.

Shammas, Carole. "Changes in English and Anglo-American Consumption from 1550 to 1800." In *Consumption and the World of Goods*, edited by John Brewer and Roy Porter, 177–205. London and New York: Routledge, 1993.

– *The Pre-industrial Consumer in England and America.* Oxford: Clarendon Press, 1990.

– "Standard of Living, Consumption, and Political Economy over the Past 500 Years." In *The Oxford Handbook of the History of Consumption*, edited by Frank Trentmann, 211–26. Oxford: Oxford University Press, 2012.

Sheppard, George. *Plunder, Profit, and Paroles: A Social History of the War of 1812 in Upper Canada.* Montreal and Kingston: McGill-Queen's University Press, 1994.

Skelton, Isabel. *The Backwoodswoman: A Chronicle of Pioneer Home Life in Upper and Lower Canada.* Toronto: Ryerson Press, 1924.

Sloane, Eric. *A Museum of Early American Tools.* New York: Ballantine, 1964.

Smith, S.D. "The Market for Manufactures in the Thirteen Continental Colonies." *Economic History Review* 51, no. 4 (November 1998): 676–708.

Smith, William H. *Smith's Canadian Gazetteer.* Toronto: H. & W. Rowsell, 1846. Reprint Toronto: Coles, 1970.

Soeurs de la Providence. *Traité élémentaire de matière médicale et guide pratique des Sœurs de Charité de l'Asile de la Providence.* Montreal: Eugène H. Trudel, 1890 [CIHM 01735].

Stokes, Melvyn. "Introduction." In *The Market Revolution in America: Social, Political, and Religious Expressions, 1800–1880*, edited by Melvyn Stokes and Stephen Conway, 1–20. Charlottesville: University Press of Virginia, 1996.

Strasser, Susan, Charles McGovern, and Matthias Judt, eds. *Getting and Spending: European and American Consumer Societies in the Twentieth Century.* Cambridge: Cambridge University Press for the German Historical Institute, 1998.

Sweeny, Robert C.H. "Accounting for Change: Understanding Merchant Credit Strategies in Outport Newfoundland." In *How Deep Is the Ocean? Historical Essays on Canada's Atlantic Fishery*, edited by James E. Candow and Carol Corbin, 121–38. Sydney: University College of Cape Breton Press, 1997.

Sweeny, Robert C.H., with David Bradley and Robert Hong, "Movement, Options

and Costs: Indexes as Historical Evidence, a Newfoundland Example."
   Acadiensis 22, no. 1 (autumn 1992): 111–21.

Sylvester, Kenneth Michael. *The Limits of Rural Capitalism: Family, Culture, and
   Markets in Montcalm, Manitoba 1870–1940*. Toronto: University of Toronto
   Press, 2001.

Taylor, Alan. *The Civil War of 1812: American Citizens, British Subjects, Irish
   Rebels, & Indian Allies*. New York: Knopf, 2010.

Taylor, Loretta M. "Fabric in Women's Costume from 1860 to 1880: A
   Comparison of Fashion Periodicals and Selected Canadian Museum
   Collections." M.Sc. thesis, University of Alberta, 1990.

A Thorough Housewife. *The Dominion Home Cook-Book, with Several Hundred
   Excellent Recipes*. Toronto: Adam Miller, 1868 [CIHM 27128].

Thorp, Daniel B. "Doing Business in the Backcountry: Retail Trade in Colonial
   Rowan County." *William & Mary Quarterly* 3rd ser. 48, no. 3 (July 1991):
   387–408.

Tiemann, Daniel F. "The Paint, Oil, and Varnish Trade." In *1795–1895: One
   Hundred Years of American Commerce*, edited by Chauncey M. Depew, vol 2,
   620–4. Reprint ed. New York: Greenwood, 1968.

Traill, Catharine Parr. *The Backwoods of Canada*. London, 1836. Reprint.
   Toronto: Coles, 1971.

– *The Canadian Settler's Guide*, 5th ed. Toronto: Old Countryman Office, 1855
   [CIHM 37099].

Trentmann, Frank, ed. *The Oxford Handbook of the History of Consumption*.
   Oxford: Oxford University Press, 2012.

Tunis, Edwin. *Colonial Craftsmen and the Beginnings of American Industry*. 1965.
   Baltimore: Johns Hopkins, 1999.

Ulrich, Laurel Thatcher. *The Age of Homespun: Objects and Stories in the
   Creation of an American Myth*. New York: Knopf, 2001.

Upper Canada Historical Arms Society. *The Military Arms of Canada*. Historical
   Arms Series, no. 1. West Hill: Museum Restoration Service, 1963.

Useful Household Helps Hints and Receipts: 3000 References. New York: Theo
   Audel, 1916.

Vallières, Marc, and Yvon Desloges. "Les échanges commerciaux de la colonie laurentienne avec la Grande Bretagne, 1760–1850. L'exemple des importations de
   produits textiles et métallurgiques." *Revue d'histoire de l'Amérique française*
   61, no. 3 & 4 (winter-spring 2008): 425–67.

Vickery, Amanda. *Behind Closed Doors: At Home in Georgian England*. New
   Haven: Yale University Press, 2009.

Walden, Keith. *Becoming Modern in Toronto: The Industrial Exhibition and the
   Shaping of a Late Victorian Culture*. Toronto: University of Toronto Press, 1997.

Weatherill, Lorna, ed. *The Account Book of Richard Latham 1724–1767*. Records
   of Social and Economic History, n.s. vol. 15. Oxford: Oxford University Press
   for the British Academy, 1990 .

– *Consumer Behaviour and Material Culture in Britain 1660–1760*. London and
   New York: Routledge, 1988.

Weaver, Martin E., and S. Buggey, eds. "A Most Significant Reference Document:
   A List of Nails and Spikes Required for the Service of the Office of Ordnance.
   17 March 1813." *Bulletin of the Association for Preservation Technology* 8,

no. 3 (1976): 88–118.

Weaver, Sharon Ann. "Making Place on the Canadian Periphery: Back-to-the-Land on the Gulf Islands and Cape Breton." PhD thesis, University of Guelph, 2013.

Welch, Evelyn. *Shopping in the Renaissance: Consumer Cultures in Italy 1400–1600*. New Haven and London: Yale University Press, 2005.

Wermuth, Thomas S. *Rip Van Winkle's Neighbors: The Transformation of Rural Society in the Hudson River Valley, 1720–1850*. Albany: State University of New York Press, 2001.

Wicken, William C. *Mi'kmaq Treaties on Trial: History, Land, and Donald Marshall Junior*. Toronto: University of Toronto Press, 2002.

Widdis, Randy William. *With Scarcely a Ripple: Anglo-Canadian Migration into the United States and Western Canada 1880–1920*. Montreal and Kingston: McGill-Queen's University Press, 1998.

Wien, Thomas. "Introduction : Habitants, marchands, historiens." In *Vingt ans après Habitants et marchands : Lectures de l'histoire des XVIIe et XVIIIe siècles canadiens / Twenty Years Later: Reading the History of Seventeenth- and Eighteenth-Century Canada*, edited by Sylvie Dépatie, Catherine Desbarats, Danielle Gauvreau, Mario Lalancette, and Thomas Wien, 3–27. Montreal and Kingston: McGill-Queen's University Press, 1998.

Wilson, Bee. *Consider the Fork: A History of How We Cook and Eat*. New York: Basic Books, 2012.

Wilson, Catharine Anne. "Reciprocal Work Bees and the Meaning of Neighbourhood." *Canadian Historical Review* 82, no. 3 (September 2001): 431–64.

Wood, J. David. *Making Ontario: Agricultural Colonization and Landscape Re-creation before the Railway*. Montreal and Kingston: McGill-Queen's University Press, 2000.

Wylie, William N.T. "The Blacksmith in Upper Canada, 1784–1850: A Study of Technology, Culture and Power." *Canadian Papers in Rural History* 7 (1990): 17–213.

– "Nebulous Substance: The Portrayal of Iron and Steel Employment in the Printed Census Reports of British North America, 1851–1891." *Archivaria* 19 (winter 1984–85): 122–6.

INDEX

Italicized page numbers refer to tables and figures.

Abbott, Joseph, 100
aboriginal customers, 104–5, 107
account books, 5, 18–20, 34, 146–7, 217–24, 231n88, 254n106, 260n42, 266n74; images of, *41–3*
Adams, James, 73, 76, *177*, *188–9*, 242n42, 264n38
addiction: to drugs, 84–5; to tobacco, 81, 244n60. *See also* alcohol
Akenson, Donald Harman, 74
alcohol, 4, 16, 25, 72–9, 80, 87, 146–7, 149, *175–7*, 242nn27–9, 242nn38–42, 243nn43–6; lists of products, *174*, *205*, *213*, *215*. *See also* local products and services: whiskey
Alnwick, 221
Andrews, Jabez, and Stephen Andrews: alcohol purchases, 72, 75–7, *176–7*, 242n42; grocery purchases, 70; local products purchases, 117, *188–9*, 256n13
animal products. *See* local products and services
animals: cattle and oxen, *41*, 115, 117, 118, 122, 124, 248n27, 257n17; food for, 117, 123–4, 192, 256n13, 259n31, 259n33, 260nn37–41; horses, 115, 117, 124, 248n27, 257n15; other products for, 58, 84, 94–5, 98, 145, *182*, 248n28, 265n55, 266n70; pigs, 27, 117, 124, 127, 257n16; purchases of, 115, 118, *189*, 234n39, 256n8, 256n13; in the rural economy, 4, 26, 27, 95, 112, 124, 128, 145, *189*, 255n108; sheep, 39, 48, 51–3, 61–2, 65, *168*, 237n39, 259n34

Appadurai, Arjun, 10, 19
Archibald, Adams G., 37, 234n7
artisans, 27, 53, 62, 63, 65, 91, 93, 96, 98, 113, 116, 119, 128, 152, 192–3, 246n10; in samples, 160–1, 220–4. *See also individual trades and tradesmen*
Asphodel Township, 31, 33, *159*, 221
Avery, James, *165*, *188–9*
Avery, William, 71, 257n18

Bank of Montreal, 32
Baskerville, Peter, 226n5, 246n11
Bastard Township, 31, *159*, 219; mill in, 21. *See also* Scovil's store
Bedford Township, 30, 121, 219, 258n30
Belisle, Donica, 8, 9, 14, 229n50, 230n72, 231n92
Bingham, Dr James, 63, 85
Birdsall, Richard, 31
Bittermann, Rusty, Robert MacKinnon, and Graeme Wynn, 114
blacksmiths, 27, 90–1, 222, 224, 246n8, 246n10, 247n13, 248nn26–7, 254n106; supplies for, 86, 93–6, 98, 100, *183–4*, 248n20, 250n47. *See also individual tradesmen*
Blanchard, Miss, 125, 260n45
blankets and bedding, 15, 38, 43, 46, 58, 59, 131–2, 134, *135*, 145, 147, *164*, 235n21, 262nn14–16, 166n70. *See also* textiles; weaving and weavers
Bolton, George, 81–2, *193*, 245n64
Bolton, Thomas, 122, *193*
Bonnycastle, Sir Richard, 101–2
Bouchard, Gérard, 267n6
bourgeois consumers, 11, 12, 63, 125, 151, 246n84
Breen, T.H., 10, 12, 17–18, 227n20, 230n76, 243n45